"Bütz integrates a wide breadth of theory and knowledge for this valuable contribution to the expanding literature on Parental Alienation and Factitious Disorder by Proxy. Bütz elucidates a model derived from systems theory to situate both phenomena within the overarching construct of interrelated multidimensional diagnoses. This model provides a multi-tiered framework that accommodates categorical and dimensional aspects of individual and family system dynamics. Thought-provoking and sure to generate additional scholarship and debate in the field."

Richard A. Warshak, PhD, author of *Divorce Poison: How to Protect Your Family from Bad-mouthing and Brainwashing*. He is a former clinical professor of Psychiatry at University of Texas Southwestern Medical Center, and best known for his expertise and publications on child custody, shared parenting, and Parental Alienation

"By taking on the whole of the pathological dynamics that create Factitious Disorder by Proxy and Parental Alienation, Michael Bütz has provided an unflinching set of challenges to our healthcare and legal systems in a creative and thoughtful read. This book is a potent reminder of the intrafamilial dynamics that can affect families."

Ted Epperly, MD, President and CEO, Family Medicine Residency of Idaho; Clinical Professor, University of Washington School of Medicine; Past President and Board Chair, American Academy of Family Physicians

"In his newest book, Michael Bütz has taken yet another important step in bringing the critical importance of complex interactions, this time to the literature on parent alienation. In doing so, he goes well beyond the subject into a seminal discussion on diagnosis that is lightyears ahead of current thinking."

F. Barton Evans, PhD, Professor of Psychiatry and Behavioral Sciences (ret.), East Tennessee State University. He has also coauthored *Forensic Psychological Assessment in Immigration Court* and *The Handbook of Forensic Rorschach Assessment*

"Michael Bütz has transformed the understanding of how illness can be transferred in a brilliant new paradigm that is relevant to healers in all facets of clinical work and challenges existing notions that continue to pathologize children and families. Providers in the psychological arena will be given a new insight into the meaning of transference in the therapeutic relationship as Bütz delineates modern ways of diagnosing and treating a serious ailment that has collective ramifications."

Eduardo Duran, PhD, clinical psychologist and author of *Healing the Soul Wound: Counseling with American Indians and Other Native Peoples. Buddha in_ _̣_ _̣_ _̣_ and coauthor of ?

"Dr. Bütz has done a great service for the field of psychology and beyond. In this masterful text, he provides both historical context and a philosophical/epistemological knowledge-base which is unparalleled in the literature. Further, he has a unique sense of psychopathology and aptly uses metaphors, case studies, and examples to reach his cogent conclusion that, in order to affect real change, IMD dynamics require policies, procedures, and action across healthcare, legal, and governmental spheres of influence. Clinicians, researchers, caseworkers, and those within the court system will find this text to be of enormous heuristic and applied value. I strongly urge you to read it, process it, and use it. It is a real winner!"

Philip Bornstein, PhD, clinical psychologist
and former Professor at University of Montana, Missoula,
with over 150 papers and publications. Coauthor of
Marital Therapy: A Behavioral Communications Approach
and coeditor of *The Handbook of Clinical Behavior Therapy with Children*

Parental Alienation and Factitious Disorder by Proxy Beyond *DSM-5*: Interrelated Multidimensional Diagnoses

Using Munchausen's Syndrome by Proxy/Factitious Disorder by Proxy and Parental Alienation as exemplars, this book advances a new diagnostic category for addressing complex pathological phenomena that integrates individual characteristics and symptoms, family as well as other system dynamics, under one diagnosis.

The author examines why current diagnostic categories within the *DSM-5* are inadequate and provides a framework for this new category—Interrelated Multidimensional Diagnoses—to better capture the complexity of MSBP/FDBP and Parental Alienation. The book begins with case studies and other examples to make the material accessible, and then proposes step-wise processes of examining family systems to determine if the phenomena exist to a reasonable degree of scientific certainty. After new diagnostic processes and criteria are provided, several interventions and recommendations for treatment are offered in a novel way that attends to the core aspects of these pathologies.

This text will provide practitioners, professionals, and researchers with a unique vantage point from which to understand and treat these pathologies.

Michael R. Bütz, PhD, is a licensed psychologist in Montana who specializes in forensic psychology with Aspen Practice, P.C., and clinical psychology and neuropsychology at St. Vincent Healthcare. He is a fellow of the American Psychological Association's Society of Clinical Psychology and recipient of numerous awards from APA's Provincial and Territorial Psychological Association Affairs Division (31). Dr. Bütz has been best known for his previous work on nonlinear dynamics as the author of *Chaos and Complexity: Implications for Psychological Theory and Practice* (1997) and as coauthor of *Strange Attractors: Chaos, Complexity and the Art of Family Therapy* (1997) and *Clinical Chaos: A Therapist's Guide to Nonlinear Dynamics and Therapeutic Change* (Routledge, 1998).

Parental Alienation and Factitious Disorder by Proxy Beyond *DSM-5*: Interrelated Multidimensional Diagnoses

MICHAEL R. BÜTZ

NEW YORK AND LONDON

First published 2020
by Routledge
52 Vanderbilt Avenue, New York, NY 10017

and by Routledge
2 Park Square, Milton Park, Abingdon, Oxon, OX14 4RN

Routledge is an imprint of the Taylor & Francis Group, an informa business

© 2020 Taylor & Francis

The right of Michael R. Bütz to be identified as author of this work has been asserted by him in accordance with sections 77 and 78 of the Copyright, Designs and Patents Act 1988.

All rights reserved. No part of this book may be reprinted or reproduced or utilized in any form or by any electronic, mechanical, or other means, now known or hereafter invented, including photocopying and recording, or in any information storage or retrieval system, without permission in writing from the publishers.

Trademark notice: Product or corporate names may be trademarks or registered trademarks, and are used only for identification and explanation without intent to infringe.

Library of Congress Cataloging-in-Publication Data
Names: Bütz, Michael R., author.
Title: Parental alienation and factitious disorder by proxy beyond DSM-5 :
    interrelated multidimensional diagnoses / Michael R. Butz.
Description: New York, NY : Routledge, 2020. | Includes bibliographical
    references and index.
Identifiers: LCCN 2019059290 | ISBN 9780367338077 (hardback) |
    ISBN 9780367345815 (paperback) | ISBN 9780429326677 (ebook)
Subjects: LCSH: Parental alienation syndrome—Diagnosis. | Munchausen
    syndrome by proxy—Diagnosis. | Psychodiagnostics.
Classification: LCC RJ506.P27 B88 2020 | DDC 618.92/89—dc23
LC record available at https://lccn.loc.gov/2019059290

ISBN: 978-0-367-33807-7 (hbk)
ISBN: 978-0-367-34581-5 (pbk)
ISBN: 978-0-429-32667-7 (ebk)

Typeset in Dante MT Std
by Apex CoVantage, LLC

For the children, young and old, and those who stand in defense of their futures . . .

Contents

Acknowledgments		*xiii*
Preface		*xv*
1	**Diagnostic Confusion and Delays That Endanger Children**	**1**
	Inherent Challenges Describing Novel Insights and Phenomena	3
	Dangers, IMDs, Case Examples, and Patterned Research	9
2	**Sparks That Ignite Fires, Symphonic Orchestras, and Interrelated Multidimensional Diagnoses**	**21**
	Meanderings and Systemic Thought	21
	Stress, the Progenitor of Differentiation	23
	Reality and Causality	24
	Metaphors That Offer a Different Vantage Point	28
	Fire and FDBP	29
	Orchestras, Symphonies, and PA	33
	Neutrality, Amid Dynamics, and Dimensions	37
	Perhaps, Taking a Step Back, It's Not So Complex After All	39
	Case Example: Factitious Disorder by Proxy	40
	Case Example: Parental Alienation	45
3	**"'Tis but thy name that is my enemy"**	**53**
	Munchausen Syndrome and Factitious Disorder by Proxy	57
	Factitious Disorder Imposed on Another (FDIA)	59
	Potential Precursors for Proliferation	63

x Contents

AIBP, CAMS, CFIC, FII, MCA, and PCF	67
Naming Conventions and the *Platypus Paradox*	74
Parent Alienation, Problems With Clarity, and Support	77
Early Descriptions	79
Alignment	80
Parental Alienation Syndrome	81
Alienated Children	84
Contemporary Literature, Parental Alienation, and the *DSM-5*	86
Debating Parental Alienation	86
DSM-5 and Where the Pathological Dynamic Lies	87
IMD and Organizing Principles	90

4 Interrelated Multidimensional Diagnoses — **93**

Punctuated Steady States and the Moment an IMD Is Realized	96
The *DSM-5*, Real Diagnoses, and the Alternative Model for Personality Disorders	98
An IMD, Not a Relational Problem or a Syndrome	101
Scientific Certainty: Daubert vs. Merrill Dow Chemical (1993)	105
Courts and PA	110
Proofs: Characteristics, Interrelationships, and Dimensions	111
Splitting and/or Triangulation and IMDS	112
Proposition: FDBP and PA Are Interrelated Multidimensional Diagnoses	118
Practical Examples of IMDs, FDBP, and PA	122
Variable Exclusion and Inclusion Criteria	124
Weighing IMD Prospects	125
Systems, Systems, Systems, a Systemic Diagnosis, and Other Diagnoses	131
Diagnosing IMDs: Suspicion and Further Study	132
IMDs and Exemplars	133

5 Factitious Disorder by Proxy and Interrelated Multidimensional Diagnoses — **137**

Revisiting "The Complaint"	137
Parental and Systemic Background in FDBP	141
Personality Traits and Pathological Lying	143
A List of Characteristics Associated With Factitious Disorder by Proxy	144
Tabled Variable Criteria and Redistributing Table 1 From 2009	151
Revisiting FDBP as an IMD and Building Tables	156
An Individual Diagnosis, a Dynamic Diagnosis, or Both, Revisited	158

Contents **xi**

The Topic of Motivation and FDBP — 160
*Revisiting the List of Characteristics Associated With
Factitious Disorder by Proxy* — 164
IMD Implications for FDBP — 169

**6 Parental Alienation as an Interrelated Multidimensional
Diagnosis** — **175**
The Psychological Surround of PA: Background, Percentages,
and Environment — 175
Percentages — 176
Environmental Forces — 177
Individuals, Behaviors, and Experiences — 180
Parent Characteristics — 180
Parent Personality Traits — 181
Rejected Parents — 184
Gender Considerations — 185
Parent Alienating Behaviors — 187
Child Characteristics — 192
Age Matters — 192
A Child's Expression of Alienating Behaviors — 193
*Not All Transformations Are Good: Identification
With the Aggressor, Internalized Oppression, and PA* — 196
Triage, Agreement, and What's in a Name — 201
*The Psychological Surround and the Optional Family–Legal
System Subdynamic* — 203
Counter Productive Parenting, Parental Denigration, Sabotage,
and Estrangement — 205
Counter Productive Parenting and Parental Sabotage — 205
Parental Estrangement — 208
What Is, and What Is Not, Parental Alienation? — 210
Psychological Abuse — 211
Discerning and Weighing PA — 214
Parental Alienation as an IMD — 221

**7 Parallel Characteristics and Variables: Factitious
Disorder by Proxy and Parental Alienation** — **231**
Stress, History, and the Nexus of an IMD in Time — 233
Three Forms of Stress and IMDs — 236
Variable Responses to Stress: Exclusion and Inclusion Criteria — 238
Family Systems in IMDs — 241

xii Contents

Baumrind's and Olson's Models 242
Larger Systems and IMDs 245
    The Child(ren) 246
IMD Symbolic Language and a Common Representation System 249

8 Interventions, Motions, Policies, Procedures, and Potential IMDs **253**

How to Intervene and the Moral Courage to Intervene 256
Other Considerations and Mild IMDs 261
FDBP Intervention and Reunification 264
PA Intervention and Reunification 269
A Model for Reunification in PA 271
    Introduction 273
Procedures, Policy, and the Best Interests—Health and Welfare of Children 275
Future IMDs 277
    Undue Influence 279
    Intergenerational Trauma 280

References 283
Appendix A Key IMD Symbolic Language 307
Index 309

Acknowledgments

As with any project there are those that I am indebted to, and in those rare moments of reflection that I have been afforded I have come to appreciate the unique capabilities bestowed on me by my parents, one an artist, one an engineer, one a pianist, one a pilot. Those diverse capabilities live on through me and my children, abilities for which I am grateful. It has also been my good fortune to know the riches of a family and the wealth provided by friends and colleagues. My wife and children have, as always, my gratitude for bearing with me during the many hours spent on this project and for supporting the work that has been involved in it. To Carlos and Ann Wagner as well as Gail Johnson for their support, and the lessons I learned from each as a boy and as a man.

There has been many a valued friend and colleague who has worked with me on this project and the material surrounding it, but none closer than Barton Evans, who stuck his neck out not once but twice to address these very controversial and difficult topics. To Cara Chamberlain, who corresponded as my proofreader late into the night and early in the morning in order to be of assistance in getting across the ideas in this text with the intelligibility these ideas deserved. Also, to my wife and children, as well as Paul and Joyce Evanson, who served as my "pre-proofreaders" on occasions when I simply could not sort out an idea or notion. Other professional colleagues across the state, such as Hallie Banziger, Phil Bornstein, and Kathleen Rock, provided invaluable feedback. I have been fortunate enough to knock around ideas and observations with my colleagues at Behavioral Health Associates as well, and I have appreciated their candor and the playful nature of our dialogue in entertaining different perspectives.

xiv Acknowledgments

As for my distinctly professional life, I could not conceive of how to be more appreciative of the fine and exceptional mentors I have been fortunate enough to know across my career. The programs at San Francisco State University and Wright Institute in Berkeley, California, could not possibility have served me better, and the education that I received from both institutions continue to provide one insight after another as I contemplate the lessons those professors taught me. In fact, I do mention several of them within these pages. There are the obvious appreciations to Nina Guttapalle, my editor, and for those at Routledge who chose to take on a topic as controversial and complex as the combination of phenomena that constitute the pages of this book. Likewise, my thanks go out to the American Psychological Association and Taylor & Francis for recognizing these concepts and assisting with the publication of this book and other related pieces. There are my collaborators on this project as well, Ron Miller and Kathleen Rock, whose assistance with the inventories and motions concepts will no doubt prove to be of assistance to practitioners, professionals, and researchers in recognizing and intervening in these matters more readily. Also, my thanks to librarian extraordinaire Pamela Trudell, at St. Vincent Healthcare, whose research and vigilance proved to be very valuable. With such enterprises there are also other colleagues too numerous to mention, such as the host of them who are practitioners and professionals I have worked with on these cases, those in Montana Psychological Association, and others across the country for whom I have a deep appreciation for the grace and knowledge each brings to the field.

With publications past, there has always been a coffee shop or two that served as a refuge, but with this project the places that I found ended up being more uncomplicated way stations between work conducted on the road. Places where I was grateful to sit, stare off into space, and think my way through this piece include Many Glacier Lodge north of St. Mary's, Montana; Meadowlark Public House in Sidney, Montana; New Belgium Brewing at the Denver Airport; and Sage Lodge outside of Pray, Montana.

Preface

The text that follows is a group of proposals borne from the necessities of clinical practice, informed by the literature, and refined by collegial discussions as well as legal cases across the state of Montana. For those of you who may not be familiar with the geography of this part of the world, it is five hundred rugged miles in any direction to the next major city from Billings, Montana. What that means for a practitioner, such as this author, is that the scope of practice is unusually broad and need for sound services high. Every day and each case is different, demanding in its own way, and oftentimes requires a renewed familiarity with the area of practice as well as with its literature. It follows that unless the referral request is addressed thoroughly, many a time these clients will need to travel to Denver, Salt Lake City or Seattle to have her or his needs met. The concept of an Interrelated Multidimensional Diagnosis was derived out of such needs in our state and this author's inability to find a more useful way to approach these phenomena.

What is an Interrelated Multidimensional Diagnosis? That will be answered in a myriad of ways over the balance of this book. The short version is that this term was meant to define a set of diagnoses[1] that holistically describe interrelated individual and system characteristics. These characteristics, together with subdynamics, cumulatively create a multidimensional pathological dynamic. It will be argued that the pathological dynamic created is known, for example, by one of the three other terms that are the focus of this book: Munchausen's Syndrome by Proxy, Factitious Disorder by Proxy, or Parental Alienation.

These phenomena each describe a pathological dynamic, wherein Munchausen's Syndrome by Proxy or Factitious Disorder by Proxy is the

xvi   Preface

number one health concern for most child protection agencies, since estimates are that between one-in-ten and one-in-twenty children who carry the diagnosis dies. Meanwhile, the latest estimates are that Parental Alienation here in the United States impacts between twenty-two and forty-four million children, and recent estimates are far higher in other countries.

So, this approach was developed to address a need in my community. This conceptualization of an Interrelated Multidimensional Diagnosis will not answer every problem given the convoluted nature of these phenomena. What you will find across the pages of this book are a series of proposals, one proposal after another intended to address the needs and problems related to these phenomena. What is being offered here is admittedly a conceptual leap too. My colleague Dr. Evans and I put it this way in our most recent article (2019):

> We recognize that what we are proposing throughout this article may seem radical. Yet, we argue that clinicians have continually wrestled with ways to more fully describe the experiences they have encountered with these sorts of complex multidimensional phenomena. In many cases these clinicians have been dissatisfied with the status quo and struggled to stem the suffering and/or death of the children whom they ultimately serve in medical and legal systems.

What follows in the pages ahead is a journey, and it is my hope that it will prove to be worthy of the reader's time and attention.

Practitioners and professionals should, I hope, find this an interesting read with multiple vantage points from which to examine these phenomena. There will be conceptual analogies, real-world practice applications and discussions, as well as innovations that include, for example, a new diagnostic approach to each phenomena at the end of Chapters 5 and 6. For those of you who are academics and researchers, there will be plenty of citations, details, and patterns that are repeated over and over by different authors in different parts of this text that clarify some of the remarkable consistencies within the literature on these two diagnostic topics. To start with, heroes and heroines from different disciplines and different fields will be discussed to demonstrate the inherent challenges of articulating novel insights. Do not be alarmed when quantum physics and the structure of DNA are discussed at the outset, since it will also be argued that behavioral scientists, practitioners in healthcare, and professionals in law have long been dealing with equally complex phenomena.

Understanding the concept of an Interrelated Multidimensional Diagnosis may sound insurmountable, but there are daily encounters with similar phenomena. Further, the concept is no more difficult to understand than a campfire or, at times perhaps, the workings of an orchestra. On this journey there are awful sounds, such as those produced by the Portsmouth Sinfonia, and still thoughts will turn toward understanding what Leonard Bernstein envisioned as art. There will also be examples of how an Interrelated Multidimensional Diagnosis may be revealed in practice early on, both with regard to the matter of Parental Alienation and in cases where there is Factitious Disorder by Proxy.

There are, as stated earlier, some highly technical theory and definition matters that do need attention in Chapter 3. These matters will be intertwined with a progression through the history of Munchausen's Syndrome by Proxy and Factitious Disorder by Proxy, as well as Parental Alienation, to provide a grounding in each phenomenon. Simultaneously, there will be attention to challenges with naming conventions. These matters will be tackled with a set of novel solutions to the Gordian Knot that these matters have created at present, and even the *Platypus Paradox* will be offered with a cartoon to illustrate the point.

After these clarifications, it will be time to get down to the nuts and bolts of what an Interrelated Multidimensional Diagnosis is, how it develops, how it is structured, how individuals and systems interact, and how it turns into a pathological dynamic. This phenomenon has interrelationships on multiple dimensions, wherein one dimension builds on the other and under the right circumstances creates a pathological dynamic—a pathological dynamic that punctuates as a new steady state that describes a change in one member of the family system whose behavior creates a change in the whole system.

Once an Interrelated Multidimensional Diagnosis has been defined, the concept will be applied first to Munchausen's Syndrome by Proxy and Factitious Disorder by Proxy to see whether its architecture and dynamics are fitting and explanatory. Parental Alienation will follow, and the literature associated with each phenomenon will be reviewed in detail as each is applied to the psychological surround of these phenomena with background dimensions. These considerations will be followed by individual characteristics and symptoms, systemic interactions and subdynamics, which again under the right conditions create a pathological dynamic. Tables and proofs will be developed from each phenomenon's literature and research in order to derive a diagnosis and diagnostic process that allows these pathological dynamics to be recognized and studied to the extent that each either conforms to a qualitative description and may be measured against a quantitative cut-off of more probable than not.

These data- and literature-rich chapters are followed by a shift back to conceptual matters. In Chapter 7 the journey leads to a discussion of how all Interrelated Multidimensional Diagnoses hold a number of characteristics in common, even though the two phenomena under discussion are very different and occur in very different environments. Each phenomenon also has variable criteria unique to the individuals in the system and the quality of the systems with which they interact. To clarify these matters, the role of stress in time and space will be discussed by way of its lasting impact in development stresses, which, coupled with contemporary and situational stresses, amplify the symptoms that create pathological dynamics. Also within that chapter the Interrelated Multidimensional Diagnosis Symbolic Language will be introduced in order to facilitate gathering information from family systems in a fashion consistent with the concepts herein, and to create a ready medium with which to converse about the structure and functioning of these family systems and the individuals and other systems they interact with.

Chapter 8 then deals with the prospect of intervention and the necessity of follow-through with an active Interrelated Multidimensional Diagnosis. Several aspects of intervention will be described with Factitious Disorder by Proxy and Parental Alienation. These discussions will eventually lead to the necessity for systems change in healthcare and law, as well as change in governmental policies and procedures in order to arrest, intervene and treat Interrelated Multidimensional Diagnoses as a larger societal matter. With these discussions behind us, then, four Interrelated Multidimensional Diagnoses will be proposed for future consideration.

It is this author's hope that this journey will prove challenging and informative, and that it will promote a new way of considering these phenomena and the families and individuals they impact.

Note

1. In the mathematical sense.

Diagnostic Confusion and Delays That Endanger Children

1

"We create the world that we perceive, not because there is no reality outside our heads, but because we select and edit the reality we see to conform to our beliefs about what sort of world we live in."

—Mark Engel, 1972[1]

—Forward to "Steps to an Ecology of Mind" By Gregory Bateson

Phenomena communicated, experienced, perceived and/or thought about in the behavioral sciences all share the same basic limitation: our capacity to reconcile them with reality. We struggle to bring these phenomena forward and are limited in our ability to describe what "it" is that is before us. Bateson (1972) made this dilemma clear in his work:

> *The perception* of an event or object or relation is real. It is a neuro-physiological message. But the event itself or the object itself cannot enter this world and is, therefore, irrelevant and, to that extent, unreal. Conversely, a message has no reality or relevance qua message, in the Newtonian world: it there is reduced to sound waves or printer's ink.
>
> By the same token, the "contexts" and "contexts of con-texts" upon which I am insisting are only real or relevant insofar as they are communicationally effective, i.e., function as messages or modifiers of messages.
>
> (p. 255)

Those of us in the behavioral sciences constantly face this struggle with the terminology we use in order to describe the phenomena before us as terms advance, morph, or are laid aside. Our field is fraught with these struggles

2 Diagnostic Confusion and Delays

(Hoffman, 1981), and those of us in day-to-day practice regularly wrangle with philosophical, epistemological challenges too numerous to mention here. These wranglings are not mere philosophical quandaries to be debated in our literature, since these terms speak to the quality of the lives our clients experience.

Given this conundrum, the purpose of this book is to discuss and define specific, particularly resistant terms in order to illustrate how a subset of *pathological* dynamics (Bütz, 1997, pp. 71–84) has lethal or detrimental impacts on the lives of children. Over the course of this book, it will be argued that Abnormal Illness Behavior by Proxy, Child Abuse in Medical Settings, Fabricated and/or Induced Illness in children, Factitious Disorder Imposed on Another, *Factitious Disorder by Proxy*, Medical Child Abuse, Munchausen Syndrome by Proxy, Pediatric Condition Falsification, an Alienated Child, Alignment, Parental Alienation Syndrome and *Parental Alienation* are all arguably similar phenomena, if the practitioner, professional or researcher understands how to identify the characteristics of what has been described as an Interrelated Multidimensional Diagnosis (Bütz & Evans, 2019). The term *Interrelated Multidimensional Diagnosis* (IMD) was proposed to describe a set of diagnoses[2] that holistically describe interrelated individual and system characteristics. These characteristics, together with subdynamics in the case of an IMD, cumulatively create a multidimensional pathological dynamic. It is argued that the pathological dynamic created is known, for example, by one of the terms above.

By unpacking the term *IMD*, it can be argued that these phenomena are diagnoses in their own right. Further, IMDs are the result of a systemic dynamic, with all the implications that this unique theoretical discipline in the behavioral sciences may suggest. As will be explained, individuals in an IMD dynamic offer their own distinctive contribution through their response to stress coupled with unique behaviors, characteristics and interactions that contribute to the unfolding of the pathological dynamic. Likewise, systems—family, legal, and healthcare systems—also contribute by way of their behaviors, characteristics, and interactions. These individuals and systems are interrelated, and, under the right conditions, interactions occur across multiple dimensions in order to cumulatively create one of the pathological dynamics that will be discussed in this text: Factitious Disorder by Proxy or Parental Alienation.

The intention behind creating this set of diagnoses was to fill the void in the current diagnostic nomenclature that neglects individual-individual, individual-system/system- individual, and system-system pathological dynamics. Further, within this diagnostic set there is an array of potential diagnoses that have shared interrelationships, characteristics and symptoms among individuals and systems. These diagnoses manifest largely under certain stress-related conditions that engender maladaptive behaviors and enact particular traits across individuals and systems, which collectively transform into a pathological dynamic. Although the title of this book might suggest that the matters being addressed are straightforward, that is far from the truth. The impetus for this book, as well as the prior articles (Bütz & Evans, 2019; Bütz, Evans, & Webber-Dereszynski, 2009), was to describe these phenomena in a comprehensible fashion for practitioners, professionals and researchers. Notwithstanding the inherent difficulties of explaining these phenomena, as witnessed in at least the last forty to fifty years or more of debate and literature on these topics, those of us in the behavioral sciences are not alone in the scientific struggles associated with the advancement of our field when principles and terms have proven difficult to define (Horgan, 2012; Kuhn, 1962).

Inherent Challenges Describing Novel Insights and Phenomena

> But numbers decide, and the result is that the roles, compared with earlier times, have gradually changed. What initially was a problem of fitting a new and strange element, with more or less gentle pressure, into what was generally regarded as a fixed frame has become a question of coping with an intruder who, after appropriating an assured place, has gone over to the offensive; and today it has become obvious that the old framework must somehow or other be burst asunder. It is merely a question of where and to what degree.
>
> (Max Planck, 1920)

Figure 1.1 Portrait of Max Planck. Photograph by Transocean, Courtesy Smithsonian Libraries Image Gallery.

4 Diagnostic Confusion and Delays

In 1920 Max Planck made this statement while accepting the Nobel Prize for his work on the services he rendered to the advancement of Physics by his discovery of energy quanta. Though far afield from behavioral health, healthcare, and law generally, this quotation from Planck's speech, delivered nearly a hundred years ago, has important things to say about the undertaking that will follow. He described several important matters in his research on radiation, such as quantitative "numbers," "changes" across time, the "strangeness" of new insights, and the heretofore "fixed frame" of contemporary scientific thinking. Planck furthered his observations by describing how, in science, "the old framework must somehow or other be burst asunder." In other words, the advancement of scientific ideas and change is inevitable. Given the challenges at that time of accounting for the particulars in classical physics, his insights back in 1900 on radiation were greeted with limited understanding of their far-reaching quantum implications, implications that we struggle with to this day. It would appear that Planck's contribution sat unnoticed until Einstein lent his support in 1905 and then advanced his discoveries further by applying Planck's ideas to light in 1907 (Bembenek, 2018).

> During the investigation of both these children, we came to know the mothers well. They were very pleasant people to deal with, cooperative, and appreciative of good medical care, which encouraged us to try all the harder. Some mothers who choose to stay in hospital with their child remain on the ward slightly uneasy, overtly bored, or aggressive. These two flourished there as if they belonged, and thrived on the attention that staff gave to them. It is ironic to conjecture that the cause of both these children's problems would have been discovered much sooner in the old days of restricted visiting hours and the absence of facilities for mothers to live in hospital with a sick child. It is also possible that, without the excellent facilities and the attentive and friendly staff, the repetitive admissions might not have happened. Both mothers had a history of falsifying their own medical records and treatment. Both had at times been labelled as hysterical personalities who also tended to be depressed. We recognise that parents some times exaggerate their child's symptoms, perhaps to obtain faster or more thorough medical care of their child. In these cases, it was as if the parents were using the children to get themselves into the sheltered environment of a children's ward surrounded by friendly staff.
>
> (Meadow, 1977)

Figure 1.2 Portrait of Sir Roy Meadow. Courtesy of Sir Roy Meadow, with the assistance of Royal College of Pediatrics and Child Health.

The preceding quotation comes from an article by Roy Meadow in *The Lancet* (p. 344– 345) that is generally credited with providing the first description of Munchausen's Syndrome by Proxy. His words evoke a sense of confusion as he attempts to account for not only what he had been witnessing but what he was experiencing as a practitioner. On the one hand, he described "very pleasant people" who "flourished there as if they belonged" in the hospital setting. Moreover, these parents, "thrived on the attention that staff gave to them." Yet, the article describes how these same parents "skillfully" manipulated the healthcare situation, and as a result one of these two children died. Meadow's attempts to come to grips with these pathological phenomena are noticeable in his words and in how he presents the material. He appears bewildered by the ongoing suffering that was eventually labeled "child abuse": "Case 1 seems to be the first example of '*Munchausen syndrome by proxy*'" (p. 345).

These were extraordinary circumstances where, in both cases, Meadow was faced with very ill young children unable to describe their symptoms; seemingly attentive and caring mothers who almost appeared to function as part of the medical staff; and perplexing, stubborn illnesses that did not respond to treatment. Readers are asked to put themselves in Meadow's shoes and to consider the emotional and mental struggles he likely went through in order to arrive at the realizations that led him to the hypothesis that one of these cases could be "the first example of 'Munchausen syndrome by proxy.'"

6 Diagnostic Confusion and Delays

We wish to put forward a radically different structure for the salt of deoxyribose nucleic acid. This structure has two helical chains each coiled round the same axis (see diagram). We have made the usual chemical assumptions. namely, that each chain consists of phosphate diester groups joining ß-D-deoxyribofuranose residues with 3',5' linkages. The two chains (but not their bases) are related by a dyad perpendicular to the fibre axis. Both chains follow righthanded helices, but owing to the dyad the sequences of the atoms in the two chains run in opposite directions.

(Watson & Crick, 1953)

Figure 1.3 Portrait of James Watson and Francis Crick with their DNA model in 1953. Reproduced with permission of Science Photo Library.

Of course, the quote above comes from Watson and Crick's explanation of Deoxyribonucleic[3] Acid (DNA), otherwise known as the self-replicating stuff that runs through most living organisms and that accounts for some of the primary features of chromosomes.

Here, the reader is asked to notice that these authors know that what they have advanced is a "radical" idea and go on to explain how they have pulled together a chemical-structural model in great detail step-by-step in order to explain it to their scientific colleagues[4] in the journal *Nature*. Still, there is some scientific short-hand and/or jargon at work here, with phrases such as "usual chemical assumptions," assumptions and descriptions that are, of course, not well understood by those not working on the phenomenon of DNA or a related subspecialty. While the nature and significance of their insights would have been immediately apparent to their colleagues, it would still take some time for other scientists to comprehend the depths of their discovery.

> A very important aspect of the response of the youngsters in this age group was the dramatic change in the relationship between parents and children. These young people were particularly vulnerable to being swept up into the anger of one parent against the other. They were faithful and valuable battle allies in efforts to hurt the other parent. Not infrequently, they turned on the parent they had loved and been very close to prior to the marital separation.
>
> (Wallerstein & Kelly, 1980a)

Figures 1.4 and 1.5 Judith Wallerstein (left) and Joan B. Kelly (right). Reproduced with the permission of the New York Times (left); picture reproduced courtesy of Joan B. Kelly (right).

What these two practitioners describe above emerged as they researched the impacts of divorce on children (p. 77). This was a unique finding, since the authors were describing a "dramatic" change in the functioning of these children when interacting with their parents, dramatic in the sense that suddenly children had become "allied" to one or the other parent. Further, it was a dramatic enough dynamic, novel enough, to require its own term and description. Wallerstein and Kelly, therefore, used the term *Alignment* to describe this

8 Diagnostic Confusion and Delays

phenomenon, "a divorce-specific relationship that occurs when a parent and one or more children join in a vigorous attack on the other parent." Imagine their surprise when 25 out of 131 children and adolescents in their study (p. 77) could be expected to form such alliances as an outcome of divorce. Moreover, they found that this group of children had particular characteristics, as did the parents they aligned with. Wallerstein and Kelly also discerned that these families were engaged in high-conflict divorces (Johnston, 1994) as they interrelated with the legal systems.

All of the stepwise realizations presented above may have been underappreciated at the time. The insights described followed from a generally recognizable set of details each researcher used to glean a comprehensible construct, but it would seem that few could imagine what developments in science would follow from the big picture perspective they offered. The intention here, and across the pages to come, is to break down concepts in a fashion that speaks to practitioners, professionals, and researchers in a comprehensible way and that allows discourse on these important topics and their origins. This form of narrative, followed by an additional elemental breakdown of the ideas discussed, will appear in this text on and off throughout the pages that follow, sometimes in a descriptive fashion and sometimes with highly technical accountings as well as some labored examples that may be ill differentiated.

If, as a practitioner, professional or researcher, you have read the above with or without the encouragement offered in the preface about wandering into other scientific disciplines, you are undoubtedly ready to see how these examples apply to the topic at hand. First, these different insights addressed a problem that science faced at the time, not just a problem, but a complex problem that was difficult to explain. Second, all of these researchers in their own way took a detailed scientific approach to sharing their insights with colleagues. Third, these insights helped science to address not only problems encountered at the time but also those that lay ahead, redefining the landscape of considerations within the field.

It is, therefore, hoped that proposing the concept of an IMD to address the complex and thorny matters associated with the phenomena described so far may well impact the fields of behavioral science, law, and healthcare. Still, considering the examples offered, it will be important to clarify the problems faced with these phenomena and how to pragmatically articulate them in a manner that breeds professional consensus based on the known literature and research in these fields in order to stem the suffering of children, adolescents and other family members. Moreover, later in the book, the case will be made for how to abate, stall, or stop these pathological processes from causing further harm.

Dangers, IMDs, Case Examples, and Patterned Research

As discussed, to determine that an IMD exists is synonymous with making the determination that a pathological dynamic exists. As will be elaborated upon later in far more detail, abuse of a child or adolescent lies at the center of the conceptualization of these phenomena. The phenomena under study, Factitious Disorder by Proxy, Parental Alienation, and permutations thereof, did not come to the fore through theoretical constructs. Rather, they came to be known either through practice (Meadow, 1977) or as the result of accounting for behavioral patterns seen in research (Wallerstein & Kelly, 1980a, 1980b, 1976). As such, the literatures associated with these phenomena illustrate the dangers of these pathological dynamics that may wear different names or titles through a variety of case studies and patterned research.

In his original article on Munchausen's Syndrome by Proxy,[5] Meadow (1977) described two cases. The first was the impetus for the term, and he begins by describing the following:

> Kay was referred to the pediatric nephrology clinic in Leeds at the age of 6 because of recurrent illnesses in which she passed foul-smelling, bloody urine.
>
> She had been investigated in two other centres without the cause being found.
>
> (p. 343)

Take note that two other centers had investigated the case without the cause of the child's illness being discovered or diagnosed. As the article unfolds, it becomes evident that the child's supposed maladies began when she was just eight months old. Examinations and treatments aimed at ameliorating or curing the child involved ongoing pain and suffering and were not innocuous events in the child's life. Yet, despite the efforts of practitioners to understand the malady under study, the illness morphed and was inconsistent. In this case, one sample of urine was as described above, only to be followed by another sample in which the "foul smelling, bloody urine" had suddenly and inexplicably vanished. Numerous studies of the child were conducted, and many were repeated. Meanwhile, observation of the parent-child relationship suggested a caring and concerned parent. There was, however, also the observation that the parent was not as concerned as practitioners might have expected about examinations and procedures the child was enduring, one after the other, in order to find the illness.

10 Diagnostic Confusion and Delays

Meadow described the problem as "insoluble" until he and his colleagues decided to "work on the assumption that everything about the history and investigation were false" (p. 343). They began with detective work, which ultimately yielded the following outcomes:

> During a 7-day period, Kay emptied her bladder 57 times. 45 specimens were normal, all of these being collected and supervised by a nurse; 12 were grossly abnormal, containing blood and different organisms, all these having been collected by the mother or left in her presence.
>
> (pp. 343–344)

Thus, Meadow and his colleagues sought the mother's own urine sample in turn, a sample which had the very same properties that were so concerning when they believed these were coming from the child. Meadow reflected that the impact of the confusion and pain endured by the child was substantial:

> The consequences of these actions for the daughter had included 12 hospital admissions, 7 major X-ray procedures (including intravenous urograms, cystograms, barium enema, vaginogram, and urethrogram), 6 examinations under anesthetic, 5 cystoscopies, unpleasant treatment with toxic drugs and eight antibiotics, catheterizations, vaginal pessaries, and bacterial, fungicidal, and aestrogen creams.
>
> (p. 344)

The outcome of Meadow's second case that shared similar characteristics was as follows:

> During the period in which the local pediatrician, psychiatrist, and social services department were planning arrangements for the child, the child arrived at the hospital one night, collapsed with extreme hypernatraemia, and died.
>
> Necropsy disclosed mild gastric erosions 'as if a chemical had been ingested'. The mother wrote thanking the doctors for their care and then attempted suicide.
>
> (p. 344)

This case suggested, first and most shockingly, that these phenomena have lethal consequences. Most literature on Factitious Disorder by Proxy puts the likelihood of mortality at between one-in-ten to one-in-twenty. In addition, though the focus is on the child's health and welfare in these cases, adults, family members and even the perpetrators also suffer to a significant degree. Considerations, for these reasons, are encouraged to be systemic.

Writing on what Wallerstein and Kelly (1980a) identified as Alignment,[6] they described the case of Paul:

> Among Paul's activities during the year following our initial contact was his continuing reporting to his mother about his father's social life and presumed delinquencies, and his continued rejection of his father's increasingly desperate overtures, including gifts and expression of wishes to maintain visitation. Paul also maintained a coercive control over his younger sisters who were eager to see their father, and he made sure, by his monitoring of them, that they would not respond with affection, at least in his presence.
>
> (p. 79)

This case illustrated the impact of the Alignment on the child's relationship with his father. Wallerstein and Kelly went on to note the following about Paul and other children pulled into Alignment dynamics with one parent or the other:

> The immediate achievement of this alignment relationship, when viewed as a coping behavior at the time of the divorce, is that it serves to reduce symptomatic responses among these children, to ward off loneliness, sadness, and more serious depression. These youngsters are galvanized into exciting activity; they speak with new and ringing authority; they are given permission to express hostility and to engage in mischief; and they experience very gratifying closeness with one parent. The alignment enables them to split the ambivalent relationship with both parents into a clear and simple good parent and a bad one.
>
> (p. 80)

Although Wallerstein and Kelly report that these parent-child/child-parent states did not persist, subsequent literature and further research (Wallerstein, Lewis, & Blakeslee, 2000) revealed a markedly different and lasting outcome that follows from this pathological dynamic (Lorandos, 2014; Baker & Ben-Ami, 2011; Meier, 2010; Bow, Gould, & Flens, 2009).

As the reader may surmise, the conceptualization and research surrounding the two phenomena for which examples have been provided continue to develop. When the *Diagnostic and Statistical Manual of*

12 Diagnostic Confusion and Delays

Mental Disorders—Fourth Edition (DSM-IV) was published (1994), what were referred to as *Sourcebooks* were also offered. The purpose of these *Sourcebooks* was to explain the rational for the diagnosis and diagnostic criteria included or excluded from the *DSM-IV*. Parenthetically, these books were truly a worthy enterprise and a useful reference for practitioners, professionals, and researchers. Turning to Factitious Disorder by Proxy, we have the *Sourcebook's* (1996) description of its inclusion in the *DSM-IV*[7] and with whom the diagnosis should rest:

> [W]hether the diagnosis should be given to the person *inducing* the symptoms or to the individual *presenting* with the symptoms. They propose that the psychiatric diagnosis, 'factitious disorder by proxy' should be given to the person who induces the symptoms.
>
> (p. 880)

Plewes and Fagan's (1994) treatment of the topic of factitious disorders was well-regarded and upon reading this language directly it may be obvious that there was great emphasis on their work. At the same time, the considerations were appreciably pragmatic in addressing within whom the disorder should be seated. While the authors of the *Sourcebook's* reference on the topic described a robust and ongoing debate, this kind of patterned research offers a meaningful effort to limit the dangers of diagnostic confusion, lack of identification or misclassification.

> I have introduced this term to refer to a disturbance in which children are obsessed with deprecation and criticism of a parent—denigration that is unjustified and/or exaggerated. The notion that such children are merely 'brainwashed' is narrow. The term brainwashing implies that one parent is systematically and consciously programming the child to denigrate the other parent. The concept of the parental alienation syndrome includes the brainwashing component but is much more inclusive. It includes not only conscious but subconscious and unconscious factors within the parent that contribute to the child's alienation. Furthermore (and this is extremely important), it includes factors that arise within the child—independent of the parental contributions—that contribute to the development of the syndrome.
>
> (Gardner, 1985)

In 1985, Gardner (p. 3) introduced and argued for the term *Parental Alienation Syndrome*. He proposed that it be considered a syndrome, one that arguably lay beyond the bounds of alignment with another parent. Indeed,

Gardner contended that children "denigrated" a parent beyond any clear reason for doing so. He also asserted that one parent acted purposively, "systematically and consciously programming the child to denigrate the other parent." Gardner's focus was also on certain "factors" that make the child more susceptible to engaging in these behaviors. His conceptualization offered another vantage point from which to view the phenomenon; his perspective on these matters came from practice, and, per Gardner, hundreds of cases that patterned in the fashion described (2001):

> This formulation proposes to focus on the alienated child rather than on parental alienation. An *alienated child* is defined here as one who expresses, freely and persistently, unreasonable negative feelings and beliefs (such as anger, hatred, rejection, and/or fear) toward a parent that are significantly disproportionate to the child's actual experience with that parent. From this viewpoint, the pernicious behaviors of a 'programming' parent are no longer the starting point. Rather, the problem of the alienated child begins with a primary focus on the child, his or her observable behaviors, and parent-child relationships. This objective and neutral focus enables the professionals involved in the custody dispute to consider whether the child fits the definition of an alienated child and, if so, to use a more inclusive framework for assessing why the child is now rejecting a parent and refusing contact.
>
> (Kelly & Johnston, 2001)

As will be addressed later in greater detail, this new definition of the challenges involved with this version of a proposed IMD were drafted (p. 251) quite explicitly to contend with what Kelly and Johnston believed to be the deficiencies in Gardner's model. The reader should take notice also that this Kelly is one and the same as the Kelly of Wallerstein and Kelly, who had proffered Alignment. It was clear that this conceptualization of an Alienated Child was meant to accomplish a number of things arguably beyond Gardner's notions about the phenomenon and, among the modifications, to differentiate it from the concept of Parental Estrangement (PE):

> Thus, this unusual development, in the absence of the type of factors described above as leading to child estrangement, is a pathological response. It is a severe distortion on the child's part of the previous parent-child relationship. These youngsters go far beyond alliance or estrangement in the intensity, breadth, and ferocity of their behaviors toward the parent they are rejecting. They are responding to complex

14 Diagnostic Confusion and Delays

and frightening dynamics within the divorce process itself, to an array of parental behaviors, and also to their own vulnerabilities that make them susceptible to becoming alienated. The profound alienation of a child from a parent most often occurs in high-conflict custody disputes; it is an infrequent occurrence among the larger population of divorcing children.

(p. 254)

Adding to this rather comprehensive undertaking, Kelly and Johnston articulated individual characteristics that made the development of the pathological dynamic more likely:

In general, a child's vulnerability to alienation increases with greater psychological adjustment problems in the child (Johnston, 1993; Lampel, 1996; Wallerstein & Kelly, 1980a). Anxious, fearful, and passive children lack the resiliency to withstand the intense pressures of the custody battle and the aligned parents' alienating behaviors. It might be psychologically easier for them to choose a side to avoid crippling anxiety. Children with poor reality testing are more likely to be vulnerable, particularly in the absence of other family members or professionals assisting the child by clarifying the troubling and confusing events and behaviors associated with the divorce.

(p. 261)

In other words, children and adolescents who have already been experiencing challenges to one degree or another are put further at risk when their weaknesses are exploited in the pathological dynamic that unfolds.

There were three main ways of fabricating or inducing illness in a child, said Dr. Eminson: making up symptoms and given a false medical history; falsifying hospital charts, records and bodily fluids, such as urine samples, and finally by inducing an illness by suffocation, injections and poisoning. Such people, she said, would tell a false story to get into hospital and will use the setting to tamper with drips and body samples [sic].

(Royal College of Psychiatrists, 2006)

Obviously, this is an argument for Fabricated and/or Induced Illness in Children, and it sounds a great deal like Munchausen's Syndrome by Proxy and Factitious Disorder by Proxy. Its development came in part from the shaken confidence in Munchausen's Syndrome by Proxy due to Meadow's inaccurate testimony on the case of Sally Clark (Utley, 2005), coupled with some apparent degree of politics, and increased pressures for diagnostic clarity in child protective services work. The situation was depicted this way by the Royal College of Psychiatrists:

> Dr. Eminson said that recognition of FII had come just at the time when there had been a sustained attack on the position of professionals—not just in Britain—where the idea of professionals as a source of expertise had been discredited.

There is an ethical balance here, and one that this author is not sure Fabricated and/or Induced Illness in Children manages. It strikes this author as a rushed concept, and one that is reminiscent of companies that change their name when wrongdoing has been found. Clearly, the case of Ms. Clark is tragic, and the particulars of her case are not argued here or meant to be lessened. But the history of healthcare, regardless of the diagnosis, is full of tragedies large and small based on misdiagnoses that were made for all sorts of reasons. It is evident that these phenomena are as vulnerable to political pressures associated with the sciences as any other (Horgan, 2012); and perhaps this is more the case given the lack of sound diagnostic clarity and recognition that the proposed IMDs have long struggled with.

> Bethany is an example of a perpetrator who uses intimidation to prevent the children, relatives, and professionals from stopping or reporting her behavior. As teenagers, Bethany's children are older than most victims. Still, she has effectively controlled their ability to speak out by restricting the people to whom they can talk and topics they are allowed to discuss. She defines for health care professionals what the children's presenting problems are and uses her version of those problems to undermine the children's own credibility.
>
> (Feldman, 2013)

In 2013, Feldman addressed the matter of whether patients, most often children, were *Playing Sick?* His book addresses the topics of Munchausen's Syndrome by Proxy and Factitious Disorder by Proxy. Here he presents an unusual permutation on the theme generally seen in such cases (pp. 139–140). While Meadow (1977) describes deceptive and skillful efforts by parents, Feldman describes Bethany, who instead seemingly used efforts at domination and intimidation of those around her to continue to gain the attention she desired by proxy. Also, note that, in this example, these are not "children";

16 Diagnostic Confusion and Delays

they are adolescents. So, it would appear that by bullying those around her, including her own children, Bethany was able to extend the time in which she was able to garner the attention she sought. In fact, Feldman describes how Bethany was able to buffalo professionals and have her child placed in a residential placement due to the lack of knowledge concerning these phenomena and her unusual presentation of these dynamics. As Feldman goes on to highlight, "No one wants to believe that he or she could be duped so completely. Also, in our litigious society, doctors may worry about the consequences if they make an accusation" (p. 140). The reader is asked to consider Bethany's agency, and the healthcare provider community's lack thereof, when adolescents are put against their will into a residential placement based on the parent's report and not on clinical necessity. This case highlights not only the dangers involved with Factitious Disorders by Proxy and other IMDs but also the fact that some patterns manifested in these individual and system interactions lead to pathology while others do not, underscoring the necessity for careful study, vigilance, and professional agency.

> Jerri, Amy, and Robert were all victims of Jim's hate and revenge. Sounding self- righteous and beyond moral reproach, Jim began a subtle process of brainwashing the children against their mother. It took him two years to slowly convince them that their mother was 'a terrible person whose only concern was for herself.' The children became more confused about how to feel. They wanted to both trust their father and love their mother. As time passed, their father's arguments were too convincing for them to resist. The children learned to hate their mother. All Jerri could do was keep her composure and try to rebuild her relationships with the children. She wanted so much for someone to understand how Jim and the court victimized her and the children.
>
> (Darnell, 1998)

What Darnell offers here is an example of Parental Alienation (pp. 3–4), with a description of the very real consequences that follow when there is a lack of intervention. As will be, and has been, described to a certain extent, children are generally of a certain age for Parental Alienation to take hold. Outside of the characteristics and behavior of the adults involved, two other important variables at this stage in our discussion should be addressed: *the lack of intervention by the courts* and the *time* this creates for what will be referred to herein as the *Alienating Parent* to engage in *Alienating Behaviors* (both will be further defined later in greater detail). As will be argued in somewhat different terms in the next chapter, and then again in Chapter 6, this "time" allows the metaphorical sparks for Parental Alienation provided by the Alienating Parent through Alienating Behaviors to take hold in the children. Over time, these sparks are fanned into a flame by these behaviors, and this excerpt from Darnell makes clear how important the variables of intervention and time are in addressing Parental Alienation. As this author has often stated in assessments or in verbal or written testimony, children involved with high-conflict custody disputes or divorce cases do not have the same protections as those involved with child protection cases under the *Adoption and Safe Families Act* (U.S. Department of Health and Human Services, 1997). Not only are these Parental Alienation cases able to go on and on for many years, there is seemingly not enough attention to the final codicil of the Best Interests of the Child statute that addresses continuous amendments either. In Parental Alienation, time is one of the most dangerous and key variables to consider:

> My experience has been that judges are extremely reluctant to issue the kinds of orders necessary for the optimum treatment of PAS[8] children in the moderate and severe categories. The legal process is intrinsically a slow one. The founding fathers guaranteed us a 'speedy trial' in the U.S. Constitution. That document was written and signed in 1789. I have not once seen a speedy trial in the context of a child custody dispute. I have seen speedy issuance of restraining orders, often without proper collection of evidence. I have seen speedy decisions following a sex-abuse accusation, again without proper collection of evidence. But I have never seen a speedy decision made in a child custody dispute. The usual duration of such cases that have come to my attention has been two to three years between the time of the initiation of the dispute and the time of the court's decision. By that time, the children are significantly older and the decision is made on the basis of data that may no longer be relevant. All of this works for the alienator, because the more time the alienator has access to the children, the more deeply entrenched will become the PAS campaign of denigration. By the time the children do come to the attention of the court, they will protest vigorously any kind of a court- imposed program that might lead to reconciliation with the alienated parent. (p. 67)
>
> (Gardner, 2001)

It is likely obvious by now that the dangers described within this section are not only in the cumulative activities of the individuals and family systems

18 Diagnostic Confusion and Delays

involved in an IMD, but also in the systems interacting with them. Gardner (2001) makes a strong statement when he says, "I have never seen a speedy decision made in a child custody dispute" (p. 67). Also, the reader should be aware that Gardner presented ninety-nine of his own cases in this particular article entitled, *Should Courts Order PAS Children to Visit/Reside With the Alienated Parent? A Follow-Up Study*. The outcome of these efforts was as follows:

> The court chose to either restrict the children's access to the alienator or change custody in 22 of the children. There was a significant reduction or even elimination of PAS symptomatology in all 22 of these cases. This represents a 100 percent success rate. The court chose not to transfer custody or reduce access to the alienator in 77 cases. In these cases there was an increase in PAS symptomatology in 70 (90.9 percent). In only 7 cases (9.1 percent) of the nontransferred was there improvement.
>
> (p. 102)

Failure on the part of healthcare providers and healthcare systems to act in cases with Factitious Disorder by Proxy proves detrimental, even lethal, to children and some adolescents. Here, Gardner makes clear that without the legal system stepping in, significantly, children and adolescents who suffer in the throes of Parental Alienation dynamics have limited prospects for their situation to improve and to avoid the long-lasting effects described by the title of Baker and Ben-Ami's 2011 article, *To Turn a Child Against a Parent Is to Turn a Child Against Himself: The Direct and Indirect Effects of Exposure to Parental Alienation Strategies on Self-Esteem and Well-Being*.

The incidence for these different phenomena varies depending on the study, but two recent publications do supply useful numbers (Anderson, Feldman, & Bryce, 2018; Harman, Leder-Elder, & Biringen, 2016; American Psychiatric Association, 2013; Stirling, 2007). For Factitious Disorder by Proxy estimates range from either 2 per 100,000 or 1,000 of the 2,500, 000 annual cases of child abuse. Further, Anderson, Feldman, and Bryce (2018) note, "Studies of published cases have shown that the mortality rate of victims of MCA[9] is between 6 and 10 percent, making it perhaps the most lethal form of child abuse" (p. 65). Meanwhile, Harman, Leder-Elder, and Biringen (2016) have described Parental Alienation this way:

> Using the percentage of parents who reported being alienated from their children in our poll (13.4%), this means approximately 22,211, 287 adults are currently targets of parental alienation. Given that many parents have more than one child, our estimate also implies that there

could be 22 million, 44 million, or even more children affected by this problem, although it is uncertain whether all children in each family unit would become alienated as a result of the parent's alienating behaviors.

(p. 65)

They add, "Interestingly, over 20% of the alienated parents on our sample reported not knowing what the parental alienation term was before it had been defined for them."

It, therefore, may be instructive to consider the words of Bernet and Baker (2013) from the PA literature: "One way to prevent the misuse of PA by abusive parents (men or women) is to have consensus regarding the diagnosis" (p. 102). Practitioners, professionals, and researchers would do well to consider that all boats float in the tide regardless of the name on the stern, and that we are employed to stem human suffering and death whenever possible.

Notes

1. He wrote this in 1971, the book was not published until 1972.
2. In the mathematical sense.
3. This author's purposeful emphasis on N for readers not familiar with the term
4. This author is aware of, but uncertain of, the controversies that have been brought up involving Rosalind Franklin and her data (Cobb, 2015).
5. Herein referred to broadly under the term Factitious Disorder by Proxy, which has been more frequently referenced in contemporary literature and diagnostic manuals.
6. Which will be described as one of the permutations of the term, Parental Alienation, given its far more frequent contemporary reference in the literature and diagnostic manuals.
7. It should be noted here, as well as a few other poignant places in this text, that the "cost" for scholarship has risen dramatically in recent years. Particular publishers such as the American Psychiatric Association charge the following (correspondence November 8, 2019): ". . . any selection of over 40 words is considered an excerpt, and there will be a $300 fee for each." Yes, that is "each", and though this author very much wished to make use of several references to the texts produced by this publisher to illustrate finer points the cost was unduly prohibitive. Exorbitant fees such as this defeats the purpose of not only scholarship, but open scientific debate plain and simple, and egregious practices like these should be aired and exposed.
8. Parental Alienation Syndrome, Gardner's term introduced in 1985.
9. Medical Child Abuse.

Sparks That Ignite Fires, Symphonic Orchestras, and Interrelated Multidimensional Diagnoses

2

Meanderings and Systemic Thought

As the title of this chapter may suggest, what is hoped for in the pages to come is that the reader will have traveled a number of different streams and tributaries to arrive at the confluence of ideas concerning how the complexities intrinsic to the phenomena of IMDs resemble other phenomena in science and art. During the process of building toward such a confluence, this author will ask for the reader's patience as some tributaries to these thoughts meander, while other streams flow more directly. Also, there are discussions that ebb more practically, and still others that flow in the direction of theory building. At times it may seem that the journey has cryptic or even enigmatic points of reference, which seemingly course away from the anticipated confluence. Still, this author will request that the reader take note of these reference points and hold them until later in the chapter or even in the text to understand how they contribute to, and/or fit in to, the IMD concept. So, while there will admittedly be confusing currents that may boil within the reader's mind, be assured that this author has included each thought piece and reference to contribute to the reader's initial and deepening understanding of how IMDs come to exist.

22 Sparks That Ignite Fires

In retrospect, the initial journey that led to the concept of the IMD began in many ways even before this author undertook his master's thesis (Bütz, 1991). The thesis had the influence of systems theory stamped on it (von Bertalanffy, 1968; Wiener, 1961), and yet at the time these influences were not so clear in the author's mind. While at San Francisco State University, I was the student of a psychodynamic program where my fellow students and I came to appreciate the forces that influence the development of the psyche as the ego navigates various relationships it encounters at different developmental stages. It seemed purposive, therefore, that the program had two professors with family systems orientations, which theoretically challenged and complemented the tenets of psychodynamic theory.

The novel insights that arose from this approach led to numerous questions about the nature of therapeutically informed diagnoses and change. There were specific conversations with Dr. Julia Lewis and Dr. Karen Hwang as I struggled to appreciate concepts in family therapy as they applied to the individual, de-pathologizing notions in systems theory, and seemingly exotic ideas concerning individuals within systems and systems within systems. The shift from considering individual pathology, the nature of what is therapeutic work, and the time it takes to understand therapy's influence were all notions challenged by systems thought. Family therapy redefined the idea of pathology, how therapy is considered, and how long it takes to produce change. These professors exposed this author and his fellow students to the radically different ideas proffered by Bateson and his colleagues (1972, 1963, 1956), Whitaker's musings (1989), the Milan Group (1978), and even Hoffman's (1981) new ways of considering cybernetic- systemic familial change.

These influences led this author to learn to take a step back metaphorically from cases, and then question what it was that was being perceived, where pathology lay, and what therapeutic work there was to be done. Subsequently, this author often found himself questioning what system, or part of a system, these clients were interacting with in order to behave in a fashion that brought them to my attention as a practitioner. Further rough and undeveloped questions at the time were:

- How have these systems influenced the client?
- What did the client bring to the clinical situation at hand psychodynamically?
- Why is the client presenting now, and what stresses has the client experienced that now bring her or him into the office?

To be clear, as a practitioner, this author does make diagnoses that clients may take as pathologizing. This author does make diagnoses that include personality disorders as well, but in making these diagnoses the influences above from family systems and psychodynamics are central to the formulation. As such, this author's approach to these diagnoses suggests developmental arrest, an arrest that was clearly implied in the *Diagnostic and Statistical Manuals of Mental Disorders* prior to *DSM-5*. At that earlier time, making a diagnosis on Axis II was meant to connote a developmental delay or impediment (American Psychiatric Association, 2000, pp. 28–29).

Stress, the Progenitor of Differentiation

After much thought on these matters, this author has also come to the opinion that these clients' functioning falls within a range based on their capacity for stress tolerance. Under greater stress, they tend to regress and function in a lower register, akin to the limitations singers may have, and in a fashion consistent with the descriptive language of narcissistic traits. However, under a lower load of stresses, these clients tend to buoy themselves up and can function in a fashion that may reflect the deceptive language of avoidant personality traits. Of course, such variations are not a day-to-day affair, and, instead, adaptive-maladaptive periods reflect months or years, depending on the quality of the clients' situations. In fact, in this example, and naturally with some argument from others in the field (Leichsenring & Leibing, 2003), these adaptive-maladaptive periods of functioning tend to represent the arc of personality disorders.

Perhaps debatably, the work of therapy in these cases is to recognize the quality of the developmental arrest and reinitiate the client's progress down the path of growth (Shedler, 2010; de Maat et al., 2009; Leichsenring & Rabung, 2008). Admittedly, within behavioral science there are all sorts of thoughts on how to do this from different theoretical viewpoints and modalities (Briere, 2019; Khoury et al., 2013; Tolin, 2010), including those from family therapy (Hoffman et al., 2005), and an array of other potential interventions.

It is proposed that a systems perspective shifts the vantage point for perceiving pathology, including theoretical constructs such as the Diathesis-Stress Model (Bleuler, 1963) and Ego Strength (Freud, 1961, 1967), to meaningfully viewing maladaptive behavior from a systems' theory perspective. The question here is what sets maladaptive behavior or pathological dynamics or processes into motion? Is it causal, too complex a phenomenon to understand, or is it a-causal? Fisher, Ury, and Patton (1992), truly systemic thinkers, provided a simple maxim for the majority of their negotiation techniques: "Separate the people from the problem" (p. 17). Of course, there were exceptions in which this was not possible (p. 107, p. 129), but, even so, they asked whether

24 Sparks That Ignite Fires

causality mattered or whether there were some stressors that would predictably set maladaptive behavior and/or pathology into motion? What conditions might amplify these states or dissipate their influence?

Reality and Causality

Discussing the nature of causality is an unavoidable topic when addressing the dynamic, interrelated, and multidimensional nature of Factitious Disorder by Proxy and Parental Alienation. Though this author has long held strong beliefs about the importance of dynamics, environment, pattern, and the uniqueness of each individual's place in the larger whole (Bütz, 1997; Bütz, Chamberlain, & McCown, 1997; Chamberlain & Bütz, 1998), there are also some basic causal realities. Dynamic patterns emerge from the interaction of individuals and systems. Each also possesses certain characteristics, dimensions and symptoms as part and parcel of the experience of existence as well.

In the past, there have been questions about reality and epistemologies within the family therapy literature (Maturana & Varela, 1987; Dell, 1987). As described some time ago (Bütz, 1997), some authors felt that the nature of epistemology should overlook identity and that conventions of language needed to be conceived of carefully. However, common sense held that it may be quite difficult to go through a day without making use of one's name, or the words "me" or "I" in one's discourse with others—no less, in reference to themselves (Bütz, Chamberlain, & McCown, 1997, pp. 15–16). There was much confusion at that time in the family systems literature as well as in other fields impacted by these epistemological emphases, and in many ways causality and objectivity were questioned (Hoffman, 1985). But such questions do have limits. Indeed, there is a knowable reality, as Mahoney (1991, p. 112) pointed out, a reality filled with solid objects that we each bump into on occasion.

These epistemologies and realities are no less at work in the case of Factitious Disorder by Proxy (FDBP) and Parental Alienation (PA) when practitioners, professionals and researchers begin to interact with family systems and collect data and information that become evidence through the application of scientific principles when coupled with a sensible degree of logic and reason. Reviewing the literature and noting the accounts from practitioners and professionals about their interactions amid such phenomena, it becomes apparent that under certain environmental stresses family systems become vulnerable to the influence of FDBP and PA dynamic stresses. Further, under these stresses a parent may or may not engage in abusive behaviors. The abuse is different in PA, though, and a child may or may not act on the alienating process of rejecting the other parent. Parental Alienation reveals itself through a series of more or less "if-then" considerations. It is argued that a cascade of successive dynamic interactions between family systems, outside systems, parents, and children results additively, and causally, in a measurable pathological dynamic such as FDBP and Parental Alienation.

In the pages that follow, these causal actions involve engaging in certain behaviors that, for example, create the larger PA dynamic. Though this author has misgivings about causality and the nature of objectivity, a series of dynamic stressors leads to the action or inaction of a parent and then a child, in order to create the pathological dynamic that the term *PA* describes. The individuals involved, the parents and the children, have certain characteristics as well. It is not, therefore, enough to say that there is an Alienated Child, as will be addressed more thoroughly later. Rather, the child *has been alienated*. But by whom? Causality and reality are implied by the term itself—Parental Alienation. Deductively, it is also dubious, with all of the existing literature generated by well-meaning scientific men and women, for others to claim there is no such thing as PA (Rand, 2010, p. 54), a matter that will be addressed further in Chapter 6. Objectivity in these cases is, indeed, hard fought and requires the sound application of the sciences of the day. Still, alienating behaviors are initiated by someone, and that someone, according to the vast majority of the literature, is *not* the child. Children do not alienate themselves from a parent, no more than they create healthcare conditions that require the care and attention of practitioners. The pathological dynamics of IMD occur within a family system that responds to stresses, and logic as well as reason informs us that it must be one or both parents who engage in abusive behaviors in order to create this pathological dynamic.

Figure 2.1 was developed to describe the flow of recommended considerations practitioners may, in an objective fashion based on proofs, work their way through in coming to the determination of whether an IMD is present (Bütz & Evans, 2019). Figure 2.1 provides an if-then process for practitioners to assemble the clinical data, findings, and information before them and to differentiate other conditions from Parental Alienation. These other conditions, and the phenomenon of PA itself, will be addressed in far greater detail in Chapters 6, 7, and 8. For now, we will simply consider the topics of Parental Estrangement (PE), Parental Denigration (PD), and parent and child forms of Alienating Behaviors (ABs/ abs). Alienating Behaviors would seemingly be straightforward enough depending on the originator, but it should be underscored that while these behaviors sound the same, parents and children

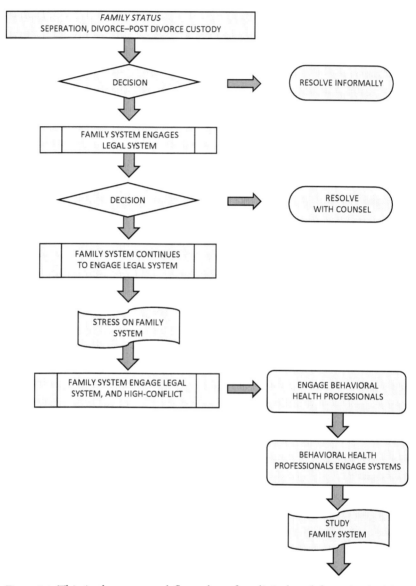

Figure 2.1 This is the proposed flow chart for clinical and forensic decision making as part of the process of ensuring whether there is proof of a PA IMDat each level, including ruling out such matters as Parental Estrangement (PE) and Parental Denigration (PD) and accounting for a parent's Alienating Behaviors (AB) as well as a child's (*ab*).

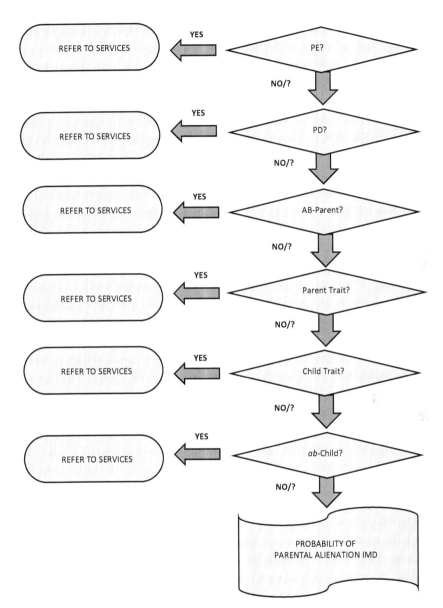

Figure 2.1 (continued)

in these situations engage in very different and specific behaviors from one another. Meanwhile, PE and PD require brief definitions. For children to be estranged from a parent (PE) is for them to have good reason to distance themselves or not to want a close relationship due to the parent's conduct (Kelly & Johnston, 2001). They are, then, "realistically estranged from one of their parents as a consequence of that parent's history of family violence, abuse or neglect" (p. 253). Thus, the rejection of the parent is both within reason and justified. On the other hand, with denigration (PD), it is simply a violation of the codicil in most parenting plans "not to speak ill of the other parent and to support the child's relationship with the other parent." Fundamentally, PD is per Rowen and Emery (2014), "the behavior of one parent disparaging or speaking negatively about the other parent in front of their children" (p. 165).

Regardless of form, an IMD has been conceptualized as additive or cumulative, wherein individual dimensional symptoms collectively interact with systems and subdynamics that transform into a larger pathological dynamic such as FDBP and Parental Alienation. An IMD is admittedly a diagnosis that is difficult to perceive without a larger objective contextual view of all the interrelated-dimensional interactions, and these conceptualizations require careful study before hypotheses about such matters are confirmed.

Metaphors That Offer a Different Vantage Point

The use of metaphors has not been, and will not be, used to downplay or minimize the impact or seriousness of FDBP or PA as Interrelated Multidimensional Diagnoses. Instead, the use of metaphors is offered to provide a substantially different vantage point in order to assist the reader in seeing, and then perhaps comprehending, both phenomena from afar. Also, these metaphors have been offered to underscore the importance of what a systems' perspective supplies by descriptively attending to how individuals and systems interact in a cumulative fashion under "certain" conditions. If, however, these conditions are not met, the pathological dynamic does not materialize. Third, these metaphors are offered to emphasize that the pathology associated specifically with FDBP or PA applies to the whole of the situation, not an individual, nor either system involved alone. It would be silly to say that a piece of wood caused a fire, or that the strings section of an orchestra alone can produce a symphonic piece. Further, though these individuals and systems may well be pathological in their own right, they are incapable of solely producing FDBP or Parental Alienation. Stress and the interactive qualities of each are what drive the cumulative forces between these individuals and systems onto the pathological dynamic.

By itself wood cannot create fire, nor can the lack of available moisture. A symphony cannot be performed by the strings section alone, nor can an orchestra with limited skills perform a complex symphony to the expectations of the composer, no matter how masterful the conductor. Thus, fuel needs to interact with other conditions to ignite, just as an orchestra needs to have certain characteristics in order to perform particularly challenging and substantial symphonies in a way that would meet the composer's intent. So, as with predicting fire danger in our national forests here in the United States, probabilities based on fuel, moisture, snowpack, and other weather conditions may include, for example, lightening. Orchestras too have dependent features, such as their skill set, the participation of certain virtuosos, and others that create a situation in which it is more or less likely that their members are able to perform a complex and technical symphony that meets or exceeds the intent of the composer. Additively, there are factors that create a higher likelihood of a wildfire or an outstanding performance by an orchestra. In the chapters to come, the same kind of additive probabilistic factors for the IMDs of FDBP and PA will be presented. It will be crucial to consider these matters from a systems perspective, again, probabilistically; that suggests a greater or lesser likelihood of the pathological dynamic association with an IMD being present or forming. The intention here is to literally account for one characteristic after another for individuals and systems in an interrelated fashion on one dimension of consideration at a time. Once these characteristics and interrelationships are accounted for across these multiple dimensions, FDBP or PA, as IMDs, may be differentiated from other phenomena.

Fire and FDBP

Over the years, many have asked the fundamental philosophical questions raised above, and there are a number of ways that this author might provide a different and explanatory vantage point for IMDs, such as breaking into a series of cryptic Buddhist koans (Nydahl, 2012; Yamada, 2005); lapsing into what was referred to in the 1980s as "epistobabble" (Coyne, 1982); or offering a discourse on epistemology (Hoffman, 1985). The reader will, however, be spared these exercises, and instead this discussion will make use of metaphors from art and nature to describe causation from a systems perspective as it applies to the concept of an Interrelated Multidimensional Diagnosis. From this author's vantage point, an IMD is no more confounding or mysterious

30 Sparks That Ignite Fires

than the summation of processes that occur with a fire. As widely known a phenomenon as fire is, it would be very difficult to describe it if an individual had never witnessed or heard the summation of such an experience in action. For example, the creation of fire requires particular kinds of fuel, a certain temperature, and a spark. It is the sum of these conditions that turns a spark into a flame. *Lexico* by Oxford (2019)[1] defines fire in this way: "A process in which substances combine chemically with oxygen from the air and typically give out bright light, heat, and smoke; combustion or burning." Fire is a common experience, but it is also a scientific phenomenon in which the end result is combustion that creates light, heat, and smoke. How would a fire be explained to someone who, almost inconceivably, had never seen one before? The reader is encouraged to ponder the same when considering how an IMD might be explained to some extent through the metaphor of fire. Consider the previous definition of fire and compare it to this one offered by Wikipedia (2019):

> Fire is the rapid oxidation of a material in the exothermic chemical process of combustion, releasing heat, light, and various reaction products. Slower oxidative processes like rusting or digestion are not included by this definition.
>
> Fire is hot because the conversion of the weak double bond in molecular oxygen, O_2, to the stronger bonds in the combustion products carbon dioxide and water releases energy (418 kJ per 32 g of O_2); the bond energies of the fuel play only a minor role here. At a certain point in the combustion reaction, called the ignition point, flames are produced. The *flame* is the visible portion of the fire. Flames consist primarily of carbon dioxide, water vapor, oxygen, and nitrogen. If hot enough, the gases may become ionized to produce plasma. Depending on the substances alight, and any impurities outside, the color of the flame and the fire's intensity will be different.

Thus, at one level of examination, the concept of fire appears to be a commonsense notion and may be explained to someone who has never seen it before. But fire is also a scientific phenomenon, and describing it as such is another matter altogether.

The differentiation between these two levels of description also holds for those involved with an Interrelated Multidimensional Diagnosis. In fact, going back to the discussion above about the origins of this author's thoughts on IMDs, the stage was indeed set during this author's graduate education at one level of description. What generated this author's interest in the phenomenon referred to as an IMD with a greater level of specificity was engendered through practice and the inability in 2006 to soundly address a referral to determine whether Munchausen's Syndrome by Proxy existed in a case. This author had a case several years before involving this phenomenon, but it was one that was a supervision case, and the facts of the case were much more developed. The referral in 2006 had both vagaries and confounding facts that required a more specific level of differentiation. These complications required a far deeper and more precise examination of the facts and relied on the diagnostic description of FDBP in *DSM- IV-TR*[2] (2000):

A. Intentional production or feigning of a physical or psychological signs or symptoms in another person who is under the individual's care.
B. The motivation for the perpetrator's behavior is to assume the sick role by proxy. (p. 783)

Criteria C and D go on to clarify that other motivations such as financial benefit is not part of the clinical picture, and that no other diagnosis offers an improved description. The limitations evident above and in this author's initial review of the literature led to an in-depth examination of the literature and research. The more this author studied the material available, the more inconsistent the criteria and titles seemed to become. As described earlier, even the *Sourcebook* from the prior *DSM-IV* was of little assistance, when even the location of the diagnosis was a matter for discussion at the time the *DSM-IV* was published (Plewes & Fagan, 1994, p. 626). Further, the same held afterward in the *Sourcebook* (1996): "A related issue considered by Fagan and Plewes was whether the diagnosis should be given to the person *inducing* the symptoms or to the individual *presenting* with the symptoms" (p. 880).

Working with several colleagues, this author ultimately generated our "Practitioner's Complaint" on the matter (Bütz, Evans, & Webber-Dereszynski, 2009). The descriptive phenomena that included Munchausen Syndrome by Proxy, Factitious Disorder by Proxy, and Fabricated and/or Induced Illness in Children at that time lacked diagnostic precision, a substantive body of controlled research, and agreement within the behavioral science community. For over forty years (Meadow, 1977; Money & Werlwas, 1976) these diagnostic phenomena remained elusive and unclear, and a point of *considerable* continued debate in professional literature as well as national policy. Not only was this a concern but it was also disconcerting that courts frequently made important decisions based on these diagnostic phenomena as if they possessed plain diagnostic criteria.

32 Sparks That Ignite Fires

Returning to our example of fire, it was as though each group of proponents for these phenomena had a new term, and many more have since followed, as described in Chapter 3. It was as though they were looking at entirely different fires, such as Classes A, "Fires in paper, cloth, wood, rubber, etc." through K, "Fires involving combustible cooking fluids such as oils and fats."[3] What made matters worse at the time was that most practitioners providing clinical services did not have ready access to extensive stores of literature and the research resources one would need to take on such a muddled subject matter as MSBP, FDBP or FII presented. There were natural limitations on time and resources that were practical considerations, and for this reason the earlier article was not held out as a comprehensive review of the subject (see Rogers, 2004; Sheridan, 2003 for such reviews). As Rogers (2004) and Sheridan (2003) described it, this literature consisted primarily of anecdotal case studies and little systematic controlled research. As a result, the nature of the complaint was that the practitioner had no solid set of resources to rely on in order to navigate this complex area of diagnosis, especially if called on to render an opinion in a clinical or forensic practice environment.

Experienced practitioners are regularly called on to make challenging and complex diagnostic determinations. Many diagnostic conceptualizations are not simple matters involving a single diagnosis or dynamic description, and, in fact, a good number frequently involve multiple diagnoses and several levels of dynamic considerations (Herman, 1992) that result in what one hopes is a well-grounded clinical conceptualization. The challenge was how a practitioner could reasonably explain to others outside of the behavioral health professions the complexities involved with the phenomena of MSBP, FDBP and FII without coming across as confusing, misinformed or even obfuscating. At the most fundamental level, these were all fires, but, in view of the import of such a diagnosis being made, the level of specificity required exceeded the earlier definition from Oxford, and it needed to be more like the definition in Wikipedia in order to speak to practitioners, professionals and researchers making important decisions. As will be described in more detail in Chapter 5, what we came to was the realization that there were particular characteristics that children involved in these phenomena had; the parents also had unique identifiable characteristics and engaged in dangerous actions or behaviors directed at their child(ren). Furthermore, the family system interacts with the healthcare system in a particular way, and in roughly one-in-twenty to one-in-ten cases, the aforementioned actions or behaviors were life-threatening abuses (Bütz, Evans, & Webber-Dereszynski, 2009). These parental behaviors, however, emerged out of a pattern of both long-standing and more recent familial interactions, even though the exact cause for these behaviors was not well known or well-studied at the time, with some exceptions (Griffith, 1988).

Consequently, a background in systems theory that steps back and examines the behavior, characteristics, interactions, and stresses proved helpful in understanding the phenomena created by these interrelated individual and system dynamics. These contingencies are no different than those seen in the scientific example of a fire. In an IMD such as FDBP, the fuel and conditions are not as clear on examination. But if the practitioner, professional, or researcher can step back from the immediate effects of the phenomenon and consider the situation from a knowledgeable systemic vantage point, the pattern of interrelated interactions and multidimensional conditions that yield the IMD pathological dynamic may become knowable.

Orchestras, Symphonies, and PA

A similar summation of processes occurs in different forms of art, such as a symphony played by an orchestra through the interactions between the woodwinds, brass, percussion, and strings. Per, again, the *Lexico* by Oxford (2019)[4], a symphony is thus: "An elaborate musical composition for full orchestra, typically in four movements, at least one of which is traditionally in sonata." Does the description offered by the Oxford do the experience of the phenomenon of a symphony performance by an orchestra justice? The sound that rises and builds across the scope of a symphony, along with those more subtle and delicate moments, is indeed something to experience. If the reader has never sat before an orchestra performing a symphonic piece that is both powerful and delicate, words to describe it prove insufficient. A symphony is the blending of, on average, one hundred instrumentalists whose efforts combine into one voice. As Leonard Bernstein (1958), the great conductor, stated:

> Any great art work . . . revives and readapts time and space, and the measure of its success is the extent to which it makes you an inhabitant of that world—the extent to which it invites you in and lets you breathe its strange, special air.
>
> (p. 124)

While the average enthusiast is certainly able to discern movements within the symphony, recognizing the contribution of one instrumentalist among the hundred when the orchestra is at full throat would require the talented and trained ear of a classical musician. To average enthusiasts, the cumulative

34 Sparks That Ignite Fires

sound produced is often enough. For them, the symphonic piece blends together into one experience across time. But what if a piece does not sound right? What level of sophistication is required to discern what aspects of the symphony are not coming together? Further, what movement does not sound right—one or all of them? Is the problem confined to a section of instrumentalists, or do one or two instrumentalists have difficulties with technically challenging parts of the score? Are there symphonies that this orchestra does not have the skill to perform as a whole, or does this lack of skill apply only to certain seats within the orchestra? For example, the Portsmouth Sinfonia were described in the following manner (Grundhauser, 2017):

> Eventually, the Portsmouth Sinfonia grew to include a rotating cast that numbered in the dozens, all doing in their level best to blast out well-known compositions. Thanks to a base level of musical knowledge among some members of the orchestra, their attempts at songs were almost always recognizable, just cringe- inducingly bad, with plenty of off-notes and random blasts of noise coloring each performance. This gave the Sinfonia a comedic appeal, but also ended up producing a raw sort of sound that gave it a distinctly emotional and human feel.

Thus, only under the right conditions, with one hundred skilled instrumentalists, strong sections of woodwinds, brass, percussion and strings, and an able conductor is an orchestra able to perform all four movements to create a sound symphonic performance.

The same may be said generally of PA, which may prove overwhelming to practitioners, professionals, and researchers attempting to discern what they have encountered and what is at work in this pathological dynamic. So much is going on in cases in which a high-conflict history exists, that these troubling dynamics often serves as a preface. In turn, stresses have built up over time from the interactions between the family system and the legal system (Johnston, 1994)[5]:

> Each of the above studies (conducted by Brotsky and colleagues, by Schaefer, Johnston, and colleagues, and by Johnston) were of children of high- conflict divorce, *whose parents had* **failed mediation, undergone evaluations,** *or had* **court-imposed settlements**.[6–12,19,29,32] According to Maccoby and Mnookin, these categories represent a small proportion, the top 10th percentile, of legal conflict in the divorcing population.

(p. 175)

It may be useful to reflect on what a high-conflict custody battle or divorce actually is. In her treatment of this matter, Johnston defined three dimensions of this state (1994):

> Divorce conflict has at least three important dimensions which should be considered when assessing incidence and its effects on children. First, conflict has a *domain dimension*, which can refer to disagreements over a series of divorce issues such as financial support, property division, custody, and access to the children, or to values and methods of child rearing. Second, conflict has a *tactics dimension*, which can refer to the manner in which divorcing couples informally try to resolve disagreements either by avoiding each other and the issues, or by verbal reasoning, verbal aggression, physical coercion, and physical aggression; or it can refer to ways in which divorce disputes are formally resolved by the use of attorney negotiation, mediation, litigation, or arbitration by a judge. Third, conflict has an *attitudinal dimension*, referring to the degree of negative emotional feeling or hostility directed by divorcing parties toward each other, which may be covertly or overtly expressed.
>
> (pp. 165–166)

Johnston further refined matters to include divorces that were troublesome when, regardless of dimension, these disputes adversely impacted the children of the family system, and she went on to cite studies that show post-separation matters involving custody and divorce are especially troubled for one particular group. Eventually, with some cautions about the size of the studies conducted and the sample itself, Johnston concluded the following about high-conflict family systems:

> Each of the above studies (conducted by Brotsky and colleagues, by Schaefer, Johnston, and colleagues, and by Johnston) were of children of high- conflict divorce, whose *parents had failed mediation, undergone evaluations, or had court-imposed settlements.*[7] According to Maccoby and Mnookin, these categories represent a small proportion, the top 10th percentile, of legal conflict in the divorcing population.
>
> To what extent are these children seriously disturbed? In each of the studies where standardized measures of maladjustment were reported, these children scored as significantly more disturbed and were two to four times more likely to have the kinds of adjustment problems typically seen in children being treated for emotional and behavioral

36 Sparks That Ignite Fires

> disturbance as compared with national norms. In general, boys were more symptomatic than girls.
>
> (p. 175)

High-conflict cases may be viewed as an environmental variable with a measurable outcome, as suggested in Johnston's article, involving the failure of mediation, parents who by necessity are psychologically assessed to clarify their capacity, or decrees due to the parents' failure to work out an arrangement. Plainly, this speaks to the maladaptive interrelationship between the family system and the legal system. It would stand to reason that any family system's members interacting with the alien and often intimidating legal system would experience this as a stressful situation. Further, family members would already be stressed due to the reason for these interactions, namely separation, divorce, change in circumstance regarding custody, parenting plan or parenting time. Stress is a fundamental part of these interactions, but some family systems, and the parents within them, weather these stresses better than others. Estimates suggest that between 5% and 15% of parents are engaged in a high-conflict divorce (Gordon, 2017; Black et al., 2016; Johnston, 1994), deductively indicating that between 85% and 95% of parents are able to resolve their relationship without these challenges. In PA, by definition, the family system, and at least one parent in that family system, does not weather these stresses well. Interactions with the legal system over time transform into high-conflict relationships for the reasons described by Johnston (1994) as well as others (Gordon, 2017; Black et al., 2016; Baker, Burkhard, & Albertson-Kelly, 2012; Birnbaum & Bala, 2010; Bala, Birnbaum, & Martinson, 2010; Saini & Birnbaum, 2007; Kelly, 2003; Hetherington & Kelly, 2002). Thus, just as an orchestra and a symphony have typical features—an average of 100 instrumentalists and four movements, respectively—the majority of PA cases include high-conflict relationships as a regular background feature.

Many times, too, one parent, sometimes both, responds poorly to these stresses due to characteristics they hold, arguably, prior to entering the family system. Characteristics that have generally been described as traits within the literature that addresses personality disordered diagnoses that fall under Cluster B in the *Diagnostic and Statistical Manual of Mental Disorders*. Once these ambivalent vulnerabilities are activated, the parent or parents begin to engage in the kind of Alienating Behaviors that are described in detail in Chapter 6. Just as certain orchestras have a weak string section, in PA one or both parents have certain maladaptive and/or pathological characteristics that leave them prone to responding poorly to stress. We, therefore, are not speaking of a broad range of orchestras, but only certain orchestras that have particular characteristics. Further, in PA, children also have certain characteristics, just as orchestras with a weak string section may have another weak section, brass or woodwinds. In PA, certain children may show similar weaknesses in the face of a parent's alienating behaviors as will be discussed in Chapter 7 through descriptors such as an Alienated/Vulnerable Child or a Naïve Child. The idea here is that different, cumulative characteristics of an orchestra are required to play a symphony as the composer intended. Leonard Bernstein's offered his thoughts on these matters (Crutchfield, 1985):

> I'm not interested in having an orchestra sound like itself. I want it to sound like the composer. That was my greatest pride with the New York Philharmonic—that they could switch on a dime from Haydn, to Ravel, to Stravinsky, to Brahms, and it would always be stylistically right.

While some orchestras abjectly fail, others manage certain symphonic passages adequately, and still others are able to "always be stylistically right." To be stylistically right would suggest a well-functioning family system, able to adapt to a variety of circumstances. Phenomena like PA, on the other hand, suggest the failure to adapt and still this family system is able to be differentiated from the more problematic Parental Estrangement dynamic which is akin to abject failure (Ludolph & Bow, 2012; Gardner, 2001; Kelly & Johnston, 2001). Moreover, under certain conditions PA, just like a great or terrible symphonic performance by an orchestra, has significant contributory factors that lead to the event. In PA, there are two sets of significant contributory acts or behaviors: the Alienating Parent (Baker, 2006; Kelly & Johnston, 2001) engages a child or children in Alienating Behaviors (Lopez, Iglesias, & Garcia, 2014; Kelly & Johnston, 2001). Then, in time, the child acts out Alienating Behaviors toward the Rejected Parent (Warshak, 2015; Kelly & Johnston, 2001). When this threshold is crossed the pathological dynamic that is PA is akin, perhaps, to the execution of an unpleasant symphony's finale.

Neutrality, Amid Dynamics, and Dimensions

No discussion of these topics and the cumulative nature of the proofs involved in discerning an IMD would be complete without literally coming to a full stop and underscoring the need for consultants and evaluators to hold an informed neutral posture in addressing these cases. That is, despite the considerable forces at work and the dizzying dimensions of consideration involved, Drozd and Olesen in particular (2004, p. 81), as well as others, warned of engaging

38 Sparks That Ignite Fires

in dichotomous thinking in a fashion that mirrors the dynamic created by these families. These practitioners, professionals, and researchers all emphasized the need to maintain a multi-determined focus on the dynamics in these cases. It was, therefore, critical for those working in this area to check their perceptions against the artificial distinctions implied within the literature on perception and personality as in, for example, the state-versus-trait discussion that has occupied the literature for many years (Allen & Potkay, 1981). In fact, in the process of completing this book, this author and his colleagues[8] had a lively debate about maintaining a healthy skepticism in such cases regarding accounts offered by one parent or the other. Just days later many of the cautions suggested above were underscored due to the forthcoming nature of a parent and the observable behavior of the other parent in the case. To this author, it was a vivid illustration of the need to focus on successive levels of proof at every dimension of consideration for characteristics, symptoms, and subdynamics before developing a theory of the case prematurely. Therefore, if practitioners and other professionals involved in these cases do not invest the time necessary to attempt to objectively perceive the scope of the dynamics associated with FDBP and PA, they may well rush to judgment based on one, or a handful, of interactions, and do so erroneously.

Much of what has been addressed regarding neutrality also centers on how practitioners and professionals in healthcare and law view the matters of FDBP and PA, and what will later be described as *variable exclusion and inclusion criteria* as well as other descriptions as part of the objective scientific community. The markers for acceptance today are several, as described above, in other work (Bütz, Evans, & Webber-Dereszynski, 2009, pp. 34–35), and as previously represented by the work of Pankratz (2006), Pagnell (2006), and Rogers (2004). There was, of course, the *Daubert Standard* or the *Federal Rules of Evidence* (i.e. Federal Rule 702), which was previously (Bütz, Evans, & Webber-Dereszynski, 2009) described by *State of Delaware vs. McMullen* ((DEF. ID. 0507014155) 6/1/2006, p. 28):

> At its core, *Daubert* dictates that Rule 702 is the governing standard for the admissibility of scientific evidence by specifying that '*if scientific,*' technical, or other specialized knowledge *will assist the trier of fact* to understand the evidence or to determine a fact in issue,' then the expert 'may testify thereto.'

Courts have had a tendency to admit evidence regarding both MSBP and FDBP, as well as the phenomena described under other terms, despite known controversies. Although, these matters will be revisited in far more detail in Chapter 4, these challenges with objective scientific measurement also hold for PA as well. Baker (2013a) and others (Saini et al., 2012) have done considerable work in this regard. In 2010, Rand also offered this to critics of PA:

> The fact that professionals are divided over PAS does not preclude widespread acceptance of the phenomenon, as evidenced by more than 150 peer-reviewed articles on PAS, and the publication of *The International Handbook of Parental Alienation Syndrome*, with 30 contributors from seven countries (Gardner et al., 2006). These contributions belie the argument that there is no empirical or scientific support for PAS. Critics like Zirogiannis overlook examples of recorded cases in which PAS was found to meet the Frye test, such as *Kilgore vs. Boyd* (2001) and *Bates vs. Peres* (2002).
> (p. 63)

By sharpening their focus on characteristics, symptoms, and subdynamics in the ways suggested herein, practitioners and professionals may well move toward the kind of scientific approach that is well accepted in the fields of healthcare and law. If this holds, then these practitioners and professionals will also be better informed and less likely to be subjectively drawn into these cases and rendered not only ineffective but complicit in the abusive dynamics. As Meadow stated in 1977, he and his colleagues had to begin their work anew and "work on the assumption that everything about the history and investigation were false" (p. 343).

Perhaps, Taking a Step Back, It's Not So Complex After All

At this point in the text, we have discussed a variety of artistic and scientific phenomena, the rough edges involved in the discovery of new phenomena, and the processes involved with creating and maintaining certain complex phenomena such as a fire, a symphony, and an Interrelated Multidimensional Diagnosis. In addition, in more recent pages we have discussed maintaining fidelity to the scientific notion of neutrality in the study of phenomena, and this author encourages the reader to keep in mind even more abstract concepts such as the significant challenges in addressing reality suggested by Heisenberg's work, the Airy Experiment, and other related concepts (Bütz, 1997, p. 87), concepts that clarify the fact that, no matter how neutral we attempt to be, we are always involved in the science at one level or another.

Although this author has pressed the reader to consider the subject matter of IMDs from a number of perspectives thus far, at this point it seems reasonable to take a step back and consider how accessible these phenomena are if one adopts

40 Sparks That Ignite Fires

a certain vantage point. Consider, for example, William Bernet's "Forward" to Baker and Sauber's text on *Working with Alienated Child and Families* (2013, p. vi).

> I am very interested in the topic parental alienation (PA). I talk about it a lot in conversations with professional colleagues, friends, and relatives, and sometimes total strangers. Most people do not recognize the phrase "parental alienation," so I usually say something like:
>
>> It's when there's a lot of fighting between parents. It's usually when they're divorced, but not always. Sometimes the children side with one parent and refuse to have anything to do with the other parent, even though they previously had a good relationship with the parent they are now rejecting.
>
> After hearing that brief explanation of PA, the person usually says they know all about it already. They tell me PA happened to himself and his first marriage or to herself when she was a child. They tell me PA happened to their brother-in-law or their best friend at work. They almost always mention how painful it was to experience or hear about PA.

The same may be said about FDBP, as most people have a passing awareness of the phenomenon, and outside of the scientific community many simply refer to it as "that Munchausen's thing that some parents do to their children."

At this point, the reader might consider that discussing or explaining these matters with the average person, or in passing, is one thing, but addressing these matters and the professional community is quite another. They would be right, and at the same time it has been this author's experience that when those in the professional community are provided a measured perspective, such as the one offered herein, they are open to listening. To provide real-world examples, this author will proffer two different cases involving, first, FDBP and then, second, Parental Alienation. What is supplied below are de-identified and paraphrased excerpts from actual prepared court testimony that addresses the basic aspects of an Interrelated Multidimensional Diagnosis.

Case Example: Factitious Disorder by Proxy

ATTORNEY: *Dr. Bütz, do you plan to diagnose Factitious Disorder by Proxy in this case?*

DR. BÜTZ: No.

ATTORNEY: *If I understand correctly, after your records review you are saying that there is a high probability that Ms. Jones' characteristics align with parents who engage in this behavior, and that she has engaged in similar acts. So, is that correct?*

DR. BÜTZ: Yes.
ATTORNEY: *So, is this how the determination of Factitious Disorder by Proxy done?*
DR. BÜTZ: In my view, yes. However, there are at least three models for making the determination, and a desk review such as this is one of the lead models being followed in this day and age.
ATTORNEY: *With regards to the standards for evidence, Daubert and the like, is Factitious Disorder by Proxy well accepted by the Courts?*
DR. BÜTZ: Yes, in the article I have provided there are references to both Delaware and Illinois. That is, despite my concerns about the diagnosis in its many forms, it is regularly accepted by the Courts.
ATTORNEY: *Are the symptoms described by the diagnosis of Factitious Disorder by Proxy rare?*
DR. BÜTZ: Yes, very rare.
ATTORNEY: *So, in combination with one another the symptoms described by the diagnosis of Factitious Disorder by Proxy is very, very rare?*
DR. BÜTZ: Yes.
ATTORNEY: *Dr. Bütz, so let's review the diagnosis again. I'm looking at Page 33 in the article, second paragraph. So, you are saying she possesses 70% of this diagnosis?*
DR. BÜTZ: No, I am saying per the desk review she possessed 70% of the symptoms from the literature in accordance with the new formulation of the diagnosis my colleagues and I have suggested.
ATTORNEY: *Dr. Bütz, you have a brief PowerPoint to illustrate these findings for the Court?*
DR. BÜTZ: Yes.
ATTORNEY: *Could you please share that with the Court and explain it?*
DR. BÜTZ: Yes, well, first of all, you can see the title slide and then the second slide that described the article by my colleagues and I.

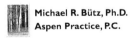

Figures 2.2 and 2.3 Introductory slide for PowerPoint presentation on probability of FDBP (left); and slide introducing the article from 2009 as the basis for the probabilities discussed (right).

DR. BÜTZ: Then, there is the third slide with the overall findings across all ten parent characteristic symptoms brought forward from the article.

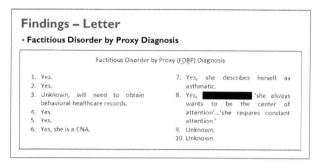

Figure 2.4 The slide describing the overall outcome across the ten variable symptom indicators in the case.

ATTORNEY: *So, pardon my interruption, but this slide indicated that seven out of the ten indicators were found in your desk review?*
DR. BÜTZ: Yes.
ATTORNEY: *Also, these indicators came out of the literature that you and your colleagues reviewed?*
DR. BÜTZ: Yes.
ATTORNEY: *Okay, please continue?*
DR. BÜTZ: Then, we have the fourth slide that described the first six parent characteristics that we had identified followed by slide five with the remaining characteristic symptoms.

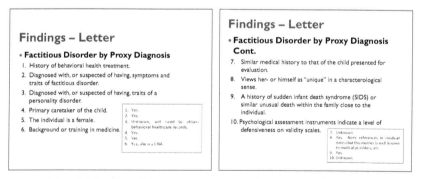

Figures 2.5 and 2.6 The slide describing the first six variable symptoms considered in the case (left); the slide describing the other four variable symptoms (right).

DR. BÜTZ: Next, we have the ten indicators from what we called the FDBP-Child Maltreatment Dynamic, and those begin with slide six, and follow through on slides seven, eight and nine.

ATTORNEY: *And, Dr. Bütz, it's not as though we have not talked about these twenty indicators earlier in this hearing?*

DR. BÜTZ: No.

ATTORNEY: *You've explained how you came up with them, and across the last few slides and the next four slides that you will show us, what I call indicators, are just presented for review to clarify your findings?*

DR. BÜTZ: Yes, that's an accurate description.

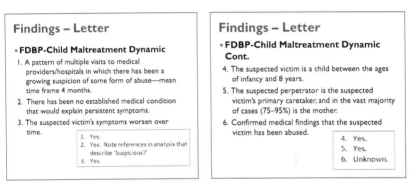

Figures 2.7 and 2.8 The slide describing the first three variable symptoms in the FDBP-Child Maltreatment Dynamic (left); the slide describing the next three variable symptoms in the FDBP-Child Maltreatment Dynamic (right).

ATTORNEY: *So, Dr. Bütz, if I'm looking at these slides correctly Ms. Jones has seven indicators out of ten that align with the kind of parent who engages in Factitious Disorder by Proxy?*

DR. BÜTZ: Yes, that's correct; it's a profile comparison.

ATTORNEY: *Again, if I'm looking at this correctly, she fits the profile for the maltreatment dynamic for seven out of ten indicators too?*

DR. BÜTZ: Yes, that would hold as well.

ATTORNEY: *So, should the authorities and her healthcare providers be concerned about this?*

44   Sparks That Ignite Fires

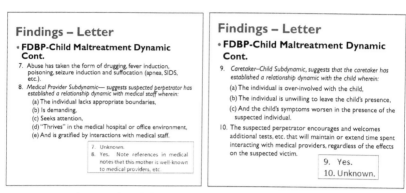

Figures 2.9 and 2.10   The slide describing variable symptoms 7 and 8 in the FDBP-Child Maltreatment Dynamic (left); the slide describing variable symptoms 9 and 10 in the FDBP-Child Maltreatment Dynamic (right).

DR. BÜTZ: Yes, it would suggest that there is a 70% probability according to the rough model that we have developed based on a reasonable review of the known literature that there is reason for concern.

ATTORNEY: *Dr. Bütz, according to the literature if someone possesses a convincingly high number of these rare traits what does it have to say about the care and custody of the child who may be a victim under their care?*

DR. BÜTZ: Place them outside of the care of the individual and see if the symptoms will relent. It's called the separation test. Further, until treatment is obtained and in good stead, only supervised visitation is recommended.

ATTORNEY: *So, remove the child?*

DR. BÜTZ: Yes, at least temporarily for investigative purposes.

ATTORNEY: *Dr. Bütz, so the other children that have been removed from her care that you have studied, did they get better—did their symptoms go away?*

DR. BÜTZ: Yes.

In this case, this author's findings were as follows; these have been paraphrased from the exact language of the conclusions reached in this case (note single quotes). Also, the reader is encouraged to take note that this case followed the 2009 article in which this author referred to an IMD as a FDBP-Child Maltreatment Dynamic.

'Per this analysis with the preliminary information that was available the quantitative probability that Ms. Jones may have been engaging in the FDBP- Child Maltreatment Dynamic and the child may have been subject to it was better than chance at 70%. Answering unknown to questions will require further research and inquiries. Thus, there is a reasonable likelihood that Ms. Jones may have these characteristics and symptoms at better than chance, at 70% again, and that the child may have been subject to the FDBP-Child Maltreatment Dynamic.'

The reader may take notice of the fact that this author came to a quantitative probability, and there will be more about calculating such probabilities as well as instruments described later in the text that specifically deals with IMD's.

Case Example: Parental Alienation

In this example, given the quality of the questions and answers that follow it may not be so readily apparent that often when this author works with attorneys on cases there is a mutual discussion of the quality of questions and the material reviewed. Then the attorney in the case often focuses in on questions he or she feels are most relevant, and creates questions based on this author's work and specific citations that get at pertinent matters.

ATTORNEY: *So, we are addressing the matter of Parental Alienation, and you have been discussing your concept of an Interrelated Multidimensional Diagnosis and how this fits the pattern of Parental Alienation. Do I have that about right?*

DR. BÜTZ: Yes.

ATTORNEY: *You have said there are, my words, building blocks to make this determination?*

DR. BÜTZ: Yes.

ATTORNEY: *So, Dr. Bütz, if I understand you correctly the first building block is that it often involves a child custody dispute?*

DR. BÜTZ: Well, actually it is referred to more properly as a high-conflict case, or a high-conflict post-separation divorce or custody case.

ATTORNEY: *Okay, the first building block is a high-conflict case?*

DR. BÜTZ: Yes.

ATTORNEY: *Why high-conflict?*

DR. BÜTZ: Stress, the stresses that result from the family system interacting with the legal system, often in very unproductive ways, creates the degree of conflict in the case.

ATTORNEY: *Like we have in the case here?*

DR. BÜTZ: Yes.

ATTORNEY: *Are there more building blocks?*

DR. BÜTZ: Yes, but first we need to take a step back and consider whether or not the case involves situations in which there is an understandable level of animosity toward an abusive or neglectful parent, versus, as Gardner has said, where there is "no justification" in Parental Alienation cases.

ATTORNEY: *So, Dr. Bütz, what is that called?*

DR. BÜTZ: Parental Estrangement.

ATTORNEY: *That is different from Parental Alienation?*

DR. BÜTZ: Yes, the child or children are understandably estranged from this parent, and there is a verifiable history of absences, abuses and/or neglect, or intimate partner violence.

ATTORNEY: *So, Dr. Bütz, if I understand you correctly the next real building block is that this pathological dynamic involves an adult who regresses into, or, who has long suffered from, what is referred to as a personality disorder and/or traits?*

DR. BÜTZ: Yes.

ATTORNEY: *So, in these cases what kind of personality disorder and/or traits; and, is there something that puts all of this into motion?*

DR. BÜTZ: Yes, Cluster B personality disordered traits . . . Also, what puts this into motion is often the person who suffers from the pressures or stressors of a custody dispute tends to feel jilted or slighted, and they regress or exist in such a state.

ATTORNEY: *Would it be fair to say that these people are self-involved?*

DR. BÜTZ: Yes.

ATTORNEY: *Would it also be fair to say that they put the child's needs second to their own?*

DR. BÜTZ: Yes.

ATTORNEY: *So, Dr. Bütz, then the next building block that I've read or that you've described to me is that these sorts of parents begin to engage in alienating behaviors?*

DR. BÜTZ: Yes.

ATTORNEY: *In the manuscript you've constructed you cited an article by* Lopez, Iglesias, and Garcia *(2014) who described a "Parental Alienation Gradient" and they described a series of alienating behaviors that described 80–90% of those parents tend to engage in, is that right?*

DR. BÜTZ: Yes.

ATTORNEY: *So, this list includes the following kinds of alienating behaviors engaged in by adults?*

DR. BÜTZ: Yes.

ATTORNEY: *So, 1. Failure to give information about the children?*

DR. BÜTZ: Yes.

ATTORNEY: *So, 2. Rewarding disrespectful behaviors in the child (toward the Rejected Parent)?*

DR. BÜTZ: Yes.

ATTORNEY: *Then, the parent who engages in alienating behavior, 3. Insulting or belittling the Rejected Parent toward the children?*

DR. BÜTZ: Yes.

ATTORNEY: *4. Add to this, Making decisions without consulting the Rejected Parent?*

ATTORNEY: *Then, also 5. Preventing Visits?*

DR. BÜTZ: Yes.

ATTORNEY: *So, Dr. Bütz, these five alienating behaviors are associated with 90% of these cases according to this article you cited by* Lopez, Iglesias, and Garcia (2014)?

DR. BÜTZ: Yes.

ATTORNEY: *The other alienating behaviors according to these authors that make up 80% included:*

1. *Interrogating child after visits to the RP,*
2. *Sharing personal/judicial information with the child,*
3. *Interfering in the child's symbolic contact with the RP,*
4. *Bindering telephone contact,*
5. *Seeking caregivers for the child alternative to the RP, and*
6. *Seeking accomplices for alienating (new partner, extended family, etc.).*

So, these alienating behaviors too?

DR. BÜTZ: Yes.

ATTORNEY: *I would like to introduce Exhibit A; which is* Lopez, Iglesias, and Garcia (2014) *who described a "Parental Alienation Gradient."*

ATTORNEY: *The next building block is that the child, themselves, has certain characteristics?*

DR. BÜTZ: Yes, in most cases.

ATTORNEY: *How old a child acts on the parent's efforts to alienate them from the other parent?*

DR. BÜTZ: In most cases, these children are between the ages of eight and their late teens.

ATTORNEY: *Is that always the case?*

DR. BÜTZ: No, there are extreme cases wherein younger children engage in these behaviors.

ATTORNEY: *Also, some authors do not refer to these behaviors that parents engage in as alienating behaviors; they use the words programming and brain washing, and say that these parents engage in behaviors often used to indoctrinate cult members—isn't that true?*

DR. BÜTZ: Yes.

ATTORNEY: *As one example you mentioned the work by Clawar and Rivlin from 2013, entitled "Children held hostage: Identifying brainwashed children, presenting a*

48 Sparks That Ignite Fires

case, and crafting solutions." It was published by the American Bar Association, wasn't it?

DR. BÜTZ: Yes.

ATTORNEY: *Am I correct that it involved work they have done since 1991, and over a 1000 case studies?*

DR. BÜTZ: Yes.

ATTORNEY: *Some authors have argued that under extreme circumstances younger children can successfully be alienated too. Is that correct Dr. Bütz?*

DR. BÜTZ: Yes.

ATTORNEY: *Dr. Bütz, I believe you are then familiar with the article by Ludolph and Bow from 2012, "Complex alienation dynamics and very young children."*

DR. BÜTZ: Yes.

ATTORNEY: *I would like to introduce Exhibit B: Ludolph and Bow from 2012, "Complex alienation dynamics and very young children," published in the Journal of Child Custody: Research, Issues, and Practices.*

ATTORNEY: *Dr. Bütz, please go to page 168, and begin reading: "Virtually all authors . . ."*

DR. BÜTZ: Okay.

"Virtually all authors who have written about alienation issues and dynamics in very young children have commented on the fact that their rejection of a parent remains fluctuating and their attitudes pliable."

ATTORNEY: *So, this would mean that for children as young as five or six, if we intervene it is not too late to stop the pathological dynamic of Parental Alienation?*

DR. BÜTZ: Yes.

ATTORNEY: *Even though it is not too late in these sorts of cases, Dr. Bütz, it is true that children can be influenced by alienating behaviors from a parent to the degree that they engage in, as Gardner put it, "a campaign of denigration against a good, loving parent, a campaign that has no justification."*

DR. BÜTZ: Yes, that is true.

ATTORNEY: *Isn't it also true that these children engage in a certain range of behaviors too, and the early work on this was furthered by Kelly and Johnston (2001)?*

DR. BÜTZ: Yes.

ATTORNEY: *I would like to introduce Exhibit C; Kelly and Johnston from 2001, "The alienated child: A reformulation of parental alienation syndrome" from Family Court Review.*

ATTORNEY: *Dr. Bütz please go to pages 262 and 263, can you read the list of behaviors that these children engage in for the Court?*

DR. BÜTZ: Yes.

- The child feels free to "express hatred or intense dislike toward the rejected parent."

Sparks That Ignite Fires **49**

- The child will "demonize and vilify that parent, often present trivial reasons to justify their hatred."
- The child is not reticent or inhibited in their "broadcasting the perceived shortcomings of the parent[9] to others."
- The child's behavior tends to be "baffling to the rejected parent, extended family and other adults knowledgeable about the prior parent-child relationship."
- The child will have also "strongly expressed resistance to visiting the rejected parent, and in some extreme cases, an absolute refusal."
- The child will express the wish to "unilaterally terminate the parent-child relationship."
- The child will, in common parlance, "want only to talk to lawyers who represent their viewpoint and to those custody evaluators and judges whom they believe will fully support their efforts to terminate the parent-child relationship."
- The child's reports of shortcomings are "replicas or slight variants of the aligned parents' allegations and stories."
- These children tend to generally sound "very rehearsed, wooden, brittle, and frequently use adult words or phrases."
- The child appears to be enjoying themselves, and "[t]here is no obvious regret."
- The child has been "given permission to be powerful and to be hostile or rude toward the rejected parent, grandparents, and other relatives."
- The child will "often idealize or speaking glowingly of the aligned parent as an adult and parent."
- The child may also report that the alienating/aligned parent has been "suffering, has been harmed economically and emotionally by the rejected parent."

ATTORNEY: *So, these behaviors are also described by Gardner in different words such as "the combination of a programming (brainwashing) and a parent's indoctrinations"?*

DR. BÜTZ: Yes.

ATTORNEY: *I would like to introduce Exhibit D, which is* Gardner's 2001 *article on "Should courts order PAS children to visit/reside with the alienated parent? A follow-up study."*

ATTORNEY: *Dr. Bütz read for me if you will from* Gardner 2001, *page 61, the bottom of the second paragraph, beginning with "When true abuse . . ."*

DR. BÜTZ: Sure.

"When true parental abuse and/or neglect is present the child's animosity may be justified, and so the parent alienation syndrome diagnosis is not applicable."

50 Sparks That Ignite Fires

ATTORNEY: *So, Dr. Bütz, when you speak of alienation, you are not speaking of what is referred to again as Parental Estrangement, where children may have reason to reject their parent?*

DR. BÜTZ: Yes, that is correct, and it's a different concept.

ATTORNEY: *But it creates confusion in the field?*

DR. BÜTZ: Yes, that is why many authors have addressed it.

ATTORNEY: *Are all forms of alienation the same?*

DR. BÜTZ: No, in fact early on Gardner described mild, moderate, and severe levels of alienation.

ATTORNEY: *So, Dr. Bütz, this is the basic framework is it not, where you have described a dynamic between a small number of contentious parents and the Court or Child and Family Services, a dynamic between one parent and the child, characteristics of each parent, characteristics of the child and that one size does not fit all in Parental Alienation? Do I have that right?*

DR. BÜTZ: Yes, that is a fair summary of what I have been describing.

ATTORNEY: *Well, that's not so difficult to understand, why is this concept such a problem?*

DR. BÜTZ: That's why I am writing the articles, in order to explain it in just this way; and because currently we do not look at clinical work from this vantage point in the field.

Notes

1. Retrieved May 18, 2018, www.lexico.com/en/definition/fire. From www.lexico.com/en ©2019 by Oxford University Press.
2. It should be noted here, as well as a few other poignant places in this text, that the "cost" for scholarship has risen dramatically in recent years. Particular publishers such as the American Psychiatric Association charge the following (correspondence November 8, 2019): "any selection of over 40 words is considered an excerpt, and there will be a $300 fee for each." Yes, that is "each", and though this author very much wished to make use of several references to the texts produced by this publisher to illustrate finer points the cost was unduly prohibitive. Exorbitant fees such as this defeats the purpose of not only scholarship, but open scientific debate plain and simple, and egregious practices like these should be aired and exposed.
3. www.osha.gov/SLTC/etools/evacuation/portable_ab
4. Retrieved May 18, 2018, www.lexico.com/en/definition/symphony. From www.lexico.com/en ©2019 by Oxford University Press.
5. Reproduced with the permission of *The Future of Children*, a publication of the David and Lucile Packard Foundation.
6. Italics and underline added by author for emphasis.
7. Italics included in this sentence for emphasis.
8. Colleagues at St. Vincent Healthcare Behavioral Health Associates. It is also worth noting, as described elsewhere in this article in different forms, these pressures create dynamics akin to splitting in the psychodynamic sense (Fairbairn, 1944; Kernberg, 1966;

Guntrip, 1968) and even parallel processes often discussed in the literature on therapeutic supervision (Searles, 1955; Hora, 1957). That is, processes within the family system or a therapeutic supervisory dynamic tend to extend beyond the realm of therapeutics and into the legal system and even into the larger community. These are not minor points to be made here; rather they are simply beyond the scope and depth of this particular chapter and will be revisited in Chapter 4

9. Obviously rejected parent.

"'Tis but thy name that is my enemy"   **3**

As described to one extent or another in the previous chapters, this author encountered a troubling situation wherein each successive venture into the literature only served to offer a more confused portrait of the phenomena described by MSBP and FDBP as well as, more recently, Abnormal Illness Behavior by Proxy (Adshead & Bluglass, 2005), Child Abuse in Medical Settings (Stirling, 2007), Fabricated and/or Induced Illness in children (Royal College of Psychiatrists, 2006), Factitious Disorder Imposed on Another (American Psychiatric Association, 2013), Medical Child Abuse (Roesler & Jenny, 2008), or Pediatric Condition Falsification (Ayoub, Alexander et al., 2002), among other names. As a diagnostician it has been this author's experience that with study the contours of pathological conditions usually come into focus. There are subtleties regarding the potential diagnosis that also come into clearer view and offer assistance with these determinations. Also, those who hold opposing viewpoints in the literature regarding symptom patterns tend to sharpen the image. In most cases these aspects of the literature serve to clarify the symptoms of, and refine the approaches to, the diagnostic issue at hand. However, no matter how deeply this author peered into the phenomena associated with MSBP and FDBP, the diagnostic image would not come into focus. Instead, the more this author attempted to adjust the image, to bring its outline and contours into view, the more clouded the image became with its multiplicity of symptoms and terms.

When this author stepped back from the term and its idiosyncratic descriptions; carefully reviewed the retrospective literature on MSBP, FDBP, and FII; and spent considerable time studying, a number of different repeating symptom patterns emerged and lists of indicators became apparent (Bütz,

54   *"'Tis but thy name that is my enemy"*

Evans, & Webber-Dereszynski, 2009). Conservatively, there were as many as two dozen lead diagnostic indicators and a number of dynamic indicators involved in attempting to determine what kinds of pathology and symptoms interacted to create these phenomena.

It was interesting at that time, too, that *DSM-IV-TR* (American Psychiatric Association, 2000, p. 781) only listed four research criteria for FDBP (a diagnosis designated for "Further Study"). In *DSM-IV-TR* (2000) the FDBP diagnosis was provided to an individual "(i.e., the perpetrator) whose presentation meets these research criteria [and] would be diagnosed as having **Factitious Disorder Not Otherwise Specified**" (p. 783). Dynamics, on the other hand, were arguably addressed within the coding system of the *DSM-IV-TR* under what are called "V Codes." Their brief description (American Psychiatric Association, 2000) of the function of V Codes stated that there was "Insufficient information to know whether or not a presenting problem is attributable to a mental disorder" (p. 5). As such, V Codes were not considered as important as so-called real individual diagnoses. At that time, this perspective appeared to be shared by third-party insurers, who commonly did not reimburse claims submitted with V Codes (e.g., Parent-Child Relational Problem, Physical Abuse of Child, Adult Antisocial Behavior, and others). From their inception, MSBP, FDBP, and FII were described mainly in dynamic terms, and their dynamic nature within the maltreatment literature has been a point of emphasis (Bütz, Evans, & Webber-Dereszynski, 2009, p. 33).

After conducting the literature review at the time, this author and his colleagues developed a list of frequently reoccurring traits that described the individual and interpersonal dynamic nature of MSBP and Factitious Disorder by Proxy (see Table 3.1). This list will be revisited and updated in Chapter 5 (Bütz, Evans, & Webber-Dereszynski, 2009, p. 35).

For now, what is important to understand is that these individual/dynamic symptoms have been described as not only rare[1] and complex but controversial. The authors' efforts to refine this list of characteristics and dynamic properties may still provoke disagreement among some professionals. In addition, since that time growing concerns have been expressed in the literature that these phenomena are far more prevalent than once imagined (Ferrara et al., 2012):

> Factitious disorders were diagnosed in 14/751 patients, resulting in a prevalence of 1.8%. Three of 14 (21.4%) patients fulfill the criteria for Munchausen syndrome. Munchausen syndrome by proxy was identified in four of 751 patients, resulting in a prevalence of 0.53%.
>
> (p. 366)

Table 3.1 Factitious Disorder by Proxy (FDBP) Diagnosis and FDBP-Child Maltreatment Dynamic

---

Factitious Disorder by Proxy Diagnosis

1. History of behavioral health treatment (I, E; Artingstall, 1995; Schreier, 1997, 2000).
2. Diagnosed with, or suspected of having, symptoms and traits of factitious disorder (I, E; Artingstall, 1995; Bools, Neale, & Meadow, 1994).
3. Diagnosed with, or suspected of having, traits of a personality disorder (I, E).
4. Primary caretaker of the child (I, E).
5. The individual is a female (I, E; Sheridan, 2003; Siegel & Fischer, 2001).[a]
6. Background or training in medicine (I, E; Artingstall, 1995; Chiczewski & Kelly, 2003; Korpershoek & Flisher, 2004; Siegel & Fischer, 2001).
7. Similar medical history to that of the child presented for evaluation (I, E; Bools, Neale, & Meadow, 1994).
8. Views her- or himself as "unique" in a characterological sense (I, E).
9. A history of sudden infant death syndrome (SIDS) or similar unusual death within the family close to the individual (I, E, O).
10. Psychological assessment instruments indicate a level of defensiveness on validity scales (I, E, O; see Rogers, 2004, for a detailed discussion of this matter, p. 232).

FDBP-Child Maltreatment Dynamic

1. A pattern of multiple visits to medical providers/hospitals in which there has been a growing suspicion of some form of abuse—mean time frame of fourteen months (I, E, O; Sanders & Bursch, 2002, suggest a chronology and table of events in most cases).[b]
2. There has been no established medical condition that would explain persistent symptoms (I, E, O).
3. The suspected victim's symptoms worsen over time (I, E, O).
4. The suspected victim is a child between the ages of infancy and 8 years (I, E, O).[c]
5. The suspected perpetrator is the suspected victim's primary caretaker, and in the vast majority of cases (75–95%) is the mother (I, E; Sheridan, 2003; Siegel & Fischer, 2001).[d]
6. Confirmed medical findings that the suspected victim has been abused (I, E, O).[e]

(Continued)

56 "'Tis but thy name that is my enemy"

Table 3.1 (Continued)

FDBP-Child Maltreatment Dynamic

7. Abuse has taken the form of drugging, fever induction, poisoning, seizure, and suffocation (apnea, SIDS, etc.; I, E, O).
8. *Medical Provider Subdynamic*—suggests suspected perpetrator has established a relationship dynamic with medical staff wherein:
   (a) The individual lacks appropriate boundaries (I, E; Siegel & Fischer, 2001),
   (b) Is demanding (I, E),
   (c) Seeks attention (I, E),
   (d) "Thrives" in the medical hospital or office environment (I, E),
   (e) And is gratified by interactions with medical staff (I, E).
9. *Caretaker—Child Subdynamic*, suggests that the caretaker has established a relationship dynamic with the child wherein:
   (a) The individual is overinvolved with the child (I, E),
   (b) The individual is unwilling to leave the child's presence (I, E),
   (c) And the child's symptoms worsen in the presence of the suspected individual (I, E, O).
10. The suspected perpetrator encourages and welcomes additional tests, etc. that will maintain or extend time spent interacting with medical providers, regardless of the effects on the suspected victim (I, E, O; Siegel & Fischer, 2001).

Note: I = criteria for inclusion; E = criteria for exclusion; O = criteria for outcome.
[a] While it is far less prevalent, men and close relatives have been identified as perpetrators.
[b] Their emphasis was on establishing, in short, what has come to be known as pediatric condition falsification (PCF) via a thorough records review. They stated: "The cornerstone of an MBP evaluation is the assessment of the veracity of claims made by the suspected caregiver" (p. 114).
[c] Some authors have put this age up to 16.
[d] Though it is far less prevalent, men and close relatives have been identified as perpetrators.
[e] This element and 7 are where the idea of pediatric condition falsification (PCF) would best apply.

For this reason, the discussions that follow address what constitutes the individual and/or dynamic symptoms involved with MSBP and FDBP, joined later by FII, and the proliferation of other terms for the phenomena as well as their permutations. The import of acquiring a thorough understanding of these matters was best summarized in Artingstall's (1995) comments from *The FBI Law Enforcement Bulletin*: "The more investigators know about MSBP, the better able they will be to identify perpetrators, clear innocent suspects, and most importantly, protect children" (p. 5).

Munchausen Syndrome and Factitious Disorder by Proxy

In 1951 Asher initially used the term *Munchausen Syndrome* to describe adults who fabricated illnesses to obtain medical attention with no secondary gain except to adopt the "role of illness" through unnecessary medical procedures and treatments (Abdulhamid & Siegel, 2006). Munchausen Syndrome was subsequently recognized in 1980 in the *Diagnostic and Statistical Manual of Mental Disorders—Third Edition* (*DSM-III*) under the heading of Factitious Disorder (p. 287); during the thirty-plus years between the *DSM-III* and the *DSM-5*, the diagnosis has not changed much or moved beyond the "intentional production or feigning of physical" or "psychological" symptoms, coupled with "a psychological need to assume the sick role, as evidenced by the absence of external incentives for the behavior" (American Psychiatric Association, 1987, pp. 318–319). Arguably, one of the most notable changes across the span of time was with the *DSM-5*, which moved these diagnoses under Somatic Symptom and Related Disorders, coupled with the criteria shift that included the following language (American Psychiatric Association, 2013): "C. The deceptive behavior is evident even in the absence of obvious external rewards" (p. 324). Thus, there was a shift with *DSM-5* to include language that identified "deception" in Criteria A (2013, p. 324) and then an elaboration of this in Criteria C. As will be explained later in this chapter, some practitioners, professionals, and researchers in the field have taken exception to this particular wording.

The additional term *by proxy*, therefore, extended the diagnosis beyond the individual with the need to fabricate illness on toward another through whom this dynamic is acted out upon (DSM-IV-TR, 2000):

A. Intentional production or feigning of physical or psychological signs or symptoms in another person who is under the individual's care.
B. The motivation for the perpetrator's behavior is to assume the sick role by proxy. (p. 783)

While it is conceptually possible that FDBP could involve another adult, the literature to date suggests that in most cases the *by proxy* is a child, which becomes crucial when considering the current estimates for the age of a child

58 "'Tis but thy name that is my enemy"

and the mortality and disability estimates (Yates & Bass, 2017; Bass & Glaser, 2014).

There has been substantial disagreement about MSBP and FDBP within the literature. One position (Fisher & Mitchell, 1995) held was that these disorders did not constitute "a diagnosis in a traditional sense but an observational description with implications regarding cause" (p. 532). Rogers's (2004) comprehensive article provided one of the most thoughtful distillations of the complex matters that surround these diagnostic symptoms. While Meadow (1977) first described MSBP, Rogers (2004), citing Rosenberg's work (1987), described the four main characteristics of the phenomenon:

a.   The child's illness simulated or produced by the parent/caretaker;
b.   Often persistent presentation for medical evaluation and treatment;
c.   The perpetrator's denial of any knowledge about the etiology of the illness; and
d.   The abatement of acute symptoms when separated from the perpetrator. (p. 226)

Other literature at that time also indicated that the alleged MSBP/FDBP parent/caretaker engaged in a "relationship" with healthcare providers in which attention-seeking behavior might become evident (Donald & Jureidini, 1996; Schreier & Libow, 1993). This suggested that in FDBP the *DSM-IV-TR* research criteria might have been too narrow. Despite Meadow's initial description of MSBP, and his continued remarks on the topic as a diagnosis (1995), it was Rogers's (2004) impression that FDBP was "more encompassing than MSBP in allowing *the classification of persons other than parents*.[2] However, it is more circumscribed in its delimitation of patients' putative motivation to the adoption of a 'sick role'" (p. 226). This creates a fine but important turn on the idea of Factitious Disorder by Proxy. Parenthetically, Meadow (1995) had recommended expanding the notion of motivation from "adoption of a sick role" to include "attention-seeking behavior." Such references that are more encompassing and address both adopting a sick role as well as engaging in attention-seeking behavior are quite important amid proliferating terminology for these phenomena, which seemingly has not heeded or recognized Meadow's earlier recommendation.

Rogers (2004) had also clearly elucidated substantial fundamental flaws involved with these individual and/or dynamic diagnoses. In a classic sense, diagnoses are made based upon fundamental rubrics, such as criteria for *inclusion*, *exclusion*, and *outcomes*. Citing Syndeham via Murphy et al. (1974),

Rogers (2004) clarified that, fundamentally, "every disorder must have inclusion, exclusion, and outcome criteria" (p. 227). Rogers (2004) further illustrated the challenges with the diagnosis of FDBP by stating:

> The proposed inclusion criteria do not delineate symptoms for the person with FDBP, but rather the *effects* of apparent symptoms on others and the putative *motivation* for producing these effects. In addition, the sole exclusion criterion ('not better accounted by another mental disorder'; American Psychiatric Association, 1994, p. 727) is simply too vague to be useful. Finally, studies of outcome criteria (e.g. Bools, Neale, & Meadow, 1993; Libow, 1995) tend to focus on the child victims rather than the FDBP parents.
>
> (p. 227)

He also pointed out that, when larger issues such as motivation are considered, incentives extend beyond a circumscribed sick role. Rogers called for consideration of the possible diagnosis of *Malingering by Proxy*. With this diagnosis, the individual would be conceptualized as not only consciously feigning signs and symptoms but also as being motivated to do so in order to obtain an external incentive.

Factitious Disorder Imposed on Another (FDIA)

Given the landscape described by Rogers and others regarding the use of the term *FDBP*, it certainly was surprising, as much as it was baffling, for the American Psychiatric Association (2013, pp. 325–326) to throw into the mix one more term to describe the phenomenon, *Factitious Disorder Imposed on Another* (FDIA). After this author conducted a thorough, but certainly not exhaustive, literature review, little explanation was evident for the change in terminology. This author has been left to observe that the workgroup on Somatic Symptoms and Related Disorders did not make any mention of FDIA in its update to the professional community (Dimsdale & Creed, 2009). Although the workgroup did reportedly address FDBP (2009, p. 475), it did not explain, per Ford (2011), that, "The proposed criteria for *factitious disorder imposed on another* are the same except there is the presentation of another person (the victim) to others as ill or impaired (Dimsdale & Creed, 2009, pp. 291–292)". Also, subsequent correspondence did not identify this matter either amid other concerns that were addressed to the workgroup (Dimsdale & Creed, 2010).

60 "'Tis but thy name that is my enemy"

Preceding the update above, and it would seem thereafter, the larger matter of whether or not to include Factitious Disorders (FD) as a category under Somatic Symptoms and Related Disorders engendered a significant debate (Hamilton, Feldman, & Janata, 2009):

> As revisions to the fifth edition of the *Diagnostic and Statistical Manual of Mental Disorders* (DSM-V) are being contemplated, numerous articles on the fate of the somatoform disorder (SD) category have been published . . . However, only one of these analyses has even mentioned factitious disorder (FD) [15] despite the phenotypic resemblance between SD and FD. Some analyses have specifically addressed the fate of the FD category, but they are far fewer in number.
>
> [15–21]

In fact, these same authors provided a refrain reminiscent of Rogers's work (2004), described earlier, in the following excerpts (Hamilton et al., 2009):

> First, a given category can be regarded as valid if research confirms that it is characterized by epidemiologic or etiologic features that distinguish it from other disorders . . .
> Second, categories have practical value if the persons who are assigned to them are distinct in clinically meaningful ways from those who are not . . .
> It is worth mentioning a third way of evaluating a diagnostic category, although it is not technically an indicator of validity. This is a question of whether a diagnosis is actually used in clinical practice.

The reader is encouraged to remember these benchmarks as well as Rogers's earlier observations, since later in this chapter what this author has called the *Platypus Paradox* will be discussed to address these and other challenges with terminology.

Krahn, Bostwick, and Stonnington (2008) have made the argument that the *DSM-5* should have included FD as a subtype of somatoform disorders, noting that, "Both Disorders feature medically unexplained physical symptoms, and it is widely agreed that both are organized around trying to meet emotional needs in maladaptive ways" (p. 277). In their response to Turner's advocacy of his position, these authors also observed that defining the boundary of what is a lie is problematic:

> Turner has called for creating a specific DSM—V category for patients with "lying or deliberate autobiographical falsification."[8] Such a

"'Tis but thy name that is my enemy" **61**

category would combine malingering and factitious disorders, as well as the phenomenon of *pseudologia fantastica*.

(p. 278)

Krahn and his colleges also remarked that practitioners regularly commit errors in their documentation of cases and seemingly asked aloud, "Is that a lie?" Then, obviously, we have Turner's view (2006), which, speaking to Criteria A, focused on the intentional production of physical or psychological signs or symptoms and then, in regard to Criteria B, addressed the motivation to assume the sick role. He stated: "The two criteria need reformulating in terms of lies and self-harm, respectively. Criterion C causes misdiagnosis by pushing factitious disorders into the somatoform and malingering categories and should be abandoned" (p. 23). Ford (2011, p. 291), then, has also observed that several had proposed it "is a syndrome of misbehavior" (Bass & Halligan, 2007; Ford, 2005; Turner, 2006); though others supported "maintaining factitious disorder as an Axis I diagnosis" (Hamilton, Feldman, & Janata, 2009; Krahn, Bostwick, & Stonnington, 2008). The term *FDIA* was plainly in the wind with Ford's specific mention of it in this book chapter, but explanation of its justification and use has proven to be elusive.

Moving beyond FD, with the publication of *DSM-5*, not only did FDBP change to Factitious Disorder Imposed on Another (FDIA) but the language shifted (American Psychiatric Association, 2013) to include the phrase "deceptive behavior" (p. 325). The term *deception* is again included with the following considerations for making the diagnosis:[3]

Differential Diagnosis

Caregivers who lie about abuse injuries in dependents solely to protect themselves from liability are not diagnosed with factitious disorder imposed on another because protection from liability is an external reward.

(p. 326)

The passage goes on to state that deception must still be apparent without outward incentives. While FDs may perhaps have been suitably placed in the section on Somatic Symptoms and Related Disorders, an argument can be made that FDIA would have been better placed under the "Trauma and Stressor-Related Disorders" subgroup (Friedman, 2013). Friedman and his colleagues described what follows as threshold criteria for inclusion: "All diagnoses within this chapter stipulate that onset or worsening of symptoms

62 *"'Tis but thy name that is my enemy"*

was preceded by exposure to an aversive event" (p. 549). This workgroup also made clear a refrain of sorts that will be repeated throughout this chapter and the next one:

> The *DSM-5* adopted a very conservative approach. Recognizing that any change to any diagnostic criterion has important clinical and scientific consequences, the evidence had to be very strong to modify, delete, or add a new symptom to any psychiatric disorder.
>
> (p. 548)

Although such decisions are now in the past, given the aspirations above and the many controversies that have been described, the diagnosis may have been better placed in the aforementioned section or under "Other Conditions That May Be a Focus of Clinical Attention." In light of the matters above, the advantage or necessity of using FDIA as one more descriptive permutation in an already crowded field was, in this author's view, certainly questionable. Regardless of the cautions described above and this author's own misgivings, the term is now in use as a form of somatic symptom, being explained to practitioners as such (Bursch, 2014), and case examples are being provided (Faedda et al., 2018).

Interestingly, out of the debate on these matters came what may well prove to be a very useful schematic model (Bass & Halligan, 2007) that articulates the span between psychopathology and subjective choice:

> To this purpose we propose a simple schematic model for conceptualizing illness deception that involves both psychopathology and subjective choice (Figure 3.1).
>
> Considered as an act of willful deception, illness deception can be meaningfully conceptualized within a socio-legal or moral model of human nature that recognizes the capacity for choice and the potential for pursuing benefits associated with the sick role. This pervasive and deep-seated notion of choice and individual responsibility provides a reasonable framework from which to explain and discuss illness behavior not produced by disease, injury, psychopathology or psychosocial factors.
>
> (p. 83)

While this author, as described elsewhere, obviously disagrees with Bass and Halligan's conclusions, the argument they have made, and the schematic model supplied in particular (see Figure 3.1), may well provide a useful

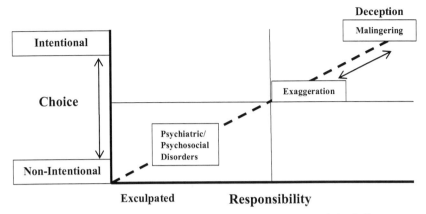

Figure 3.1 Bass & Halligan's Figure 3.1 (2007, p. 83), Model of Illness Deception, reproduced by the author for illustrative purposes here and in Chapter 5.

continuum to address the proliferation of new terms or even entertain new diagnostic distinctions.

Potential Precursors for Proliferation

To take on these new terms it is necessary to go back and revisit a few articles that may well have created the proliferation of terms spoken to thus far in the text, and that will be addressed specifically in the next section of this chapter. Two works have often been cited: the article put forward by the task force from the American Professional Society on the Abuse of Children (APSAC) that addressed definitions of MSBP (Ayoub, Alexander et al., 2002) and the considerable review article by Sheridan (2003), which it would seem apropos to note also included step-by-step comparisons to the earlier work done by Rosenberg (1987). Publication dates do not reflect the length of these studies, and one must take into consideration publication lag. The APSAC task force began its work in 1996, while Sheridan submitted her manuscript in 2000. It is worth mentioning, therefore, that the *DSM-IV-TR* was issued during these time frames, and with its publication FDBP was brought forward as a diagnosis (American Psychiatric Association, 2000):

> Fundamentally the aforementioned task force was assembled to (Ayoub, Alexander et al., 2002, p. 105): . . . develop working definitions

64 "'Tis but thy name that is my enemy"

for the constellation of behaviors currently described as Munchausen by proxy (MBP). The aim of the task force was to develop a synthesis of the most current thinking in pediatrics, psychiatry, psychology, child protection, and law and to articulate the current consensus among professionals to facilitate the identification and treatment of this complex clinical problem.

(p. 751)

This task force observed at that time an estimated growing prevalence:

Furthermore, experts now agree that MBP cases are likely to go undetected because of the covert nature of their presentation, the striking ability of the perpetrators to fool those around them, and the many obstacles to the identification of these cases by professionals.

(pp. 105–106)

With that said, three tasks needed to be addressed: to create a working definition, to ensure that this definition reflected current thinking, and, most importantly, to "facilitate the identification and treatment of this complex clinical problem" (p. 105).

This task force argued that in its current form MSBP had but two components, the child victim and the adult perpetrator, whose actions they described in this way: "[The] caregiver, most often the child's mother, intentionally falsifies history, signs, and/or symptoms in her child to meet her own self-serving psychological needs" (p. 106). Interestingly, the task force went on to comment on the fact that MSBP had been described as a "family disorder," and that healthcare providers "frequently play a central role in contributing to the interactions in MBP" (p. 106). This treatment of the subject matter actually suggested four components that interact with one another, rather than simply two. Instead of describing one term for practitioners, professionals, and researchers to rally around, the task force bifurcated the phenomenon into two terms: Pediatric Condition Falsification (PCF) and Factitious Disorder by Proxy. The only apparent difference, however, was the notion of attribution in FDBP, i.e., "persons who intentionally falsify history, signs or symptoms in a child to meet their own self-serving psychological needs" (p. 106). But, in all honesty, are not those very attributes implied by the term *Pediatric Condition Falsification*? Does not the term *falsification* indicate the same thing, no matter in which phrasing you use it? Compared side-by-side (pp. 106–107) these two terms appear indistinguishable on the aforementioned metric of "facilitate the identification and treatment of this complex clinical problem" (p. 105).

PCF is a form of abuse. Some of the documented physical conditions alleged in these children include but are not limited to. . . . The first course of action when MBP is suspected is to identify and report the presence of maltreatment in the child, herein defined as child abuse by PCF.

Persons who intentionally falsify history, science, or symptoms in a child to meet their own self-serving psychological needs are diagnosed with factitious disorder by proxy (FDP) . . . . Different kinds of self-serving psychological needs may motivate this behavior.

The perceptible difference seems to lie in the contortion of language this task force used as they made the case that PCF is somehow a more straightforward phenomenon and/or clearly a form of child abuse per the citation above. The task force later suggested that motivations in FDBP are again somehow different:

However in FDP, they are not primary in the sense that the driving force for the parent is other than these coexisting incentives. Motivation in this condition as in others is often arrived at through the careful scrutiny and understanding of circumstantial evidence.

(p. 108)

Reviewing these and other proposed distinctions only serves to raise the question as to whether the very same may be said of the other term. More perplexing still is that the task force offers a subsection entitled "Conditions That May Be Confused With Abuse by PCF and/or FDP" (p. 108). This was perplexing, in that the distinctions between PCF and FDBP were, perhaps arguably, not all that clear in the first place. It is suggested that, rather than truly facilitating identification, the task force, though likely well intentioned, only confused matters more, artificially bifurcated the dynamic, and thereby added support for one more term as well as perhaps the proliferation of others. *DSM-IV-TR* had already been published, and FDBP was the consensus term described in that manual.

Then we have Sheridan's more actuarial work in 2003, where she benchmarked her findings against Rosenberg's research from 1987. She analyzed 451 cases and found the following patterns with these cases of MSBP:

- Victims were "usually 4 years of age or older"
- "Six percent of victims were dead"
- 7.3% "were judged to have suffered long-term permanent injury"
- "Twenty five percent of victims' known siblings are dead"

- 60.3% "of siblings had illnesses similar to those of the victims or raised suspicion of MBP"
- "Mothers were perpetrators in 76.5% of cases" (p. 431)

Sheridan (2003) went on to articulate more distinctions while noting that in Rosenberg's work she found a higher rate of deaths and permanent injuries, and that mothers were exclusively the perpetrators, "Rosenberg's 98% of birth mothers and 2% [of] adoptive mothers" (p. 436). She also highlighted concerns about a small percentage, 5.3% of her sample, where there appeared to be secondary gain (p. 439), a finding that did not fit with the Rosenberg's previous patterns. She also stated the familiar refrain in this literature, citing Rosenberg as well as others, that cases of FDBP "should be considered a minimum estimate of actual occurrences" (p. 440). Sheridan concluded with four points, which included:

> The finding that MBP may co-exist with elements of secondary gain or with other injuries in a minority of cases may make formal definition and theorizing more difficult. In practice, however, those interested in child protection should be aware that such "mixed cases" exist, and do not preclude the presence of genuine MBP as Rosenberg defines it.
>
> (p. 444)

What we have with these two articles are very different approaches to the phenomenon: arguably a more top-down approach by the task force (Ayoub, Alexander et al., 2002) compared to the bottom-up approach represented by Sheridan (2003) and, by extension, Rosenberg (1987). Two developments are marked by these articles, among others, and again by the publication of the *DSM-IV-TR* in 2000. First, the task force (2002) endorsed the use of PCF by seemingly isolating falsification as an a-motivational phenomenon in comparison with those motivations described by the term *Factitious Disorder by Proxy*. Second, Sheridan (2003) concludes her review by describing what she refers to as "mixed cases," but she cautions that these kinds of cases "do not preclude the presence of genuine MBP as Rosenberg defines it" (p. 444). In turn, Sheridan leaves space between PCF and FDBP, and at the fringes of MSBP, and she seems, perhaps unwittingly, to open proliferation and speculation on phenomena that had heretofore been contained under MSBP initially and then later under FDBP with the publication of the *DSM-IV-TR*.

AIBP, CAMS, CFIC, FII, MCA, and PCF

At the time the earlier article with my colleagues was written (2009), a number of new terms were introduced to describe the phenomenon under study through several articles. To maintain a sense of continuity and retain the focus in the *DSM* series on factitious disorders as discussed above, the term *FDBP* was maintained in order to underscore its consistent use since 2000 with the *DSM-IV-TR*. Also, there was the convention of using of Factitious Disorder in prior manuals in the *DSM* series to connect to this author's prior article (Bütz, Evans, & Webber-Dereszynski, 2009), and also in light of a more recent article that addressed Interrelated Multidimensional Diagnoses (Bütz & Evans, 2019). Thus, for these and other reasons that will be explained, FDBP was maintained as the term to describe the phenomenon. However, among the many challenges associated with the *DSM-5* (Bütz, 2014), the language of this diagnosis also changed to *Factitious Disorder Imposed on Another*. The rationale for that change appears to be largely absent in the literature. As described above, there are just a few sources that speak to this change in language that seemed, again, to contribute to the spread of proliferating titles, including terms such as *Abnormal Illness Behavior by Proxy* (Adshead & Bluglass, 2005), *Fabricated and/or Induced Illness in children* (Bools, 1996; Royal College of Psychiatrists, 2006), *Medical Child Abuse* (Roesler & Jenny, 2008), *Pediatric Condition Falsification* (Ayoub, Alexander et al., 2002), and *Child Abuse in Medical Settings* (Stirling, 2007). Still other terms have not been mentioned here, and the trend toward proliferating terms has continued.

Taking on these new terms somewhat alphabetically, we have Abnormal Illness Behavior by Proxy (AIBP), which has been described seemingly as a subvariant of FII anchored in attachment theory (Adshead & Bluglass, 2005, 2001). These authors (2005) described, first of all, illness behavior as "a term that refers to the ways individuals perceive, experience and respond to illness" (p. 330). Further, they reported that this involves "individual, social and cultural experiences and constructs of illness and may be subject to special expectations" (2005, p. 330). Per the account of Adshead and Bluglass (2005), then, "Factitious illness by proxy behavior involves three forms of abnormal illness behavior: false accounts of symptoms, fabricated symptoms and induction of symptoms (Bools, 1996, p. 330)". Here, again, terms and descriptions are proliferating wherein these authors appear to state that the notion of FII has subvariants, such as *abnormal illness behavior, false accounts of symptoms*, and *induction symptoms*. Although the title of Adshead and Bluglass's article and its focus muddy the waters associated with the phenomenon under

68 *"'Tis but thy name that is my enemy"*

study with one more term, some important contributions from the attachment literature are brought into this discussion by these authors. Those that have come from the attachment literature and entered into this discussion (Bass & Glaser, 2014; Kozlowska, Foley, & Crittenden, 2006) have attempted to describe the psychological makeup of these mothers, the family and the family background, as well as what psychological dynamics they may be acting out consciously or unconsciously, inclusive of the notion of motivation. After a number of considerations, Adshead and Bluglass (2005) described the following: "Our main finding is that mothers with factitious illness by proxy are more like a clinical group than not, and therefore are likely to have unmet needs, which may be relevant to future risk" (p. 332). It follows that, if these mothers may be understood, they might also be amenable to treatment:

> We would argue for the development of psychological treatment services for all maltreating patients, to include psychological therapy, psychoeducational interventions and medication where appropriate, and an active approach to risk management. From our own clinical experience, we know that these women are people who need to deal with their rage, shame and hostility to their children if they are to be safe in the future.
>
> (pp. 332–333)

These suggestions will be revisited in Chapter 8, which addresses intervention, but, in keeping with this chapter's focus on defining the phenomenon, it is important to step back and reassert that another change in terminology as represented in AIBP simply does not serve these mothers or these children. It only seems to further confuse matters. Notwithstanding this author's concerns, symptomatology described by these authors may be used to augment existing work in a way that adds to descriptive criteria and addresses important symptoms on a continuum for this phenomenon.

Following Chapter 2, it is likely that the reader knows this author's views on the sudden and inexplicable rise of the term FII (Royal College of Psychiatrists, 2006). Still, FII will not be stepped around, since there were earlier efforts at introducing this term (Bools, 1996). Further, from a nosological point of view, a number of artificial distinctions have been hung on FDBP, wherein FII somehow shifts the focus rather than simply adjusting or augmenting the former term (Bass & Glaser, 2014). Such matters will be dealt with shortly as we discuss the *Platypus Paradox* later in this chapter. Despite this author's frustrations with the permutations involved with one more term that confuses the matters around this phenomenon, there is good work being done under this moniker, such as the aforementioned attachment focus some authors have been pursuing, the actuarial revisiting of Sheridan's work (2003), and an elaboration of the patterns that suggested that these mothers themselves were diagnosed with Factitious Disorder or Somatoform Disorder, or both, and that 89% suffered from characterological traits (Bass & Glaser, 2014). Earlier studies, among others, supported a combination of the attachment and actuarial literature (Bass & Jones, 2011), again with important insights about potential therapeutic techniques that will be addressed in Chapter 8 as we deal with intervention.

Among the many pieces of literature reviewed to address the matters in this portion of the chapter, there is yet another reference for the reader to address in the book by Roesler and Jenny (2008) on Medical Child Abuse (MCA). These authors, however, seemed to share several of the same concerns expressed in the pages above and below: "In conclusion, despite many efforts by experts such as Meadow, more and more conditions have come to be called MSBP. We are continually reminded of the lack of a clear definition about what is meant by the term" (p. 27). They also made this summary observation: "Not only is there a disagreement about whether motivation is relevant, those who cite the importance of motivation described many different motivations that underlie the behavior" (p. 28). Further, this author appreciated the following statement: "As helpful as it would be to have a profile procedure we could use for screening, efforts made to date do not even begin to address the complexity of the problem" (p. 33).

Despite the many useful parts of the synthesis of ideas provided by Roesler and Jenny, the term MCA ultimately did not enjoy a solid foundation even within the organization that proposed it: "We first presented the concept of *medical child abuse* at the annual meeting of the American Professional Society on the Abuse of Children (APSAC) in Tucson, AZ, in 1995" (p. 47). Obviously, with the earlier discussion regarding the APSAC's task force from 2002, this group endorsed a bifurcated path with PCF and Factitious Disorder by Proxy. Roesler and Jenny later explained the definition of MCA and their reasoning for maintaining the term:

> These authors used *medical abuse* as a synonym for MSBP. Rather than using the term as a convenient synonym for MSBP, factitious disorder by proxy, pediatric condition falsification, or some other variation, we have advocated simply calling this class of child maltreatment what it really is, child abuse.
>
> (p. 47)

70 "'Tis but thy name that is my enemy"

Although the American Academy of Pediatrics (AAP) published their book in 2008, and thereby seemingly lent support to the term, only five years later the AAP went another way by introducing a far more muddled term (Flaherty et al., 2013, p. 590), which was Caregiver-Fabricated Illness in a Child (CFIC). There were really no significant differences between what was described as CFIC and prior terms, and yet MCA had been set aside. This occurs along with setting aside the term Child Abuse in a Medical Setting (CAMS). That is, just in 2007, Stirling described CAMS as harm by way of exaggeration, fabrication or induced symptoms that results in child abuse in this way:

> Whatever it is called, it is important to remember that harm incurred when a caregiver exaggerates, fabricates, or induces symptoms of a medical condition may still simply be termed "child abuse, which happens to occur in a medical setting."
>
> (p. 1027)

The language of that guidance was, colloquially, all over the place; in one instance he was describing FII intermixed with an MSBP, and in another describing FDBP and PCF, without offering a true definition beyond what has been supplied above, as well as making statements such as those that follow:

> The motive of the caregiver, although useful to the therapist, is unimportant in making the diagnosis of abuse. In no other form of child abuse do we include the perpetrator's motives as a diagnostic criterion.
>
> (p. 1028)

> ——

> Although multidisciplinary input can be very helpful in diagnosis and essential in treatment, psychologists, social workers, and others are not in a position to make or confirm this diagnosis.
>
> (p. 1028)

As described earlier, attending to the role of motivation in these phenomena is controversial, but it is necessary in order to limit false positives and for the purpose of describing severity and possible intervention, as will be described in Chapters 5, 7, and 8.

Regardless, the definition that remains, "child abuse, which happens to occur in a medical setting," is neither descriptive nor useful in addressing such complex phenomena diagnostically, despite Roesler and Jenny's (2008) many articulate and useful observations. Nonetheless, Yates and Bass (2017) made use of this term, considering the guidance of the American Psychiatric Association (2013) while noting Stirling as well (2007, p. 46). This article fundamentally extends the work of Sheridan (2003) under the moniker of Medical Child Abuse. Yates and Bass (2017) clarified their findings regarding the known patterns within this phenomenon in a fashion that mirrored Sheridan, and they also made distinctions in their discussion:

- Almost all perpetrators of MCA in the reviewed cases were women and the mother of the victim.
- A healthcare-related occupation was mentioned in nearly half of the cases. This finding must be treated with caution, as pathological lying was also common.
- A history of childhood maltreatment was common (30%) and our analysis returned higher rates of its associated psychiatric problems [. . .]
- FDIOS[4] was identified in nearly a third of perpetrators, and we found support for Meadow's (1998) claim that: "periods of most active fabrication and induction of illness follow sequentially and alternate between perpetrator [and] child" (p. 216).
- Perpetrators of MCA have been found to be high users of obstetrics and gynecological services (Bass & Jones, 2011).
- Fatality nonetheless occurred in a disturbingly high proportion of cases: 7.6%. The rate we found is slightly higher (+1.6%) than was reported in Sheridan's (2003) review of only MSBP/FDIOA[5] cases.
- Children must not be considered safe in hospital unless separated from the perpetrator or placed under surveillance (Vennemann et al., 2005), as in 54.4% of the cases included in the study the abuse continued even when the victim was hospitalized.
- Of these, the two variables found to have most predictive value were 'Caregiver has features of Munchausen syndrome' and 'Caregiver has personal history of child abuse' (p. 41–42). Bass and Jones (2011) also identified 'abuse/neglect' and 'current factitious disorder' as strong risk factors for MCA.

(pp. 50–51)

Returning to PCF, other authors have made use of the term, and, of these authors, it was remarkable that Clarke and Skokauskas (2010) seemed to make use of it as an umbrella term: "As has been emphasized, the motivation of the mother (her psychological needs), is important in distinguishing MSBP

72 *"'Tis but thy name that is my enemy"*

from other forms of Paediatric Condition Falsification (PCF)" (p. 39). Meanwhile, others, such as Kucuker, Demir, and Resmiye (2010) seemed to lump PCF with another grouping of terms:

> Pediatric condition falsification (PCF), also known as Munchausen syndrome by Proxy or Medical Child Abuse, is a somewhat rare form of child abuse and neglect. Its association with a history of adult factitious disorder (AFD) or Munchausen syndrome in the perpetrator is also well known.
>
> (p. 572)

These two articles are offered simply to underscore the point that, despite the backing a term may have, the chosen term should clearly and demonstrably (Ayoub, Alexander et al., 2002) "facilitate the identification and treatment of this complex clinical problem" (p. 105). Fundamentally, it should enjoy agreement among practitioners with known case examples at a level of 70–80% in order to make such a diagnosis. Parenthetically, the *DSM-5* certainly had its failings in this area, with low levels of agreement and inter-rater reliability (Frances, 2013). As is evident above, there is not even agreement that these terms clearly distinguish the phenomenon or convey the same meaning.

Ultimately, the result of this proliferation of terms for, broadly, the same phenomenon has produced significant and nearly unprecedented confusion in the field, no less in other professional communities and the public. In this author's experience, the average informed person understands and can articulate the basic contours of MSBP with the statement of, "Oh yeah, that's the thing where . . ." This holds to a lesser extent with Factitious Disorder by Proxy. But ask the average informed person about AIBP, CAMS, CFIC, FDIA, MCA, and PCF, and it is likely that these terms will engender a blank stare. As a possible exception, FII seems to have become a term of art in the United Kingdom and perhaps Canada for the reasons mentioned in Chapter 2. Joined by colleagues, this author issued a "practitioner's complaint" at an earlier time about the conditions associated with identifying and diagnosing this phenomenon (Bütz, Evans, & Webber-Dereszynski, 2009). At this point, it would not only be more accurate but also more reasonable to describe this author's stated frustration with this literature as a rant. The authors cited above have engaged in the seemingly careless rhetorical proliferation of these terms, which has simply put children in danger and at greater risk. As stated earlier, this phenomenon is the most lethal of those child protection specialists face in the field. While PA, the companion phenomenon described to illustrate IMDs, has suffered confusion concerning the observation of similar characteristics within legal systems, the terminology has largely been held to four main variants. Of late, the literature has seemingly solidified around the term *Parent Alienation*. What has been created here with regard to MSBP, FDBP, and so on is diagnostically similar to the Gordian Knot.

Each new term and/or wrinkle on existing terms adds another piece of rope to be disentangled. Though tempted to take an Alexandrian approach to addressing these matters, it will ultimately be argued that the "symptoms" described beneath these terms do elaborate the phenomenon's scope and the appropriateness of considering the notion of variable criteria. All the same, these steps forward could have been accomplished through careful scholarship and support of existing terms accompanied by better descriptions and added phenomenologically relevant criteria.

Figure 3.2 The reader is asked to imagine that for each new term, it is like throwing one more rope into the Gordian Knot, so the fellow on the top may be weaving a rope in for PCF, then the fellow to the left pulling tight another rope for CFIC, and still another to the right twisting two ropes together as the term FDIA is added. Reproduced with the kind permission of Patrick Corrigan, an artist from Toronto, Canada.

Naming Conventions and the *Platypus Paradox*

The level of support the terms above have received varies, but what does come through is that the proliferation of monikers, names and titles for this phenomenon has been counterproductive and has resulted in leading the field of study hither and yon in a manner suggestive of the parable about the blind men and the elephant. This metaphor would seemingly fit better with the descriptive challenges associated with PA, given the limited number of terms. Wrestling with thoughts on these matters and recollecting how certain animals were considered to be mythical by the scientists of the 1800s and 1900s, the conventional wisdom in Europe and the United States came to mind regarding the study of biology. By the way, it seems reasonable to point out that these animals were not all that mythical or unknown to the local peoples of those areas of the world.

This author came across two useful media articles that would speak to the larger audience of this text, one a piece from the popular television series *Animal Planet* (Staff, 2015)[6] and the other an article from *The Guardian* (Hone, 2013).[7] First, the piece from *Animal Planet* addresses the topic of *Mythical Animals That Turned Out to Be Real*. This article seemed most apropos to address the phenomenon under study in this chapter, no less the whole of the contents of this book. The term *cryptozoology*, introduced by staff writers at the outset, refers to "the study of creatures whose existence is rumored but unproven." The article speaks to providing proof by means of western scientific notions, such as providing the carcass, for example, of an enormous prehistoric lizard that roamed Komodo Island in 1910. The species is, of course, the *Varanus komodensis*, more commonly known as the Komodo dragon. Then, in 1799, regarding the platypus and its carcass, the reportedly esteemed zoologist George Shaw noted that, "a degree of skepticism is not only pardonable, but laudable; and I ought perhaps to acknowledge that I almost doubt the testimony of my own eyes." The piece went on to describe okapis, gorillas, and manatees as well. But what it does not describe is six or more names for the same creature once it has been presented and acknowledged scientifically, at least per scientific conventions in Europe and the United States. It may seem unwieldly to describe a platypus, or fantastical to describe a manatee. However, once the fundamentals had been described, biological scientists tended to modify the *description* about the animal, but not the *name* of the animal itself. This is a convention that the science of healthcare might learn from.

The second piece describes the intent of the author simply by putting forth the following title: *How a New Species Is Named*. The author, Dave Hone, begins with the following:

"'Tis but thy name that is my enemy" **75**

> Sadly this is not just a case of dreaming up an interesting moniker and announcing it to the world (though that is part of it), but a reliable source of information and documentation of the identity of the species is required for the new form.

He goes on to explain that, first, a holotype is necessary to serve as a starting point for identifying a specimen for the whole of the species and to "mark it out as unique and new." A description of the new species follows and serves to "mark it out as being unique and new, and how can it be distinguished from close relatives." Creating a new two-part name—genus and species—is the next step in designating biological nomenclature. Last, of course, is publishing the findings. Hone, nevertheless, cautioned his readers about this process:

> So avoiding messing with names unnecessarily or incorrectly is a serious issue and making sure the whole system can be followed and works is thus a major undertaking, and is why names are taken so seriously. Calling *Apatosaurus* by the out of date name '*Brontosaurus*' is not just a harmless quirk, but belies what a species (or in this case, genus) is and what that name represents, and hence is taken seriously and the persistence of an incorrect name is more than academic pettiness and nit-picking, but fundamental to how we see organisms and their place in the evolutionary tree of life.

Thus, embarking on the task of describing new terms for the phenomenon that has been under study in this chapter has been approached with a similar degree of caution and skepticism to that held by both Hone and Shaw. In this author's view the holotype for the phenomenon was supplied by Meadow in 1977 with MSBP, and the working description that has been accepted by the largest body of scientists to date remains FDBP per the *Diagnostic and Statistical Manuals of Mental Disorders* across the last nineteen years . . . sort of. As alluded to earlier, the *DSM-5* has run into several problems, including, for example, failing its clinical trials (Frances, 2013). With the discussion of FDIA behind us as well, the question becomes how it is that each of the terms described, each new permutation thereof, served to "mark it out as being unique and new, and how can it be distinguished from close relatives." Given the interpretations provided in the pages above, MSBP and FDBP remain the most legitimate terms to describe the phenomenon on that basis.

It is proposed at this juncture to those in the field who are working with and attempting to refine the symptomatology that has been described for the phenomenon heretofore referenced as MSBP and FDBP, that they consider what this author suggests as the *Platypus Paradox*. Though, as mentioned earlier, this creature like others was described by several terms by local people who lived in eastern and southeastern Australia as well as Tasmania, it has come to be known the world over as the platypus. Shaw originally named it, per the scientific conventions of the 1800s and 1900s, *Platypus anatinus*. This name, a mixture of Greek words with a Latin term added for good measure, was intended to be descriptive (Australian Platypus Conservancy, 2019)[8]: "'platys' (meaning flat or broad) and 'pous' (meaning foot) and a Latin word meaning duck-like ('anatinus')." Later on, it was discovered that a group of beetles had already been described as *platypus*, and in turn the creature's name was changed to *Ornithorhynchus anatinus*. Even with this adjustment in accord with the naming conventions of science, the most recognized term for the creature remains *platypus*, and, paradoxically, this name has endured. The platypus was one of those creatures that were, per *Animal Planet* (2015), described as *Mythical Animals That Turned Out to Be Real*.

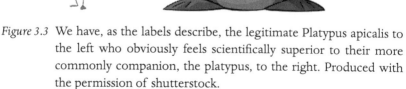

Figure 3.3 We have, as the labels describe, the legitimate Platypus apicalis to the left who obviously feels scientifically superior to their more commonly companion, the platypus, to the right. Produced with the permission of shutterstock.

Such descriptions, it would seem, hold much in common with MSBP and FDBP, no less in the seemingly common experience of professionals, practitioners and researchers attempting to describe these phenomena in healthcare, legal and scientific communities. It is an experience akin to Shaw's earlier description of a platypus (*Animal Planet*, 2015), "I almost doubt the testimony of my own eyes." Scientifically, using the term *platypus* is a paradox; still, with the use of the term, a very specific creature does come to mind. It is, therefore, proposed that the *Platypus Paradox* be applied to the phenomenon associated with MSBP and FDBP in order to acknowledge that this phenomenon is still best recognized by the term MSBP by the general public and that FDBP was described by the largest credible scientific community to date in the *DSM-IV-TR* after having been anchored by the diagnosis Factitious Disorder which had existed in the *DSM Series* for many years prior. For the sake of these children, the field needs to settle on a rallying point, and it is this author's suggestion that this can be achieved by acknowledging the *Platypus Paradox* and endorsing MSBP and FDBP in order to move forward.

Parent Alienation, Problems With Clarity, and Support

Though Parental Alienation (PA) has not suffered the remarkable proliferation of terminology seen in MSBP and FDBP, this field of study has struggled to holistically describe the complex phenomenon under study. Parental Alienation and related concepts have similarly been mired in decades of skepticism (Bernet, Verrocchio, & Korosi, 2015; Sanders et al., 2015; Clemente & Padilla-Racero, 2015; Baker, 2013a; Bernet & Baker, 2013; Ertelt & Van Dyke, 2013; Fidler, Bala, & Saini, 2013; Lowenstein, 2013; Whitcombe, 2013; Houchin et al., 2012; Ludolph & Bow, 2012; Saini et al., 2012; Carrey, 2011; Garber, 2011; Bernet, 2010; Bernet et al., 2010; Jaffe, Ashbourne, & Mamo, 2010; Rand, 2010; Walker & Shapiro, 2010; Ackerman, 2006; Drozd & Olesen, 2004; Warshak, 2001; Kelly & Johnston, 2001). Furthermore, it has also been recognized that Wallerstein and Kelly (1976, 1980a) described a state of, "alignment." Gardner (1985) articulated what he described as Parental Alienation Syndrome. Kelly and Johnston (2001) later proposed a shift toward describing what they termed an "alienated child" (p. 251). Still others (Baker, Burkhard, & Albertson-Kelly, 2012) have cited Reich (1949) as "the first person to write about this phenomenon from a clinical perspective" (p. 179). Notwithstanding these descriptions, another author suggested that such dynamics have been present for 200 years (Lorandos, 2014, p. 324). Even with these different viewpoints, there has not been the proliferation of terms

78 "'Tis but thy name that is my enemy"

beyond the dialogue provided to debate differing positions and to establish the phenomenon.

Rand (2010), among others, has made it clear that, "The controversy over PA/PS[9] has been divisive and vitriolic at times" (p. 65). Meier (2010) made it plain that, in her view, "Nothing is more polarizing in the family law field than the debate over domestic abuse and parental alienation" (p. 220). Some of these authors (Saini et al., 2012) have also described the mired terminology associated with what has been generally referred to as Parental Alienation:

> This phenomenon has been variously described in the literature as "alienation", "parental alienation," "parental alienation syndrome," "child reluctance or refusal to visit," "child alienation," the "Medea syndrome," and "malicious mother syndrome."
>
> (p. 401)

The literature has been rather harsh in a number of ways, and still it has homed in on articulating what is and what is not Parental Alienation. One such example was commentary made by Nichols in 2014, followed by debate over the quality of the exchange in *Children and Youth Services Review* in 2015. In the latter example, scholarship was deemed to be so poor that an appeal was made to withdraw an article from the literature (Clemente & Padilla-Racero, 2015; Bernet, Verrocchio, & Korosi, 2015). There was attention to, and propositions about, the notion of PA being included during the time when the *Diagnostic and Statistical Manual for Mental Disorders—Fifth Edition* (American Psychiatric Association, 2013) was being developed (Bernet & Baker, 2013; Lowenstein, 2013; Whitcombe, 2013; Houchin et al., 2012; Carrey, 2011; Bernet, 2010; Bernet et al., 2010; Walker & Shapiro, 2010; Kelly & Johnston, 2001).

The calls for addressing what is, and what is not, Alignment, Parental Alienation Syndrome (PAS), an Alienated Child (AC),[10] and Parental Alienation (PA) have not stopped, which is where this author initially entered the fray by introducing the notion of an Interrelated Multidimensional Diagnosis (Bütz & Evans, 2019). There has been misinformation, also, about the concept, such as when PA was being proposed as a diagnosis in the *DSM-5* as Bernet and Baker (2013) described. For example, Nichols reported in 2014 that the phenomenon described by these terms had been rejected. The definition that was envisioned by the proponents of the term PA for inclusion in the *DSM-5* was, in reality, the diagnostic equivalent of the AC put forward by Kelly and Johnston in 2001. It was, therefore, incorrect to assert the following without clarifying terms: "At the very least, the American Psychiatric Association's explicit rejection of PAD,[11] in light of the significant lobbying effort by some professionals advocating its acceptance" (p. 673). Authors' voices over the years have made clear their concerns about this confusing and perplexing state of affairs (Drozd & Olesen, 2004):

> Some evaluators, on the other hand, have not recognized the reality that a parent can convince a child of something that is not true, nor have they appreciated the pernicious effect of alienating or sabotaging behavior by one parent that tries to turn the child against the other parent.
>
> (p. 68)

While there have been calls like this one for simple awareness, there are other calls as well, including *Parental Alienation: Time to Notice, Time to Intervene* (Whitcombe, 2014). Whitcombe not only offered a provocative title but stated the following:

> Although there are hundreds of peer-reviewed articles by psychologists, psychiatrists, legal and social work professionals attesting to the concept and the presence of PA in highly conflicted divorce cases, it has rarely been openly or formally discussed in the UK.
>
> I feel driven to raise awareness in the general public, so that PA can no longer be denied or swept under the carpet in the same way as childhood sex abuse use to be. This lack of awareness exacerbates the alienation process and its impact on children and parents alike.
>
> (pp. 33–34)

It follows that there certainly is a need to clarify these phenomena and determine which term has assembled the most contemporary consensus. The focus of the latter part of this chapter will be to articulate the descriptions over the years that add up to the proposed pathological dynamic of Parental Alienation. In order to do so, a brief history will be provided regarding Alignment, PAS, AC, and PA that describes how the field came to the considerations that now exist.

Early Descriptions

Obviously, there is a history here that pertains to the terms *Alignment*, *PAS*, *AC*, and *PA*, and each term has its author or authors as well as its proponents. Although the terms *Parental Alienation* (PA) and *Parent Alienation Syndrome*

80 "'Tis but thy name that is my enemy"

(PAS) have dominated more recent literature, it is appropriate to address the other two terms descriptively and consider what they were intended to convey given their history and the centrality of the authors involved with this body of literature.

Alignment

Two particular works are cited when the term *Alignment* is used in this context (Wallerstein & Kelly, 1976,1980a). In order to be true to the concept being described, it would seem best to simply cite what these authors have described in both references. The concept of Alignment also has other implications for the kinds of attributes and characteristics shared by the adults and children who engage in, and/or suffer from, this phenomenon, as will be described later in more detail. Turning to the 1976 reference, Wallerstein and Kelly described the following:

> Among the 31 children in this cohort, eight (or 26%) formed a relationship with one parent following the separation which was specifically aimed at the exclusion or active rejection of the other. These *alignments*[12] were usually initiated and always fueled by the embattled parent, most often by the parent who felt aggrieved, deserted, exploited, or betrayed by the divorcing spouse. The angers which the parent and the child shared soon became the basis for complexly organized strategies aimed at hurting and harassing the former spouse, sometimes with the intent of shaming him or her into returning to the marriage. More often the aim was vengeance.
>
> (p. 266)

Plainly, what is being articulated here is that the parents have had a conflicted relationship, and then one parent who has felt spurned begins a campaign for the child to reject the other parent. Wallerstein and Kelly go on to report what lies below regarding these dynamics.

> A central part of the dynamic of this behavior is the splitting of the ambivalent relationship to the parents into that with the good parent and the bad parent. Moreover, in our findings, these alignments have the hurtful potential for consolidation and perpetuation long past the initial post-separation period, especially in those families where the child is aligned with the custodial parent.
>
> (pp. 266–267)

These early descriptions of the phenomenon under study were remarkable in laying out a pattern that still holds today and is described in current literature. Wallerstein and Kelly further elaborated on these observations and the term *Alignment* in their 1980 book entitled, *Surviving the Breakup: How Children and Parents Cope with Divorce*. There, once again they brought forward the notion of an Alignment, and, with one section of their book entitled "Alignment with One Parent," they offer the following:

> A very important aspect of the response of the youngsters in this age group was the dramatic change in the relationship between parents and children. These young people were particularly vulnerable to being swept up into the anger of one parent against the other. They were faithful and valuable battle allies in efforts to hurt the other parent. Not infrequently, they turned on the parent they had loved and been very close to prior to the marital separation.
>
> The most extreme identification with the parents cause we have called an "alignment"—a divorce-specific relationship that occurs when a parent and one or more children join in a vigorous attack on the other parent. It is the embattled parent, often the one who opposes the divorce in the first place, who initiates and fuels the alignment, not infrequently as he or she discovers the involvement of the other partner in a new relationship.
>
> (p. 77)

In this treatment of the subject we learn more about the qualities involved with the child who is vulnerable and becomes swept up in the anger of the parent(s)[13] who feels spurned. The child aligns with whomever they perceive to be, and/or are persuaded is, the so-called good parent as opposed to the bad parent. Further, the parent being attacked and rejected had a loving and close relationship to the child(ren)[14] prior to this onslaught. As will be discussed later, these attacks do not simply denigrate and/or, more colloquially, talk down the other parent. What Wallerstein and Kelly have described in the passages above are attacks that are "hurtful," "vigorous" and "shaming" with long-lasting impacts after the post-divorce/separation period.

Parental Alienation Syndrome

When Gardner (1985) first rolled out his notion of the phenomenon conceptually, he offered a description that was cautious but clear:

82 "'Tis but thy name that is my enemy"

Of the many types of psychological disturbance that can be brought about by such litigation, there is one that I focus on here. Although this syndrome certainly existed in the past, it is occurring with such increasing frequency at this point that it deserves a special name. The term I prefer to use is parental alienation syndrome. I have introduced this term to refer to a disturbance in which children are obsessed with deprecation and criticism of a parent—denigration that is unjustified and/or exaggerated. The notion that such children are merely "brainwashed" is narrow. The term brainwashing implies that one parent is systematically and consciously programming the child to denigrate the other parent. The concept of the parental alienation syndrome includes the brainwashing component but is much more inclusive. It includes not only conscious but subconscious and unconscious factors within the parent that contribute to the child's alienation. Furthermore (and this is extremely important), it includes factors that arise within the child—independent of the parental contributions—that contribute to the development of the syndrome.

Typically, the child is obsessed with "hatred" of a parent. (The word *hatred* is placed in quotes because there are still many tender and loving feelings felt toward the allegedly despised parent that are not permitted expression.) These children speak of the hated parent with every vilification and profanity in their vocabulary, without embarrassment or guilt. The vilification of the parent often has the quality of a litany. After only minimal prompting by a lawyer, judge, probation officer, mental health professional, or other person involved in the litigation, the record will be turned on and a command performance provided. Not only is there the rehearsed quality to the speech but one often hears phraseology that is identical to that used by the "loved" parent. (Again, the word *loved* is placed in quotations because hostility toward and fear of that parent may similarly be unexpressed.)

(p. 3)

This, in a nutshell, was Gardner's early description of Parent Alienation Syndrome. Gardner also described how he felt the phenomenon expressed itself:

At this point I will discuss the pathogenesis of this disorder, with particular emphasis on three contributing factors: parental "brainwashing," situational factors, and the child's own contributions.

(p. 4).

"'Tis but thy name that is my enemy" **83**

In that 1985 article he went on to describe each aspect, noting that in most cases brainwashing was a conscious act by a parent that involved maneuvers and situational factors, including the ambiguity of joint custody at that time. But, during that time period, relatively little was known or described about the child's own contributions, per his narratives.

Later on, Gardner (2002) suggested a different definition, one with three subtypes and eight primary symptomatic manifestations:

> The parental alienation syndrome (PAS) is a disorder that arises primarily in the context of child-custody disputes. Its primary manifestation is the child's campaign of denigration against a good, loving parent, a campaign that has no justification. It results from the combination of a programming (brainwashing) parent's indoctrinations and the child's own contributions to the vilification of the target parent. When true parental abuse and/or neglect is present the child's animosity may be justified, and so the parent alienation syndrome diagnosis is not applicable.
>
> —
>
> There are three types of parental alienation syndrome: mild, moderate and severe. . . . In the mild type, the alienation is relatively superficial, the children basically cooperate with visitation, but are intermittently critical and disgruntled with the victimized parent. In the moderate type, the alienation is more formidable, the children are more disruptive and disrespectful, and the campaign of denigration may be almost continual. In the severe type, visitation may be impossible so hostile are the children, hostile even to the point of being physically violent toward the allegedly hated parent.
>
> —

These are the primary symptomatic manifestations of parental alienation syndrome:

1. A campaign of denigration
2. Weak, absurd, or frivolous rationalizations for the deprecation
3. Lack of ambivalence
4. The "independent thinker" phenomenon
5. Reflexive support of the alienating parent in the parental conflict
6. Absence of guilt over cruelty to and/or exploitation of the alienated parent
7. The presence of borrowed scenarios

84 *"'Tis but thy name that is my enemy"*

8. Spread of the animosity to the friends and/or extended family of the alienated parent. (pp. 192–193)

In this article, Gardner (2002) described being wedded to the concept of a syndrome, and that the underlying cause was "programming by an alienating parent in conjunction with additional contributions by the programmed child" (p. 195).

Alienated Children

Later on, after Kelly's earlier work with Wallerstein, she began working with Johnston, and in 2001 they wrote *The Alienated Child: A Reformulation of Parental Alienation Syndrome*. Thus, the origin for this term is unmistakable. They proposed a new way to describe the phenomenon, but, first, they articulated their objections to the use of the term *PAS:*

> The controversy regarding PAS has focused on a number of criticisms, only some of which will be discussed here (see also Faller, 1998; Williams, 2001 [this issue]). First and foremost, PAS focuses almost exclusively on the alienating parent as the etiological agent of the child's alienation. This is not supported by considerable clinical research that shows that in high-conflict divorce, many parents engage in indoctrinating behaviors, but only a small proportion of children become alienated (Johnston, 1993). In other cases, it can be shown that some children (especially adolescents) develop unjustified animosity, negative beliefs, and fears of a parent in the absence of alienating behaviors by a parent (Johnston, 1993). Hence, alienating behavior by a parent is neither a sufficient nor a necessary condition for a child to become alienated.
>
> Second, Gardner has formulated a definition of PAS that includes its hypothesized etiological agents (i.e., an alienating parent and a receptive child). This renders his theory of the cause of PAS unfalsifiable because it is tautological (i.e., true by definition). Third, because there is no "commonly recognized, or empirically verified pathogenesis, course, familial pattern, or treatment selection" of the problem of PAS, it cannot properly be considered a diagnostic syndrome as defined by the American Psychiatric Association (1994). If PAS is considered a "grouping of signs and symptoms, based on their frequent co-occurrence," it could be considered a nondiagnostic syndrome, but this sheds no light on cause, prognosis, and treatment of these behaviors. Hence, the term *PAS* does not add any information that would enlighten the court, the

clinician, or their clients, all of whom would be better served by a more specific description of the child's behavior in the context of his or her family. Fourth, using the terminology of a medical syndrome to explain the behavior of family social systems engenders controversy among mental health professionals of different philosophical orientation and training, ensuring that the validity of PAS will continue to be debated.

(pp. 249–250)

Accordingly, for these and other reasons Kelly and Johnston proposed the concept of an Alienated Child:

> This formulation proposes to focus on the alienated child rather than on parental alienation. An *alienated* child is defined here as one who expresses, freely and persistently, unreasonable negative feelings and beliefs (such as anger, hatred, rejection, and/or fear) toward a parent that are significantly disproportionate to the child's actual experience with that parent. From this viewpoint, the pernicious behaviors of a "programming" parent are no longer the starting point. Rather, the problem of the alienated child begins with a primary focus on the child, his or her observable behaviors, and parent-child relationships. This objective and neutral focus enables the professionals involved in the custody dispute to consider whether the child fits the definition of an alienated child and, if so, to use a more inclusive framework for assessing why the child is now rejecting a parent and refusing contact.
>
> (p. 251)

It follows that what Kelly and Johnston have focused in on is manifest symptomatology, which as they had proposed is an "objective and neutral focus." Another notable distinction they made was that they couched this within systems theory:

> To adequately diagnose and effectively intervene when a child is presented as alienated, a systems framework that assesses the multiple and interrelated factors influencing the child's response during and after separation and divorce is critical.
>
> (p. 254)

These latter shifts seemed to be intent upon pulling attention to this phenomenon from the medical field and/or the medical model, and into the context of behavioral healthcare and systemic thought processes.

86 *"'Tis but thy name that is my enemy"*

Contemporary Literature, Parental Alienation, and the *DSM-5*

Debating Parental Alienation

Rand wrote an article in 2010 entitled, *Parental Alienation Critics and the Politics of Science*. It is a somewhat lengthy treatment of the topic addressing these phenomena, and provided a history that involved competing ideas. Rand's (2010) focus throughout was, as she described it, "what is known" (p. 48) about the phenomenon that clinicians, researchers and various professionals had been observing. She (2010) went on to articulate two of the camps and their objections to the term PAS:

> Today, there are two main groups of critics who oppose use of the term PAS, and the concept of parental alienation (PA) generally. The first group . . . I refer to this group as the Johnston/Kelly critics. According to these critics, the two most contentious issues in the PAS debate are Gardner's emphasis on the causal role of the alienating parent and the seemingly radical interventions which flow from that, such as changing custody to the hated parent.
>
> PAS critics in the second group identify themselves as advocates for abused women and children. . . . I refer to this group as the feminist and child advocates. Critics in this group object to Gardner's views on child sex abuse and frequently equate false allegations of sex abuse with his definition of PAS, which is a misunderstanding.
>
> (p. 49)

Meier (2010) observed that these factions were "often identified with the opposing political movements that have popularized their use: feminism and women's rights on one hand, and 'father's rights' on the other" (p. 220). This represents a sentiment echoed differently by others, such as Ludolph and Bow (2012): "Alienation has been much maligned by advocates for abused women, believing that it is a fabricated manipulation of violent men to gain control over their wives" (p. 154). Other conceptualizations, such as the one offered by Moné and Biringen (2012, pp. 159–160), center their approach on theoretical constructs from family systems theory, feminist theory, and attachment theory whilst constructing an instrument to measure for such dynamics (Relationship Distancing Questionnaire). Citing Kuhn, Rand (2010) further explained that, "Debate between seemingly competing schools of thought is a necessary part of scientific advancement" (p. 50). Perhaps debatably, she does not dismiss the concerns put forth by these competing conceptualizations of the phenomenon. Instead, Rand (2010) goes on to represent these concerns, and in part answer them in order to observe a "common understanding" about "what is known" (p. 65). In turn, Rand's analysis offers an important set of considerations and contemplations that entertains the concept of what forms this phenomenon in an inclusive fashion by way of describing all three competing models. What Rand's article also described is that this field of study has largely condensed around the use of the term Parental Alienation (PA) in order to describe the phenomenon.

Outside of what has been offered by way of Rand's descriptions above, there are multiple and somewhat different descriptions of this phenomenon under the heading of Parental Alienation, such as the one offered by Saini, Johnston, Fidler, & Bala in 2012:

> "Parental alienation" (PA) is a generic term used broadly to refer to a child who has been influenced to reject one parent, in extreme cases 'brainwashed' or indoctrinated by an embittered/malicious other parent.
>
> (p. 399)

Garber (2011) had described it in this way: "Specifically, I use the word 'alienation' to describe the convergence of relationship dynamics which together cause an individual to express unjustifiable and disproportionately negative reactions to a targeted individual" (p. 322). Debate over the term may be found in nearly every corner of this literature, and yet there was a push several years ago to unify these descriptions in order to ensure that Parental Alienation was recognized by a larger audience in the *DSM-5*. Such efforts served to clarify and further the discussion about this phenomenon. It is for these reasons that it will henceforth be referred to as Parental Alienation (PA).

DSM-5 and Where the Pathological Dynamic Lies

Recognizing the contributions of the definitions and terminology above, there was a large movement to include the term *PA* in the *DSM-5* with the following description (Bernet et al., 2010):

> We define parental alienation as a mental condition in which a child— usually one whose parents are engaged in a high-conflict divorce—allies

88 "'Tis but thy name that is my enemy"

himself or herself strongly with one parent (the preferred parent) and rejects a relationship with the other parent (the alienated parent) without legitimate justification.

(p. 76)

This group went on to focally state that, "parental alienation is not a minor aberration in the life of a family, but a serious mental condition" (p. 77). Although there was much to agree with in what Bernet, Baker and their colleagues (2010) in this immediate group offered (including a considerable number of more peripheral colleagues), the diagnosis that they proposed centers itself problematically on *the child* and not on a parent or parents, or on a larger dynamic:

Regarding our proposed diagnostic criteria, we argue that the essential feature of *parental alienation* is that *a child*[15]—usually one whose parents are engaged in a high-conflict divorce—allies himself or herself strongly with one parent.

(p. 78)

This extends to other descriptors, too: "The primary behavioral symptom is that *the child*[16] refuses or resists contact with a parent" (p. 78). Likewise, Bernet and Baker further characterize these symptoms as residing in the child: "The primary mental symptom is *the child's*[17] irrational anxiety and/or hostility toward the rejected parent." The apparent origin for these notions, as described earlier, came from Kelly and Johnston, as well as their colleagues from a work group in 2001. The concept of the AC was developed in opposition to Gardner's model, and Kelly and Johnston proposed:

Hence, the term *PAS* does not add any information that would enlighten the court, the clinician or their clients, all of whom would be better served by a more specific description of the *child's behavior*[18] in the context of his or her family.

(p. 250)

——

This formulation proposes to focus on the alienated child rather than on parental alienation. An *alienated child* is defined here as . . .

(p. 251)

As discussed, and alluded to in a number of articles, books and book chapters on the topic, the focus has been to unburden the child and to clarify boundaries (Garber, 2011). But there has been considerable confusion about these notions. For example, note the quote from Godbout and Parent (2012):

> This study adopts this systemic approach, and thus, examines parental alienation as a problem that reflects difficulties associated with the family system as a whole, rather than as a disorder diagnosed in the child.
>
> (p. 35)

Yet, Kelly and Johnston, per the quote above, did propose the term "Alienated Child," and so the diagnosis is "in" the child and not located in the family system dynamic. Bernet and Baker (2013) did acknowledge this criticism in their piece responding to those with differing opinions regarding the *DSM-5* proposals: "Some colleagues have expressed concern about labelling children of high-conflict divorce with a mental condition" (p. 98).

It is argued here with some support (Walker & Shapiro, 2010) that the diagnosis should not lie in the child: "It is not appropriate to diagnose a child with a mental illness based on the parents' behavior" (p. 277). Instead, as is proposed in earlier articles (Bütz, Evans, & Webber-Dereszynski, 2009; Bütz & Evans, 2019) and in this text, the pathology lies in the systems dynamic, a pathological dynamic ultimately put into motion by one or both parents and reflecting in most cases the pressures and stresses associated with high-conflict divorce and/or developments associated with custody arrangements, parenting plans or parenting time. The pathology, therefore, lies within these interrelated multidimensional systems dynamics and manifests out of the stresses associated with an environmental context with individuals and subdynamics across family as well as legal systems. The aforementioned *DSM-5* group certainly went to some considerable efforts, and this author is in agreement with much of what was proposed. However, fundamentally placing the disorder in the child misses the point not only of the diagnosis, but of intervention and treatment efforts as well (Warshak, 2015; Gardner, 2001).

The challenges and problems with PA are that it is a pathological systems dynamic created through environmental stresses and put into motion by the actions of the parent who subjects the child to alienating behaviors within the context of a family and legal system dealing with a high-conflict divorce or custody proceeding. Yes, the child ultimately colludes in order for the PA dynamic to be realized, but that is neither how the pattern begins nor how it is instigated according to the vast majority of this literature. At the same time, keep in mind the comments of Lowenstein in 2015, where he stated his opinion quite clearly:

> The child cannot be blamed for this rejection of a parent. The fault lies totally with the alienating parent who has manipulated the child due to the justified or unjustified hostility that the parent feels toward the other parent.
>
> (p. 659)

The aforementioned *DSM-5* group put the onus on the child for the pathology, when, in fact, the pathology rests in the interrelated systems dynamic, a dynamic brought about through processes involved with an adversarial legal system, subdynamics, and certain characterological predispositions in parents who are activated under these stresses.

Even with the discussion above, it would be remiss not to mention that the *DSM-5* group proposed two forms of diagnoses for introduction in the *DSM-5* (Bernet et al., 2010, pp. 183–187): Parental Alienation Disorder and Parental Alienation Relational Problem (Bernet & Baker, 2013, p. 183). Though the emphasis was placed on Parental Alienation Disorder, in this author's view the more appropriate emphasis was the relational problem. In fact, with some exceptions, a serviceable diagnosis that describes a relationship dynamic may be achieved simply by abandoning Parental Alienation Disorder and applying much of the criteria to Parental Alienation Relational Problem. Thus, modestly revised language might be used in this manner: *The essential feature of parental alienation relational problem is that amid high-conflict divorce or custody proceedings (with some exceptions) one or both parents engage in a dynamic with behaviors that alienate a child or children from one or both parents.*

IMD and Organizing Principles

Metaphors such as the Gordian Knot, the platypus, and the blind men and the elephant have been called forth to help clarify the contours of the difficulties with naming conventions in the fields of healthcare and law regarding phenomena that are as complex as MSBP, FDBP, and Parental Alienation. At this point in our discourse the most appropriate and relevant metaphor to take us out of the so-called weeds of academic discussion and move the conversation forward toward practice is that of those blind men and the elephant. This involves taking a step back and perceiving the whole of each phenomenon, recognizing that those researchers whose descriptions have gone before had

"'Tis but thy name that is my enemy"   91

Figure 3.4   With Parental Alienation, it may be argued that each theoretical model has had a piece of the elephant, with Alignment, Parental Alienation Syndrome, Alienated Child, and Parental Alienation via proposals for *DSM-5*. Perhaps now with a systemic interpretation, the practitioners, professionals, and researchers involved with this work may be able to mutually benefit from one another. The image has been reproduced with the permission of Sam Gross.

a piece or pieces of the phenomena that have been described herein as IMDs and noting that IMDs take form in a number of different ways, as will be discussed further in Chapter 7. The elephant is a particular form of IMD, and the blind people are the practitioners, professionals, and researchers who have attempted to feel their way toward describing what is before them.

Now that the dimensions of these disagreements about naming conventions are behind us, we can articulate what the contours of FDBP are scientifically as an IMD and what is and is not PA as an Interrelated Multidimensional Diagnosis. After the concept of an IMD is thoroughly introduced in the next chapter, FDBP and PA are set off in their own succeeding chapters. One of the benefits that unification brings under an IMD is the ability to measure and probabilistically describe, and perhaps detect, the presence of each phenomenon under study.

Notes

1. Estimates range from .0002 to .000003 (Alexander, Smith, & Stevenson, 1990; Sheerin, 2006; Huynh, 2006; Volz, 1995); but is it also often stated that legal authorities and providers simply do not know, as it is believed that many cases go undetected. Stated another way, per Siegel and Fischer (2001) citing Schreier (1997), "criteria suggests that 625 new cases per year can be expected in the United States" (p. 33).
2. Italics added for emphasis.
3. It should be noted here, as well as a few other poignant places in this text, that the "cost" for scholarship has risen dramatically in recent years. Particular publishers such as the American Psychiatric Association charge the following (correspondence November 8, 2019): "any selection of over 40 words is considered an excerpt, and there will be a $300 fee for each." Yes, that is "each", and though this author very much wished to make use of several references to the texts produced by this publisher to illustrate finer points the cost was unduly prohibitive. Exorbitant fees such as this defeats the purpose of not only scholarship, but open scientific debate plain and simple, and egregious practices like these should be aired and exposed.
4. Factitious Disorder Imposed on the Self (FDIOS).
5. Factitious Disorder Imposed on Another (FDIOA).
6. Retrieved on June 4, 2019, www.animalplanet.com/tv-shows/monster-week/mythical-animals-that-turned-out-to-be-real/
7. Retrieved on June 4, 2019, www.theguardian.com/science/lost-worlds/2013/jun/21/dinosaurs-fossils
8. https://platypus.asn.au/evolution-names/
9. Reference offered by this author indicating both descriptions of Parent Alienation (PA) and Parent Alienation Syndrome (PS).
10. Hereafter there will be two abbreviations of the phrase or term Alienated Child. One abbreviation, AC, is meant to describe the concept by Kelly and Johnston (2001). The other, *ac*, is descriptive, i.e., a child who has been alienated. The latter abbreviation is used to describe children who are in the midst of these IMDs, and the lower case and italics are used to clearly differentiate these and their behaviors from those of adults. This serves two purposes: first it more clearly differentiates parents from children when abbreviations are used, and second it provides a clearer set of abbreviations for the IMD Symbolic Language that will be introduced at the end of Chapter 7.
11. Parental Alienation Disorder (p. 668).
12. Italics included for emphasis by the author.
13. Although, henceforth referred to as simply a parent or the parent, it is acknowledged and agreed that both biological parents and possibility additional parents may well engage in these behaviors. It would, however, be cumbersome to continue to address parent(s) in the fashion of an implied singular or plural reference.
14. As with the footnote above, it is also acknowledged and agreed that one child or more than one child may become entangled in these dynamics. It would, still, prove cumbersome to continue to address child(ren) in the fashion of an implied singular or plural reference.
15. Bold and italics added for emphasis.
16. Ibid.
17. Ibid.
18. Italics added for emphasis.

Interrelated Multidimensional Diagnoses

4

After many years of working with these concepts across clinical, forensic, and neuropsychological work, this author realized that individual and system symptoms not only fell into a pattern but were related at multiple levels in certain phenomena. In this author's forensic work, the matter generally referred to as Parental Alienation (PA) kept coming to the fore. However, it was this author's perception that his services had not included much in the way of this work when the FDBP article was written (2009), whereas after 2012 there was a remarkable uptick in the number of PA cases presented with questions about this kind of phenomenon. Also, retrospectively, this author came to realize that there were both subtle and obvious traits of PA in his prior cases that were simply missed or overlooked. In turn, over the next several years one case after the other followed, exhibiting similar patterns with individual and system characteristics, behaviors engaged in by these individuals and interactions that resulted in pathological dynamics. The comparability of these patterns led to the consideration that the overall diagnostic frame of reference needed to be changed.

It eventually became evident that my colleagues and I were just flat missing something, or a lot of things, with these cases, and after months of contemplation, reading and reviewing cases this author reluctantly came to the concept of an *Interrelated Multidimensional Diagnosis*. It was, in a word, admittedly radical. As a construct it was in no way in keeping with the conventions of the *Diagnostic and Statistical Manuals* or the *International Classification of Diseases*, but it was in keeping with the lessons learned about systems thinking during this author's graduate education and since (Bütz, 2017; Bütz, Carlson, & Carlson, 1998; Proskauer & Bütz, 1998; Bütz, Chamberlain, & McCown, 1997;

Bütz, 1995); and more importantly it was in keeping with clinical observations, forensic outcomes and the repeated patterns in the literature.

Once again, working with this author's colleague Barton Evans, we worked out how to present it and to speak to both FDBP and PA in the process of proposing the term *Interrelated Multidimensional Diagnosis* (2019). This term was intended to describe a *set* (in the mathematical sense) of diagnoses that holistically addresses interrelated individual and system characteristics, symptoms and subdynamics in a dimensional way that cumulatively create a pathological dynamic. This set of diagnoses was envisioned as satisfying a portion of the existing diagnostic descriptive void that neglects the importance of individual-individual, individual-system/system-individual, and system-system pathological dynamics. The term was intended to propose a diagnostic set in which there is an array of potential diagnoses that have shared interrelationships, characteristics, and symptoms among individuals and systems. These are, importantly, diagnoses that manifest under the right conditions, conditions in which interrelated and subdynamic phenomena interact to transform into a larger pathological dynamic. Parenthetically, the term *pathological* was chosen here rather than *disease* or *disorder* for specific reasons (Bütz, 1997):

> Pathology is disease—pain or discomfort. Or, a disease is a disorder—lack of order. Pathology, symptomatology, diagnostics, and nosology are all tied, by definition, to the ideas of dis-ease or dis-order. Language becomes a trap, used to describe everything that is troubling as an issue of ease or order.
>
> (p. 72)

It is simply not this reference to pathology, but the concept as whole that merits contemplation (1997, pp. 71–84). We have proposed five dimensions to explain each pathological condition (Bütz & Evans, 2019):

> On the first dimension, there is a unique set of characteristics and/or symptoms that individuals possess. On the second dimension, there are interrelated symptoms among individuals, which may be called groups, but we call family, legal and medical *systems*. For example, a parent and child are representatives of a family system, just as medical providers are representatives of a medical system (Bütz, Evans, & Webber-Dereszynski, 2009). A third dimension of consideration involves multiple systems interacting, which create stresses that develop into symptoms, and it is the quality of these interactions between

individuals and systems that produce a fourth dimension that we refer to as subdynamics.

(p. 367)

In earlier work it was described that the parent interacted in a certain way with staff members from a medical system, and vice versa (Bütz, Evans, & Webber-Dereszynski, 2009). As will be explained in more detail later, that is what is meant by a subdynamic as the fourth dimension with the pathological dynamic serving as the fifth. The subdynamic subsumes a range of interactive behaviors, and it is a more descriptive and encompassing account than the maltreatment dynamic and other related terminology expressed in 2009. Here, it must be underscored that these pathological dynamics only manifest under the right conditions, conditions wherein these individuals, systems, and subdynamics collectively interact in such a way that they create the fifth dimension, which is a pathological dynamic.

The conceptualization of an IMD made novel use of categorical, dimensional and hybrid diagnostic conceptualizations in an integrated fashion. For this reason, it has been proposed that these conceptualizations are then interrelated through a progressive multidimensional sequence of events best understood by virtue of an integrated vantage point, one that reveals a comprehensive accounting of the pathological dynamic. It follows that the prior conceptualization of FDBP offered by this author and his colleagues would be improved by revising it under the proposed concept of an Interrelated Multidimensional Diagnosis (IMD); this will be addressed in Chapter 5.

For the time being, it should be clarified that an IMD was not intended to follow the customs associated with a unitary descriptive diagnosis in an individual, such as anxiety or depression. At this point, these experiences are believed to be mental states categorically and dimensionally located within the individual and generally without the consideration of the larger psychosocial context. In turn, such individually focused diagnoses have described impairment in the individual-to-environment context, and generally not vice versa. An IMD, therefore, was intended to surpass the limited conventions of the so-called "Relational Problems" touched on earlier from the *Diagnostic and Statistical Manual of Mental Disorder's* nomenclature. Relational problems, and other similar conventions in the *DSM* systems, are simply seen as diagnostic modifiers that describe the quality of a relationship or a system on one dimension. Often, diagnoses in the *DSM* system have been made without specific links to the nature of disorders they purportedly modify. Should such diagnostic limitations be addressed, it is possible for the notion of relational problems to create a conceptual in-between set, a bridge, between the diagnoses described in the *DSM* system and Interrelated Multidimensional Diagnoses. It is proposed that an IMD moves the bar for complexity and sophistication a significant step further quantitatively and qualitatively with a combination of unique individual characteristics and symptoms, interrelated symptoms among individuals, systemic interactions, and subdynamics that cumulatively result in a pathological dynamic. An IMD combines all of these aspects into a singular diagnosis that, by definition, results in a pathological dynamic requiring symptomatic proof at each dimension of consideration. In short, an IMD manifests when the whole of these characteristics and interactions transform into something greater than the sum of its parts to create a pathological dynamic. So, as described, it is important to understand that an IMD manifests when the entirety of these characteristics and interactions manifest into a phenomenon that goes beyond certain symptoms and subdynamics, a summation of factors and processes that create a pathological dynamic.

Punctuated Steady States and the Moment an IMD Is Realized

The article that introduced IMDs (Bütz & Evans, 2019) described them as phenomena that may or may not form. For either of the proposed diagnoses, FDBP or PA, to be made scientifically as an IMD, there is a set of successive proofs necessary at each dimensional- symptomatic level of examination. Consider, for example, the popular short-hand phrase known as the "butterfly effect," which is often used to describe chaos theory or nonlinear dynamics through an iconic example. This phrase, more formally, is Sensitive Dependence on Initial Conditions and was coined by Lorenz to describe the unexpected sensitivity of weather systems (Gleick, 1987). To be brief, the story goes that a storm may manifest in an unstable weather system by way of an input so small as a butterfly flapping its wings. By the same token, though, when the system is stable enough, a storm may not form, even if the butterfly flaps its wings. Thus, a storm's development is "dependent" on how environmental conditions impact the weather system. By comparison, the development of the pathological dynamic in an IMD is dependent on how different individuals and systems respond to a series of environmental conditions.

Many kinds of considerations are involved with both nonlinear dynamics and systems thinking, as will be described in more detail later in this text. For the moment, one example from the field of nonlinear dynamics will illustrate the multidimensional nature of such phenomena. The term *Punctuated*

Equilibria (Gould & Eldredge, 1972, 1993) was developed to discuss threshold events from an evolutionary perspective. As Gould and Eldredge (1972) wrote:

> The history of life is more adequately represented by a picture of "punctuated equilibria" than by the notion of a phyletic gradualism. The history of evolution is not one of steely unfolding, but a story of homeostatic equilibria, disrupted only "rarely" (i.e., rather than often in the fullness of time) by rapid and episodic events of speciation.
>
> (p. 84)

The concept Gould and Eldredge introduced in 1972 and continued to describe (1993) was that the Darwinian notion of gradual evolution was fundamentally incorrect in any number of instances. Based on their extensive research, they postulated that under environmental stresses new forms of life and/or new variations on life forms emerge suddenly, uniquely, and may hold distinctive adaptive advantages. Similarly, a family system develops pathological dynamics that may emerge gradually or suddenly based on its features and how it interacts with the environment. Thus, the development of an IMD may be subject to a sort of Darwinian gradualism or to Gould and Eldredge's concept of punctuated equilibria, via either the FDBP or the PA manifestation. Designating threshold events set these pathological dynamics apart from other family dynamics. That is, the emergence of a parent harming or subjecting their child to harm in order to interact with healthcare professionals (FDBP), or, a child beginning to reject a good and loving parent for no apparent reason (PA). Thus, the cumulative factors that create an IMD either form to the extent that this threshold behavior is exhibited from the family system, or it does not manifest. In FDBP the mother's functioning under stress punctuates, and her behavior toward one of her children changes based on her own needs, or it does not. With PA, the functioning of a child under stress punctuates, and they begin to reject one or both of their parents in the ways described, or they do not.

The term *Steady State* (Von Bertalanffy, 1968) is used in the title of this section to describe what this author believes is a more accurate description of stability and, conversely, transformation (Bütz, Schwinn, and Chamberlain, 2019; Bütz, 2017, 1997). Accordingly, it may be said that the functioning of a family system in these cases remains in a steady state absent stresses that set IMDs into motion or in the presence of more resilient individual and familial characteristics. By contrast, if the family's functioning shifts or degrades toward a more regressive state, it may transform under these stresses, and its former steady state begins to buckle. After a period of time in a transformative state, an IMD pathological dynamic may well emerge, punctuate, as a new steady state that connotes the family's functioning.

The *DSM-5*, Real Diagnoses, and the Alternative Model for Personality Disorders

The widely discussed issue of categorical and dimensional diagnoses has continued its development as well (e.g., Kraemer, Noda, & O'Hara, 2004), and this discussion is an important one for reconceptualization of FDBP and Parental Alienation. This debate has received important updates too (see Nazem et al., 2014; Biondi et al., 2018; Mermis, 2018). Of significance are those who have taken the long view regarding the artificial distinction imposed on diagnostic phenomena by categorization at the expense of dimensional considerations in the *DSM-5*. For example, Carragher et al. (2015) stated,

> Revolutionizing psychiatric classification to include dimensions would align the field with other medicine areas [13]. Fourth and the focus of this review, converging lines of research indicate that disorders co-occur more often than expected by chance, challenging the DSM conceptualization that disorders are discrete entities.
>
> (p. 340)

Similarly, Blashfield and his colleagues (2014) made the following observations:

> The DSM-5 intended to add dimensional measures of symptoms and severity (First, 2010; Lopez et al., 2007; Narrow & Kuhl, 2011; Regier, 2007). Problems that are frequently encountered with categorical diagnoses include high rates of comorbidity, frequent use of NOS diagnoses, and boundary lines between disorders drawn on the basis of tradition rather than empirical data
>
> (Jones, 2012; Widiger & Simonsen, 2005).

Although the leaders of the DSM-5 supported the move toward a more dimensional system, the internal controversies associated with the DSM-5 were intense around this dimensional versus categorical split. The DSM-5 proposal to create a *hybrid*[1] categorical-dimensional system for the PDs was rejected by the Board of Trustees of the APA (American Psychiatric Association, 2013, Kupfer et al., 2002). The dimensional components of workgroup proposals (aside from the creation of diagnostic spectra) were included in Section III of the manual, indicating the controversial and unsettled views within the DSM-5.

(p. 42)

Still others have addressed how to incorporate dimensional aspects of diagnosis, such as the proposal of the Alternative Model for Personality Disorders (AMPD). Specifically, Waugh et al. (2017) opined that:

Severity and style of personality dysfunction are evaluated conjointly through ratings for overall level of personality impairment and specific pathological personality traits. These ratings generate hybrid categorical-dimensional PD diagnoses in addition to dimensional indices of personality psychopathology. Psychological evaluation conducted through the lens of the AMPD generates both psychiatric diagnosis and a psychometric profile of clinical data that can serve as a relatively comprehensive personality assessment.

The AMPD joins two conceptual planes of personality pathology.[2] The first plane covers disturbances in self and interpersonal functioning. The second involves dimensions of maladaptive personality traits assessed through 5 broad trait domains that are partitioned into 25 narrower trait facets.

(p. 80)

These authors also stated, "Importantly, the AMPD accommodates clinicians of varying backgrounds much in the same way that the psychotherapy integration movement bridges theoretical orientations." Thus, it appears that a conceptual shift has been in the wind, one that speaks to the combined use of categorical and dimensional approaches to diagnosis. This shift naturally suggests hybrid diagnoses, an approach that underscores what had been described by Reed (2010):

the clinical utility of a classification construct or category for mental and behavioural disorders depends on: a) its value in communicating (e.g., among practitioners, patients, families, administrators); b) its implementation characteristics in clinical practice, including its goodness of fit (i.e., accuracy of description), its ease of use, and the time required to use it (i.e., feasibility); and c) its usefulness in selecting interventions and in making clinical management decisions.

(p. 461)

100 Interrelated Multidimensional Diagnoses

In addition, Blashfield and his colleagues (2014) indicated that

> Humans naturally attempt to sort and make sense of their environments, including how to classify psychopathology. Different methods are developed (taxonomies) in an attempt to most accurately represent reality. There are scientific pros and cons to each method, and politics play a role in deciding which methods are used. Throughout the histories of the DSMs, the researchers and clinicians have been struggling with similar issues, and these issues have not been resolved with the newly released DSM-5. We still do not know the etiology of mental disorders or when dimensions are better to use in classifying them as opposed to discrete categories. Theoretical positions oppose one another, which is good for science in that it allows theories to be falsified.
>
> (Popper, 1985, pp. 46–47)

It follows that there has been much to consider about current diagnostic considerations and matters central to building scientific consensus on developing a more complex, sophisticated, and clinically useful approach to diagnosis (and hopefully intervention and/or treatment).

With the continued dialogue on the nature of diagnosis as backdrop, we return to FDBP as a critical example of the diagnostic complexity spoken to in this debate. To review, FDBP was conceptualized as: "a forerunner of the more sophisticated practice of wedding individual diagnoses and group, social, family and legal dynamics together" (Bütz, Evans, & Webber-Dereszynski, 2009, p. 37). If FDBP is to be considered a model for advancing diagnostic sophistication and clarity, how might more common diagnoses such as anxiety and depression be comprehended from a next-generation diagnostic-category perspective that moves beyond linear, individual-focused, categorical conceptualization? If psychosocial dimensions are directly incorporated into diagnoses, questions also arise regarding the value of separate social diagnostic modifiers such as those described historically by Relational Problems or V-Codes in the *Diagnostic and Statistical Manuals of Mental Disorders*. Further, it is both possible and useful to broach a hybrid diagnosis that integrates individual and system characteristics and interrelationships to advance a discussion that has been stalled for over half a century, i.e., *Patients have families* (Richardson, 1948). These considerations are but a few examples of those necessary to discuss the next generation of complex sophisticated diagnoses. It was after many hours of contemplation that this author felt that the necessity of the shift was so profound that it called for a term to describe diagnostic conceptualizations similar to FDBP and the process of elucidating other similar interactive symptom patterns that transform into pathological dynamics.

An IMD, Not a Relational Problem or a Syndrome

To illustrate the necessity or value of introducing the concept of IMD, it is proposed to compare it to similar scientific terms and concepts, most notably the *DSM*'s "Relational Problem" and the broader concept of a syndrome. According to the *DSM-5*, the term *Relational Problem* is found under the section on "Other Conditions That May Be a Focus of Clinical Attention." Relational problems are considered "not mental disorders" (p. 715). Moreover, this approach from the *DSM-5* suggests that relational problems only hold value by elaborating conditions for "true disorders." The authors of the *DSM-5*[3] (American Psychiatric Association, 2013) note that this category of "Other Conditions" was intended to address these three matters:

> conditions and problems that may be a focus of clinical attention or that may otherwise affect the diagnosis, course, prognosis, or treatment of a patient's mental disorder.
>
> (p. 715)

This rationale goes on to include whether it is the justification for the session or clarifies the necessity of other interventions, as well as whether it has valuable information about the person's situation that may impact service delivery. Thus, regardless of the descriptions provided about abuse, neglect, domestic violence, war, and other very important psychosocial matters, the *DSM-5* approach is that this term does not describe, or even largely consider, the presence of a diagnosable pathological dynamic. In fact, in the eyes of the authors of the *DSM-5*, such problems have only ancillary or contextual value, and are not in and of themselves diagnosis worthy. Indeed, these "other conditions" are essentially optional descriptors, and in this author's experience are rarely even used in most diagnoses.

By contrast, the conceptual shift suggested with the term IMD takes a much different approach in valuing these matters. Relational-problem interactions at the individual- system/system-individual level are an important bridge to the concept of IMDs. To perhaps reiterate points made earlier in this text, with IMDs individual-system/system-individual interactions are critical to the architecture of providing a comprehensive description of the complex interrelated and multidimensional individual and systemic subdynamics, which, together, more fully elucidate a pathological dynamic. Thus, if certain challenges with relational problems are worked out, these "other conditions" may serve as an intermediary diagnostic "set" between individuals and Interrelated Multidimensional Diagnoses.

Naturally, others might argue for the term *syndrome* instead of Interrelated Multidimensional Diagnoses. Per Merriam-Webster, a syndrome is defined in one of these two ways[4]:

1. a group of signs and symptoms that occur together and characterize a particular abnormality or condition
2. a set of concurrent things (such as emotions or actions) that usually form an identifiable pattern

Merriam-Webster's definition notes that the modern usage of the term *syndrome* first occurred in 1541 and elaborates that

> Combining its two Greek roots, *syndrome* means basically 'running together'. So when diagnosing a condition or disease, doctors tend to look for a group of symptoms existing together. As long as a set of symptoms remains *mysterious*, it may be referred to as a specific syndrome. But if that name is used for a while, *it may become the condition's permanent name, even after an underlying cause has been found.*[5]

This elaboration accurately describes the two meanings by which the *syndrome* tends to be regarded. On the one hand, it describes a mysterious "running together" of symptoms. On the other hand, it may become simply a convention of description by way of repeated use.

It is not surprising then that the psychological literature is replete with discussions about the confusion surrounding syndromes, and then conventional terms that are eventually adopted as a term of art, that is, *"the condition's permanent name, even after an underlying cause has been found."* For example, in *Diagnoses, Syndromes and Diseases: A Knowledge Representation Problem,* Calvo et al. (2003) wrote that terms such as "syndrome," "disease" and "diagnosis" are used improperly, are at times ambiguous, and compound the difficulties in how medical information or knowledge is employed. These authors argued,

> Diagnostic categories (diseases and most syndromes) are simply concepts. They are justified only if they provide a useful framework for organizing and explaining the complexity of clinical experience in order to derive inferences about outcome and if they guide decisions about treatment.

Interrelated Multidimensional Diagnoses **103**

> A **syndrome** is a recognizable complex of symptoms and physical findings which indicate a specific condition for which a direct cause is not necessarily understood. Thus in practice doctors refer to the infamous "viral syndrome" as such because of the uncertainty regarding the legion of viral agents that is causing the illness. Once medical science identifies a causative agent or process with a fairly high degree of certainty, physicians may then refer to the process as a **disease**, not a syndrome. Mucocutaneous lymph node syndrome became Kawasaki syndrome which in turn metamorphosed into Kawasaki disease; the latter is properly a disease, no longer a syndrome, by virtue of its clearly identifiable diagnostic features and disease progression, and response to specific treatment.
>
> (p. 802)

Previously, when there has been an array of co-occurring symptoms, or a collection of symptoms to one degree or another, the use of the term *syndrome* has been discounted and / or set aside in favor of better-known diagnostic presentations. At the same time, paradoxically, if this array of symptoms has been present long enough, whatever name becomes attached to the syndrome becomes a term of art and represents some disease, disorder, or pathology, even in the absence of empirical support.

The concept of a syndrome proved difficult in addressing the phenomenon considered under the term *PA* as well, and Gardner (2002) posed the question of whether or not Parental Alienation Syndrome was "a true syndrome," defining the phenomenon in these ways:

> Some who prefer to use the term parental alienation (PA) claim that the PAS is not really a syndrome. This position is especially seen in courts of law in the context of child-custody disputes. A syndrome, by medical definition, is a cluster of symptoms, occurring together, that characterize a specific dis-ease. The symptoms, although seemingly disparate, warrant being grouped together because of a common etiology or basic underlying cause.
>
> (p. 96)

Later, Bernet et al. (2010) elaborated these difficulties and differences as well:

> Richard Gardner commented on this topic in his article, "Does DSM-IV have equivalents for the parental alienation syndrome (PAS) diagnosis?" Gardner thought that parent-child relational problem and PAS "have some symptoms in common," but they are not equivalent. He said, "In

104 Interrelated Multidimensional Diagnoses

> the PAS situation there is a pathological dyad between the alienating parent and the child and another pathological dyad between the alienated parent and the child . . . Examiners using this criterion do well to emphasize that two separate parent-child relational problems are manifested."
>
> (Gardner, 2003, p. 84)

It would appear that Gardner (2003), in his efforts to explain a syndrome, had hit on one major difference between parent-child relational problem and PAS, and reiterated that, "There is a pathological dyad between the alienating[6] parent and the child and another pathological dyad between the alienated parent and the child" (p. 11).

These are two separate but interrelated behaviors that result ultimately in a pathological dynamic, just as the parent-child and the parent—healthcare provider relationships ultimately produce a pathological dynamic in Factitious Disorder by Proxy. But, in these cases, these are not two sets of separate phenomena or groups of symptoms that simply run together. Instead, an intricate interaction of phenomena occurs on several different dimensions over time in an interrelated pattern, which cumulatively produces a pathological dynamic. The buildup of symptoms in individuals and systems over time is not mysterious once the interrelated natures of the characteristics and the subdynamics have been studied adequately as an Interrelated Multidimensional Diagnosis. Rather, the pattern is readily revealed as an IMD by way of a symptom-by-symptom examination of the phenomenon across individuals and systems on multiple dimensions of examination. Also, by virtue of the clarity offered by describing the phenomenon as an IMD, once the elements associated with these pathological dynamics are revealed, this pathological pattern can be dealt with therapeutically, disrupted, halted, or stopped altogether, as will be explained in Chapter 8.

As we have seen, throughout the various iterations of the *DSM*, relational problems and complex interactions between individuals and systems have not been intended to describe diagnoses. On the other hand, the term *syndrome* has proven too broad, has been overused, and has often been misapplied in a fashion that creates significant confusion within the literature broadly. This confusion has indeed made elaborating the phenomena under study as an IMD challenging, as the examples from the literature described earlier attest. It is proposed that the concept of an IMD specifically describes a cumulative process across individuals and systems that, by definition, produce a pathological and diagnosable dynamic. It is also argued that the very weaknesses which have set aside relational problems and syndromes may well mark them as the next step in offering a new generation of holistic conceptual diagnoses, or IMDs, which are proposed as a set of diagnoses that describe complex interrelated and multidimensional phenomena in a scientific fashion.

Scientific Certainty: Daubert vs. Merrill Dow Chemical (1993)

The standards developed for the level of scientific certainty acceptable in legal proceedings require consideration here. A simple, but telling, literature review was conducted pertinent to the matters at hand in 2008 (Bütz, Evans, & Webber-Dereszynski, 2009). The criteria for the literature search included the words "Daubert," "Scientific Certainty," "Factitious Disorder by Proxy," and "Munchausen Syndrome by Proxy." *PsychNet*, the main search engine available for psychological publications at the time, returned no results. The majority of professional references found by other means expressed the same sentiment, that, as an individual and/or dynamic diagnosis, MSBP and/or FDBP were difficult to define at best. At worst, as Lucire (2000) stated, "Experienced practitioners agree that this phenomenon has reached epidemic proportions and has all the characteristics of mass hysteria, now termed *moral panic*" (p. 45).

In fact, at that time in 2008, MSBP and FDBP were considered so unreliable in the United Kingdom (Adshead, 2005; Pagnell, 2006)[7] that there was active discussion about abandoning them altogether in favor of still another term, *Fabricated and/or Induced Illness in Children (FII)* (See Press Release by the Royal College of Psychiatrists, July 11, 2006). This additional term, *FII*, had been actively debated for several years preceding the earlier article (Bütz, Evans, & Webber-Dereszynski, 2009). The press release from the Royal College of Psychiatrists had stated, "FII had come just at the time when there had been a sustained attack on the position of professionals—not just in Britain— where the idea of professionals as a source of expertise had been discredited." Yet, despite the critical opinions in this literature at the time, represented best in Pankratz (2006), Pagnell (2006) and Rogers (2004), as well as public opinion that apparently called for change, courts frequently accepted these diagnoses through the *Daubert Standard* or the *Federal Rules of Evidence* (i.e., Federal Rule 702). As described by *State of Delaware v. McMullen* ((DEF. ID. 0507014155) 6/1/2006):

> At its core, *Daubert* dictates that Rule 702 is the governing standard for the admissibility of scientific evidence by specifying that *"if scientific,"*

106 Interrelated Multidimensional Diagnoses

technical, or other specialized knowledge *"will assist the trier of fact to understand the evidence or to determine a fact in issue,"* then the expert *"*may testify thereto.*"*

(p. 28)

Also, the *People of the State of Illinois v. B.T.* ([No. 1-05-0638] 9/23/05) illustrated these considerations further:

> The crux of respondent's argument is that factitious disorder by proxy has not achieved general acceptance because it is not a formal diagnosis under the DSM IV standards (American Psychiatric Association, *Diagnostic and Statistical Manual of Mental Disorders*, at 781–83).
>
> (4th rev. ed. 2000)

> We note that all the experts, including respondent's, testified consistently at trial that factitious disorder by proxy was a recognized research criteria diagnosis by the American Psychiatric Association instead of a formal diagnosis because more research was needed before it could appear in the body—rather than appendix—of the diagnostic manual and researchers had not yet developed a specific profile regarding what symptoms indicated the disorder. We also note that other jurisdictions have found evidence regarding factitious disorder by proxy, earlier known as MSBP, admissible under either *Frye, Daubert v. Merrell Dow Pharmaceuticals, Inc.*, 509 U.S. 579, 125 L. Ed. 2d 469, 113 S. Ct. 2786 (1993), or state rules of evidence. See *People v. Phillips*, 122 Cal. App. 3d 69, 86–87, 175 Cal. Rptr. 703, 713–14 (1981) (testimony regarding objectively verifiable symptoms leading to a diagnosis of MSBP was admissible as garden variety expert testimony, was not a new scientific development, and it made no difference that the syndrome might be an unrecognized illness or not listed in the diagnostic manual of mental disorders); *State v. Hocevar*, 300 Mont. 167, 184–85, 7 P. 3d 329, 341–42 (2000)
>
> (expert testimony regarding MSBP was not novel to the field of pediatrics or law and was admissible under the rules of evidence).

Given the tendency of courts to admit evidence of MSBP and FDBP, as well as under other terms based on the earlier work from 2008, the aforementioned search was updated.

During the summer of 2019, this author circled back to the exercise that was conducted in 2008, but this time Google's Scholar application was used and given the same search parameters. This search generated thirteen hits outside of this author's own previous work with his colleagues (Bütz, Evans, & Webber-Dereszynski, 2009), and as it turned out some pertinent articles were missed in the earlier review (Adshead, 2005; Dahir et al., 2005; Sutherland, 2005; American Prosecutors Research Institute & National Center for the Prosecution of Child Abuse, 2004). Though some references only supplied an investigative approach (American Prosecutors Research Institute & National Center for the Prosecution of Child Abuse, 2004), others, such as Adshead (2005), made a number of useful descriptions and, in particular, described the following:

> The British courts have not examined the status and admissibility of expert testimony as the U.S. Courts have, for example, in *Daubert v. Merrell Dow Pharmaceuticals, Inc.*[23] The duties of the expert are set in *Anglo Group Plc v. Winther Brown & Co Ltd.*[24] The expert should be able to provide evidence that it is not clear to the ordinary person (*R. v. Turner*[25]). The test of the status of the medical evidence would probably mirror the test for negligence; it should reflect a reasonable body of medical opinion (*Boulam v. Friern Hospital Management Committee*[26]), which does not mean that there are not opposing opinions (*Maynard v. West Midlands Regional Health Authority*[27]) and it should be logical (*Bolitha (deceased) v. City & Hackney HA*[28]).
>
> (p. 104)

These are critical considerations that address the necessity of scientific evidence in these cases. We also have Sutherland (2005) and her review titled, "Undue Deference to Experts Syndrome?" Although work in this piece was dedicated to the shortcomings of Sir Roy Meadow's work on a particular set of cases, she offered this useful descriptor:

> It should be remembered that the standard of proof in child protection cases requires proof on the balance of probabilities, while the standard in criminal cases is proof beyond reasonable doubt.[50] In short, what is insufficient in the criminal context, may be enough in a child protection case.
>
> (p. 388)

The work of Dahir et al. (2005) would have also proven very useful had this author's original literature search uncovered it. This group of researchers

108 Interrelated Multidimensional Diagnoses

made inquiries with over two hundred judges and came to several important insights:

> When asked what factors they would consider when assessing psychological syndrome and profile evidence, respondents tended to revert to the legal use of pre-*Daubert* standards (i.e., qualifications of the expert, relevance, in general acceptance, as determined by case precedent, as well as wide acceptance in the relevant scientific field) more often than reliability generally, and to ignore the newer *Daubert* guidelines of falsifiability and error rate that were intended by the *Daubert* court to be measures of scientific validity.
>
> (p. 74)

They also noted that judges have far less experience with syndrome-like evidentiary profiles (p. 75), and that earlier research found that between 6% and 4% of state trial court judges understood *Daubert* guidelines. They (2005) wrapped up their discussion with the following nodal observation:

> Regardless of debates among philosophers of science, Popper's approach was embodied in the *Daubert* decision, specifically regarding falsifiability as outlined by Justice Blackman's quote: "The criterion of the scientific status of the theory is falsify ability, or refute ability, or testability" (*Daubert*, p. 2797). The justices were influenced by his arguments, as evidenced by the Court's announcement that evidentiary reliability-trustworthiness is to be determined by scientific validity. None of the four guidelines has been rejected or superseded by subsequent Supreme Court decisions (i.e., *General Electric Co. v. Joiner*, 1997, or *Kumho Tire Co. v. Patrick Carmichael*, 1999), and the importance of testability continues to be accepted by many philosophers of science, even if they reject a straight Popperian falsifiability definition of science.
>
> (p. 77)

Later on, Pienaar (2013) discussed the notion of a "collective-mind" in another discussion on certain psychological instruments that could be taken as evidence of FDBP (Abidin, Austin, & Flens, 2013), and, via FII, the description (Scaife, 2012) that courts are "reluctant to accept that the behaviour constitutes a syndrome, whilst it is clear that some care-givers do deliberately harm children in a manner which results in unnecessary medical attention and can be fatal" (p. 78).

In 2016 Artingstall described the multifaceted role expert witnesses play in these cases and the accumulation of evidence. Then, she also discussed the *Daubert* versus *Frye* Standards, explaining that she:

> Concluded that *Kelly/Frye* formulation (*Kelly* formulation) should remain a prerequisite to the admission of expert testimony regarding new scientific methodology.
>
> Such factors include (1) whether a theory or technique has been or can be tested; (2) whether the theory or technique has been subjected to peer review and publication; (3) the known or potential rate of error; and (4) whether the technique has been accepted by a relevant scientific community.
>
> (p. 305)

Clearly, the science involved with MSBP and FDBP has been and continues to be discussed in a scholarly fashion that can be tested and has been subjected to peer review. However, questions remain about the error rate and whether these phenomena are accepted in the scientific community. It is this author's hope and intention with the use of the concept of an IMD that both of these matters will be soundly addressed later in this text.

Despite the foregoing efforts, as well as, no doubt, other literatures outside of the scope of behavioral health, this author considered that he may not be aware of treatises such as the one offered by Eichner (2016), who has argued that, "Despite the rising number of parents faced with these charges, this phenomenon has received no critical attention whatsoever in legal literature" (p. 206). She does not stop there but at the same time goes on to state: "In short, the MCA theory developed by physicians and enforced by child protection officials is bad constitutional doctrine, bad law, bad science, and bad medicine" (p. 206). A year later Howe (2017) offered a piece that proposed "De-Junking MSBP Adjudication." In fact, Howe said the following[8]:

> MSBP cases are subject to high levels of false positives. Whether subject to dependency adjudication or other forms of child-welfare interventions, accused parents are deprived of their children. Underlying these false positives are serious defects in the types of evidence used to support MSBP adjudications.
>
> (p. 201)

She also provided examples of how *Daubert* comes to bear on these cases:

The factors enumerated in the *Daubert* test vary in their ability to evaluate reliability and validity of the differential diagnosis. For testability, the judge can look to whether alternative cases were tested or ruled out to falsify the diagnosis.[82] However, for the most part, the differential diagnosis is considered a valid methodology as it is generally accepted, peer-reviewed, and most often correct.

(p. 211)

She went on to review fifty cases and provide what she described as a decision matrix to better evaluate evidence in MSBP cases, which will be discussed later in more detail.

Other pathological dynamics in addition to FDBP have faced similar descriptive challenges, including the phenomenon variously represented as Alignment (Wallerstein & Kelly, 1976), Parent Alienation Syndrome (Gardner, 1985), the Alienated Child (Kelly & Johnston, 2001) and Parent Alienation (Bernet et al., 2010). Collectively, this phenomenon is more contemporarily described by the term *Parental Alienation* (PA), and this phenomenon has also encountered difficulties with recognition in the scientific community as well as admissibility in court, which has been addressed within its literature (Baker, 2013a; Lorandos, 2013; Lowenstein, 2013; Gardner, 2001).

Courts and PA

Legal controversies around PA, like FDBP, persist, suggesting that it has been difficult for courts to discern what the phenomenon is and when it is present (Baker, 2013a; Lowenstein, 2013). As will be described further in Chapter 6, these difficulties play out in a legal context in two ways. The first is through the legal system itself and how it adds to environmental stressors that create high-conflict divorces, custody disputes, parenting plans and parenting time. The second matter addresses how courts determine the potential reliability and validity of PA as a scientific concept according to legal standards, that is, *Daubert* and related standards of proof. While the first matter will be discussed in detail in Chapter 6, legal standards such as *Daubert* will be addressed in this segment.

As but one marker of these matters, Lowenstein (2013) had described that, "Many judges still do not recognize PA or parent alienation syndrome (PAS) because they have not yet been included in the *International Classification of Diseases* (11th ed. *[ICD-11]*) or *Diagnostic and Statistical Manual of Mental Disorders* (5th ed. *[DSM-5]*)" (p. 658). In her chapter on the research about PA and its relationship to "The Daubert Standards," Baker (2013a) made the case that guidelines for admitting scientific expert testimony include the passage of three thresholds of proof:[9]

1. The judge is the gatekeeper, ensuring that scientific expert testimony truly proceeds from scientific knowledge.
2. The trial judge must ensure that the expert's testimony is "relevant to the task at hand" and that it rests "on a reliable foundation."
3. The judge must find it more likely than not that the expert's methods are reliable and reliably applied to the facts at hand.[10] (p. 324)

Now, obviously, this characterization of *Daubert* and related case law that serves as legal standards sounds different from the earlier discussion on Factitious Disorder by Proxy. Still, after providing a very good review of the scientific method, at the time of her article Baker (2013a) wrote: "PA and/or PAS have been subjected to two *Daubert* hearings and one *Mohan* hearing[11]" (p. 344). It was found that PA was admissible under *Daubert*, but PAS was not in these two cases. Baker then described the Mohan ruling:

> The judge concluded that the 17 parental alienation behaviors and the 8 child manifestations of alienation "are supported by Dr. Baker's own research and appear to be well accepted in the literature and scientific community."
>
> (p. 344)

Even so, she described that her questionnaire (Baker Strategies Questionnaire [BSQ]) and Bricklin and Halbert's (2004), Bricklin and Elliot's (2002) Perception-of-Relationship Test (PORT) were "helpful but incomplete because they do not map onto the eight behavioral manifestations" (p. 344). Something is lacking in how PA has been considered, and it is this author's contention that what has been lacking is addressing the pathological family dynamic that develops in an IMD, coupled with the accompanying knowledge that PA arises out of a certain background environment, as described above.

Proofs: Characteristics, Interrelationships, and Dimensions

It follows from what has been described above that the aforementioned characteristics, interrelationships, and dimensions require proofs that correspond

112 Interrelated Multidimensional Diagnoses

to known symptom presentations in individuals and systems that have been reliably and validly addressed in the literature on each specific Interrelated Multidimensional Diagnosis. As will be described later, these IMD symptom profiles include considerations that have been described as continuous composites (e.g., see Viglione et al., 2014) or as *variable* exclusion, inclusion, and outcome criteria that may serve as markers of proof corresponding with the idea of differentiating criteria (Rogers, 2004). Comparison proofs may include categorical and dimensional considerations, or, in some cases, even hybrid considerations, as in the PA dynamic that will be described in Chapter 6.

This process of gathering proofs begins with the practitioner, professional or researcher addressing the clinical situation and cataloging certain individual characteristics, the severity of symptoms, the kind and quality of relationship interactions, and systemic interactions that collectively produce subdynamics. Different properties of the process represented in an individual or in a system may be described by its strength or weakness, or even absence, as well as by the aforementioned continuous composites or variable criteria (Bütz & Evans, 2019). These criteria more fully address the scope of dimensional considerations for symptom presentations in individuals and systems, and whether these symptoms are evident to a greater or lesser degree. For example, when considering presentation of symptoms in the case of either FDBP or PA, one question is whether a child's age falls within the range expected. Further questions are whether, on a different continuous variable dimension, the family system in FDBP is prone to symptomatic interrelationships to the point that a *folie à deux* between the parents may be present, and whether there is active conflict between the parents about the symptoms materializing in the child. In PA, does the child engage in Alienating Behaviors? Moreover, are these mild, moderate, or severe disparaging remarks against the Rejected Parent? Thus, even if most of these conditions for poof are met, the question remains whether a pathological dynamic is created out of the collective sum; that is, does the butterfly flapping its wings produce a storm? Consequently, by definition, an IMD cannot be made without clear clinical articulation, descriptive proof that symptom-by-symptom, interaction-by-interaction, a pathological dynamic becomes evident.

Splitting and/or Triangulation and IMDS

While discussing IMDs, practitioners, professionals and researchers discuss experiences they have when encountering these phenomena. Having worked in these circumstances for some time, this author felt obliged to illuminate to one degree or another the emotional, mental and physical experiences of working with IMDs, experiences that are at times talked about among those working with these families and systems as bewilderment, anger, the favoring of one parent over another, and being astonished by the apparent actions of one parent or another. Discussing what some may view as an old-world topic rooted in the theoretical discipline of Psychoanalysis, *splitting* is one term that describes these dynamics (Kohut, 1971; Kernberg, 1967, 1968; Guntrip, 1961; Klein, 1946; Fairbairn, 1941; Freud, A., 1927; Freud, S., 1910). The other that may be more agreeable and/or familiar is the notion of *triangulation* within the theoretical literature on Family Therapy (Minuchin, Rosman, & Baker, 1978; Weakland, 1976; Minuchin, 1974; Bowen, 1972). The intention here is not to stir up any more controversy than the implications of these ideas will likely bring, nor to endure more of the kinds of criticisms that likely will follow given this author's experience with novel topics (Bütz, 1993b, 1993c, 1992a, 1992b). However, the focus of this text is to be of assistance to those working with families who find themselves in the tumult of these pathological dynamics. A number of professionals, practitioners and researchers may simply be unaware of, or perhaps avoid, topics such as transference or countertransference (Searles, 1978; Reich, 1951). In this day and age of simplifying therapeutic processes, it is possible that some practitioners are unacquainted with the kinds of dynamics that can, and do, play out in these situations while interacting with these systems in healthcare and/or legal environments.

In this author's view, it would be unfair to those practitioners, professionals, and researchers not to at least hazard a description of experiences that have been in the literature for approximately one hundred years, experiences that many a clinician has struggled with emotionally, mentally, and physically. Admittedly, this discussion is not for everyone, and this author will not be suggesting the use of chaise lounges in the psychoanalytic sense or the employment of a one-way mirror and call-in from family therapy practices. Each modality and practice is useful in its own right. What will be described is the experiential piece of this work, and an effort to help make sense of the experience of working with these families as well as some names with which to build a language that helps navigate the confusing and complicated nature of these interpersonal and systemic interactions.

Of the more bewildering experiences a person may have in working with individuals and family systems that have regressed or are regressed in their functioning is splitting. Recognizing that this book has been developed for professionals, practitioners, and researchers, the long and detailed history of the development of splitting, splitting of the psyche, splitting of the ego, splitting of an object, and splitting as a defense will not be addressed here.

There are whole books written on each topic, and it has been an active area of research and theoretical work for a very long time. Parenthetically, it is worth looking into this research further if one actively and regularly works in this field.

Very briefly, splitting of the ego or psyche was discussed in contemporary science as early as the work of Janet (1889) and Freud (1910). It was also addressed as part of early primitive interpersonal relationships by Anna Freud (1928). Further, splitting has been conceived of as a normal part of development in very young children as a transition period in Object Relations Theory, which is a discipline within the larger umbrella of Psychoanalytic or Psychodynamic theoretical thought (Klein, 1946; Fairbairn, 1941). But all of these references are to very early on in life, during the so-called primitive stages of development for the ego, located around two years of age, plus or minus. Unresolved, these conflicts are also where progress may stall and result in personality traits or a personality disorder that is evidence of the developmental arrest. Further, under great strain, others with slightly more developed defense mechanisms can, and do, regress into these sorts of primitive defense mechanisms (Kohut, 1971; Kernberg, 1967, 1968; Guntrip, 1961). Hence, this is where long-term psychotherapy has proven to be particularly useful; that is, when an individual's emotional and interpersonal development has stalled and with individuals who are fortunate to have more developed ego functions but have regressed in the face of stress. (Shedler, 2010; Leichsenring & Rabung, 2008).

Speaking to even the basics of splitting from this literature is not an easy task to accomplish with practitioners, professionals and researchers who have had no exposure to this literature, since there is a whole language that may be unfamiliar as well as precedents and theoretical schools of thought that speak to this era of development and conflicts. Mindful of this, and its hazards, in the most basic sense, splitting is a defense that preserves the functioning of an individual's ego in the face of "objects", i.e., people whom children learn they cannot trust. As noted, splitting happens in healthy development as a phase, but splitting remains an active defense into adulthood when children have grown up in environments where they do not feel trust in their parent figures, or what are referred to as "primary objects." Most often when splitting holds into adulthood, or when there is a ready path to regression, parents in these homes abuse or neglect the child. In so doing, these parents frustrate or obscure the child's need to develop a sense of consistency, to hold internal representations of objects, and to learn to self- sooth in even the most basic of ways. It is due to this lack of internal structure that individuals have a limited sense of themselves and are almost constantly attempting to discern whom they can trust. Depending on the level of pathology, this effort can occur, for example, from day-to- day or even moment-to-moment. In turn, these individuals have no barometer of whom they can and cannot trust, and they work off the slimmest of information at times to inform these discernments, or at other times they require a mountain of evidence. Neither is enough, or too much, as there is no internal benchmark for whom they can trust and those they cannot. So, it is a rather agonizing and constant process for these individuals to attempt to recognize so-called "good objects" and "bad objects." Their sense of confusion and disorganization is very real, and it tends to move beyond the individual and into the dynamics of the family system where these conflicts get played out in one way or another. One day a person in the family can be a good object when the person is feeling good and they are not frustrated by their actions; and the next day, due to the person's own internal instability, this same member of the family becomes a bad object. Obviously, this would be very confusing to children within the family system, and to those practitioners, professionals and researchers interacting with a parent who does engage in splitting. Again, this author has only touched on the most elemental dynamics of splitting here, but this gives some sense of the challenges faced as we begin to entertain the interpersonal and family dynamics in these cases.

In the Family Therapy literature, *splitting* is rarely used as a term due to its theoretical background; an arguably similar dynamic has been described by the term *triangulation* (Dallos & Vetere, 2012; Fivaz-Depeursinge & Favez, 2006). Dallos and Vetere (2012) described triangulation in the following manner:

> Triangulation can be conceptualized as a noun and a verb, in that we can speak of dynamic triangular relationships between intimates, and processes of triangulation that draw a third person into consideration with a dyad. Early systems theory drew on Mills' sociological idea that the basic human relationship was a triad, not a dyad, in that when any two people get together they are influenced by a third.
>
> (p. 118)

They spoke to the matter of early attachment in this article in a fashion comparable to the developmental time frame discussed by Psychoanalytic Theory, but obviously drew from a different body of literature as well:

> Essentially triangulation contains the idea that what is happening in a significant relationship between two people in a family can have

116 Interrelated Multidimensional Diagnoses

a powerful influence on a third family member, and vice versa, in mutually reinforcing ways. Early systemic practitioners, such as Weakland (1976) and Minuchin (1974), Minuchin, Rosman, and Baker (1978), observed that families may engage in a variety of triangular processes that could lead to stable coalitions or less stable and shifting alliances.

(p. 119)

As with the above descriptions of splitting, triangulation may be viewed as a normal part of a family system's development, or it may result from, and in, pathology (Fivaz-Depeursinge & Favez, 2006):

One of the key notions in family process is triangulation, or the recruitment of a third person to lessen the tension or anxiety in a dyadic relationship (Bowen, 1972). In childhood, at its worst, this process may lead a child whose parents are in an intractable conflict to play the role of go-between or scapegoat and risk emotional development disturbance (Minuchin, 1974). Given the exacerbation of distress known to occur in couples in conflict during the transition to parenthood (Shapiro et al., 2000), this problematic process is likely to originate in infancy.

(pp. 3–4)

Although the maladaptive and/or pathological description of triangulation sounds somewhat different, it is a dynamic that fundamentally describes the kinds of challenging experiences that this section of the book attempts to address, experiences that professionals, practitioners and researchers may well step in the middle of when working with the dynamics described in an Interrelated Multidimensional Diagnosis.

The regression spoken to through either splitting or triangulation above is where our interests lie in these kinds of cases with FDBP and PA, where in many instances a parent or parents have experienced significant stress to the extent that they have and/or have begun to engage in these behaviors that initiate such pathological processes within the family system. Naturally, splitting and triangulation may also occur in children and adolescents in PA, too, but that is later in the process, after Alienating Behaviors have begun with one or both parents.

Attempting to simplify these concepts, this author looked for an acceptable general description of splitting since it was the more elusive concept to explain. Such a definition, albeit colorful, was offered in an article from *Psychology Today* on addressing clients who suffer from borderline traits

Interrelated Multidimensional Diagnoses **117**

(Allen, 2011): "Everyone else is treated either like a god or a complete pile of manure, with nothing in between." This statement does not quite do the concept justice, but Allen does get at one of the most troubling parts of the splitting dynamic. Individuals who engage in splitting create interpersonal dynamics in which the other person feels either idealized or degraded. Often, idealization suggests that the other participant in the dynamic has gone along with what the first person has asked, while the feeling of degradation often follows from either not granting this person's wishes or from in some way, shape or form eliciting other gratification than what she or he wished for. Often, people interacting with these individuals feel compelled or pulled to engage, and to gratify the person's wishes, whatever they may be. Hence, and getting a bit ahead here, this is why establishing boundaries and neutrality are so crucial in these cases.

If left unidentified, splitting can also play out in healthcare and legal settings. A very useful commentary that is not so delicate has been supplied by Kraemer (1987) in his article entitled, "Splitting and Stupidity in Child Sexual Abuse." Kraemer summarizes his opinion in the abstract:

> The discovery that sexual abuse is occurring on a far wider scale than was previously believed has divided society in two. In particular cases where abuse is known or suspected there is a similar partition of opinion, both within the minds of the individuals involved and between them, inducing a kind of stupidity which undermines the capacity for honesty and judgement, and all but the most authentic professional skills.
>
> (p. 247)

To Kraemer, this author would, however, offer that the training of many nowadays does not include a base level of understanding about splitting, no less the experience of it in cases in which trauma is being investigated.

This feeling of being pulled into a dynamic also occurs in family systems, and many in this literature speak to this experience and/or to being pulled into a triangulation. Going back to reference the original work from family therapy, Dallos and Vetere (2012) described the following:

> We can also see some parallels here with the ideas of the Bateson group (1972) regarding the double bind. The process of triangulation, or the invitation from the parents to take sides, makes the strategy of withdrawing very hard, so that in effect, it is impossible to leave the relational field. The nub of the double bind—"damned if you do and

damned if you don't"—lies in not being able to step outside the interaction and comment on it at a reflective level of understanding.

(p. 126)

This author cannot describe how many times he has heard the aforementioned expression in conducting this work. An inkling of what to do amid such experiences and/or situations has also been provided by these authors, that is, again, "step outside the interaction and comment on it at a reflective level of understanding."

The main point here is that professionals, practitioners, and researchers may feel an unconscious pull. They may feel drawn into the family dynamic to join part of the family's triangle, or they simply may well feel overwhelmed and disoriented in the face of such cases. That is the big idea here, and why the psychoanalytic literature developed the term *splitting* and the family therapy literature developed the term *triangulation*! If one does not know how to describe what they are feeling, then naturally, no matter how good the professional, practitioner, or researcher is, they will not know how to respond, *no less realize that such experiences are expected in working with these cases.* Both literatures point to maintaining one's scientific psychological distance and to addressing these dynamics with certain levels of interventions too detailed and too numerous to go into here. But let us just say that the powerful effects of these dynamics were such that the literature in Psychoanalysis is replete with instructions to therapists about maintaining professional boundaries and neutrality in the face of such dynamics (Drozek, 2019; Kwawer, 2019; Siegel, 2019). In the Family Therapy literature some woefully maladaptive cases were so powerful, their capacity to pull others into their dynamic called for one therapist to sit in the room with the family while others observed through a one-way mirror, attempting to comprehend the dynamic at work and generate interventions (Selvini-Palazzoli et al., 1978).

Proposition: FDBP and PA Are Interrelated Multidimensional Diagnoses

Returning to our example of FDBP, earlier work proposed contrasting approaches to reaching this diagnosis with either multiple standard diagnoses and relational problems consistent with current practice, or with what might be described as a higher order diagnosis that subsumes the other diagnoses, with FDBP as a unitary diagnosis (Bütz, Evans, & Webber-Dereszynski,

2009), that is, an Interrelated Multidimensional Diagnosis. Without getting fully into the fundamentals of our reconceptualization of FDBP, the following earlier narrative is in keeping with current diagnostic practice:

> We offer a ready heuristic that exists within the *DSM-IV-TR*. For example, a child is traumatized and suffers from posttraumatic stress disorder (PTSD) after he or she has been physically abused. Both issues are commonly coded, that is, PTSD and Physical Abuse of Child. PTSD provides the individual diagnosis, while Physical Abuse of Child provides the etiology and social context of the diagnosis, or what we refer to as its *dynamic* aspect when it refers to the victim (American Psychiatric Association, 2000, p. 738). When the Physical Abuse of Child refers to the alleged perpetrator, then a V Code is also given and again implies a *dynamic* aspect, though the *DSM-IV-TR* does not state it as such. We suggest that experts consider the matter of FDBP as both an individual diagnosis and as a dynamic diagnosis, with coding systems that integrate both aspects to capture the individual, interpersonal, social, and legal complexity of the phenomenon.
>
> (pp. 36–37)

In order to present a unified description of FDBP, four dimensional criteria were offered at that time (American Psychiatric Association, 2009) in a supporting table, which defined *"Factitious Disorder by Proxy (FDBP) Diagnosis* and *FDBP-Child Maltreatment Dynamic"* (pp. 36–37). As noted, advancing the concept of an IMD changed these dimensional considerations to five generally, and parenthetically it will be agreed that each form of IMD may have a different number of dimensions for consideration beyond four (Bütz & Evans, 2019). Addressing the example (2009) that will follow, the order provided below should have been reshuffled, since the process of proofs builds dimensionally and is cumulative:

a. Intentional production or feigning of physical or psychological signs or symptoms in another person who is under the individual's care (*DYNAMIC*).

b. The motivation for the perpetrator's behavior is to assume the sick role by proxy (*DIAGNOSIS/DYNAMIC*).

c. External incentives for the behavior (such as economic gain) are absent (*DIAGNOSIS/DYNAMIC*).

d. The behavior is not better accounted for by another mental disorder (*DIAGNOSIS*).

As the reader is able to see, in our opinion, three out of four research criteria describe an interpersonal dynamic rather than an individual mental disorder diagnosis, and only one of the criteria cleanly provides a traditional diagnostic basis for FDBP.

Bearing these concerns in mind, we hope that Table 1 will supply characteristics that describe both the individual and dynamic diagnostic features of FDBP in order to create some level of objective points of comparison.

(p. 36)

The order of the criteria above was inconsistent with a dimensional cumulative process, and the most consistent progression within the IMD conceptualization would be: b, c, a, d.

So, by way of comparison to PA, we begin with individual characteristics under "b," wherein the adult wishes to gain attention by assuming the sick role through the child. At the same time, there are also the characteristics of a child who is very young and unable to protect her- or himself from the activities of the adult. This is the first dimension of consideration, and these variables are valid for both inclusive and exclusive criteria à la Rogers (2004). The second- dimension addresses criterion "c," wherein external incentives are absent; thus, if there are external incentives, it is not Factitious Disorder by Proxy. In this example, the first dimension speaks again to exclusion criteria in "d," since this phenomenon is not better accounted for by other known diagnoses.

As an earlier conceptualization, "a" contains elements of "b" and "c" and speaks to IMD dimensions four and five. The classification was correct, though, as the fifth- dimension pathological dynamic spoken to throughout was evident. These criteria incorporated the *FDBP—Child Maltreatment Dynamic*, which required ten broad criteria and eight subcriteria that represented a combination of inclusion criteria, including individual traits and what we suggested be referred to as *subdynamics*. These dimensions collectively reflect the individual presenting the child by way of individual symptoms that are absent and individual symptoms that are present. In our original article, the characteristics, criteria, dynamics, and subcriteria were supported by the literature, suggesting both reliable and valid symptoms, which are accounted for one by one as proof and according to a process of building proofs across dimensions, leading to the current IMD conceptualization. Also, as described above, it was added that these criteria may not be all-or-none propositions, but a variable approach to criteria, which has been proposed to accompany the concept of an IMD with such proposed intentional phrases "as more or

Interrelated Multidimensional Diagnoses **121**

less probable," i.e., in such criteria as "History of behavioral health treatment" (Bütz, Evans, & Webber-Dereszynski, 2009, p. 35). Stated another way, an individual may have no behavioral health history, a limited history, or an extensive history. The fourth dimension of consideration simply states that another diagnosis does not better account for the diagnostic situation. Again, Rogers (2004) rightly attempted to move forward the discussion about FDBP-related diagnoses by clarifying that, "every disorder must have inclusion, exclusion, and outcome criteria" (p. 227). The outcome in this case is the fifth dimension of consideration: whether a pathological dynamic has formed once the symptom-by-symptom accounting has been completed.

After further consideration about the previous work, and to come in line with the concept of an IMD, it is suggested that two of the dynamics cited above would more properly be described as *individual dimensional symptoms*. Symptom "a" represents the pathological dynamic described by the proposal of an Interrelated Multidimensional Diagnosis. Individual dimensional symptoms such as "b" and "c" are a product of the parent's individual psychopathology or symptomatology. It is also true that these symptoms feed into the larger pathological dynamic that will be discussed as a diagnostic procedure shortly.

Obviously, PA is also proposed as an example of an IMD, and, without the considerable background supplied by the prior article on FDBP (2009), several examples will be fleshed out further in Chapter 6. But, for example, there is a history and literature on PA, and its known, reliable, and valid individual and system characteristics, interrelationships, and symptoms. The literature clearly has shown that PA emanates in most cases from high-conflict divorces or disputes regarding custody, parenting plans, or parenting time (Howe & Covell, 2014; Baker, Burkhard, & Albertson-Kelly, 2012; Kelly & Johnston, 2001). Again, as described in Chapter 2, Johnston (1994)[12] defined high-conflict cases in the following manner:

> Each of the above studies (conducted by Brotsky and colleagues, by Schaefer, Johnston, and colleagues, and by Johnston) were of children of high-conflict divorce, whose parents had failed mediation, undergone evaluations, or had court-imposed settlements.[12,19,29,32] According to Maccoby and Mnookin, these categories represent a small proportion, the top 10th percentile, of legal conflict in the divorcing population.
>
> (p. 175)

Second, it is a dynamic that arises out of the stresses and demands of the environment created by a family system's interactions with a legal system (Saini

122 Interrelated Multidimensional Diagnoses

et al., 2012; Garber, 2011; Kelly & Johnston, 2001). Third, this process is put into motion by a parent or parents responding to these stresses and demands (Lopez, Iglesias, & Garcia, 2014; Godbout & Parent, 2012; Saini et al., 2012; Garber, 2011; Baker & Ben-Ami, 2011). Fourth, children involved in these cases have certain characteristics (Baker, Burkhard, & Albertson-Kelly, 2012; Ludolph & Bow, 2012; Kelly & Johnston, 2001) and experience interactions with this parent who attempts to entrain the child to engage in Alienating Behaviors. Fifth, if the child responds in kind at a certain level of intensity (Nichols, 2014; Vijoen & van Rensburg, 2014), then, sixth, this pathological dynamic manifests. As was mentioned in the prior chapter, the pathology and/or pathological dynamic do not lie in the child in either FDBP or Parental Alienation. The child's behavior is symptomatic of the pathological dynamic, it is simply a representation of these individuals and systems characteristics, and exhibits symptoms coupled with environmental contingencies that produce enough stress to create this significant degree of dynamic pathology. These matters will be addressed in further specific detail in Chapters 5, 6, 7 and 8.

Practical Examples of IMDs, FDBP, and PA

Arguably, one of the greatest problems with providing healthcare services and remedying legal disputes lies in recognizing just what dynamics or situations are presented in either system. Each system does have a way of making use of categorical, dimensional, and even hybrid criteria. For our purposes, in healthcare, there is the *DSM-5* and *ICD-11* to address diagnoses. In legal settings, there are state and federal laws, which have criteria and a burden of proof required before a legal finding may be made. Yet, each also requires the interpretation of these criteria by individuals, such as healthcare providers or judges. Thus, if these individuals are unable to recognize the phenomenon before them, how would they possibility make a correct diagnosis or legal finding? In the case of FDBP, the weight of such considerations may well be life threatening, while in PA the consequences have been described as children losing their ability to trust adults, the world around them, and themselves, as the title of Baker and Ben-Ami's article (2011) emphasizes: "To Turn a Child Against a Parent Is to Turn a Child Against Himself: The Direct and Indirect Effects of Exposure to Parental Alienation Strategies on Self-Esteem and Well-Being." By addressing these phenomena as IMDs, as has been proposed, those in healthcare and legal systems are called upon to recognize these criteria in a systematic fashion and adapt to the suggested interrelated-dimensional-approach variable criteria associated with FDBP and PA in order to better serve these children.

Understanding that these cases conform to credible recognizable patterns that create pathological dynamics puts the onus on those in authority in each of these systems to recognize their nature. These systems need not only recognize these dynamics but also make important judgments and decisions about them once a reasonable accounting has been taken. There are well-known inclusion and, thereby, exclusion criteria to rely upon that have been repeatedly addressed in both literatures. For example, in FDBP this author and his colleagues documented ten traits regarding individuals known to commit these acts (2009, p. 35). Ten behaviors are also involved with maltreatment acts in FDBP, which were also documented in our earlier work. Turning to PA, most authors recognize that this phenomenon arises from high-conflict separation, divorce, and post-divorce custody cases, and that parents engage in characteristic Alienating Behaviors. In addition, certain predisposing characteristics are found in parents and in children. Further, judges have accepted as credible evidence (Baker, 2013a) a number of these characteristic behaviors and assessment methods, such as the Baker Strategies Questionnaire designed to address these characteristics (Baker & Eichler, 2014; Baker & Verrocchio, 2013). There are other measures that have since been developed, too, and actually one that was recently discovered by this author that actually measures splitting in PA germane to our discussion earlier in this chapter, i.e., the Parental Acceptance—Rejection Questionnaire (Bernet et al., 2018). Then, there has been the development of the Parental Alienation Scale (Gomide, Camargo, & Fernandes, 2016) and the Rowlands' Parental Alienation Scale (Rowlands, 2019). Recognizing the patterns associated with these proposed IMDs will allow those within healthcare and legal systems to better identify these pathological dynamics and intervene more expediently for the sake of these children.

In his work on the ICD-11, Reed (2010) has suggested that the following three aspects of diagnoses be considered to gauge their utility:

a. its value in communicating (e.g., among practitioners, patients, families, administrators);
b. its implementation characteristics in clinical practice, including its goodness of fit (i.e., accuracy of description), its ease of use, and the time required to use it (i.e., feasibility); and,
c. its usefulness in selecting interventions and in making clinical management decisions. (p. 461)

The topic of intervention in FDBP and PA is beyond the scope of this chapter and will be addressed in Chapter 8. The question to consider here is whether an IMD provides a different set, or vantage point, from which to communicate and work on these complex phenomena in healthcare and legal systems. There is, for example, nearly universal acceptance that both FDBP and PA are forms of abuse (Harman, Kruk, & Hines, 2018; Clawar & Rivlin, 2013a; Godbout & Parent, 2012; Baker & Ben-Ami, 2011; Drozd & Olesen, 2004; Kelly & Johnston, 2001). It may also be instructive to consider the words of Bernet and Baker (2013) from the PA literature: "One way to prevent the misuse of PA by abusive parents (men or women) is to have consensus regarding the diagnosis" (p. 102). It remains to be seen whether the concept of an IMD will meet Reed's suggested benchmarks, but for now let these serve as markers for future contemplation about an IMD's utility.

Variable Exclusion and Inclusion Criteria

A number of other matters are seemingly similar but actually different from the kind of pathological dynamic involved with PA, for example, as the very detailed chapter on PA coming later in the text will discuss. There, certain terms will be used to describe different dynamics and forms of pathology that are categorically different from Parental Alienation. More will be added to these terms later, but for now the reader is encouraged to consider them as different but related phenomena. So, in addition to such dynamics as Parental Estrangement (PE) that redirect considerations toward more prevalent and straightforward cases of abuse and neglect, there has also been the description of Parental Denigration (PD) that is a lesser form and has likewise been suggested as an exclusion criterion in Figure 2.1. These considerations will be further elaborated on in Chapter 6. Descriptors such as these have taken different forms, and others have entertained the term *sabotage* as well (Drozd & Olesen, 2010): "we proposed that in abuse cases, when there is an alienating kind of behavior" (p. 259). (See also Drozd & Olesen, 2004, p. 88) As these authors (2010) have pointed out, it is not an all-or-none set of considerations since, "Research shows that abuse is more common in disputed child custody cases than is alienation; any way you look at it, both are real. Simply ask the families plagued by one and/or the other" (p. 263). In their earlier work, Drozd and Olesen (2004) provided important distinctions:

> It is our suggestion that the term alienation should be used only in those cases where there is no abuse, and that estrangement, sabotaging,

Interrelated Multidimensional Diagnoses **125**

and counterproductive parenting should be used in abuse cases where a child rejects his or her parent. Each of these terms is meant to be used descriptively.

(p. 94)

Drozd and Olesen went on to describe specific and meaningful use of these terms in making these propositions (pp. 94–98) and establishing three potential exclusionary criteria. Yet, they (2004) highlighted that, "Alienation and abuse are not dichotomous variables; instead, they may occur across continua" (p. 101). What it seems these authors attempted to describe were variable criteria. Within the PA literature, Meier (2010) has framed the work conducted by Drozd and Olesen admiringly, as attending to "the unenviable challenge of weaving a neutral path between these highly polarized fields" (p. 220). She also follows their work with a discussion about the difference between fundamentally what has been described as PA, PE and what Drozd and Olesen (2004) had proposed with the notion of a hybrid kind of case assessment. The latter, in Meier's view (2010), "has gained substantial attention in the field," (p. 221) with an accompanying multivariate assessment approach. There are other wrinkles, too, such as those presented by Friedlander and Walters (2010) as well as Garber (2011). Ludolph and Bow (2012) noted that "most cases with issues of alienation also have either aspects of estrangement or enmeshment or both, and they term these cases 'hybrid cases'" (p. 154). The work done by these authors was important, and for the purposes here it is fundamental to be aware of these distinctions without going too far afield entertaining them.

Weighing IMD Prospects

As an example of working through proofs and addressing variable criteria in PA, there was first of all the flow chart described in Chapter 2 and earlier (Bütz & Evans, 2019), which illustrated the flow of recommended considerations practitioners may work their way through in coming to the consideration of whether or not an IMD is present. These considerations will also be revisited in far more detail in Chapter 6. Variable criteria suggest more of a weighted process, with leanings this way or that, rather than the prospect of all-or-none categorical thinking. Instead, variable criteria suggest a dimensional thought process and shared categorical characteristics and symptoms that are not mutually exclusive. These other conditions and the phenomenon of PA itself will be addressed in far greater detail in Chapter 6.

126 Interrelated Multidimensional Diagnoses

For now, one considers a series of metaphorical balancing scales labeled, for example, with the designations PA, Parental Estrangement (PE), Parental Denigration (PD), Parental Sabotage (PS) and Counter Productive Parenting (CPP). Parental Estrangement, PD, PS and CPP do require brief definitions for the purposes here. For a child to be estranged from a parent (PE), is for the child to have good reason to distance her- or himself or to not want a close relationship with a parent due to that parent's conduct, i.e., the child is "realistically estranged from one of their parents as a consequence of that parent's history of family violence, abuse or neglect" (Kelly & Johnston, 2001, p. 253). Thus, the rejection of the parent is both within reason and justified. On the other hand, with denigration (PD), it is simply a violation of the codicil in most parenting plans not to speak ill of the other parent and to support the child's relationship with the other parent, i.e., "the behavior of one parent disparaging or speaking negatively about the other parent in front of their children" (Rowen & Emery, 2014, p. 165).

In 2004, Drozd and Olesen offered a "Decision Tree" and queried the reader in their concluding remarks, "Is it abuse, alienation and/or estrangement?" This challenge was followed by the paragraph below:

> This Decision Tree offers the field of child custody an alternative approach to the either-or thinking that sometimes characterizes debates about abuse and alienation in divorcing families. *Alienation* and *abuse* are not dichotomous variables; instead, they may occur across continua. We have also provided the reader of this article an invitation to use new terms to explain the reasons that any given child might reject a parent: alienation, in non-abuse cases, and estrangement, sabotaging, and counter productive parenting in cases where there is abuse.
>
> (pp. 99–100)

Thus, it would appear that they felt that PA and PE, essentially, each represented an extreme on the same continuum organized in the following manner: (non-abuse cases) PA severe, moderate, mild—mild, moderate, severe PE (abuse cases). They also seemed to argue that what they referred to as Counter Productive Parenting (CPP) was a lesser form of abuse, followed by Sabotaging (PS), which suggested a moderate form of abuse, with PE being the most severe manifestation of abuse. Stated another descriptive way: (non-abuse cases) PA severe, moderate, mild—CPP, PS, PE (abuse cases). Drozd and Olesen's elaboration of these concepts only seems to confuse matters, unless this author is taking their meaning incorrectly, and, indeed, PS has been described by Drozd and Olesen (2004) as a variable or

Interrelated Multidimensional Diagnoses **127**

offshoot of particular alienating behaviors reflecting the efforts of more aggressive parents:

> We have found that the aggressor parent may engage in behavior designed to sabotage the child's relationship with the victim parent. The aggressor takes advantage of the victim parent's vulnerabilities and convinces the child or children in the family that the victim parent is not a good parent and that he, the aggressor, has the power and can do best for the children. This behavior formerly may have been called alienating behavior, though inasmuch as it occurs in the context of an abusive family, we are calling it *sabotaging* behavior.
>
> (p. 88)

Then, as for CPP, there was also Drozd and Olesen's description (2004) of Rejected Parents' counterproductive behaviors, but these behaviors are enacted by a non-abusive parent:

> *Victim parent may engage in counter productive protective parenting.* Victim parents may conduct themselves in ways that result in the child further rejecting the abusive parent. This behavior by the victim is similar to the abuser's sabotaging behavior inasmuch as both may involve an authoritarian style of parenting as well as a child's rejection of a parent (see Figure 17). The two are dissimilar inasmuch as the non-aggressive parent's behavior not only may involve an authoritarian parenting style, but it also may be a manifestation of the victim parent's fear of the abuser.
>
> (p. 95)

So, realigning this continuum, a better representation may well be offered by describing a continuum for the (PA) Alienating Parent—Estranging Parent (PE) and then for the (PA) Rejected Parent—Victimized Parent (PE). Taking up these matters, then, we have Figures 4.1–3, which provide a visual reference to help practitioners sort out whether or not there is more of one particular dynamic at work than the other, some clearly pathological (PA, PE, and arguably PS) and others involving one parent denigrating the other before the child (PD) or a Rejected Parent engaging in counterproductive behaviors (CPP).

Thus, what is revealed is a mix of both variable exclusion and inclusion criteria, rendering a delineation of whether PA is tenable. If there are variable criteria, these may address exclusion or inclusion by way of the weight of

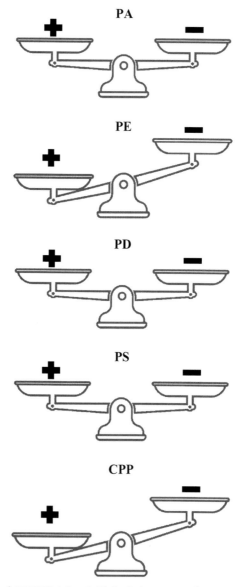

Figure 4.1 PE and CPP Weighted: If the balances on these scales are weighted toward PE and CPP, that is one thing, and suggests that this case is not a PA case. Instead, PE seems like the more probable hypothesis.

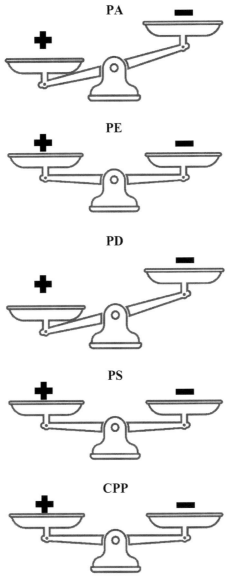

Figure 4.2 PA and PD Weighted: If the weight solely falls to PA or PD, as in this example, the findings and information collected in the case suggest perhaps a mild to moderate form of PA, or PD.

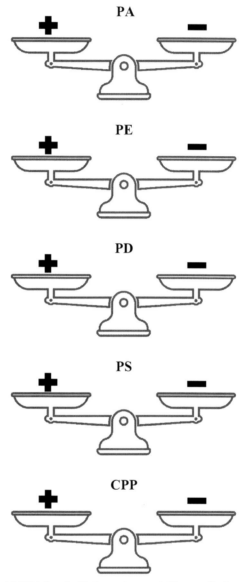

Figure 4.3 Hybrid Weighted: If there is no ability to distinguish among the weighting of these different scales, then it would appear that a hybrid case has been revealed.

Interrelated Multidimensional Diagnoses   **131**

the evidence available, such as the accumulated data, findings, and information associated with the case. It follows that system-wide PA symptoms are clarified by the accumulated weighting of individual and system symptoms by the patterns that they create. On the one side of these scales is a symptomatic weighting assigned to a variable set of exclusion criteria, while on the other side is a variable weighting that represents inclusion criteria. An IMD is admittedly a difficult diagnosis to perceive without a larger contextual view of all the interrelated-dimensional interactions, and to make such a determination requires careful study to confirm or disconfirm hypotheses practitioners may have.

Systems, Systems, Systems, a Systemic Diagnosis, and Other Diagnoses

If this section heading appears to sound emphatic, that is the intention, and this author will be brief on this point. One underpinning to the idea of IMDs that has been implied, but not stated clearly thus far, is that an IMD is literally intended as a diagnosis for the system(s) under study. So, the FDBP IMD is intended to diagnose the pathological dynamic that exists between a family and healthcare system and all that that implies, just as a PA IMD is intended to diagnose a pathological dynamic that exists between the family and legal system. They naturally impact individuals, children most focally, but all members of those systems are impacted to one degree or another by the pathological dynamic created between the systems. As such, there is no intention of diagnosing the child with an IMD, nor a parent with an Interrelated Multidimensional Diagnosis. It may be part of their diagnostic picture, even the lead diagnosis among many, but the individual themselves are not diagnosed with "it" per se.

The emphasis here is on understanding, rather than pathologizing: all of the individuals within these systems are suffering to one degree or another from the pathological dynamic created by the Interrelated Multidimensional Diagnosis. Debatably, second only to the children in these cases are the parents who engage in either physical abuse (FDBP) or psychological abuse (PA). They are not well and are responding out of their own pathology to the stresses that they have encountered as these systems interact. The impact of stress on members of these systems, and the types of stress, is a topic that will be amplified further in Chapter 7. If we are to help the children in the midst of these pathological dynamics, then we need to understand the parents in these family systems and the stresses they are responding to as well

132 Interrelated Multidimensional Diagnoses

as the professionals in the healthcare and legal systems and the stresses they are responding to in turn. Because the focus clinically is on the family system, diagnosing individual professionals is not included, although they may well have their own diagnoses that interact unfavorably with the Interrelated Multidimensional Diagnosis. Additionally, as will be described in the chapters that follow, a number, though not all, of the parents involved in these cases have their own diagnostic characteristics that are often symptomatic of the interactions in the Interrelated Multidimensional Diagnosis. As will be discussed in Chapter 8 to some extent, intervention includes addressing these parents' own diagnoses as part of the efforts to contain the IMD pathological dynamic. Interventions will also be suggested for other systems as well, but in this respect it is through laws, policies, and procedures that healthcare and legal systems may be guided to engage these families differently and prevent, stall, or dissipate the impact of an Interrelated Multidimensional Diagnosis.

Diagnosing IMDs: Suspicion and Further Study

It has probably occurred to the reader by now that when addressing IMDs there are matters in which there are observable changes and symptoms and then there are characteristics and history that require further examination and study. Thus, there may be different dimensions of observable changes and symptoms that are more apparent and easier to discern. Still, there are other characteristics and/or historical events in the life of an individual or family that require further study and even investigation. It is also suggested that these proposed IMDs often come to light by way of allegations that are made, allegations that require a timely answer. With the pressing need for recognition that regularly accompanies the allegation of an IMD it would be reasonable to ask how is it possible to accomplish both the necessities of expediency and a thorough examination?

Looking to functional diagnostic conventions from the *DSM* series in order to address this conundrum, there are the designations in the *DSM-5* of suspected and confirmed abuse, intimate-partner violence, or neglect (American Psychiatric Association, 2013, pp. 717–722). Although there were no objective criteria provided for either designation, this suspicion–confirmation step-wise process does supply a ready and suggestive heuristic when it comes to IMDs. Thus, what is observable may lead to suspicions of larger dynamics, and yet the "probability" of a larger dynamic cannot be established without further study. It is proposed that a two-step process for diagnosing an IMD would accomplish both the task of expedient identification and the need for careful further study. A benchmark for observable symptoms and studied characteristics may both be reasonably set at the marker of *better than chance*. This would suggest that a marker of better than half of the observable symptoms would merit suspicion, just as further study brings the prospect to bear on all the criteria of an IMD, and these findings may be considered against the standard of *more probable than not* or *a preponderance of the evidence*.

As a preliminary diagnostic convention for IMDs then we have the stage of suspicion that would logically signal consultation with another practitioner as a best practice, and this consultation is envisioned as generating three possible clinical determinations: the need for further study of observable symptoms, intervention of some form depending on the severity of the IMD, or a more thorough level of intervention is initiated and the process of further study regarding characteristics and history of the IMD is undertaken to determine its probability. This process will be described more explicitly for each IMD in Chapters 5 and 6, and then in Chapter 8 when it comes time to consider intervention based on an IMD's probability and severity.

IMDs and Exemplars

What has hopefully been communicated in this chapter is that FDBP and PA are not diagnoses that can reasonably be described through one dimension or even two; rather, these are symptomatically interrelated diagnoses that must be explained on multiple dimensions all at the same time. These are integrative diagnoses that are not singular in focus and that incorporate individual dimensional symptoms as well as subdynamics, all of which are interrelated within the context of time. Thus, FDBP and PA have sufficient criteria based on prior research and in the existing literature described to be the first diagnoses termed *Interrelated Multidimensional Diagnoses*.

The need to elucidate FDBP was clear enough before 2009, as was seen in the work of the American Professional Society on the Abuse of Children (APSAC) task force on Munchhausen's Syndrome by Proxy (Ayoub, Alexander et al., 2002; Ayoub, Schreier, & Alexander, 2002; Schreier & Ayoub, 2002). In addition, Munchhausen's Syndrome by Proxy and FDBP were considered unreliable in the United Kingdom to the extent that there were active discussions about abandoning these diagnoses (Adshead, 2005; Pagnell, 2006). Similarly, PA was not included in the *DSM-5* despite substantial debate and efforts (Bernet & Baker, 2013; Houchin et al., 2012; Bernet et al., 2010). The PA discussion has been ongoing for over forty years (Wallerstein & Kelly, 1976). Perhaps these kinds of preceding debates and discussions within the field may

134 Interrelated Multidimensional Diagnoses

well foretell the developmental stirrings of an emerging Interrelated Multidimensional Diagnosis.

Certainly, there are shortcomings with the proposed approach thus far described, as is the case in any exploratory endeavor. The two most prominent shortcomings center on the conceptual leap forward suggested by the concept of an IMD and how to measure its presence. As for the first, at present the discourse simply addresses difficulties associated with moving from singular categories to integrating multiple dimensions, as described above. Others may argue the validity of using only observable behaviors and known neurobiology in developing diagnoses, despite the evidence for the empirical underpinnings of our explorations into complex psychosocial phenomena. It is certainly understandable, given the different historical vantage points and leanings within the field of psychiatric diagnosis, that yet others may view the IMD as a vast and overbroad conceptual leap. At the same time, the conceptual bases of such complex ideas as an IMD have been entertained for decades and decades (Rogers et al., 1976; Wallerstein & Kelly, 1976; Meadow, 1977; Gardner, 1985), and as scientists are we not obligated to seek explanations when a reasonable degree of scientific certainty exists within the literature?

The second potential weakness thus far is how to examine such complex diagnostic structures symptom-by-symptom in a cumulative, perhaps even actuarial, fashion: to measure various parts while arriving at the sum of these parts in order to describe the whole pathological dynamic quantitatively. Previously, this author and his colleagues (Bütz, Evans, & Webber-Dereszynski, 2009) proposed to additively measure the weighted symptoms to come to a more probabilistic approach in discerning whether or not FDBP was a viable diagnosis:

> The reader is encouraged to think of these lists as comparable attributes in terms of percentages of agreement (e.g., 1 out of 10 being 10%). While no magical cutoff point is proposed, the reader is encouraged to consider these percentages qualitatively within the larger context of an overall assessment, as well as what may tip the scales (DeMatteo & Edens, 2006, pp. 231–233). These comparisons are based on probabilities clustered together that result in a set of individual and dynamic diagnostic profiles. Not all FDBP cases entail the same diagnostic features in the alleged perpetrator or alleged victim or with the same maltreatment dynamic properties. Siegel and Fischer (2001) have offered this useful caution, "Some FDP perpetrators are uneducated, dramatic, emotionally labile, hostile, and obviously dishonest (Parnell, 1998), whereas others are out to harass physicians, hoping to profit from

malpractice suits (Rosenberg, 1995) or benefit from governmental services and programs (Artingstall, 1995).

We offer 20 points of consideration about what comprises FDBP. This list (Table 4.1) reflects both the complexity of the phenomenon and provides a set of concrete reference points to incorporate individual and dynamic comparisons for a proposed revision of the FDBP diagnosis that is more holistic and inclusive. We suggest that both the individual traits and the maltreatment dynamic be present before an FDBP diagnosis is made.

(p. 36)

To clarify, another way of thinking about these matters is deriving weighted factors in a fashion comparable to the reliability and validity associated with the subscales of an intellectual measure. These subscales produce a measurement outcome that contributes to an overall standardized score but one that has its own singular reliability and validity as well (such as a composite score or a full-scale intellectual quotient [see Roid, 2003; Wechsler, 2008]). But, in such cases, the overall number or outcome could conceivably represent the probability of a pathological dynamic with a quantitative index. Of course, this is not an original idea, and it is proposed here as a possible approach that addresses the quantitative measurement of these phenomena. At the same time, perhaps, behavioral health has advanced to the point wherein more sophisticated hypothesis-drawn models may be employed, such as Bayesian statistics (see Bütz, Evans, & Webber-Dereszynski, 2009, p. 36), as has also been elaborated by others (Sorias, 2015; Van de Schoot et al., 2014; Wollert, 2006).

Such considerations have led to the development of new measures with a colleague (Bütz & Miller, 2019a, 2019b) anchored in the IMD conceptual framework that offer both options: a probabilistic outcome that speaks to legal standards and iterative Bayesian outcomes that address the degree to which the hypothesis advanced by the practitioner has been confirmed or not. These new instruments have been developed for use by appropriately trained practitioners and are referred to as Interrelated Multidimensional Diagnostic Inventories[©], or IMD-I[©] for short. Each has been specifically developed for a particular pathological dynamic. Each carries the name of the condition, such as Interrelated Multidimensional Diagnostic Inventories—Factitious Disorder by Proxy[©] or IMD-I-FDBP[©], and Interrelated Multidimensional Diagnostic Inventories—Parental Alienation[©] or IMD-I-PA[©]. The specifics and the literature that support these instruments will be described across the chapters that remain.

Notes

1. Italics added for emphasis.
2. Italics added for emphasis.
3. It should be noted here again that the "cost" for scholarship has risen dramatically in recent years. Particular publishers such as the American Psychiatric Association charge the following (correspondence November 8, 2019): ". . . any selection of over 40 words is considered an excerpt, and there will be a $300 fee for each." Yes, that is "each", and though this author very much wished to make use of several references to the texts produced by this publisher to illustrate finer points the cost was unduly prohibitive. Exorbitant fees such as this defeats the purpose of not only scholarship, but open scientific debate plain and simple, and egregious practices like these should be aired and exposed.
4. Retrieved August 19, 2018, www.merriam-webster.com/dictionary/syndrome. By Permission. From Merriam-Webster.com ©2019 by Merriam-Webster, Inc. www.merriam-webster.com/dictionary.
5. Italics added for emphasis.
6. Italics added in this quote for clarity.
7. "MSBP/FII has also been the subject of contentious debate in the U.K. Parliament on several occasions, and in a Parliamentary debate on 17 October 2004, Earl Frederick Howe said of MSBP/FII that, "(it is) one of the most ill- founded and pernicious theories to have gained currency in child care and social services over the past ten to fifteen years."
8. Copyright 2017 by Arizona Board of Regents and Janet Howe. Reprinted with permission of the author and publisher. This student note originally appeared in *Arizona Law Review*, vol. 59, no. 1, p. 201.
9. This excerpt published courtesy of Charles C Thomas Publisher, Ltd., Springfield, Illinois.
10. "That is, the knowledge is gained through the scientific method . . ."
11. A hearing comparable to Daubert in Canada.
12. Reproduced with the permission of *The Future of Children*, a publication of the David and Lucile Packard Foundation.

Factitious Disorder by Proxy and Interrelated Multidimensional Diagnoses

5

Revisiting "The Complaint"

Back in 2007, when the original manuscript was written on MSBP, FDBP and FII, this author made a somewhat more ardent statement than the one created with his colleagues and the editorial staff at *Professional Psychology: Research and Practice* given here (Bütz, Evans, & Webber-Dereszynski, 2009).

> As a practitioner one hopes that the referral question provided by a client has clean and clear boundaries, is well-researched in the literature, discernable through recognized sources such as the *Diagnostic and Statistical Manual of Mental Disorders, Fourth Edition, Text Revision* published by the American Psychiatric Association (APA (*DSM-IV-TR*)) and the *International Statistical Classification of Diseases, 10th Revision (ICD-10)*, etc., and that there is agreement within the professional community.
>
> (p. 31)

As discussed in Chapter 2, it has been forty years since MSBP was first described (Meadow, 1977; Money & Werlwas, 1976), and, as Chapter 3 made clear, the situation regarding clarity of terms has not improved. This set of diagnostic symptoms has remained elusive and unclear, and the point of considerable debate in professional literature and national policy. Still, healthcare providers and courts frequently make important decisions based on these diagnoses as if this phenomenon enjoyed agreement and unified terminology.

The motivation for generating the manuscript penned in 2007 and 2008 was to make at least a limited argument to improve terminology and suggest a path forward. Due to natural limitations on time and resources, most practitioners do not have ready access to extensive stores of literature or to the research resources necessary to take on such a muddled subject. Most also lack ready access to records in emergency rooms or other primary care sites, despite the growing presence of behavioral health providers in these environments (Bütz & Tynan, 2019). Even so, a careful review of the most representative aspects of the voluminous literature (Korpershoek & Flisher, 2004) revealed several different explanatory models with several dozen lists of indicators that had been regularly cited (Rogers, 2004; Sheridan, 2003; Rosenberg, 1987). As many as two dozen lead diagnostic indicators and approximately the same number of dynamic indicators were involved in making a determination of MSBP, FDBP and Fabricated or Induced Illness.

Per the rather lengthy discussion in Chapter 3, the updated literature review conducted with this author's current work herein and elsewhere (Bütz & Evans, 2019) demonstrated a largely similar pattern. It was interesting to take note of the works not accounted for in more recent literature and the discussions that remained between, broadly, behavioral and medical healthcare, as well as legal treatises. The terminology has, as described in Chapter 3, proliferated into a mind-numbing level of complexity along these divisions and national interests to the extent that this author invoked the Gordian Knot as a metaphor and meanwhile offered the *Platypus Paradox* to help resolve matters. It follows that reference to broad public discussions about this phenomenon will be referred to as MSBP, while more scientific references will feature FDBP regardless of the terminology used in the citation (i.e., AIBP, CAMS, CFIC, FII, MCA, and PCF). The task now is once again to describe how the characteristics and symptoms are similar, or even the same, across these different references, and to discover if there are findings to discuss. In addition, the literature has broadened, adding family and healthcare systems to the discussion. Therefore, this author will build on prior work with his colleagues, expanding potential characteristics and symptoms, as well as addressing system interactions to update and align these matters with the IMD conceptualization described in prior work (Bütz & Evans, 2019) and described within the pages of this text.

Since the earlier article by this author and his colleagues, others have addressed this diagnostic reconceptualization in various ways, not only by focusing on the continued lack of definitional clarity and usage (Lazenbatt, 2013) but also by assessing rare or unusual diagnoses (Dombrowski, Gischlar, & Mrazik, 2011). Still another group has looked at the identification and management of FDBP (Dye et al., 2013), while a number of authors have explored additional diagnostic conceptualizations (Koetting, 2015; Dombrowski, Gischlar, & Mrazik, 2011; Walk & Davies, 2010).

Further, following our earlier article on FDBP, progressive considerations within the literature on diagnostic concepts have shifted this landscape, as discussed at length in Chapter 3, but the landscape has also changed in association with the publication of the *Diagnostic and Statistical Manual of Mental Disorders, Fifth Edition (DSM-5*; American Psychiatric Association, 2013) and the *International Classification of Diseases, Eleventh Edition (ICD-11*; World Health Organization, 2018). The revision of these classification systems has had varied impacts on the field of behavioral healthcare (Reed et al., 2016; Blashfield et al., 2014; Reed, 2010). There has also been continued progress in expanding notions about the relevance of cultural considerations (La Roche, Fuentes, & Hinton, 2015), along with persistent efforts to connect the vast majority of behavioral health disorders to observable behavior and neurobiology (Cuthbert & Insel, 2013). It is this author's belief that a great deal may be learned from development of the ICD-11 and from taking a broad and inclusive psychosocial focus that captures the breadth and complexity of making accurate and useful clinical diagnoses (Reed et al., 2016).

For the purposes here, this process begins with the introductory article on IMDs in which we adjusted the order for reviewing characteristics and symptoms (Bütz, Evans, & Webber-Dereszynski, 2009, p. 36) in the FDBP—Child Maltreatment Dynamic (Bütz & Evans, 2019), noting the difference between *"subdynamics or individual dimensional symptoms."* The larger pathological dynamic described in IMDs had to be accounted for as well, and other matters were echoed in Chapter 4. For these reasons, the order of consideration will follow the progression suggested by the dimensional model described in IMDs, building toward a pathological dynamic. Notably, there have been some advances in how the notion of proofs is dealt with in more recent works in this literature.

Some authors have discussed a "decision matrix," profiling described as soft signs, and direct evidence as a more robust sign of Factitious Disorder by Proxy (Howe, 2017, pp. 226–234). Further, Bass and Jones (2011) found that over half of the parents studied had histories of self-harm and three quarters had received psychiatric care and/or counseling, and these parents also had histories that involved significant trauma. Bass and Jones described the following (2011):

> Our findings also suggest that no clinician should attempt to carry out an assessment of a woman suspected of this form of child abuse without access to extensive previous medical (and other) records. Neither should any opinion be expressed by the examining doctor about the mother's competence to look after a child based on a single assessment in an out-patient clinic. Our findings also imply that great care be taken in validating symptom reports by these women, especially those where evidence of pathological lying is suspected or has been established. In practice this means that the clinician needs to corroborate clinical data

using a variety of different sources, both medical and nonmedical, and a degree of healthy skepticism is required throughout the management of such cases.

(p. 117)

These authors also noted that 61% of these mothers were known to lie and fabricate stories and engage in "pathological lying," and that the following also held true:

We found high rates of chronic somatoform disorders in these women, with enduring somatoform disorders in 57% and fabricated symptoms in 64% (11 individuals had both chronic somatisation and factitious illness). In many participants the use of healthcare services was chaotic, with frequent visits to different accident and emergency departments, frequent changes of GP (often instigated by the GP) and lack of continuity of care.

(p. 115)

Bass and Halligan (2007), whose work was addressed in Chapter 3, discussed the array of symptoms of MSBP and FDBP as a matter of noteworthy concern. They provided a "model of illness deception" (p. 83), which involved a figure, reproduced in Figure 5.1, that described different continua, with a focus on choice and responsibility.

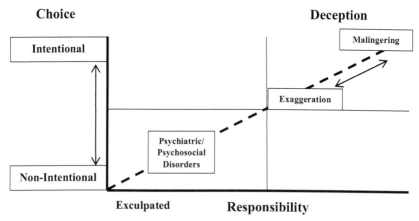

Figure 5.1 Bass and Halligan's Figure 1 (2007, p. 83), Model of Illness Deception, reproduced by the author for illustrative purposes here and in Chapter 3.

Factitious Disorder by Proxy and IMDs **141**

This figure may be particularly valuable in plotting different understandings represented in the literature on the dimensions spoken to earlier as well as in explaining the role of motivation to disentangle the Gordian Knot created over the years. The reader is asked to simply take note here, and we will return to Bass and Halligan's figure shortly.

Given these progressive and seemingly positive developments, an updated list of frequently reoccurring characteristics and symptoms that mirror the language proposed under an IMD will be suggested for addressing the nature of Factitious Disorder by Proxy. Despite the clear reoccurrence of characteristics and symptoms across individuals and systems, there are still, as before, areas of disagreement among professionals, practitioners and researchers represented most accurately by earlier literature (Sanders & Bursch, 2002). In 2009 the import of gaining a detailed understanding of these matters was still best articulated in a condensed fashion by Artingstall's (1995) comments from *The FBI Law Enforcement Bulletin*: "The more investigators know about MSBP, the better able they will be to identify perpetrators, clear innocent suspects, and most importantly, protect children" (p. 5). It should also be noted that, prior to the published proposal of an IMD, Artingstall (2016) issued a thorough treatment on this topic.

Parental and Systemic Background in FDBP

Since the earlier work with this author's colleagues in 2008, increased attention has been paid to how parents develop characteristics that seemingly make them prone to engage in Factitious Disorder by Proxy. As described earlier in Chapter 3, there has also been a set of articles that paralleled the actuarial focus of Sheridan (2003) and Rosenberg (1987). Several references fit this description and have extended the work by Sheridan and Rosenberg (Yates & Bass, 2017; Yates & Feldman, 2016; Bass & Glaser, 2014; Bass & Jones, 2011). These articles have proven to be very useful in updating individual, and deductively systemic, characteristics and symptoms that are more and more evident in the literature as pre-symptomatic indicators in parents, predominantly mothers (Yates & Bass, 2017):

> Many have been sexually or physically abused, (21.7%–79%). Personality disorders (8.6–75%), mood disorders (5.3–50%), and somatoform disorders (52%–72%) are common, as are features of 'Factitious Disorder Imposed on the Self (FDIOS)' (29.3–64%) which is a psychiatric disorder in which sufferers intentionally fabricate their own illness for psychological gratification (American Psychiatric Association, 2013; Yates & Feldman, 2016).
>
> (p. 46)

142 Factitious Disorder by Proxy and IMDs

In turn, Bass and Glaser (2014) have offered the following observations:

> The early attachment experiences of these mothers are likely to affect both parenting capacity and personality development.[45] These findings suggest an important association between abnormal forms of attachment, childhood adversity, adult somatisation, and, in some women, transmission of abnormal illness behaviour to their offspring.
>
> (p. 4)

According to Bass and Jones (2011),

> The most striking abnormality in the childhood experiences of these women was the high rate of early family disruption and loss. Only 2 of the 28 had not experienced loss of the parent (through death, separation/divorce or removal of a parent to prison) before the age of 11 years, and over a third had spent time in foster care during their formative years. High rates of physical and sexual abuse have been reported by others,[14] and in another study insecure attachment as well as high rates of unresolved trauma and loss reactions was identified in the mothers.
>
> (p. 116)

In order to get at these background factors, a number of practitioners in the field have focused on attachment theory and, in their research, have made use of the Adult Attachment Interview (AAI) by George, Kaplan, and Main (1994). The work of Adshead and Bluglass (2005) assessed 85 mothers initially, but their sample was winnowed down to 67, and, as they described it, "In all but three cases, a court had established that the mother had carried out some sort of abnormal illness behavior by proxy or that there were reasonable grounds for child protection intervention" (p. 328). After discussing a number of matters and their evaluations of these mothers, Adshead and Bluglass attended to the following:

> The fact that these mothers involve their children in abnormal illness behavior suggests that their attachment to the children, and related capacity to care for them, has become disorganized. The argument that their experience of illness in childhood affects their proxy care-eliciting behaviours is consistent with the work of Craig et al. (2002) on somatising mothers and research by Hill et al. (2004), who found that a mother's experience of maternal care affected how she related to professionals involved in the care of her child's health.
>
> (p. 331)

Similar findings were provided by Kozlowska, Foley, and Crittenden (2006), whose focus appeared, in part, to leave open "parental intention" (p. 92) in these cases. To articulate their concerns, this group presented the case example of Rosie:

> A key difficulty in treating families presenting with "factitious illness by proxy" is parents' ability to explain their behaviour in ways that fit professionals' reality, and clinicians' inability to generate explanations that fit parents' reality.
>
> (p. 92)

Fundamentally, the focus that both sets of practitioners addressed was an explanatory model for, as Kozlowska, Foley, and Crittenden (2006) put it, "parents' harmful health-seeking behaviour on behalf of their children [that] is referred to as 'maladaptive caregiving' or 'misguided protective behaviour'" (p. 92). Similarly, Griffith analyzed two family systems in 1988, with a focus on the following:

> Munchausen Syndrome by Proxy may be a systemic syndrome generated when a mother already possessing a somatoform or factitious disorder joins an enmeshed, authoritarian family system possessing a systemic history of exploitation of children. We suggest that measures instituted to protect the abused child must take into account the systemic function of the Munchausen by Proxy behavior in maintaining family stability, lest such measures be rendered ineffective by family members.
>
> (p. 423)

Personality Traits and Pathological Lying

Although it has been well-established that a large proportion of parents who engage in these activities suffer from personality traits or disorders per the language in the *DSM Series*, a group of practitioners suggests that these parents also have histories of pathological lying (Dike, Baranoski, & Griffith, 2005). Initially, Bass and Glaser (2014) explored this condition as part of the record review and parental characteristics in the literature: "Detailed examination of both primary care and extensive medical and social-work records might uncover episodes of illness deception and pathological lying,[32] often coexisting with somatoform presentations" (p. 3). They also provided a descriptive example as well: "Denial of past actions and their consequences and pathological lying—e.g., 'I used to lie because it made me feel happy and got me friends'; 'is it possible that I put the drugs into Jack's bottle without knowing

144 Factitious Disorder by Proxy and IMDs

that I did it?'" (p. 8) Bass and Jones (2011) described that pathological lying was part of these parents' dispositions from a very early age and is, at times, referred to as pseudologia fantastica:

> These lies were often compulsive, habitual and sometimes self-aggrandizing, and occurred throughout adolescence in many. In some they emerged at times of life stress and the episode of fabricated or induced illness was often accompanied by the re-emergence of lying and other deceitful activity such as repeated hoax telephone calls to police about "harassment," which occurred in two women, financial fraud in one and nomadic wandering in another.
>
> (p. 116)

The literature is still developing on this characteristic (Sousa Filho et al., 2017), but Bass and his colleagues made a compelling argument to include pathological lying in the parents' individual dimensional symptoms.

The literature of the past and present has also repeatedly addressed the fact that a significant number of these parents have a form of Cluster B personality disorders and/or traits (Yates & Bass, 2017; Bass & Glaser, 2014; Bass & Jones, 2011; Sheridan, 2003; Rosenberg, 1987). This often-cited association, however, has been debated by a few who have suggested more in the way of attachment problems (Kozlowska, Foley, & Crittenden, 2006), with only 20 out of 67 in their sample who demonstrated these symptoms (Adshead & Bluglass, 2005, pp. 329–330). Though all of these discussion points had been addressed in a variety of studies, in their more actuarial bent Yates and Bass (2017) focused in on the work of Greiner et al. (2013) and stated, "Caregiver has features of Munchausen syndrome" and "Caregiver has personal history of child abuse" (pp. 41–42). Bass and Jones (2011) also identified "abuse/neglect" and "current factitious disorder" as strong risk factors (p. 51).

A List of Characteristics Associated With Factitious Disorder by Proxy

In this author and colleagues' article from 2009, a list of FDBP characteristics that appeared frequently in the literature was provided in Table 1 for direct comparison between an alleged perpetrator diagnosis (FDBP) and what at the time was referred to as the FDBP—Child Maltreatment Dynamic (p. 35). Revisiting these lists, each characteristic will be presented in the original form (see Table 5.1) and then separated into Table 5.2 for the FDBP—Child Maltreatment Dynamic and Table 5.3 for review.

Table 5.1 Factitious Disorder by Proxy (FDBP) Diagnosis and FDBP—Child Maltreatment Dynamic

---

Factitious Disorder by Proxy Diagnosis

---

1. History of behavioral health treatment (I, E; Artingstall, 1995; Schreier, 1997, 2000).
2. Diagnosed with, or suspected of having, symptoms and traits of factitious disorder (I, E; Artingstall, 1995; Bools, Neale, & Meadow, 1994).
3. Diagnosed with, or suspected of having, traits of a personality disorder (I, E).
4. Primary caretaker of the child (I, E).
5. Female (I, E; Sheridan, 2003; Siegel & Fischer, 2001).[a]
6. Background or training in medicine (I, E; Artingstall, 1995; Chiczewski & Kelly, 2003; Korpershoek & Flisher, 2004; Siegel & Fischer, 2001).
7. Similar medical history to that of the child presented for evaluation (I, E; Bools, Neale, & Meadow, 1994).
8. Views her- or himself as "unique" in a characterological sense (I, E).
9. History of sudden infant death syndrome (SIDS) or similar unusual death within the family close to the individual (I, E, O).
10. Psychological assessment instruments indicate a level of defensiveness on validity scales (I, E, O; see Rogers, 2004, for a detailed discussion of this matter, p. 232).

FDBP—Child Maltreatment Dynamic

---

1. A pattern of multiple visits to medical providers/hospitals has established a growing suspicion of some form of abuse—mean time frame fourteen months (I, E, O; Sanders & Bursch, 2002, suggest a chronology and table of events in most cases).[b]
2. There has been no established medical condition that would explain persistent symptoms (I, E, O).
3. The suspected victim's symptoms worsen over time (I, E, O).
4. The suspected victim is a child between the ages of infancy and 8 years (I, E, O).[c]
5. The suspected perpetrator is the suspected victim's primary caretaker, and in the vast majority of cases (75–95%) is the mother (I, E; Sheridan, 2003; Siegel & Fischer, 2001).[d]
6. Medical findings have confirmed that the suspected victim has been abused (I, E, O).[e]

(Continued)

Table 5.1 (Continued)

FDBP—Child Maltreatment Dynamic

---

7. Abuse has taken the form of drugging, fever induction, poisoning, seizure induction, and suffocation (e.g., apnea, SIDS, etc.) (I, E, O).

8. *Medical Provider Subdynamic*—suggests suspected perpetrator has established a relationship dynamic with medical staff wherein the individual:
   (a) Lacks appropriate boundaries (I, E; Siegel & Fischer, 2001),
   (b) Is demanding (I, E),
   (c) Seeks attention (I, E),
   (d) "Thrives" in the medical hospital or office environment (I, E),
   (e) And is gratified by interactions with medical staff (I, E).

9. *Caretaker–Child Subdynamic*—suggests that the caretaker has established a relationship dynamic with the child wherein:
   (a) The individual is overinvolved with the child (I, E),
   (b) The individual is unwilling to leave the child's presence (I, E),
   (c) And the child's symptoms worsen in the presence of the suspected individual (I, E, O).

10. The suspected perpetrator encourages and welcomes additional tests that will maintain or extend time spent interacting with medical providers, regardless of the effects on the suspected victim (I, E, O; Siegel & Fischer, 2001).

Note: I = criteria for inclusion; E = criteria for exclusion; O = criteria for outcome.

[a] While it is far less prevalent, men and close relatives have been identified as perpetrators.

[b] Their emphasis was on establishing, in short, what has come to be known as pediatric condition falsification (PCF) via a thorough records review. They stated: "The cornerstone of an MBP evaluation is the assessment of the veracity of claims made by the suspected caregiver" (p. 114).

[c] Some authors have put this age up to sixteen.

[d] Though it is far less prevalent, men and close relatives have been identified as perpetrators.

[e] This variable and variable 7 are where the idea of pediatric condition falsification (PCF) would best apply.

Table 5.2 FDBP—Child Maltreatment Dynamic

1. A pattern of multiple visits to medical providers/hospitals has established a growing suspicion of some form of abuse—mean time frame fourteen months (I, E, O; Sanders & Bursch, 2002, suggest a chronology and table of events in most cases*).
2. There has been no established medical condition that would explain persistent symptoms (I, E, O).
3. The suspected victim's symptoms worsen over time (I, E, O).
4. The suspected victim is a child between the ages of infancy and eight years (I, E, O).**
5. The suspected perpetrator is the suspected victim's primary caretaker, and in the vast majority of cases (75–95%) is the mother (I, E; Sheridan, 2003; Siegel & Fischer, 2001).***
6. Medical findings confirm that the suspected victim has been abused (I, E, O).****
7. Abuse has taken the form of drugging, fever induction, poisoning, seizure induction, and suffocation (e.g., apnea, SIDS, etc.) (I, E, O).
8. *Medical Provider Subdynamic*—suggests suspected perpetrator has established a relationship dynamic with medical staff wherein the individual:
   (a) Lacks appropriate boundaries (I, E; Siegel & Fischer, 2001),
   (b) Is demanding (I, E),
   (c) Seeks attention (I, E),
   (d) "Thrives" in the medical hospital or office environment (I, E), and
   (e) Is gratified by interactions with medical staff (I, E).
9. *Caretaker–Child Subdynamic*—suggests that the caretaker has established a relationship dynamic with the child wherein:
   (a) The individual is over-involved with the child (I, E),
   (b) The individual is unwilling to leave the child's presence (I, E), and
   (c) The child's symptoms worsen in the presence of the suspected individual (I, E, O).
10. The suspected perpetrator encourages and welcomes additional tests that will maintain or extend time spent interacting with medical providers, regardless of the effects on the suspected victim (I, E, O; Siegel & Fischer, 2001).

Note: I = criteria for inclusion; E = criteria for exclusion; O = criteria for outcome.
* Their emphasis was on establishing, in short, what has come to be known as Pediatric Condition Falsification (PCF) via a thorough records review. They stated: "The cornerstone of an MBP evaluation is the assessment of the veracity of claims made by the suspected caregiver."
** Some authors have put this age up to sixteen.
*** Though it is far less prevalent, men and close relatives have been identified as perpetrators.
**** This element and G are where the idea of Pediatric Condition Falsification (PCF) would best apply.

148 Factitious Disorder by Proxy and IMDs

Table 5.3 Factitious Disorder by Proxy Diagnosis

1. History of behavioral health treatment (I, E; Artingstall, 1995; Schreier, 2000, 1997).
2. Diagnosed with, or suspected of having, symptoms and traits of Factitious Disorder (I, E; Artingstall, 1995; Bools, Neale, & Meadow, 1994).
3. Diagnosed with, or suspected of having, traits of a personality disorder (I, E).
4. Primary caretaker of the child (I, E).
5. Female (I, E; Sheridan, 2003; Siegel & Fischer, 2001).[*]
6. Background or training in medicine (I, E; Artingstall, 1995; Chiczewski & Kelly, 2003; Korpershoek & Flisher, 2004; Siegel & Fischer, 2001).
7. Similar medical history to that of the child presented for evaluation (I, E; Bools, Neale, & Meadow, 1994).
8. Views themselves as "unique" in a characterological sense (I, E).
9. History of a Sudden Infant Death or similar unusual death within the family close to the individual (I, E, O).
10. Psychological assessment instruments indicate a level of defensiveness on validity scales (I, E, O; see Rogers, 2004 [p. 232] for a detailed discussion of this matter]).

Note: I = criteria for inclusion; E = criteria for exclusion; O = criteria for outcome.
[*] While it is far less prevalent, men and close relatives have been identified as perpetrators.

The contents of these tables have been redistributed to reflect the progressive dimensional considerations, with an IMD formulation prefaced by the Background Dimensional Symptoms discussed earlier and described in more recent years in Table 5.4 (Yates & Bass, 2017; Bass & Glaser, 2014; Bass & Jones, 2011; Kozlowska, Foley, & Crittenden, 2006; Adshead & Bluglass, 2005). Parent Individual Dimensional Symptoms and then Child Individual Dimensional Symptoms will be provided in Tables 5.5 and 5.6. The Parent–Child Subdynamic and the Parent–Provider (Healthcare) System Subdynamic will be provided in Tables 5.7 and 5.8.

At the time these concepts were put forward, this author and his colleagues relied heavily on the work of Rogers (2004) and Artingstall (1995), the *DSM-IV-TR*'s research criteria, and Rosenberg's description of MSBP (1987) in formulating this list of FDBP characteristics, as well as the work of Korpershoek

Factitious Disorder by Proxy and IMDs **149**

and Flisher (2004), Rand and Feldman (1999), Siegel and Fischer (2001) and other literature. Additional points were cited that were not so closely tied to the work above; some appeared only in certain articles, or there was some level of disagreement surrounding the question as an indicator of Factitious Disorder by Proxy. In turn, the contents of Table 1 reflected a set of comparisons based on our opinion at the time that FDBP was both an individual diagnosis and an interpersonal dynamic diagnosis (see Tables 5.1–5.3). It has been proposed that the literature on the matter is so confounding because of the lack of an integrated conceptualization. As such, we attempted both to capture a diagnosis that exists for one individual, or perhaps two (*folie à deux*), and to describe a larger complex dynamic between the alleged perpetrator, the alleged victim, and the medico-legal system. We were also aware of the known hazards of addressing larger complex dynamics that had been described throughout the bodies of literature on abuse and neglect, family systems, groups, and industrial-organizational matters. We also took heed of Artingstall's (1995) warning that 60% of mothers accused of MSBP and FDBP "attempted suicide"[1]:

> Despite seemingly strong circumstantial evidence present in some cases of apparent FDBP or MSBP abuse, child protection officials, healthcare professionals, and law enforcement officers must make every effort to refrain from making false allegations. Accusations based on insufficient investigation and absent forensic analysis can have disastrous consequences.
>
> (pp. 8–9)

Howe (2017) has since likewise cautioned the healthcare and legal communities on these matters:

> While Patricia was never officially accused or diagnosed with MSBP, the prosecution's theory against her, as well as the problematic medical evidence, are illustrative of typical MSBP cases.[16] Currently, a medical professional or child-welfare employee will allege MSBP if they think a parent is intentionally harming a child or fabricating the symptoms of a child for the purpose of presenting the child for unnecessary medical treatment.[17] A parent who suffers from MSBP often seeks to gain the attention of medical personnel, outsmart doctors, or fill psychological and emotional voids.[18] These parents can be dangerous to a dependent child; however, both the diagnosis and adjudication of suspected MSBP are prone to error.
>
> (pp. 203–204)

150 Factitious Disorder by Proxy and IMDs

Howe (2017) goes on to state what has become more and more the reality: "Cases are being reversed and defendants exonerated as newer scientific techniques debunk former techniques and expose their lack of scientific foundation.[21] At the very least, methods are being questioned and prompting deeper consideration" (p. 204). Previously, Rogers (2004) had also suggested, "A research priority is the establishment of symptoms and other characteristics that reliably differentiate FDBP from other disorders" (p. 229). He suggested three categories for inclusion: FDBP criteria, proxy-victim characteristics, and relationship variables (parent-victim and parent-physician). Concerns about the loss of objectivity were at the center of the problem of false positives, which both past and present literatures have described.

There was an essential need to clarify these concepts in order to stem false positives and at the same time take necessary precautions to ensure the health and welfare of the children largely involved in these cases, since also in many cases the child under study had siblings who may have, or had, been similarly impacted (Bools, Neale, & Meadow, 1994; Ayoub, Alexander et al., 2002; Bass & Glaser, 2014). Given research criteria for FDBP at the time (American Psychiatric Association, 2000, p. 783) and in light of Rogers's (2004) comments on inclusion, exclusion, and outcome criteria (p. 227), each criterion was labeled according to whether or not it was an element of an individual diagnosis or a dynamic diagnosis in Tables 5.2 and 5.3 above. Parenthetically, in this author's view, the criteria and descriptions in *DSM-IV-TR* were much more consistent with the overall literature. Given the redistributed order of characteristics, symptoms, and subdynamics per the IMD formulation that preceded this book (Bütz & Evans, 2019) and this author's review of the same in Chapter 4, we have Tables 5.4 through 5.8 to consider as well. It was our hope that Table 1 would supply characteristics that described both the individual and dynamic diagnostic features of FDBP in order to create some level of objective points of comparison (Bütz, Evans, & Webber-Dereszynski, 2009, p. 35). The list was, as stated at the time, "by no means exhaustive nor the product of controlled research; rather, it comes from the suggestions of experts in the field and recurring characteristics seen within the literature" (p. 36). It was, however, true that the list was meant to serve as a practical starting point for examination of FDBP following thirty years of literature on the topic.

Tabled Variable Criteria and Redistributing Table 1 From 2009

The approach that this author and his colleagues took at the time was that the child maltreatment was the most frequent social/interpersonal system dynamic associated with FDBP, and could be clearly defined (Sanders & Bursch, 2002) as a situation "in which an adult falsifies physical and/or psychological signs and/or symptoms in a victim causing that victim to be regarded as ill or impaired" (p. 112). But, as described, what was labeled as the FDBP Pathological Dynamic in Chapter 4 is really the culmination of the collective processes involved with the FDBP Interrelated Multidimensional Diagnosis. It should, in fact, be the last consideration, and/or the point at which these processes culminate.

The redistribution of Table 1 into Table 5.2, the FDBP—Child Maltreatment Dynamic, and Table 5.3 for the FDBP Diagnosis on the caretaker, was initially done for illustrative purposes. It also helped differentiate the dynamics from the person who allegedly engaged in the act, though in this case it was an artificial distinction in much the same way that Ayoub and colleagues (Ayoub, Schreier, & Alexander, 2002; Ayoub, Alexander et al., 2002) made their distinctions, as discussed in Chapter 3. The intention of the proposals in 2009, as here with an IMD, had been to convey a holistic concept and to make clear that what had been described was not simply an act or a diagnosis saddled on one member of a family system. Instead, the focus had been on the entire process. Further, if the practitioner began to suspect FDBP, the maltreatment subdynamic spoken to in Table 5.2, the question was whether the caretaker had the characteristics described in Table 5.3 in a fashion that would affirm the practitioner's suspicions to a reasonable degree of scientific certainty. The sample of court testimony in Chapter 2 and Figures 2.2–2.10 were the fundamental read-world application of that conceptual model. Was it more probable than not? That was, in essence, our thinking on these matters in 2009.

With the further conceptual shift to an IMD, the array and order of characteristics and symptoms has expanded beyond the data points or variables described at this earlier time. Thus, the contents of Table 1 now require a practical redistribution into tables that will describe the full extent of FDBP as an Interrelated Multidimensional Diagnosis. This new conceptual structure includes Background Dimensional Symptoms as described above with Table 5.4. This table is followed by Table 5.5 for Parent Individual Dimensional Symptoms, Table 5.6 for Child Individual Dimensional Symptoms,

152 Factitious Disorder by Proxy and IMDs

Table 5.7 for the Parent–Provider System Subdynamic, and Table 5.8 for the FDBP Pathological Dynamic. The whole of the variables in these tables is conceptualized, again, as leading to a cumulative statistical outcome wherein the threshold for FDBP as an IMD is, or is not, *more probable than not*. As a larger, more inclusive conceptualization, an IMD necessarily requires considering more points of data before a hypothetical FDBP can be considered.

Table 5.4 Background Dimensional Symptoms

The parent has allegedly engaged in the pathological dynamic of abuse (FDBP) and has a history that includes the following life events:

- (a) Has experienced physical or sexual abuse, or both, and/or neglect.
- (b) Experienced a heighten level of familial disruption.
- (c) Has disturbed attachments and suffers from attachment insecurity.
- (d) Experienced parent loss through death, illness, or separation.
- (e) Was placed in an out-of-home placement such as foster care.

It follows that by redistributing them, the variables in our prior Table 1 in 2009 flow into these five new tables. Apropos of this discussion, an argument could be made for a parent–child subdynamic, but in this author's view such a conceptualization duplicates the gist of the FDBP Pathological Dynamic. Also, this list of tables could include the known list of illness states in these cases, but at this point the variables described herein are thought to be higher-order considerations. The same holds with the often-nebulous description of the fathers in these cases as well. The focus here is to address well-defined high-frequency variables across the landscape of characteristics and symptoms in an Interrelated Multidimensional Diagnosis. Beginning with Table 5.2, which addresses the FDBP Child Maltreatment Dynamic, variables 1 and 2 best fit in Table 5.7 within the Parent–Provider System Subdynamic. Variables 3 and 4 from Table 5.2 are aptly redistributed to Table 5.6 and are most fitting as a Child Individual Dimensional Symptom, while Variable 5 was placed on Table 5.5 as a Parent Individual Dimensional Symptom.

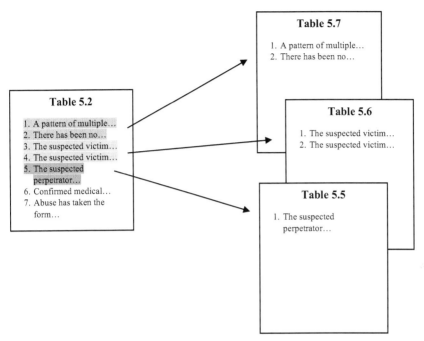

Figure 5.2 Table 1 from our work in 2009 was redistributed to address the basic dimensional conventions associated with an IMD, divvying up characteristic and symptom variables in a way that described each unique contribution, such as those belonging to the parent's behavior and characteristics at the center of these allegations, as well as the child's characteristics.

Table 5.5 Parent Individual Dimensional Symptoms

---

1. The suspected perpetrator is the suspected victim's primary caretaker, and in the vast majority of cases (75–95%) is the mother (I, E; Sheridan, 2003; Siegel & Fischer, 2001).
2. The individual has a history of behavioral health treatment (I, E; Artingstall, 1995; Schreier, 2000, 1997).
3. The individual has been diagnosed with, or suspected of having, symptoms and traits of Factitious Disorder (I, E; Artingstall, 1995; Bools, Neale, & Meadow, 1994).

(*Continued*)

Table 5.5 (Continued)

4. The individual has been diagnosed with, or suspected of having, traits of a personality disorder (I, E).
5. The individual lacks appropriate boundaries (I, E; Siegel & Fischer, 2001).
6. Is demanding (I, E).
7. Seeks attention (I, E).
8. Primary caretaker of the child (I, E).
9. The individual is a female (I, E; Sheridan, 2003; Siegel & Fischer, 2001).*
10. The individual has a background or training in medicine (I, E; Artingstall, 1995; Chiczewski & Kelly, 2003; Korpershoek & Flisher, 2004; Siegel & Fischer, 2001).
11. The individual has a similar medical history to that of the child presented for evaluation (I, E; Bools, Neale, & Meadow, 1994).
12. The individual views themselves as "unique" in a characterological sense (I, E).
13. Psychological assessment instruments indicate a level of defensiveness on validity scales (I, E, O; see Rogers, 2004, for detailed discussion of this matter [p. 232]).

Note: I = criteria for inclusion; E = criteria for exclusion; O = criteria for outcome.
* While it is far less prevalent, men and close relatives have been identified as perpetrators.

Table 5.6 Child Individual Dimensional Symptoms

1. The suspected victim's symptoms worsen over time (I, E, O).
2. The suspected victim is a child between the ages of infancy and eight years (I, E, O).*

Note: I = criteria for inclusion; E = criteria for exclusion; O = criteria for outcome.
* Some authors have put this age up to sixteen.

Continuing the redistribution from the original, as shown in Table 5.1, then, variables 6 and 7 would belong under Table 5.8 as confirmatory evidence of the FDBP Pathological Dynamic. Variable 8 would be divided into letters a–c as belonging to Parent Individual Dimensional Symptoms on Table 5.5, while d and e would more accurately belong in Table 5.7, and the Provider-Healthcare System Subdynamic that was previously named the "Caretaker–Child Subdynamic" would now be referred to as the Parent–Provider (Healthcare) System Subdynamic under Table 5.7 since the vast majority of the literature has described a parent, in most cases the mother, as the perpetrator of the act against the child. Thus, 9a and 9b and 10 would simply be placed under Table 5.7, while 9c would fit under Table 5.8 since it is a more causal symptom.

Table 5.7 Parent–Provider (Healthcare) System Subdynamic

---

1. A pattern of multiple visits to medical providers/hospitals has established a growing suspicion of some form of abuse—mean time frame fourteen months (I, E, O; Sanders & Bursch, 2002 suggest a chronology and table of events in most cases*).
2. There has been no established medical condition that would explain persistent symptoms (I, E, O).
3. The individual is overinvolved with the child (I, E).
4. The individual is unwilling to leave the child's presence (I, E).
5. The individual "thrives" in the medical hospital or office environment (I, E).
6. The individual is gratified by interactions with medical staff (I, E).
7. The suspected perpetrator encourages and welcomes additional tests that will maintain or extend time spent interacting with medical providers, regardless of the effects on the suspected victim (I, E, O; Siegel & Fischer, 2001).

Note: I = criteria for inclusion; E = criteria for exclusion; O = criteria for outcome.
* Their emphasis was on establishing, in short, what has come to be known as Pediatric Condition Falsification (PCF) via a thorough records review. They stated: "The cornerstone of an MBP evaluation is the assessment of the veracity of claims made by the suspected caregiver."

156 Factitious Disorder by Proxy and IMDs

Table 5.8 FDBP Pathological Dynamic

---

1. Child's symptoms worsen in the presence of the suspected individual (I, E, O).
2. A history of a Sudden Infant Death or similar unusual death within the family close to the individual (I, E, O).
3. Confirmed medical findings that the suspected victim has been abused (I, E, O)
4. Abuse has taken the form of drugging, fever induction, poisoning, seizure induction, and suffocation (e.g., apnea, SIDS, etc.) (I, E, O).

Note: I = criteria for inclusion; E = criteria for exclusion; O = criteria for outcome.

Similarly, in the FDBP Diagnosis from the original Table 1, provided herein under Table 5.3, variables would be divvied up into this new table structure with variables 1 through 8 and 10 placed under the Parent Individual Dimensional Symptoms in Table 5.5. Meanwhile, variable 9 would rightfully fall under the FDBP Pathological Dynamic in Table 5.8. As before, each comparison in these lists has markers in parentheses beside it to indicate that it meets Rogers's (2004)[2] criteria of inclusion (I), exclusion (E), and outcome (O). The reader was previously also encouraged to think of these lists as comparable attributes in terms of percentages of agreement, (e.g., 1 out of 10 being 10%) or per the developed terminology herein identified as *variable criteria*. There was no "magical" cut-off point proposed at that time, and the reader was encouraged simply to consider these percentages qualitatively within the larger context of an overall assessment, as well as what might "tip the scales" (DeMatteo & Edens, 2006, pp. 231–233). These comparisons were considered probabilities clustered together that could result in a set of individual, or now subdynamic, diagnostic profiles that were additive.

Revisiting FDBP as an IMD and Building Tables

With the IMD conceptualization, rather than designating every variable's origin in the literature, a representative set of literature was pulled together to create these tables and the IMD Inventory for FDBP© that would follow. The conformance of this literature to these variables would be discussed as part of the supporting literature for the IMD Inventory© on FDBP, including the actuarial efforts by Yates and Bass (2017); the suggested "decision matrix," profiling as soft signs, and direct evidence as more robust signs from Howe (2017); and the screening items offered by Greiner et al. (2013), among others (Bass & Wade, 2019; Velso & Rogers, 2018; Day et al., 2017). There were three groups of literature used to inform the tables that followed, describing characteristics, symptoms, subdynamics and, under the right conditions, the development of the IMD pathological dynamic. These were seminal pieces that have been cited and referred to repeatedly in the literature. Other works included those that came to the fore after conducting a search on Google Scholar that resulted in references that were either directly pertinent to the search terms or that had amassed numerous citations. In this case, the key phrases were "Munchausen's Syndrome by Proxy" and "Factitious Disorder by Proxy." In most cases, even with the variety of terms described in Chapter 3, these search terms would trip articles written to these different terms, such as AIBP, CAMS, CFIC, FII, MCA, and PCF, and so on. The first two pages of results were then reviewed, and those pieces that were perhaps arguably the most referenced or directly relevant were included. The third group of work consisted of promising studies that contributed new insight or research but had not been part of this body of literature long enough to be considered seminal or to accumulate a substantial number of citations. Seminal pieces were also divided into two groups, the first directly relevant to the broader topic of the IMD under study and the second related to those considerations described in background dimensional symptoms. With some exceptions, works either critical of FDBP or PA or at the fringe were not included in this group of literature, (e.g., Frye & Feldman, 2012; Feldman, Bibby, & Crites, 1998). The controversies and differences of opinion about these phenomena have been well represented throughout this text; there is no need to further revisit them here since this aspect of the book is how to identify IMDs, not to argue whether they exist at all. To be clear, as in 2009, not all FDBP cases are described by the same FDBP pathological variables in the parent or the child, individual–healthcare provider interactions, or FDBP pathological dynamic properties.

Consider, for a moment, the weight of these determinations: for example, the fate of Meadow after opening up this area of inquiry or the known impact that such a determination may have on mothers who have been falsely accused of Factitious Disorder by Proxy (Howe, 2017). In 2009 this author and his colleagues offered the aforementioned eighteen points to consider the probable characteristics and symptoms that may comprise Factitious Disorder by Proxy. At the time these variables both reflected the complexity of the phenomenon and provided a set of reference points to incorporate individual and subdynamic comparisons for a proposed revision of the FDBP diagnosis with the potential to be more holistic and inclusive. Since that time, these cautions have been buttressed through important updates to certain characteristics and symptomatic variables, while at the same time others have been added, all of this while entertaining how to conceptualize FDBP as a pathological IMD dynamic. Therefore, at this point in our discussion it makes sense to pause and revisit earlier considerations about whether or not FDBP is an individual or dynamic diagnosis, or both, in order to articulate new developments and clarify characteristics and symptoms variables.

An Individual Diagnosis, a Dynamic Diagnosis, or Both, Revisited

It is likely apparent that the fundamentals of this question have already been addressed with the proposal of an Interrelated Multidimensional Diagnosis. However, these prior considerations from 2009 create a platform from which to update the discussion, to reconsider variables, and to add new ones to the conceptualizations offered if appropriate to do so. Since at least its initial description, MSBP has been considered a complex four-fold dynamic rather than a diagnosis per se (Meadow, 1977; Money & Werlwas, 1976; Robins & Sesan, 1991; Rosenberg, 1987). Rand and Feldman (1999) had considered misdiagnoses of MSBP and questioned the premise of whether it was a diagnosis or not (p. 95). According to Rand and Feldman (1999), this description distills to what one might describe as a dynamic that could be seen as a "complex maltreatment interaction dynamic between the parent/caretaker, child and medical staff" (p. 100). As this author alluded to earlier in this chapter, certain background characteristics and symptoms may well have led to the interactions that have also been discussed as subdynamics.

In Chapter 2 the American Professional Society on the Abuse of Children (APSAC) task force on MSBP was discussed (Ayoub et al., 2002; Ayoub, Alexander et al., 2002; Schreier & Ayoub, 2002); the task force's work suggested that MSBP be abandoned as the primary descriptive term (Schreier & Ayoub, 2002) and instead encouraged clinicians to take a step-wise approach to identify child abuse first, that is, *Pediatric Condition Falsification* (PCF). Then, as a second step, FDBP could be identified via the criteria from *DSM-IV-TR* (American Psychiatric Association, 2000). However, in this author's view such changes were simply a matter of semantics. As Pankratz (2006) had pointed out, this was no easy matter either, as PCF was based on the notion that the parent/caregiver has "falsified" the medical record. Pankrantz stated:

During careful interviews, ordinary mothers provided information that was not consistent with the medical records of their children. The findings in this study suggested that mothers say what they believe at the time.

The base rate for misinformation in the pediatric setting may be high, but this does not necessarily reflect evil intentions. Falsification can arise from simple mistakes or complex psychodynamic drives; clinicians must evaluate and minimize these risks. Yet, attorneys comb the massive records of chronically disabled children looking for the smallest discrepancies, which are then paraded before the court as falsifications. This has a powerful effect on the whole process because anything that the mother says thereafter in her own defense can be dismissed as a part of her pattern of lies.

Many articles on MSBP recommend comprehensive evaluations, but the diagnostic labels of pediatric condition falsification and MSBP often divert the assessment process and management planning into a contentious legal battle. The purpose of a multidisciplinary team, of course, is to assess different domains of function and, one hopes, to avoid viewing the patient through a diagnostic peephole.

Once a problem is perceived as MSBP or pediatric condition falsification, the focus easily turns to simplistic blaming instead of assisting the mother in the management of her child. Most often, the planning sessions of child protective services result in the assignment of burdensome tasks for the parents to earn back their child even when there has not been evidence of harm.

(pp. 92–93)

At the time it was possible to describe an identifiable, though to an extent incomplete, pathological dynamic for FDBP with the work of Rosenberg (1987) and the APSAC task force on Munchausen Syndrome by Proxy (Ayoub, Alexander et al., 2002).

As noted in 2009 the task force's schematic for understanding this proposed maltreatment dynamic (one endorsed by a sizable number of practitioners) still had noteworthy problems aside from those described in Chapter 2; both the first arm that describes PCF (Pankratz, 2006) and the second arm on the diagnosis of FDBP, which Rogers (2004) had described, were problematic at best. These considerations did not yield an answer to the question of whether FDBP was an individual or dynamic diagnosis. Instead, the discussion suggested that elements of both were at work.

The Topic of Motivation and FDBP

This author and his colleagues earlier used Siegel and Fischer's (2001) work to describe certain cautions when approaching this phenomenon:

> Some FDP perpetrators are uneducated, dramatic, emotionally labile, hostile, and obviously dishonest (Parnell, 1998), *whereas others are out to harass physicians, hoping to profit from malpractice suits*[3] (Rosenberg, 1995) or benefit from governmental services and programs (Artingstall, 1999).
>
> (p. 36)

The passage in this citation on Rosenberg's concerns above (1995) re-opens an important discussion on motivation that has been touched on a number of times thus far. Although many potential references may be of use here, Velsor and Rogers (2018) have provided a thoughtful update to the factitious disorders matter generally within the *DSM-5* and described some of the major changes that were dealt with in Chapter 3. Still, they also hit on crucial aspects of these matters in the following passage:

> Factitious Disorder Imposed on the Self (FDIOS) and Factitious Disorder Imposed on Another (FDIOA). FDIOS involves the fabrication of physical or psychological symptoms or the induction of injury or disease on oneself, whereas FDIOA encompasses the same criteria but focuses on another person (the victim) as impaired, injured, or ill.
>
> (p. 4)

Thus, a parent is in a dynamic interaction with her or his child—two people and one dynamic. Velsor and Rogers importantly expanded the discussion by including the description below and with a context that comes later:

> A third important change with DSM-5 eliminates the requirement from factitious disorders that the evaluated person is motivated to adopt a sick role. Indeed, the word "motivation" is removed entirely. Instead, non-specific language indicates that deceptions must be present "even in the absence of obvious external rewards" (American Psychiatric Association, 2013, p. 325). This crucial adjustment was aimed at shifting focus away from an attempt to understand underlying motivation for feigning in favor of more objective measures, such as identifying false symptoms (Yates et al., 2018). While the desire for diagnostic objectivity is laudable, turning a blind eye to motivation completely disregards

the complexity of factitious presentations. Especially with FDIOA, it is critically important to understand—however imperfectly—the underlying motivation. In hurting one's child, for example, the FDIOA motivation could vary from unmet dependency needs to sadistically motivated behaviors.

(p. 4)

Subsequently, Velsor and Rogers (2018) provided a rather pithy, but exacting, series of rhetorical questions and concluded that, "motivation cannot be willed out of existence."

Can researchers and practitioners even agree whether basking in the unmerited attention of health care professionals resulting from an FDIOA induced medical mystery constitutes an obvious external reward? If so, can they reach diagnostic agreement? Specifically, how much basking objectively qualifies for this external reward? Conceptually, the absence of observed external rewards cannot be equated with the presence of internal motivation. Moreover, external rewards may be overshadowed by internal motivations.

(p. 4)

In turn, motivation lies in the parent and cannot generally be said to exist in a child, and that motivation creates the beginnings of a pathological dynamic.

Considerations for motivation do not stop there, and Velsor and Rogers (2018) go on to propose a Factitious Psychological Presentation (FPP) through four different explanatory "Models" (pp. 5–10): Pathologenic, Criminological, Adaptational, and Nurturance. These terms are generally true to what one might imagine, and a number of familiar references are provided as well in their Table 1 to describe explanatory models of motivation, such as Pathologenic (Feldman, 2004) and Criminological (Yates & Feldman, 2016), while others are new, as with Adaptational (Lawlor & Kirakowski, 2014), and still others lie outside the field of inquiry, as in Nurturance (Rogers, Sewell, & Gillard, 2010).

This range of models for motivation is well suited to the distinction that seemed to spawn the proliferation of terms in the field, as described in Chapter 3, and to clarify language about motivation in *DSM-5*. As described previously, the Model of Illness Deception figure by Bass and Halligan (2007) will be of use for considering the matter of motivation (see Figure 5.1 (repeated again on page 162)), particularly with an overlay of Velsor and Rogers's Models (see Figure 5.2) to clarify these matters.

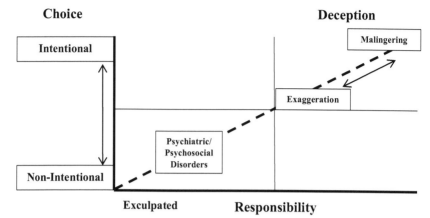

Figure 5.1 (repeated) Bass and Halligan's Figure 1 (2007, p. 83), Model of Illness Deception, reproduced by the author for illustrative purposes here and in Chapter 3.

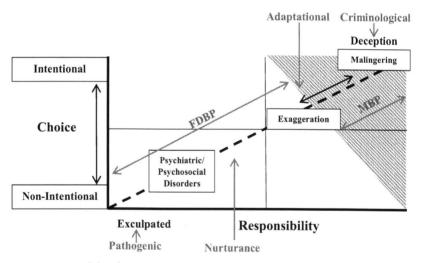

Figure 5.3 Models of Deception and Motivation: Bass & Halligan's Figure 5.1 (2007, p. 83), Model of Illness Deception; reproduced to include Velsor & Rogers's Table 5.1 (2018, pp. 8–10) Models of Motivations.

Turning our attention to Figure 5.3, this author is of the belief that Velsor and Rogers were correct when they identified a range of motivations involved more broadly with MSBP and more narrowly with Factitious Disorder by Proxy. Yet, in either respect there is a line when diagnostic considerations shift to what Rogers (2004) described some time ago as Malingering by Proxy (p. 227). Further, he deduced that, "If diagnostic formulations continue to insist that FDBP be limited to a 'sick-role' motivation, then important variations (e.g., malingering by proxy) must also be considered" (p. 235). Though Velsor and Rogers (2018) have created relationships from their "Models" that reflected Pathologenic, Criminological, Adaptational and Nurturance in their Table 1 or the discussion on these matters (pp. 8–10), Figure 5.3 shows a different relationship among these descriptions, and places Pathologenic and Criminological at the outermost markers while Adaptational and Nurturance hold the innermost part of the continuum. The reasons for this may be apparent, but even so the literature would suggest that Pathologenic and Criminological are opposites, and that the more nominal motivations are Adaptational and Nurturance. Second, this continuum provides a line of demarcation between what would properly be considered FDBP and Rogers's notion of Malingering by Proxy. In this author's view, that line would best be set within the midline of the Adaptational Model with the focus there (Velsor & Rogers, 2018),

> Sometimes described colloquially as being stuck "between a rock and a hard place," persons with FPP[4] are motivated to achieve the best—or the least detrimental—outcome. A recurring theme of cost—benefit analysis appears to be a compelling explanation for the adaptive motivations underlying FPP.
>
> (p. 9)

Parenthetically, this description might better be served by the term *maladaptive* or *adaptive-maladaptive*. The placement of this line between FDBP and Rogers's proposed MBP occupies the third described by the terms Adaptational and Criminological, which represent the maladaptive region of the continuum, hence the suggested replacement terms. Again, these are rare conditions (Bass & Wade, 2019), but as Velsor and Rogers (2018) have noted above, it is reasonably clear that there is no getting around some of the realities associated with these situations and the motivations involved. Meanwhile, FDBP continues to represent two-thirds of the range of the continuum, which is consistent with the literature's ongoing

164 Factitious Disorder by Proxy and IMDs

description of Pathologenic, Nurturance and Adaptational motivations. The origins for the more pathological end of this range find their best footing in the historical orientation to MSBP; for FDBP, more recent works cited earlier in this chapter have described different views on motivation, such as maladaptive or misguided efforts at nurturing (Bass & Jones, 2011; Kozlowska, Foley, & Crittenden, 2006; Adshead & Bluglass, 2001, 2005). The ground has now been set to take up the dimensional characteristics and symptoms that were spoken to in 2009 in order to refine this list and to clarify the subdynamics.

Revisiting the List of Characteristics Associated With Factitious Disorder by Proxy

Symptomatic variables of FDBP that regularly appear in the scientific literature have been preliminarily provided in Tables 5.4 and 5.8. There are also the considerations entertained in Figures 5.1 and 5.3 about the nature of motivation in these cases and the line of demarcation between FDBP and Munchausen Syndrome by Proxy. This analysis allows a necessary comparison between the known list of characteristics and symptoms described previously (Korpershoek & Flisher, 2004; Rogers, 2004; Siegel & Fischer, 2001; Rand & Feldman, 1999; Artingstall, 1995; Rosenberg, 1987) and in more recent literature as each table will be revisited. In updating these dimensional characteristics and symptoms, all have been given relatively equal footing and naturally include the array of terms discussed in Chapter 3. This discussion references the *Platypus Paradox* that this author proposed, which described MSBP as a common term for laypersons and FDBP as the scientific term for professionals, practitioners, and researchers.

Addressing FDBP as an IMD would not be complete without at least presenting hypotheses about Background Dimensional Symptoms, symptoms that may be akin to the condition of the soil in which the seeds of an IMD grow. The discussion in more recent literature yielded four potential symptoms that for now are seated within the parent's experience of her or his developmental home life in Table 5.4 above, and it is not much of a stretch to consider the kind of family dynamic this parent grew up in (Olson, 2000) and the parenting style in such families (Baumrind, 1991, 1971). Such considerations would likely prove fruitful areas for further research and will be discussed later in the book.

Factitious Disorder by Proxy and IMDs   **165**

Parents who grew up within such a family dynamic have been regularly described by the characteristics and symptoms in Table 5.5, which lists Parent Individual Dimensional Symptoms; these variables have been redistributed from our earlier work in 2009. Given changes in the recent literature, Table 5.9 supplies a needed update that reflects a more advanced conceptualization with higher probabilities first, the inclusion of new variables, and the removal of a rarely cited variable that has little practical probabilistic value even though there was some more recent work on this subject (Day et al., 2017; Rogers, 2004; Parnell, 1998; Schreier & Libow, 1993).

Table 5.9 Revised Parent Individual Dimensional Symptoms

---

1. The suspected perpetrator is the child's mother.
2. The individual has been diagnosed with symptoms and/or traits of Factitious Disorder and Somatisation Disorder.
3. The individual suffers from a personality disorder and/or traits that include borderline, narcissistic, and histrionic descriptors and they may
    (a) views themselves as "unique" in a characterological sense.
4. The individual has engaged in the past and present in a pattern of pathological lying.
5. The individual has a similar medical history to that of the child presented for evaluation.
6. The perpetrator has a history of behavioral health treatment, and they may have also :
    (a) Experienced mood disorder (%) and/or,
    (b) Been psychiatrically hospitalized.
7. The individual has a background or training in medicine.

To begin, there were some redundancies in Table 5.5, where variables 8 and 9 had already been collapsed into the first variable, which enjoys wide agreement within this literature, that is, that in the vast majority of cases the perpetrator is the child's mother. More recent literature has found a greater incidence of what has been described in variable 3 in Table 5.5, where not only have there been prior diagnoses of factitious disorder, but somatisation disorder as well (Bass & Glaser, 2014; Greiner et al., 2013). This pattern has proven so strong that it merits moving it to the second position in Table 5.9. Though understandably debatable according to certain groups within the literature, what was then variable 4 in Table 5.5 was moved to the third position in Table 5.9, as the perpetrator has regularly been discussed in the past and present literature as suffering from what amounts to a personality disorder and/or personality disordered traits in the range of Cluster B per the *DSM* series. There is also considerable overlap between variables 5, 6, 7, and 12, which have been collapsed into variable 3 in Table 5.9, with the exception of antisocial traits that may well be better used to describe the parents who engage in MBP, as discussed above and as will be discussed in Chapter 8. More recent literature has also shown a new finding and/or trend of pathological lying that appears to have strong support for taking up the fourth position in Table 5.9 (Bass & Glaser, 2014; Bass & Jones, 2011). There was also growing support for the idea of the parent having many of the same challenges as the child, and so variable 11 from Table 5.5 was moved to the fifth position in Table 5.9. Addressing variable 2 from Table 5.5, it has become more and more apparent that these parents have had a significant history of behavioral health treatment. Noting the diagnoses referenced earlier with factitious disorder and somatisation disorder, as well as the personality disorder and/or traits mentioned above, the literature has also discussed mood disorders as a significant ailment, and a number of these parents have been psychiatrically hospitalized (Bass & Jones, 2011). Thus, variable 2 in Table 5.5 was moved to the sixth position, contextually noting the percentage of these parents who have a mood disorder and have had psychiatric hospitalizations as subvariables. Variable 10 remains unchanged, although with the attrition of other variables it moved up to the seventh position and continues to be discussed in the literature regularly. Variable 13, having little practical use probabilistically, was dropped (although it may be considered as an element of the assessment process suggested in Chapter 8).

In turn, these seven individual dimensional symptoms should be seen as variables that are more or less present in the profile of the person suspected of engaging in these injurious behaviors toward their child. As noted earlier, any of these variables need to be present to a significant degree to fit with the notions about profile characteristics. As will be seen later, these profile characteristics are best borne out of a thorough record review initially and each is included as one among a number of other variables considered.

Table 5.10 Child Individual Dimensional Symptoms

1.	The suspected victim's symptoms worsen over time.
2.	After multiple visits to providers, no definitive diagnoses have been provided that ameliorate the child's illness.
3.	The suspected victim is a usually a child (some place the age between infancy and eight years, and other studies show mortality risk is greater in the first two years of life).
4.	The child's siblings have often suffered related or similar illnesses, or have died.

The Child Individual Dimensional Symptoms in what is now Table 5.10 also includes several modifications. The lack of a firm diagnosis after multiple visits has been included as variable 2, and the previous variable 4 from Table 5.2 has been moved to the third position and clarifies that the victim is often simply a child. More recent literature has provided variations on this characteristic symptom, though most pieces explain that the younger the child, the greater the potential for sustaining lethal injuries (Bass & Glaser, 2014; Greiner et al., 2013). What has been treated in the literature and perhaps arguably become more and more evident as a part of the characteristics associated with the child is the illness or death of a sibling. This variable will be placed fourth in the order, as clearly the prior three variables are more common, and it is perhaps debatable whether it is an attribute that needs to be known about the child. There are repeated references to sibling illness and/or death, and this variable could be placed in a number of tables in this model, but it does comment on the child and her or his existence within the family.

Table 5.11 Parent–Provider (Healthcare) System Subdynamic

1.	The parent is ingratiating, comfortable, and unexpectedly at ease interacting with healthcare providers and healthcare systems.
2.	The parent has left the hospital against medical advice or insists on transfer to another facility for themselves and/or does so regarding their child.
3.	After multiple visits to healthcare providers/healthcare systems over a period of time, providers develop a growing suspicion of some form of abuse—mean time frame fourteen months.
4.	There has been no established medical condition that would explain the child's persistent symptoms.

168 Factitious Disorder by Proxy and IMDs

As for the Parent–Provider (Healthcare)System Subdynamic, the more-or-less sterile description of the parent's interactions with healthcare providers as an essential characteristic and/or symptom was, after much contemplation, misleading in 2009. It did not describe the quality of that relationship accurately in this author's view. Meadow (1977) originally captured the nature of one of the significant attributes and/or characteristics in this subdynamic in the following passage:

> They were very pleasant people to deal with, cooperative, and appreciative of good medical care, which encouraged us to try all the harder. Some mothers who choose to stay in hospital with their child remain on the Ward slightly uneasy, overtly bored, or aggressive. These two flourished there as if they belonged, and thrived on the attention that staff gave to them.
>
> (p. 344)

He reiterated these characterizations in 1995 as well (p. 535). These characterizations do precede all others, and, due to the parent's history, it would seem are coupled with their familiarity with adversity and healthcare. As a distillation it could be said in this author's words, "These parents are ingratiating, comfortable, and unexpectedly at ease interacting with healthcare providers and healthcare systems." This description has been repeated to one extent or another across this literature, but not quite with the quality of narration Meadow provided. This, in turn, should be the first variable spoken to in Table 5.11.

It also follows that a second variable is inserted in this revision: it is only after multiple visits to healthcare providers/healthcare systems over a period of time, that providers hold a growing suspicion of pathology. While there is a mean time frame (Bass & Glaser, 2014; Greiner et al., 2013), given the text of variable 2 in Table 5.2, changes are required. Variable 2, in turn, changes to variable 3 for reasons that will be explained shortly. These variables require further elaboration when attending to the predominant symptom presentation and subvariables involved here. Although addressed in the FDBP Pathological Dynamic, which is more an aggregate of evidence, what was not provided was a pattern to look for as providers struggled to clarify just what potential pathology they were dealing with.

In this regard, the more actuarial work of Greiner et al. (2013) provided a useful list of characteristics and symptoms. As stated earlier, Bass and Glaser (2014), Greiner et al. (2013) and Bass and Jones (2011) have been particularly useful, and out of these works another addition is merited. That is, it would seem, there are circumstances in which a parent may not obtain the satisfaction he or she seeks from healthcare providers, or the parent may suspect providers have grown suspicious of their intentions. In these situations, these parents may suddenly and unexpectedly withdraw from services themselves or withdraw their child from services (Greiner et al., 2013): "Caregiver leaves hospital against medical advice or insists on transfer" (Table 2, p. 42). For obvious reasons, this should be in the second position, since regardless of the degree of suspicion a provider may have, this particular action may well mark "the time to act" and/or intervene. The details of these matters will be further explained in later chapters.

Therefore, the subdynamic now includes the parents appearing to thrive by way of interactions with healthcare providers; the sudden withdrawal by parents and/or withdrawal of their child from healthcare settings, after multiple visits providers beginning to suspect the possibility of abuse; and the lack of a firm diagnosis amid those most frequently feigned in these situations. A list of these conditions most commonly associated with FDBP could be a subvariable here and regularly appears in this literature. Ultimately, this leads us back to the FDBP pathological dynamic.

IMD Implications for FDBP

Most scientists are aware that correlation does not equal causation, and addressing the multifaceted elements of FDBP is not as simple as cataloging individual and dynamic diagnostic variables (Palermo & Kocisc, 2005; Sanders & Bursch, 2002) by way of a parent's alignment with a profile. Matters are more complex than they seem (Shah, 1989), and some time ago the respected researcher Kerlinger (1979) offered the following:

> Behavioral science and research does not offer certainty. (Neither does natural science!) It does not even offer relative certainty. All it offers is probabilistic knowledge: If A is done, then B will probably occur.
>
> (p. 28)

Given the interrelated and multidimensional considerations of the last several chapters, a probabilistic approach is proposed to describe whether FDBP may well be at work in cases in which sufficient efforts have been made to address background dimensional symptoms, individual dimensional symptoms, and subdynamics. With the number of variables that have been described in the tables above it comes time to define the pathological dynamic by way of proposing diagnostic criteria informed by the foregoing discussion. As addressed in the latter portion of Chapter 4 IMD diagnoses involve a two-stage process.

Suspicion based on observable symptoms, and second the further study of characteristics and historical variables in order to generate an overall probability for the IMDs presence. For this reason, IMD diagnoses require a two-stage, arguably a three-stage process, before arriving at *a more probable than not determination*. As described in Chapter 4, not only is the suspicion derived by a marker of *better than chance* observable variable symptoms, but best practices also suggest that this determination is followed by consultation with another practitioner.

Possible observable symptom variables have been brought forward from the characteristics and symptoms supplied and Tables 5.4–5.12. Table 5.12 has been provided in order to describe the FDBP IMD diagnostic criteria. Initial considerations go to criteria I–VI, or alternatively VII alone, or some combination of I–VI and VII that equates to a likelihood of *better than chance* that the practitioner in the case has a good scientific reason to suspect the pathological dynamic. Other variable characteristics and history follow in criteria VIII–XI based on the known literature regarding FDBP. As noted, establishing these criteria require further study by the practitioner or another member of the multidisciplinary team. Once these criteria have been studied, analysis follows based on conformance to the diagnosis in Table 5.12 and/or their broad conformance to Tables 5.4–5.11, or perhaps to the outcome of the IMD Inventory—FDBP©. These methods are intended to arrive at a quantitative probability for the FDBP IMD that is considered in concert with the studies of a multidisciplinary team.

Table 5.12 Proposed FDBP IMD Diagnosis

The fundamental aspect of Factitious Disorder by Proxy (FDBP) is that it is a family systems diagnosis that involves the deliberate production or feigning of physical or psychological signs or symptoms in another person who is under the individual's care. Typically, the victim is a child under the age of four, and the person engaged in the act(s) is the child's mother. The apparent motivation for the mother's behavior is the psychological need for attention by proxy, and thus she presents a sick child to healthcare professionals. External incentives are absent, and the existence of a usual or rare disorder has been eliminated to a reasonably degree of scientific certainty.

As an Interrelated Multidimensional Diagnosis (IMD), this diagnosis is meant to be made fully only after a two-stage process. The first stage, suspicion, is reached by a *better than chance* occurrence of criteria I–VI, or VII alone if the evidence is strong enough, or a combination of I–VI and VII. The second stage requires further study of characteristics and history to determine an overall probability for the diagnosis, which involves the additional considerations involved with criteria VIII–XI. *If the whole of variable criteria meet a probability of .50+, and/or more probable than not, then the FDBP IMD diagnosis should be made.*

SUSPICION STAGE

I.   Intentional production of, or feigned, physical or psychological symptoms in a child by a parental figure in most cases.
II. The child in most cases is under four years of age but may be up to eight years of age.
III. The parent's suspected motivation is to assume the sick role by proxy.
IV. The child's condition has not improved over multiple visits to healthcare providers, and there is no definitive diagnostic hypothesis after repeated episodes.
V.   The parent in most cases is uncommonly at ease in a healthcare setting, ingratiating, and comfortable despite the child's condition.
VI. The parent in most cases does not appear to be distressed by the potential of significant diagnoses for their child and/or by the need for significant procedures or studies their child must endure.

AND/OR

VII. Based on one or more of the criteria above, studies or video surveillance have provided evidence of induced or feigned illness to the child by the parent.

(Continued)

Table 5.12 (Continued)

FURTHER STUDY STAGE

VIII. After a period of separation from the parent and/or tightly supervised visitation with the parent, and the provision of appropriate care, the child's condition improves markedly; that is, there are no lingering symptoms that may suggest a complicated or rare diagnosis.

IX. The parent in question in most cases has a background history that includes the following:
   A. Experienced abuse or neglect as a child or adolescent.
   B. Experienced a high level of family disruption such as loss of a parent due to abandonment, divorce, death, illness, or separation.
   C. Lived in an out-of-home placement or been in foster care or its equivalent.
   D. Assessment or clinical documentation suggests that the parent suffers from attachment insecurity.

X. The parent in question has the following characteristics:
   A. The parent is the child's mother.
   B. The parent has been diagnosed previously with symptoms and/or traits of Factitious Disorder and Somatization Disorder.
   C. The parent has been diagnosed with a personality disorder and/or traits that include borderline, narcissistic, and histrionic descriptors, and/or they may view themselves as unique.
   D. The parent has engaged in a pattern of behavior referred to as pathological lying.
   E. The parent has a similar healthcare history to that of the child presented for examination.
   F. The parent has a history of behavioral health treatment.
      i.   The parent has been diagnosed with a mood disorder.
      ii.   The parent has required in-patient behavioral healthcare services.
   G. The parent has a background or training in healthcare.

XI. The events or history of the family or the parents includes the following:
   A. The parent or parents have removed one or more of their children from a healthcare setting Against Medical Advice on at least one occasion.
   B. The family has children who have suffered or are suffering from a similar pattern of illness.
   C. A sibling has died from a healthcare-related illness (not an accident or by other means).

It is this author's hope that the reader would agree that a sound systemic diagnosis may be made based on these diagnostic criteria, and that a practitioner, professional or researcher would be able to derive a useful probabilistic outcome based on the forgoing discussion and tables. The development of the new inventory too has been designed to further these efforts, since it is anchored in the IMD conceptual framework for addressing FDBP and offers a quantitative probabilistic outcome that speaks to all of these variables. At the same time, the inventory is also intended to provide an iterative Bayesian outcome and a weighting of evidence gleaned from more robust sources such as laboratory findings, the separation test, and video surveillance. The IMD Inventory—FDBP© has been designed based on the tables that have been offered above and the IMD proof process described herein.

Provided these considerations, FDBP may be conceived of as one IMD with a number of underlying variables worthy of their own diagnoses as well in the parent, or perhaps regarding particular subdynamics. Such considerations should, hopefully, inform child protection officials, healthcare practitioners, and professionals in the legal community. Perhaps such considerations may also impact policy and procedures in these larger systems, as will be discussed further in Chapter 8. There are real-world prospects for over- and underreacting in these cases, and these too will be addressed in more detail in later chapters.

Notes

1. It is vague in her article whether or not she is referring to a demographic preceding the accusation, or if this occurred after being accused of the crime—it seemed the latter.
2. "A research priority is the establishment of symptoms and other characteristics that reliably differentiate FDBP from other disorders."
3. Italics added for emphasis.
4. Factitious Psychological Presentation.

Parental Alienation as an Interrelated Multidimensional Diagnosis

6

The Psychological Surround of PA: Background, Percentages, and Environment

As with the sparks that ignite FDBP, the experiences in PA may be seen to rise out of the collective interactions among members of a disjointed sinfonia to create a pathological dynamic from the psychological surround, created by certain background of characteristics and symptoms. Indeed, Ludolph and Bow (2012) referred to "the psychological surround" (p. 155) of alienation dynamics. In particular, they announced the following: "We will call this psychological surround 'alienating dynamics,' thinking not only of what is present in the minds and actions of older family members, but also in the day-to-day atmosphere of the family" (p. 155). Although the vast majority of separating or divorcing couples with children are able to resolve their differences amicably by putting the health and welfare of the children, and each other, at the center of their considerations, other couples and/or parents manage these tasks poorly and fail to navigate these interactions with the legal system and hold the aforementioned priorities close. Discussing the environment created broadly in these situations, Kelly and Johnston (2001, pp. 255–256) described the conception of an Alienated Child and an array of interactions that occurred with these families, including the child being triangulated in the intense marital conflict; separation experienced as deeply humiliating by one or both parents; a high-conflict

176 Parental Alienation as an IMD

divorce with litigation; and maladaptive contributions of new partners, next of kin, and professionals. At the risk of being repetitious, this author noted in Chapter 2 that Johnston (1994, p. 175) had defined high-conflict cases as suffering from unsuccessful mediations, the necessity of parental capacity assessments, and court-imposed settlements. She indicated that these kinds of cases only constituted 10% of separating or divorcing parents. Since these earlier days, high-conflict cases have been regularly discussed in the literature associated with Patient Alienation. Ben-Ami and Baker (2012) identified these matters as central to the PA dynamic as well: "One distinct form of parental conflict that can sometimes emerge under high-conflict situations has been termed parental alienation (PA)" (169). Likewise, Baker, joined by Burkhard and Albertson-Kelly (2012), noted the centrality of high conflict, "Children's alignment and alienation in response to high-conflict divorce is a long-standing problem" (p. 179). Generally speaking, Kelly (2003, p. 37) made the case that in PA a high-conflict divorce was more or less an umbrella background characteristic and that PA was at work in just 8–12% of all high-conflict cases.

Percentages

Not all high-conflict divorces involve PA, however. Drozd and Olesen (2004, p. 66) cited percentages between 11% and 27% per the available literature at the time (Wallerstein & Kelly, 1980a; Johnston, 2003; Johnston, Lee, et al., 2005). Still other estimates of the incidence of PA have ranged as high as 25–29% of divorcing parents (Howe & Covell, 2014, p. 156). Meanwhile, others such as Meier (2010) made clear that in her view, "Johnston's credible empirical research demonstrates that child alienation occurs in only a small fraction of cases" (p. 219). In addition, she stated that, "Only in a very small proportion of cases—something less than 2% (i.e., 20% of 9%) of the total population of divorcing families—require courts' involvement concerning alienation" (p. 240). More recently, Harman, Leder-Elder, and Biringen (2016) have stated:

> Results revealed that 13.4% of parents (or 9.03% of the entire sample) have been alienated from one or more of their children. Our findings suggest that tens of millions of adults and their children may be impacted by parental alienation, which is much higher than previous estimates.
>
> (p. 62)

Also, perhaps there are questions of terminology in the world's literature on these matters since numbers such as nearly half of separations and a third of divorces are suggested to involve PA (Siracusano et al., 2015), and still if such statements hold that certainly raises questions about prevalence. It follows that, to address PA, those working with these cases need to recognize that there are very specific background considerations, such as high-conflict separation, divorce, and post-divorce interactions. Further, within those cases that make up that 10%, some result in PA, which is a finding repeated throughout this literature, though estimates of the number vary and appear to be on the rise.

Environmental Forces

Much of the literature on PA has described contextual environmental forces, or stresses, involved in the aforementioned high-conflict cases (Kelly & Johnston, 2001). These descriptions are coupled with reports about certain characteristics that parents as well as children in these situations possess: "The profound alienation of a child from a parent most often occurs in high-conflict custody disputes; it is an infrequent occurrence among the larger population of divorcing children" (p. 254). Other, more recent, authors also have made similar observations: "It appears to be greatest in high-conflict divorcing families . . . especially when custody and visitation arrangement are court ordered" (Howe & Covell, 2014, pp. 156–157). Consider the import of the article by Nichols in the *Michigan Law Review* (2014) regarding the legal environment and its impact, which emphasized the notion that with high-conflict divorces there was a need to involve a guardian ad litem regularly. By virtue of this statement, Nichols has made clear that the health and welfare of these children are at risk, no less considerations about their best interests. The article by Vijoen and van Rensburg (2014, pp. 260–262) discussed provider experiences and noted that high-conflict divorces were a context for PA. They went so far as to categorize comments, noting the "High-conflict caused by partners 'decoupling' at different times from the relationship" and "Parental pathology involved in high-conflict divorces and PAS" (p. 261). Pertinent to the considerations within this portion of the chapter, Vijoen and van Rensburg (2014) described that PA was a "process with PAS as a consequence" (p. 262). It was a process so powerful that these authors warned about the dangers of the PA dynamic: "One of the greatest challenges for any health care professional is the necessity to remain as objective as possible and not to 'become sucked into'" (p. 262), a sentiment described earlier in Chapter 4

178 Parental Alienation as an IMD

under the section on splitting and triangulation. These thoughts were very recently amplified by Bernet et al. (2018) in actually discussing how to measure splitting within these family systems. It stands to reason what these practitioners, professionals and researchers have described with this article, since the higher the degree of splitting, the greater the pathology in the family system.

It has also been noted that there may well be multiple causes for PA, and tying these down has proven challenging, as Garber (2011) noted: "parental alienation is seldom exclusively the result of one parent's malicious actions toward or about the other" (p. 323). He indicated that often there was a hybrid of reasons and perhaps a so-called "perfect storm of relationship dynamics" (p. 323). There are other views besides Garber's on these environmental dynamics, too. In a piece dedicated to the prospect of sorting out what empirical studies have had to say about PA, Saini et al. (2012) explained that,

> the phenomenon can occur within intact, separated and divorced or custody-litigating families. However, parental alienation occurs more frequently in disrupted families and litigating cases (#5, 7, 16, 26), suggesting that parental conflict is a formative factor.
>
> (p. 428)

These authors went on to offer that, "the problem of PA is being raised increasingly more often in custody litigation matters during the past decade" (p. 428). In summary, they found, "it is apparent that PABs[1] are characteristics often associated with high-conflict separations and post-divorce parental disputes" (p. 434).

Three groups of literature were used to inform the tables that follow describing characteristics, symptoms and subdynamics, which under the right conditions create the development of the IMD pathological dynamic. These seminal pieces have been cited and referred to repeatedly in the literature. Other works include those that came to the fore after this author conducted a search on Google Scholar, which resulted in references that were either directly pertinent to the search terms or that had amassed numerous citations. In this case, the key phrases were "Alienation," "Parent Alienation Syndrome," "Alienated Child," and "Parental Alienation." In most cases, these search terms would trip related terms and vice versa. The first two pages of results were then reviewed, and those pieces were arguably the most referenced or directly relevant to the topic. The third group of work included articles, books, book chapters, and the like that were promising and contributed new insight or research, but these pieces had not been part of this body of literature long enough to be considered seminal or to accumulate a substantial number of citations. Seminal pieces were also divided into two groups: those directly relevant to the broader topic of the IMD under study and those that were related or that included the considerations described in background dimensional symptoms. With some exceptions, works either critical of IMDs and the range of considerations within PA, or at the fringe, were not included in this group of literature, e.g., Houchin et al., 2012; Pepiton et al., 2012. The controversies and differences of opinion about these phenomena have been well represented throughout this text, and there seemed to be no need to further revisit those matters here since this aspect of the text concerns how to identify IMDs, not whether they exist at all.

Though there is essentially general agreement about high-conflict cases as a recognized background symptom, Kelly and Johnston (2001) made a number of very useful contributions that clarify the dimensions spoken to in this reformulation of Parent Alienation. While they rejected the notion of an alienating parent causally influencing an alienated child (pp. 249–250), what they did describe were factors that lead to alienated children and characteristics of alienating parents:

> these include a set of background factors that directly and indirectly affect the child, specifically, a history of intense marital conflict; a humiliating separation; subsequent divorce conflict and litigation that can be fueled by professionals and extended kin; personality dispositions of each parent; and the age, cognitive capacity, and temperament of the child. A number of intervening variables can either moderate or intensify the child's response to these critical background factors, including parenting beliefs and behaviors, sibling relationships, and the child's own vulnerabilities within the family dynamics.
>
> (p. 254)

There are indeed important considerations that will be addressed, and still Kelly and Johnston (2001) reminded those in the field "that the presence of alienating processes and typical alienating behaviors of parents do not predict that a child will become alienated with any certainty" (p. 255). The phrasing here was quite interesting, with "alienating processes" and "typical alienating behaviors" both describing a set of accumulated variables with differing values on different dimensions of consideration, as will be addressed later in this piece. Prediction is another matter, too, since, among behavioral healthcare practitioners, professionals and researchers are typically better off addressing approximations or probabilities.

180 Parental Alienation as an IMD

Table 6.1 PA Background Dimensional Symptoms

---

1. High-conflict separation, divorce, or post-divorce case per Johnston (1994); the case is representative of the top 10% of ongoing cases; and the case exhibits:
   a. Failed mediations, or
   b. Parents who have undergone psychological assessments, or
   c. Parents who have had court-imposed settlements.

It would appear that from each vantage point the psychological surround for PA is created by the interactions between separating, divorcing or post-divorce family systems and legal systems, which in time produce a high-conflict case. As such, per the IMD dimensional descriptions offered in Chapter 4, the Background Dimensional Symptoms are those associated with a high-conflict case.

Individuals, Behaviors, and Experiences

Parent Characteristics

From what has been described above beyond the psychological surround and systems involved, a number of individuals initiate the processes that create a high-conflict divorce; and, in "as many as one third of entrenched parental disputes, several years after separation or divorce, one parent is clearly *the* high-conflict parent" (Kelly, 2003, p. 38). Kelly noted that it is very important for mediators and residence evaluators to differentiate these parents from others in their documentation and reports. Meanwhile, several years earlier, Kelly and Johnston (2001) noted that many times it was incorrect to assume that these dynamics were unleashed by only one parent, and that "many parents engage in indoctrinating behaviors, but only a small portion of children become alienated" (p. 249). Still, over a decade later Warshak (2015), as well as others, described that it was incorrect to assume by default that both parents contribute to the alienation process. He indicated that these singular parents had "disturbed and disturbing behavior . . . often characteristic of borderline and narcissistic psychopathology" (p. 237). What is more, Warshak (2015) cited a number of works emphasizing that these parents are more likely than rejected parents to display controlling and coercive behavior, poorly modulated rage, paranoid traits, and parenting styles that encourage enmeshed parent—child relationships, such as intrusive and infantilizing behaviors.

(p. 237)

This suggests that some parents are more vulnerable than others to the psychological surround that stresses produce, and under these stresses they engage in Alienating Behaviors (AB). Clawar and Rivlin (2013a) have also described what they have referred to as "Common Motivational Factors" (pp. 65–113). Kelly (2003, pp. 40–47) reported characteristics of parents involved in enduring disputes by describing partnership dynamics during and after the relationship, but more specifically individuals diagnosed with antisocial, borderline, and narcissistic personality disorders, as well as mental illnesses. She wrote that individuals with characteristics such as these increased the likelihood that these parents would remain enraged, ruminate about old grievances, want vengeance, and become locked into behaviors associated with entrenched conflicts for five or even ten years. She (2003) went on to report that these individuals were worse off after a divorce or separation than others:

When parents had serious psychological problems or character disorders at separation or at final divorce, as indicated on standardized measures, they were significantly more likely to have higher levels of psychological symptoms and problems two years after divorce.

(p. 43)

Parent Personality Traits

Accounts from a number of practitioners, professionals and researchers in the PA literature have highlighted concerns about pathological behavior and Alienating Parents (AP) suffering from personality disorders or traits. Godbout and Parent (2012) reported: "Consistent with these results, Baker (2006) described patterns of alienation that involve narcissistic personalities and violent behavior, among other characteristics observed in alienating parents" (p. 37). Ellis and Boyan (2010) stated, in short, that, "the alienating parent will typically have at least some symptoms of a personality disorder" (p. 224). Lorandos (2014), describing a series of authors' contributions in this area, noted the following: "Psychological disturbance, including histrionic, paranoid, and narcissistic personality disorders or characteristics, as well as

182 Parental Alienation as an IMD

psychosis, suicidal behavior, and substance abuse are common among alienator parents" (p. 330). He (2014) also reported MMPI-2 studies addressing characteristic profiles-associated parents who engaged in ABs, which essentially boiled down to index measures and indications of borderline functioning as well as the use of primitive defenses (p. 330). Saini et al. (2012) also wrote that five of the studies included in their review had assessed the possibility of psychological profiles for the AP and the Rejected Parent (RP): "In three of four studies, the findings supported the hypothesis that alienating parents tend to use more narcissistic and primitive defensives and had poor reality testing" (pp. 430–431). Likewise, Garber (2011) described a literature in which:

> Caregiver character pathology (Earley & Cushway, 2002; Mayseles & Scharf, 2009), co-parental conflict and separation (regardless of the legal status of the adult relationship) and divorce are also commonly identified among the stressors that can compromise intrafamilial roles and interpersonal boundaries.
>
> (p. 324)

Still, the theme of characterological symptoms pervaded other works, such as Howe and Covell (2014):

> Researchers often report the presence of various personality disorders in the alienating parent (Fidler & Bala, 2010; Gordon et al., 2008). Such parents do not react to the end of a marriage with sadness or a sense of loss; rather, they respond with profound rage, pathological hatred, and desire for revenge (Demby, 2009).
>
> (p. 157)

Furthermore, Kelly and Johnston (2001) had previously described the following:

> Both empirical research and clinical observation indicate that there is often significant pathology and anger in the parent encouraging the alienation of the child, including problems with boundaries and differentiation from the child, severe separation anxieties, impaired reality testing, and projective identifications with the child.
>
> (p. 258)

Lowenstein (2015) articulated that parents who engage in ABs "are suffering from a personality disorder. . . . Many will go to great lengths to demonize, abuse, denigrate, and seek to do everything to destroy the other parents credibility and relationship with the child" (p. 659). So we have one subset of parents who are more likely to be party to a high-conflict separation, divorce, or post-divorce custody dispute. Of this subset, there is yet another subset of parents who are more likely to engage in ABs with their child than others according to the available literature. Not only does the literature suggest that there are characteristics of parents who engage in ABs, but other researchers argue that parents can themselves be the recipients of ABs and that Rejected Parents (RPs) have certain characteristics, too. Once again, we have potential variables exclusion and inclusion criteria.

The notion of organizing beliefs within parents who engage in ABs was described by Kelly and Johnston (2001); these include communicating to their children that they do not need the other parent, that the RP is dangerous, and that "the rejected parent does not and has never loved or cared about the child" (pp. 257–258). Kelly and Johnston (2001, pp. 256, 259–260) wrote as well that other stresses and dynamics set ABs into motion and that other characteristics lead to alienating. For example, the separation may be experienced as deeply humiliating, and they may allow or engage new partners and extended kin as well as professionals to participate in the alienation process. Kelly and Johnston (2001) referred to what they described as common behaviors and organizing beliefs of the parent who engages in ABs and articulated these in the following paraphrased excerpts:

- Extreme negative views of the rejected parent espoused by the alienating parent "freely, angrily, and repeatedly expressed to the child."
- A "drumbeat" about the rejected parent's shortcomings "to erode the child's confidence in and love for the rejected parent and to create intolerable confusion."
- "[I]nnuendoes of sexual or child abuse or implications that the parent is dangerous in other ways." (p. 257–258)

More recently, other authors (Saini et al., 2012) have reviewed the research on these matters and found "at least eight studies . . . [have] produced a set of remarkably concordant findings, derived from researchers with diverse perspectives" (p. 430). These authors (2012) went on to note the following:

> Mothers, fathers, children, young adults, and counselors alike have been able to describe the explicit behaviors that may be perpetrated by one parent and have the capacity to distance, damage, or destroy a child's relationship with the other parent.
>
> (p. 430)

184 Parental Alienation as an IMD

Garber (2011, pp. 324–328) also described as a central concern the corruption of the RP's relationship with the child, which he conceived of as being manifested through parentification, adultification, and infantilization.

Rejected Parents

In 2001 Kelly and Johnston described some of the dynamics associated with an RP:

> Subsequently, these toddlers had difficulty with psychological separation and individuation from a needy, dependent primary parent, usually the mother. The other (rejected) parent was effectively pushed out of his parenting role or was inconsistently available to the young child.
>
> (p. 255)

They (2001, pp. 259–260) also indicated that RPs share certain characteristics as well, including passivity/withdrawal in the face of high conflict, counter-rejection of the child being alienated, being self-centered and immature, and having critical and demanding traits. These rejected parents also seem to suffer diminished empathy for the child being alienated. As Kelly and Johnston (2001) highlighted, these characteristics do not warrant the child's response, but it is still important to be aware of these characteristics. In the literature, there are other traits to describe the RP, but these are not described with the same consistency or prevalence as those of the AP and should be gauged differently. This does not seem to be spoken to consistently within the literature. In this author's experience as a practitioner, the pattern described in this portion of the literature fits about 50% of the time; on the other hand, the correspondence to the literature regarding APs was more robust and existed in 75–80% of this author's cases. Clearly aware of the experience base of those cited in this literature in this section of the text, this author would, of course, defer to those with more experience and access to sources of research should these colleagues have different experiences or knowledge. Describing this and other work, Godbout and Parent (2012) reported the following list of characteristics that RPs may possess:

> These behaviors include passivity in the face of conflict, rejection of the child in reaction to being rejected, a rigid parenting style, immaturity and egocentrism, placing exaggerated demands on the child, and displaying little empathy toward the child.
>
> (p. 37)

They also described, citing Johnston in 2003, that matters were made worse by "the lack of warm involvement from the rejected parent during the year following the separation and up to 2 years afterward" (p. 37). Saini et al. (2012) have also indicated that, largely per their research, "In litigated custody cases, fathers are more likely to be the rejected parent" (p. 428).

Gender Considerations

The matter of which gender tends to engage in more ABs naturally comes up in the process of identifying characteristics of APs and RPs, even with the different factors described earlier in this piece. Studies and anecdotal accounts vary, and it is plain that these sorts of binary considerations are basic and focused on heterosexual relationships. At the same time, it is necessary to be mindful of how these dynamics may play out among lesbian, gay, bisexual, transgendered and queer-questioning (LGBTQ) marriages and partnerships (Gates, 2012; Pleak, 2012; Green, 2006). Gardner revised his estimate in 2002 from largely describing women earlier in his work to reporting that the "ratio is now 50/50" (p. 198). Other studies, such as the one from Bala, Hunt, and McCarney (2010), note that, in "Canadian Court Cases 1989–2008," the ratio was one-third fathers to two-thirds mothers (p. 166). But these authors also noted that, "differences in gender are reflective of custody and child care arrangements rather than a maternal predisposition to alienate children" (p. 167). Parenthetically, this study also provided a remarkably sound metric for substantiated cases of PA when the matter came up as a topic in custody or divorce proceedings:

> It is notable that the rate of substantiation of alienation remained essentially unchanged, at 60 percent in 1989 to 1998, and 61 percent in 1999 to 2008, suggesting that the increase in cases does not reflect an increase in unsubstantiated claims being made.
>
> (p. 166)

Baker and Ben-Ami (2011) made a rather powerful set of observations about parents who engage in ABs as they related to psychological abuses:

> The psychological foundation of parental alienation—lack of empathy and inability to tolerate the child's separate needs and perceptions—is

also the foundation of psychological maltreatment and other forms of child maltreatment more generally.

(p. 473)

The review of the literature has supplied a remarkable set of concordant findings largely regarding APs, but it has also been informative about RPs as well. Though these parent characteristics may well not have equal weight in the literature when compared to one another, each parent's individual symptoms add to the whole of the building dynamic that may become the PA Interrelated Multidimensional Diagnosis.

Table 6.2 Parent Individual Dimensional Symptoms

Alienating Parent (AP)

---

1. The parent who engages in Alienating Behaviors (ABs) has a history that includes many of following events or possesses the following characteristics:
   (a) This parent has been diagnosed with a personality disorder or its traits that are largely in Cluster B of the *DSM* series,
   (b) This parent may have demonstrated a posture toward the failed relationship in which they experienced the separation or divorce as embarrassing or humiliating, and respond with reprisals toward their former partner,
   (c) Under the stress of the legal process (high conflict), this parent's prior level of functioning may regress and this parent may engage in less productive parenting behaviors, and
   (d) This parent may demonstrate difficulties with reality testing per practitioners involved with the case.

Rejected Parent (RP)

---

1. The parent who has Alienating Behaviors (ABs) acted out against them has a history that includes many of following events or possesses the following characteristics:
   (a) This parent tends to be passive and withdrawn, and this holds true in the face of conflict,
   (b) This parent may be less involved and more distant,
   (c) This parent may be immature, egocentric and somewhat rigid, and
   (d) This parent may act like a Counter Productive Parent (noun) or engage in Counter Productive Parenting (verb).

Parent Alienating Behaviors

The literature and research on these behaviors come from a wide variety of sources, and still it seems there are compelling retrospective sources that provide accounts largely in keeping with one another:

> Baker's research provides strong support for Gardner's concept of PAS. The adults alienated as children who Baker . . . interviewed gave graphic accounts of how the alienating parent had deceived and manipulated them into turning against the other parent.
>
> (Rand, 2010, p. 61)

In turn, the fundamental conceptualization by Warshak (2015) and others (Clawar & Rivlin, 2013a; Kelly & Johnston, 2001) has been that their clinical work and research revealed "programming as the primary dynamic behind a child's alienation, and they regard such programming as psychologically abusive" (p. 237). Clawar and Rivlin (2013a) described what they referred to as brainwashing, programming, and various pathological dynamics. They also labeled many of these techniques:

- " 'Who Me?' "
- "Middle-Man"
- "Circumstantial"
- " 'I Don't Know What's Wrong with Him' "
- "Ally"
- "Morality"
- "Threat of withdrawal-of-love"
- " 'I'm the only one who really loves you' "
- "You're an Endangered Species" (pp. 1–64)

Meanwhile, Howe and Covell described several patterns of behavior in their 2014 article, as paraphrased below:

- vilifying the target parent,
- inducing conflict with the child and the target parent,
- telling the child the target parent does not love the child,
- making unfounded allegations of abuse and neglect, and
- making unfounded allegations about dangerous behavior or criminal behavior against the target parent (p. 157).

These authors (2014) added that "the child's emotions are manipulated through becoming angry and eliciting a fear of rejection if the child shows any positive regard for the target parent . . . In essence, the child is taught to hate the target parent" (p. 157).

As the literature has developed on PA, there is a range of behaviors so consistent that back in 2001 Kelly and Johnston observed: "alienating behaviors on the part of the aligned parent have long been recognized as contributing to a child's alienated stance" (p. 257). However, as Drozd and Olesen (2004) and others have pointed out in more recent years, "Alienation is not a dichotomous variable to be noted as present or absent. It is a complex variable that ranges in several dimensions: from mild to extreme, from situational and temporary, to part of an ongoing pattern" (p. 77). This description of alienation brings up an important consideration. Not only does it clarify that alienation is not an all-or-nothing enterprise to examine, but, in this small excerpt, these authors have also presented characteristic considerations in describing complex phenomena that occur in the face of crises and have more than one pattern (Bütz, Schwinn, Chamberlain, 2019; Bütz, 2017). These patterns are, at the very least, challenging to consider as a dynamic. As Howe and Covell (2014) described, however, certain patterned ABs do characterize and provide evidence of the PA dynamic, or one part of the whole:

> To be considered evidence of parental alienation, however, these behaviors must be *intentional, strategic,* and involved consistent efforts to *create an alliance*[2] with the child against the other parent (Baker, 2010). The strategies used are assumed pathological because they reflect the five core manifestations of psychological maltreatment as defined by the American Professional Society on the Abuse of Children: spurning, terrorizing, isolating, corrupting, or exploiting, and denying emotional responsiveness (Binggeli, Hart, & Brassard, 2001).
>
> (p. 157)

By definition, these patterns of interacting with children, these ABs, are a pathological manifestation, even if considered just within that interrelated dimension. As will be described in a later section of this chapter, engaging in ABs with children is plainly a psychologically abusive act.

Although there are a number of different descriptions of ABs, thus far one of the most accessible listings appears to have been proffered by Baker and her colleagues, who have produced two measures: the Baker Alienation Questionnaire (Baker, Burkhard, & Albertson-Kelly, 2012) and the Baker Strategy Questionnaire (Baker & Ben-Ami, 2011). The Baker Alienation Questionnaire

(BAQ) inquires about the degree of alienation experienced by the child retrospectively and inquires whether the child has already been alienated. The Baker Strategy Questionnaire (BSQ) addresses the strategies employed to alienate in the past and potentially in the present. One measure addresses what has happened (BAQ), while the other addresses not only what has happened but what may be happening. The BSQ described nineteen different alienating strategies (Baker & Ben-Ami, 2011, p. 472) in a series described and endorsed in their research with adults who have reported being subject to PA as a child or adolescent. Their description of the most prominent strategies was described in the following manner: "The most commonly cited parental alienation strategy is denigration by one parent ('alienating parent') of the other parent ('targeted parent') in a consistent and total expression of negativity" (p. 473). They further elaborated that, "there are nearly limitless negative statements one parent can say about the other" (p. 474). Baker (2007) argued that such a strategy always involves the message that the targeted parent is *unsafe, unloving* and *unavailable*.[3] Baker and Ben-Ami (2011) also cited concerns about five forms of maltreatment described by the American Professional Society on the Abuse of Children (Binggeli, Hart, & Brassard, 2001). Baker and Ben-Ami's (2011) research on adults ultimately found the following percentages:

> 90% of the sample endorsed bad-mouthing, 80% of the sample endorsed confiding, 70% of the sample endorsed made communication difficult and required favoritism, 60% of the sample endorsed six items (limited contact, appeared upset when child was positive about the other parent, made the child choose, encouraged reliance on himself or herself, encouraged disregard of the other parent, and made it hard to be with the extended family of the other parent). Further, 50% of the sample endorsed said other parent was unsafe and fostered anger at the other parent; 40% of the sample endorsed three items (made communication difficult, said other parent was unloving, and asked child to keep secrets); and 30% or fewer endorsed the remaining items, including withheld or blocked messages, asked child to spy on the other parent, called other parent by first name, and referred to new spouse as Mom/Dad).
>
> (pp. 481–483)

Further, the work of Lopez, Iglesias, and Garcia (2014) has described a *Parental Alienation Gradient*, in which these authors have put forward strategies that were used repeatedly and differentially both by gender and according to whether or

190 Parental Alienation as an IMD

not the parent(s) had custody of the child. As one passage in the article described, these five alienation strategies were used in 90% of cases in their study[4]:

1. Failure to give information about the children,
2. Rewarding disrespectful behaviors in the child (of rejection toward the RP[5]),
3. Insulting or belittling the RP toward the children,
4. Making decisions without consulting the RP, and
5. Preventing Visits. (p. 224)

By adding the following strategies, 80% of alienating behaviors were captured within their study:

6. Interrogating child after visits to the RP,
7. Sharing personal/judicial information with the child,
8. Interfering in the child's symbolic contact with the RP,
9. Bindering telephone contact,
10. Seeking caregivers for the child alternative to the RP, and
11. Seeking accomplices for alienating (new partner, extended family, etc.). (p. 224)

Thus, according to this study these are the most readily apparent alienating strategies. Five alienating strategies were used differentially per gender (pp. 224–225). Women were described as employing these four primarily:

1. Frequently telephoning the children during their stay with the RP,
2. Seeking accomplices for alienating,
3. Frightening the children by telling them that the RP will cause them some kind of harm, and
4. Seeking medical and/or psychological reports as "evidence."

The strategies used by men were less involved, per their description: "Men, on the other hand, are more likely to use the strategy of *encouraging the children to challenge or defy the RP's[6] rules and authority*" (p. 225). As most literature showed, parents who engaged in ABs were largely those with custody, and the kinds of alienating strategies employed by those parents largely included the following kinds of behaviors:

1. Making decisions without consulting the RP,
2. Preventing visits,

Parental Alienation as an IMD **191**

3. Seeking caregivers for the child alternative to the RP,
4. Seeking accomplices for alienating, and
5. Encouraging the children to reject the RP's extended family. (p. 225)

Lopez, Iglesias, and Garcia (2014) highlighted the following critical point as a result of their studies:

> Indoctrinating children in the ways described here is a *complex, deliberate process* that requires *considerable persistence*, involving the *application of a group of premeditated and organized strategies applied with perseverance to achieve an aim.*[7]
>
> (p. 229)

The upshot of this statement, and their research, was that employing alienating strategies is both conscious and deliberate.

At its most basic level, PA plays out as two ends of a continuum, per Drozd and Olesen (2004): "alienating behavior can range from mildly belittling and hostile comments about the other parent to intense and active campaigns to rewrite history and to assert there is only evil in the ex-spouse" (p 78). The description above by Drozd and Olesen (2004) plainly articulated dimensions of alienating behavior—situational, pervasive and/or ongoing, and subtle as well as obvious (p. 79). Alienating behaviors set the PA dynamic into motion, and, therefore, these behaviors have an origin.

In PA, as has been discussed, the background and psychological surround are created with a family system when it is separating, divorcing, or

Table 6.3 Parent Alienating Behaviors—AP—Child/RP Subdynamic

1. Failing to give information about the children
2. Rewarding disrespectful behaviors in the child (of rejection toward the RP)[8]
3. Insulting or belittling the RP toward the children
4. Sharing personal/judicial information with or confiding in the child
5. Making decisions without consulting the RP
6. Preventing visits
7. Bindering telephone contact,
8. Interrogating child after visits to the RP
9. Interfering in the child's symbolic contact with the RP
10. Seeking caregivers for the child alternative to the RP
11. Seeking accomplices for alienating (new partner, extended family, etc.)

192 Parental Alienation as an IMD

addressing post-divorce custody matters and interacting with a legal system in a fashion that impacts one or both parents. In turn, a parent or parents become stressed to the point that they engage in ABs in order for the stirrings of the PA dynamic to begin. Often, the quality of these interactions may come on suddenly or be protracted, as will be described later as a potential subdynamic.

Child Characteristics

To begin with, as has hopefully been articulated throughout, these matters are best approached with a certain degree of clarity and caution since Kelly and Johnston (2001) have rightly pointed out that there is a considerable difference between a child who has suffered from alienation dynamics and one who has been subject to other related dynamics, including estrangement: "There are multiple reasons that children resist visitation, and only in very specific circumstances does this behavior qualify as alienation. These reasons include resistance rooted in **normal developmental processes**" (p. 251). The "normal developmental processes" that they go on to list include separation anxiety in young children, high-conflict transitions, responses to particular parenting styles, and others. Along these lines, they (2001) also differentiated what they referred to as children having an affinity toward one parent or children who are allied with another parent, with the latter differentiated in this way: "Unlike the alienated child, children allied with one parent generally do not completely reject the other parent or seek to terminate all contact. Most often, they express some ambivalence" (p. 252). So, again, when considering what appear to be symptoms of PA, the best interests of children are served when considerations are mindful of the factors discussed above as well as other potentials.

Age Matters

Ludolph and Bow (2012) addressed the complexities of alienation dynamics and went so far as to take issue with the idea that, "Infants and preschoolers living in families beset by alienation dynamics are widely thought to resist alienation because of their immature emotional and cognitive abilities" (p. 153). As they later described, "One of the few areas of discussion that has gone largely unchallenged is the idea that alienation is unusual in very young children" (p. 154). Still, it is their belief that, while this is generally true, "there is thinking in the alienation literature and related work in child development that would argue that they are affected by exposure to alienating ideas and behavior" (pp. 154–155). On the other hand, Kelly and Johnston (2001) described that children involved in alienation dynamics, in order to become alienated, require a certain level of "cognitive and emotional maturity" (p. 260). They explained that young children are simply not "useful allies or loyal soldiers; they fail to follow parental agendas" (p. 260). Moreover, these younger children "often forget their scripts, let go of their anger, and have inconsistencies in their presentations" (p. 260). While they argued that children at the age of seven or eight are on the brink, "Overall, the most common age range of the alienated child is from 9 to 15" (p. 260). Rand (2010) also cites Johnston and Campbell (1988), describing characteristics of such children and finding that, "Children ages nine to twelve were particularly vulnerable to forming such 'unholy alliances'" (p. 52). Meanwhile, Ludolph and Bow (2012) report that, "For most, the upper age boundary of the group seems to be defined as children under 7 or 8, in accord with the work of Kelly and Johnston (2001)" (p. 52). Similarly, Drozd and Olesen (2010) described that, "Alienated children are most commonly between the ages of 8 and 18, may be of either gender, and may reject either parent" (p. 258). Also, it was interesting to note that Baker, Burkhard, and Albertson-Kelly (2012) included children who were between, "6 and 17 years of age" (p. 181) in their pilot study to differentiate alienation dynamics. Ludolph and Bow (2012) did feel that children under the age of seven, and with some specificity, are impacted by PA dynamics in the short and long run. At the same time, regarding intervention, they described the following about children this young: "Virtually all authors who have written about alienation issues and dynamics in very young children have commented on the fact that their rejection of a parent remains fluctuating and their attitudes pliable" (p. 168). Thus, even if the PA dynamic has begun to take form, it is not as fixed or entrenched as it is in those children who have grown to the ages of seven, eight, nine and on into their teenage years.

A Child's Expression of Alienating Behaviors

Common behaviors for children who have been the recipients of ABs are, as paraphrased here from Kelly and Johnston (2001):

- Expressing hatred or intense dislike for the rejected parent disproportionate to the quality of the relationship,

194 Parental Alienation as an IMD

- Resisting visiting the rejected parent,
- Expressing allegations or stories that are mostly replicas of those offered by the parent engaging in alienating behaviors,
- Being empowered to treat the rejected parent with remarkable hostility and rudeness,
- Speaking in glowing terms about the parent engaging in alienating behaviors, and, oddly,
- Functioning well outside of the custody—parental situation. (pp. 262–263)

These authors (2001) reported that their view of the core behaviors demonstrated by these children were similar and that,

> By definition, the core feature of alienated children is the extreme disproportion between the child's perception and beliefs about the rejected parent and the actual history of the rejected parent's behaviors and the parent-child relationship.
>
> (p. 262)

They followed with a very specific list of behaviors that are paraphrased and quoted below, for brevity, in bullet points:

- The child feels free to "express hatred or intense dislike toward the rejected parent."
- The child will "demonize and vilify that parent, [and] often present trivial reasons to justify their hatred."
- The child is not reticent or inhibited in "broadcasting the perceived shortcomings of the parent[9] to others."
- The child's behavior tends to be "baffling to the rejected parent, extended family and other adults knowledgeable about the prior parent—child relationship."
- The child will also have "strongly expressed resistance to visiting the rejected parent, and in some extreme cases, an absolute refusal."
- The child will express the wish to "unilaterally terminate the parent–child relationship."
- The child will, in common parlance, "want only to talk to lawyers who represent their viewpoint and to those custody evaluators and judges whom they believe will fully support their efforts to terminate the parent–child relationship."
- The child's reports of shortcomings are "replicas or slight variants of the aligned parents' allegations and stories."

- These children generally tend to sound "very rehearsed, wooden, brittle, and frequently use adult words or phrases."
- The child appears to be enjoying her- or himself, and "there is no obvious regret."
- The child has been "given permission to be powerful and to be hostile or rude toward the rejected parent, grandparents, and other relatives."
- The child addresses the alienating/aligned parent by "often idealiz[ing] or speaking glowingly of the aligned parent as an adult and parent."
- The child may also report that the alienating/aligned parent has been "suffering, has been harmed economically and emotionally by the rejected parent." (pp. 262–263)

Kelly and Johnston (2001, p. 263) went on to raise some other matters that are not so apparent in such cases: these children may appear to function in a so-called normal fashion, but closer examination reveals significant difficulties, including simplistic thinking in binary terms, rigid unforgiving views, and problems with authority. In addition, they prefer to be in regular, if not constant, contact with the parent who has engaged in ABs, and then "they whisper hostile observations about the rejected parent's words, behaviors, meals and personality" (p. 263). Drozd and Olesen (2010) have also described children who persistently express strong negative feelings (such as anger, hatred, contempt, and fear) and beliefs about the RP that are unreasonable and significantly disproportionate to the child's actual previous experience with the Rejected Parent (p. 258). These beliefs are typically irrational, distorted or exaggerated (p. 258). Howe and Covell (2014) found that definitive detection of a change in the child's attitude is described through animosity, attitudes, and beliefs toward the RP:

> Parental alienation is also detected through the child's expressed attitudes and beliefs (Bernet, 2008; Evans, 2006). The child will express a false belief that the target parent is dangerous and must be avoided; in fact, that the parent is "all bad." . . . But pure animosity is characteristic of children who have been subjected to parental alienating behaviors; these children have been taught to hate.
>
> (p. 158).

They added that, "the child also expresses no remorse about behaving badly toward the target parent, behavior that includes imitating the verbal denigration modeled by the alienating parent" (p. 158). Thus, and this will be important to recognize in the pages that follow, there is a noteworthy

196 Parental Alienation as an IMD

change, a shift, in the child. References such as these in the PA literature are replete and go back in the contemporary literature to the late '70s and early '80s.

Not All Transformations Are Good: Identification With the Aggressor, Internalized Oppression, and PA

Up to this point in the text this author has been charging along describing the case made in the PA literature for the mounting evidence of a consistent set of dimensional symptoms. For a moment, however, let us step back to the more reflective tone struck in earlier chapters. This author had been struggling with just how to present this portion of the book, and in a way that was just slightly outside of his consciousness. It was a nagging and unsettling experience. Nevertheless, the writing continued, expressing the ideas, research, and thoughts of others, as is required with dutiful scholarship. One characteristic or symptom after the other was laid down in an effort to describe the processes involved with an Interrelated Multidimensional Diagnosis. Even so, this internal struggle persisted in the background until this author noticed that the rough draft of this chapter was without the child's individual dimensional symptoms table. It was bewildering. This author thought about it and was greeted with the commonly uncompromising tone of his superego: "How was it I overlooked something like that?" It was troubling, and, though it was difficult material to explain, there was really no quarter to be granted if these ideas were not expressed correctly. This author feared misleading other practitioners, professionals, and researchers, which was in reality an ongoing concern throughout. These fears and others gave way to concerns about further confusing matters to the detriment of these children and families.

So this author reviewed the list of characteristics and symptoms that had been put together for the Child–RP Subdynamic, which described a child's *alienating behaviors* based on the literature, and attended to descriptive clarity as well as frequency of reference. As this author read that list, there was a dawning awareness that roughly half to a third of these were neither actions nor behaviors, but attributes: a change in the state of the child amidst the throes of the pressures and stresses involved when an AP continues to engage in ABs directed at the child and the Rejected Parent. All at once it was clear, "That's where the child's individual dimensional symptoms had gone." While interesting, that was still a rather banal matter to get so wound up about. It was, however, not just that these were attributes that had been overlooked among actions and behaviors described by many others. These attributes marked a change, a transformation in the child's state; that is when the child's attributes shifted from the ability to have an ongoing relationship with both parents to a child who aligned with only one parent (AP) and began to actively reject the other parent (RP).

The child's state shifted from a transformative state that reflected the pressures and stresses described by the psychological surround of PA and the AP's ABs, and punctuated to a new steady state when the child became an *alienated child (ac)*.[10] In turn, the *ac*'s attributes and characteristics noticeably changed per the account of those who had known the child. Actions and behaviors also changed after this point, observably, as described in the literature on the form of children's *alienating behaviors (abs)*. A notable change in the child preceded a change in the child's actions and behaviors. Thus, the child transformed from one capable of loving interpersonal relationships with both parents to a new form, an altered form, an *ac*.

This insight was disturbing enough, but what came next was even more distressing. One insight often leads to others. Perhaps this is debatable, but in this author's view it is inherent in such processes. When the jolt from one insight strikes, it also engenders thoughts about the past as well. These thoughts led back to graduate work. There was an unusually clear case in which a young child had been abused, and the quality of the metaphor this child chose to work with in play therapy helped this author to better understand how abuse alters the quality of these children's psyches (Bütz, 1993a):

> The same can be said of the individual who has been abused; abuse is often characterized by several intrapsychic disturbances that include a loss of self, dissociative states during and after the trauma (Silber, 1979), and the delayed onset of overwhelming emotions that frequently are repressed for months, years.
>
> (p. 427)

There were other descriptors, too, in that work that roiled over and over in this author's mind until the piece was read again in an attempt to grapple with what was so unsettling about the realization that children change in PA when they become an *ac*, and that change is followed by a change in their actions and behavior (*abs*):

> Before the abuse, the individual was psychically whole; now a great loss of psychic energy occurs through defensive adaptation to the trauma, whereas previously the psyche may have been unimpinged by such

extreme adaptive measures. In the terminology of analytical psychology, the ego before trauma is fairly intact and therefore contains a limited amount of material in the personal unconscious that must be reintegrated and differentiated. After trauma, the ego is overwhelmed and must actively repress traumatic memories into the personal unconscious. This repression requires a loss of psychic energy and fragmentation of the once essentially whole being. . . . In both cases, the previous being has been destroyed, and replaced by a new and less desirable form.

(p. 428)

The child in play therapy had lost the previous self and was painfully aware that a less desirable form was walking around hollow, agitated, or lifeless, and thus was rigid in managing the new form. As it turned out, the child worked through the therapeutic process and was able to take back aspects of the former self, but was also able to move beyond prior limitations in some rather remarkable ways.

It was so extraordinary, and the case material so rich, that this author used it as the topic for a paper in a third-year graduate class on the work of Carl Jung. To this author's surprise, his professor for that course on Analytical Psychology, Dr. Eduardo Duran, not only provided it a fine grade but also encouraged the paper's publication. It was equally astonishing when the paper was published after only being submitted to one journal (Bütz, 1993a). The whole of this experience drove home how profoundly lives may be impacted by abuse, and at the same time how even a modicum of reasonable therapeutic intervention can activate the capacity for adaptive change and resilience. A related thought followed the insight above, this one more penetrating than the last and equally profound. In recent weeks, this author had been working on the final chapter for the book, and as the reader will see, the case is made for several phenomena to be put forward as potential IMDs for further study. One such phenomenon described later on is Intergenerational Trauma, and work on this topic brought back the work of Dr. Duran. He had written on the concept of Intergenerational Trauma for many years (Duran & Duran 1995; Duran, 1990) and in 2006 he seemed to have dusted off the aforementioned article (Bütz, 1993a) and used it as a way to describe the concept of Internalized Oppression as "identification with the aggressor" (pp. 17–20). The reader is encouraged to attend closely to the words he used to introduce the discussion.

One impact of the awareness of historical trauma is the notion of internalized oppression, or as it was known previously, identification with the aggressor (Freud, 1967). Identification with the aggressor is a phenomenon observed in clinical settings in which the patient presents with physical, psychological, epistemic, and cultural violence, and the victim identifies with the perpetrator in a variety of ways.

(p. 17)

Having gone over these words just weeks earlier, again this author was struck by the comparisons that held between identification with the aggressor, internalized oppression, and the experience of a child in the turmoil of Parental Alienation. In fact, to describe abuse, Anna Freud (2018/1936b) had written an entire piece entitled "Identification with the Aggressor" back in 1936 (pp. 109–121). Parenthetically, though Dr. Duran's reference was to 1967, it was only just last year that Routledge had republished the work by Freud. This author was well aware of this literature but was not certain why it had not come into focus sooner (Freud, 2018/1936b):

A child introjects some characteristic of an anxiety object and so assimilates an anxiety experience which he has just undergone. Here, the mechanism of identification or introjection is combined with a second important mechanism. By impersonating the aggressor, assuming his attributes or imitating his aggression, the child transforms himself from the person threatened into the person who makes the threat.

(p. 113)

While the concept of identification with the aggressor is well known in the literature on child abuse and neglect, it has not been a central feature of the discussion in PA with a few exceptions that this author found in a subsequent literature search (Siracusano et al., 2015; Meister, 2003). It was this distinction, this clarification, that assisted this author in unraveling the transformed attributes of a child who comes to suffer as an *ac*, that is after succumbing to the pressures and associated stressors that come with the AP's Alienating Behaviors. It follows that now these tables may be offered in order to clarify the differences between the attributes of the child and the child's *alienating behaviors (abs)*.

Table 6.4 Child Individual Dimensional Symptoms

1. The child is between the ages of eight and sixteen, +/- 1 year.
2. The child has been observed to noticeably change, and their behavior and statements (described in the subdynamic) tend to confound the RP, extended family, and others who knew the prior quality of the child–RP attachment.
3. The child appears to be superficially happy and expresses no ambivalence or regret about their actions.
4. The child idealizes the AP in actions and words in a disproportionate fashion, with an inability to entertain ideas and opinions outside of the AP's sphere of influence.

Table 6.5 Child Alienating Behaviors (*abs*)—Child–RP Subdynamic

1. The child feels free to openly state hatred toward the RP and does so.
2. The child has been permitted by the AP to engage in hostile or rude behavior toward the RP and the RP's extended family—there are no bounds to these expressions.
3. These children tend to sound coached and/or have stilted accounts, as well as employ adult phrases or words often used by the AP.
4. The child's reports of shortcomings the RP allegedly possesses are imitations, or slightly different variations, of those made by the AP.
5. The child is not reticent or inhibited in statements made about the RP.
6. The child will denigrate the RP for trivial reasons to justify hatred.
7. The child resists or refuses visits with the RP.
8. The child will singly express the wish to terminate relationship with the RP.
9. The child may also report openly that the AP has been harmed by the RP.
10. The child expresses the desire to speak to the lawyers or the judge about her or his wishes, with the belief that these wishes will be granted.

Triage, Agreement, and What's in a Name

The politics of a father's rights versus a mother's rights has been one of the stumbling blocks in getting down to clear notions about Parental Alienation. However, the lack of clarity in examining the phenomenon may well be because the path to triage has not been established either and is clouded by these politics. A level of triage would allow clinicians to address the symptoms that are most obvious first, second and so on, thus ruling out certain conditions and progressing forward with others. In 2010, Meier essentially argued this point mightily, calling for clarity by stating first what would appear to be clinical common sense:

> even a cursory look at the etiology and application of alienation theory indicates that its current significance is inseparable from its utility as a means for discrediting claims of abuse. Moreover, as the following discussion suggests, alienation's focus on the parent—child relationship is intrinsically incompatible with the focus on safety and risk called for when dealing with abuse. Treating parental alienation as an equivalent concern to abuse in custody-litigating families thus inherently devalues abuse allegations, while over-valuing a claim that is most often used to deflect responsibility for abuse. It is simply not possible or appropriate to seek a middle ground between reality and denial, which is the hallmark of many cases with competing abuse and alienation claims.
>
> (p. 221)

Meier made clear that first things must come first, and that is to separate out abuses given in the known literature since their impacts on children and adolescents are well known (such as matters involving estrangement, denigration, and others). Then, as discussed above, these first steps also include recognizing the contributions of background and environmental forces on family systems via legal systems, parent characteristics, ABs, child symptom variables and ultimately *abs* produced by children. These conditions differentiate PA from other family and systems dynamics, which may be viewed again as variable exclusion criteria.

As described in Chapter 3, there have been four main terms in the PA literature for arguably the same phenomenon, and, in addition to the opinions described; there are still other views and other voices on PA and related phenomena. As Rand (2010) has described, there are three, so to speak, broader camps on these matters. Within the literature there are those who accept Gardner's conceptualization of PAS and/or related conceptualizations, as was discussed above; those who describe what are referred to as ACs, referencing the work of a task force put together by Johnston and Kelly (2004; Kelly and Johnston, 2001) (Rand, 2010, pp. 51–53); and those described by Rand (2010) as being focused on feminism and child advocacy, whose concerns are for the potential of sexual abuse (pp. 53–55). Rather than a reformulation of PA, Rand (2010) described the latter group's orientation: "there is no such thing as PAS, PA, or pathological alienation as it is also called. All alienation is a matter of justified estrangement" (p. 54). In addition, there are those who have used the term PA, but have really described the concept of an AC, such as the proponents of the diagnosis in the *DSM-5* (Bernet & Baker, 2013; Pepiton, Alvis, & Allen, 2012). This author's impression of the utility of the concept of an AC and the *DSM-5* group's work has been commented upon earlier in Chapter 3.

It appears that when these base considerations are addressed, professional providers are able to agree upon the broader conceptual framework of Parental Alienation. Rueda (2004) has, for example, suggested that there has been agreement about these concepts when a knowledgeable group of professionals is involved. Rueda conducted a study in which the independent variable was symptoms of PA or PAS and the dependent variable was a professional's perception of it (p. 391). The study was conducted with psychiatrists, psychologists, and custody evaluators who were experts in child custody and PA or Parent Alienation Syndrome. This group was asked to review five case scenarios (p. 394), and, ultimately, Rueda concluded the following: "Based on the surveys returned, 93% of the respondents agreed with the assessment of parental alienation syndrome in all five cases. However, this study failed to firmly differentiate PAS from parental alienation[11]" (p. 400). In addition, back in 2004 when Rueda's article was written, he noted that "PAS is admissible in 21 states, for a total of 70 courts throughout the nation" (p. 392). Add to this Warshak (2015), who reported on "a survey that reported 98% agreement 'in support of the basic tenet of parental alienation: children can be manipulated by one parent to reject the other parent who does not deserve to be rejected'" (p. 237). There is indeed a building consensus here, and, where matters of PA are concerned, there is no need for any rush to judgment. However, as previously noted, and as will be discussed shortly, courts do delay action on these cases and when this occurs are certainly a contributing factor. As with FDBP, asserting PA should not be made without a solid and thorough assessment of the situation: "Gardner (1998) clearly stated, 'A proper PAS evaluation rests on the foundation of a solid and thorough child-custody assessment. An evaluation of a family embroiled in a child-custody dispute is quite complex' (p. 221)" (Rand, 2010, pp. 60–61). Rand (2010), again, has made an important distinction: "A key issue in the controversy has to do with holding a parent responsible for supporting, influencing, or encouraging a child to reject the other parent" (p. 65).

The Psychological Surround and the Optional Family–Legal System Subdynamic

Environmental stresses in these cases are largely associated with high-conflict divorces or custody disputes, which provoke one or both parents to engage in behaviors that alienate the child from a parent. This matter has been touched on a number of times, and further contemplations have suggested that there is a third subdynamic potentially at work in these cases as well, that is the aggravating and/or exacerbating effects of an unresponsive court and/or legal system that perpetuates the suffering of these children and these families with protracted evaluations, interventions and the setting of hearings. As noted in Chapter 1, but condensed here, Gardner's views on these matters were unmistakable in his 2001 article:

> The usual duration of such cases that have come to my attention has been 2 to 3 years between the time of the initiation of the dispute and the time of the court's decision. By that time, the children are significantly older and the decision is made on the basis of data that may no longer be relevant. All of this works for the alienator, because the more time the alienator has to access the children, the more deeply entrenched will become the PAS campaign of denigration.
>
> (p. 67)

As will be discussed further in Chapter 8, Warshak (2015) espoused similar views, though they were directed at the courts' limited intervention: "Case studies and clinical experience suggest that psychotherapy while children remain under the care of their favored parent is unlikely to repair damaged parent—child relationships and may make things worse" (p. 243). He also reported the following:

> [I]f one of more attempts with psychotherapy have already failed to remedy the problem, if the aligned parent is likely to sabotage treatment, and if the child is empowered to avoid contact with the rejected parent, the court should understand that ordering another round of psychotherapy without changing the amount of contact the child has with each parent is unlikely to remedy the problem and may postpone effective intervention until it is too late.
>
> (p. 243)

Therefore, a perpetuating subdynamic is proposed as an optional table that may be included to address these matters and is designed to offer additional weight to the considerations about different measures and the tables above as well as the variables on the IMD Inventory—PA©.

204 Parental Alienation as an IMD

Table 6.6 Family–Legal Systems Optional Subdynamic

1. Court's orders and actions designate the case as high conflict.
2. There have been repeated baseless vexatious motions that limit the alleged RP's contact, or an order by the AP for a change in the custody or parenting plan to limit the alleged RP's contact.
3. PA has been raised as a concern in the case, or there has been a finding from a practitioner or professional of PA.
4. The alleged AP continues to engage in ABs toward RP.
5. The alleged *ac* engages in *abs*.
6. No guardian ad litem, parenting coordinator, or special magistrate has been assigned to the case to ensure more regular monitoring or contact with the Court or its representatives.
7. The case has been before the Court for six months or more, with matters #3 and #4 stated repeatedly, and there have been no actions by the Court to address these matters.
8. Therapeutic efforts ordered are not clearly focused on resolving PA and the child or children's reunification with the RP.
9. After repeated efforts at #2, the alleged AP attempts to relocate the child.
10. After one year or more with three or more of the follow indicators (#1–5 and #8), the Court has not created a list of sanctions for the alleged AP to deter the ABs.

Finally, the reader is asked to again consider the Adoption and Safe Families Act (U.S. Department of Health and Human Services, 1997), wherein there is a time limit for child protective matters, a time limit children in PA cases are not afforded. It is not surprising then that the fundamental psychological surround provoking the stresses that produce the pathological interpersonal dynamic described by PA remain an active consideration in these cases. Time is one of the key issues to consider in these cases, since a PA IMD does gain momentum and spread across family systems and communities if not met with the boundaries and limitations supplied by legal systems. If our legal systems do not set appropriate boundaries and limitations in these cases, these systems may have not just an aggravating influence but a contributory and participatory influence on these family systems.

Counter Productive Parenting, Parental Denigration, Sabotage, and Estrangement

There have been other matters debated, too, which are similar to PA but not consistent with the progressive formulations noted above. Matters that describe different but related phenomena that are more and less detrimental to the health and welfare of the children are involved in these cases. Parental Denigration was offered by Rowen and Emery (2014) to refer to dynamics related to PA, and perhaps this term may better serve as a description of precursor phenomena since, "We define parental denigration as the behavior of one parent disparaging or speaking negatively about the other parent in front of their children" (p. 165). Denigration does not convey the same conditions as PA, since, for the reasons described above, parents' behavior must exceed the threshold of simply disparaging the other parent: "In the child custody literature, when one parent continuously and directly demeans the other to their children, it is generally termed 'parental alienation'" (2014, p. 166). But this statement does not hold; and what Rowen and Emery have described are fundamentally alienating statements that lack the specificity of Alienating Behaviors. Further, a limited number of alienating strategies crossed over in their concept of denigration (p. 171), as well as other limitations in the cases presented (pp. 174–175). The term *Parental Denigration* (PD) does, however, provide a ready subthreshold term that could serve as one of several variable exclusionary criteria, criteria that describe active alienating statements absent ABs and/or not meriting the designation Parental Alienation.

Counter Productive Parenting and Parental Sabotage

In Chapter 4, Meier (2010) had described her concerns about a variety of characteristics and symptoms related to PA as well as the unenviable but robust work that Drozd and Olesen (2004) had done to in order to create a Decision Tree that clarifies these and related phenomena for practitioners. The work that Drozd and Olesen (2004, 2010) put forward added a number of useful terms to this discussion, albeit there was some confusion about just how to define or make use of the terms *Counter Productive Parenting* (CPP) and *Parental Sabotage* (PS), as expressed in Chapter 4. Further, this author would argue that CPP's best use is both as a noun and a verb, as is suggested in Table 6.2, akin to nouns like AP and Rejected Parent. Here, more detail should be added to these descriptions to perhaps further

206 Parental Alienation as an IMD

explain Drozd and Olesen's apparent intentions. Revisiting their 2004 article, we have the following statement:

> Some mothers, often ones with serious psychopathology, use their children to avenge the abuse they have suffered. In rare instances, a victim-mother may with malice and intent sabotage her child's relationship with the abuser (frequently the father) out of rage. Again, this is not the norm in our clinical experience. Cases in which the mother's intent is malicious and in which she is acting out of revenge are labeled as *sabotaging*. Sabotaging mothers and counter productive protective mothers are different in terms of their intent. The mother whose intent is to protect her child, even if her fear causes her to do it badly, would be called counter productive.
>
> Some mothers are blamed for sabotaging (mislabeled as alienating behaviors) their children's relationships with their fathers when they intend to protect their children. Their intent is protection, not revenge. A significant problem occurs when evaluators fail to thoroughly explore the factors operating in the particular family: the abuse hypothesis as well as the specific types of parenting. Mistaking one type of interference with the child's access to the other parent for another type can have serious and pernicious effects.
>
> (p. 96)

As noted earlier, Drozd and Olesen's discussion about their Decision Tree included a query to the reader in their concluding remarks, "Is it abuse, alienation and/or estrangement?"

> This Decision Tree offers the field of child custody an alternative approach to the either-or thinking that sometimes characterizes debates about abuse and alienation in divorcing families. *Alienation* and *abuse* are not dichotomous variables; instead, they may occur across continua. We have also provided the reader of this article an invitation to use new terms to explain the reasons that any given child might reject a parent: alienation, in non-abuse cases, and estrangement, sabotaging, and counter productive parenting in cases where there is abuse.
>
> (pp. 99–100)

Attempting to discern their meaning earlier, this author felt as though they were considering a continuum that had on one end abusive behaviors and at the other end non-abusive behaviors. A reproduction of the particular portion of the Decision Tree that has been of interest would be useful here.

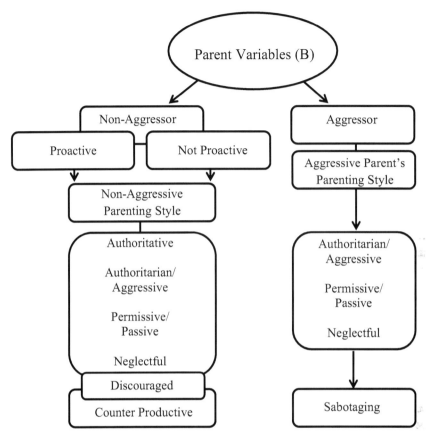

Figure 6.1 A Branch of Drozd and Olesen's Decision Tree.

Source: Drozd and Olesen, reproduced by M. R. Bütz. Permission Granted 11/7/19 by Taylor & Francis.

Reviewing Figure 6.1 above, it may be seen that what Drozd and Olesen attempt to communicate is the fact that there are two different parenting styles exemplified by aggressive and non-aggressive parents, who engage in behaviors that differ between being active (PS) and re-active (CPP). In turn, PS struck this author as less problematic than PA, and PE was more problematic than either PA or PS, which seems to occupy the space along the continuum where abuse—physical, psychological, sexual, or neglect—has been alleged but not substantiated. Parental Denigration falls below the threshold for all three, PA occupies the space of psychological abuse, while PE occupies the space that would justify a child's rejection, and PS appears to occupy the space in between PD and Parental Alienation.

Reflecting on Drozd and Olesen's work in 2004 again, PS was described as follows, and the reader should take particular note that the descriptor "abusive family", which suggested that PS is most reasonably described as occupying a space along the continuum between PD and PA:

> We have found that the aggressor parent may engage in behavior designed to sabotage the child's relationship with the victim parent. The aggressor takes advantage of the victim parent's vulnerabilities and convinces the child or children in the family that the victim parent is not a good parent and that he, the aggressor, has the power and can do best for the children. This behavior formerly may have been called alienating behavior, though inasmuch as it occurs in the context of an abusive family, we are calling it *sabotaging* behavior.
>
> (p. 88)

Still, it is unclear if abuse is alleged or substantiated per their descriptions.

Then, we have Drozd and Olesen's (2004) description of CPP, and for all intents and purposes this is reactive behavior, seemingly responding to PD, PS, PA or Parental Estrangement. These are behaviors that are enacted, albeit by the RP or the non-abusive parent:

> *Victim parent may engage in counter productive protective parenting.* Victim parents may conduct themselves in ways that result in the child further rejecting the abusive parent. This behavior by the victim is similar to the abuser's sabotaging behavior inasmuch as both may involve an authoritarian style of parenting as well as a child's rejection of a parent (see Figure 17). The two are dissimilar inasmuch as the non-aggressive parent's behavior not only may involve an authoritarian parenting style, but it also may be a manifestation of the victim parent's fear of the abuser.
>
> (p. 95)

CPP is an important consideration all by itself, be it used as a noun or a verb, since in this condition the parent's response is maladaptive, too, and yet he or she is not the Alienating Parent. Even so, in the fray of such cases it may be a challenging determination to make for practitioners and professionals.

Parental Estrangement

Parental Estrangement has served as a large contextual factor that is equally binary in comparison with the criteria above and that includes the distinction of differentiating PA from PE as an exclusion criterion (Bütz, Evans, & Webber-Dereszynski, 2009, pp. 36–37; Rogers, 2004). In fact, it also may prove to be an IMD, as will be discussed in Chapter 8. Citing Kelly and Johnston, Ludolph and Bow (2012) described the dynamics of "'estrangement' [as] a child's rejection of a parent who is *psychologically* or *physically abusive, neglectful*, absent or *otherwise realistically incompetent*[12] in his or her parenting" (p. 154). Several authors have also highlighted how estranged parents have engaged in behaviors, such as abuses and neglect, that served to alienate or estrange them from their children (Gardner, 2001; Kelly & Johnston, 2001). In turn, "the child's animosity may be justified, and so the parental alienation syndrome *explanation for the child's hostility is not applicable*" (Gardner, 2001, p. 61).[13] It should be added that PE is no minor matter and is more regularly encountered with forms of abandonment, abuse, intimate partner violence and neglect, and that it is more prevalent and more damaging than PA. In differentiating it from PS, however, the literature is mixed on the need for substantiated abuses, neglect, intimate partner violence, or abandonment. Restraining orders are often readily available regardless of the quality of the evidence or even the capacity to challenge the allegation, which Gardner (2001), as well as many others, has described in the literature. When this author speaks of PE herein, substantiated evidence is implied, while the use of the designation PS does not connote this level of verification.

Clearly, there are valid reasons for a child to be estranged from, or to reject, a parent, and these should be conceptualized as exclusion criteria (Saini et al., 2012; Garber, 2011). At the same time, it is clear that the greater complexity involved with these cases requires investigations by specialists to tease apart alienation from estrangement cases (Walker & Shapiro, 2010, p. 273; Drozd & Olesen, 2010, p. 258).

> Alienated children are distinguished from children and adolescents who experienced child abuse or violence in the family toward the other parent or themselves, and have become emotionally estranged from that parent and/or traumatized and do not want continued contact
> (J.B. Kelly, April 23, 2009).

As will be touched on in Chapter 8, therapeutic activities with the aim of reuniting children with parents from whom they have been estranged may well require more skill on the part of the professionals and practitioners involved. It is a much more common problem than Parental Alienation. There is good reason for an estranged child to distrust such a parent's intentions. Forcing a child to reunify with an estranged parent, who in a number of cases has made

210 Parental Alienation as an IMD

no effort to better her or his behaviors, strikes this author as an abusive act in and of itself. Fundamentally, if these kinds of "re-unification" interventions are going on, professionals and practitioners are both failing these children and colluding with the estranged parent, unless they have engaged in the kind of extensive interventions often described in many child protection family re-unification plans *beforehand*. These and other matters suggest that PE poses an even greater danger to the health and welfare of children than Parental Alienation.

What Is, and What Is Not, Parental Alienation?

In regard to the proposition that PA is a pathological dynamic composed of individual and systems interactions, Drozd and Olesen supplied a very interesting description in their article from 2004 on the topic:

> Said another way, the analysis of alienation is not two dimensional and certainly not dichotomous; rather, it is multi-dimensional and should be reported as such. Discussions of these continua are found in Lee and Olesen (2001), Kelly and Johnston (2001), Sullivan and Kelly (2001), and Johnston, Walters, and Friedlander (2001).
>
> (p. 78)

In fact, many writing on this topic refer to PA in a similar fashion. A multidimensional description is a regular part of what these authors and theorists struggle to bring forward with clarity amid the reductionistic leanings of others in the field who voice skepticism about the whole enterprise (Ertelt & Van Dyke, 2013; Houchin et al., 2012). Saini et al. (2012) had this to offer after carefully reviewing thirty-nine papers and dissertations that fit the characteristics they sought in an empirical review of the literature on the topic:

> Almost all viewed it as a multidimensional construct. In some studies there was no consensus, and in other studies the majority did not endorse PAS as a syndrome meeting either Frye or Daubert standards for admission as a diagnosis by an expert witness.
>
> (p. 433)

Although there are exceptions to every rule, as described above, the vast majority of PA cases are described in association with either a high-conflict separation, divorce or post-divorce custody dispute or involvement with child protective services (Schwartz, 2015; Ludolph & Bow, 2012; Baker, Burkhard, & Albertson-Kelly, 2012; Garber, 2011; Jaffe, Ashbourne, & Mamo, 2010; Rueda, 2004; Kelly & Johnston, 2001). Authors and researchers in this area have sounded cautions about identifying Parental Alienation. While somewhat casual in tone, the point made by Baker, Burkhard, and Albertson-Kelly (2012) merits contemplation: "Of course, identifying alienation is just the first step in what is a complex undertaking fraught with its own controversies and concerns" (p. 180). That is, complexities arise as one goes about the task of collecting clinical data, findings and information in a neutral fashion (Reamer, 2018; Glancy et al., 2015: Herlihy & Corey, 2014; American Psychological Association, 2010). This diagnosis occurs within a particular environment, and this background and/or psychological surround serves to open the door for considering what is, and what is not, Parental Alienation.

So, to be quite clear on these points, it is this author's view on these matters that PA has been described, first, as a multidimensional construct emanating in most cases from high-conflict divorces or disputes regarding custody, parenting plans or parenting time. Second, it is a dynamic that arises out of the stresses and demands of the environment created by a family system's interactions with a legal system. Third, this process is put into motion by a parent's or the parents' response to these stresses and demands. Fourth, children who have certain characteristics experience interactions with a parent or parents who attempt to entrain the child to engage in Alienating Behaviors. Fifth, the child might respond in kind at a certain level of intensity. Sixth, if this holds true, the PA pathological dynamic manifests. But, as noted earlier, the diagnosis and/or pathology *does not lie in the child; the child's behavior is symptomatic of the pathological dynamic.* These individuals and systems are engaged with environmental contingencies that produce enough stress to create this degree of dynamic pathology, and in some cases legal systems perpetuate it (see Table 6.6). Without getting into intervention at this point (see Chapter 8), it has repeatedly been shown that, if the environmental contingencies are changed, the pathology subsides (Warshak, 2015; Gardner, 2001, 2002).

Psychological Abuse

No treatment of what is, and what is not, PA would be reasonably inclusive without considering the matter of psychological abuse, or what is often termed *emotional abuse* in the literature. While the background or the psychological surround has been used to describe the conditions that set these dynamics in motion, their outcome when PA is created is the pathological psychological abuse of the child or children involved. It is hard to imagine that the purposive mistreatment of a child by a parent to achieve a certain result in court is not both a pathological dynamic and psychological abuse. As Kelly and Johnston (2001) have stated, "Whether such parents are aware of the negative impact on the child, these behaviors of the aligned parents (and his or her supporters) constitute emotional abuse of the child" (p. 433). This implies that the pathological dynamic that PA becomes is able to stretch from within a familial reference, to the courtroom and on into the larger community. As stated by Drozd and Olesen (2004), "Abuse comes in many packages" (p. 84). They also note that, "It is imperative that the custody evaluator considers psychological and emotional abuse as well as other kinds of abuse, including physical, sexual, financial, and legal" (p. 84). Quite recently, Harman, Kruk, and Hines (2018) have proposed that PA is a form of family violence and have made their case across a lengthy and thoughtful article that may, in short, be encapsulated by the following:

> Parental alienating behaviors do not just contribute to child abuse; they are direct and indirect attacks that an AP[14] makes on the TP.[15] Intimate partner violence (IPV) describes aggressive and abusive behaviors perpetrated by a current or former intimate partner (i.e., spouse, boyfriend/girlfriend, coparent, dating partner, or ongoing sexual partner; Breiding et al., 2015) and, like child abuse, has been a difficult form of violence to define due to the many forms it can take.
>
> (p. 1280)

Godbout and Parent's (2012) work on the topic has, likewise, continued to extend the notion of psychological abuse out into the future and described it this way: "The conception of parental alienation as a form of maltreatment implies long-term effects on the mental health and well-being of children who experience this phenomenon" (p. 38). Add to these voices those of Baker and Ben-Ami (2011), who have stated quite clearly that,

> Parents who exhibit parental alienation strategies can be considered to be psychologically maltreating their children because of the expression of the strategies inevitably and directly results in children feeling

'worthless, flawed, unloved, unwanted, endangered, or only of value in meeting another's needs.'

(p. 473)

Baker, Burkhard, and Albertson-Kelly (2012) have previously stated similar sentiments (Baker, 2007), and elaborated that, "To the extent that parents play a role in instigating, fostering, or encouraging these polarized views, this could be considered a form of emotional abuse" (p. 188). Updating their research, Clawar and Rivlin (2013a) also described the following: "We continue to find that this form of social-psychological child abuse is likely to be as damaging as physical abuse" (p. xxvii). Citing Gardner, it was described by Lorandos (2014) that " 'these behaviors of the aligned parent (and his or her supporters) constitute emotional abuse of the child' " (p. 324). Still later, there were Baker and Verrocchio (2015): "Research has linked these types of parental alienation behaviors to poor outcomes and to psychological maltreatment in a number of independent samples" (p. 3048). Then, Lowenstein (2015) stated, "Keep in mind that PA is a form of emotional abuse in using a child or children in a vindictive manner against an often good parent" (p. 657). We then have Lopez, Iglesias, and Garcia (2014), who had stated,

> Child Protection Services of different autonomous regions of Spain (Arruabarrena, 2011; IAASIFA, 2008) define the instrumentalization of children in martial conflicts as emotional maltreatment. As a form of psychological maltreatment, it has highly negative effects on the health and wellbeing of children that are as strong as or stronger than other types of child maltreatment.

(p. 218)

The nature of these psychological abuses is importantly described by Baker and Verrocchio (2015, pp. 3054–3055), wherein they described *acs* are made to feel that RPs are unworthy, and therefore the *ac* is unworthy. Also, the AP has also conveyed that the RP is unworthy of love, and therefore the *ac* is likewise unworthy of love. Thus, they concluded, "the child is internalizing the negative messages that the parent is conveying to the child about the other parent as a negative message about *himself*" (p. 3055). In turn, PA is a form of psychological abuse that persists so long as the pathological dynamic continues.

Discerning and Weighing PA

Examples described previously will be reconsidered now that there have been more substantive discussions on the phenomena involved, as well as on a number of other matters that are similar, but essentially different, from the kind of pathological dynamic involved with PA cases. As described above, in addition to Parental Estrangement (PE) and the description of Parental Denigration (PD), still other descriptors have been addressed in their different forms with Counter Productive Parenting (CPP) and Sabotage (PS), which Drozd and Olesen (2010) added to their work from 2004: "Research shows that abuse is more common in disputed child custody cases than is alienation; any way you look at it, both are real" (p. 263). Drozd and Olesen (2004) had also previously highlighted the observation that, "Alienation and abuse are not dichotomous variables; instead, they may occur across continua" (p. 101).

What it seems these authors were attempting to describe were variable criteria, and Meier (2010) again frames the work conducted by Drozd and Olesen admiringly when she recognizes "the unenviable challenge of weaving a neutral path between these highly polarized fields" (p. 220). She follows their work with a discussion about the fundamental differences between what has been described as PA and PE, and revisiting what Drozd and Olesen had proposed as a *hybrid* kind of case assessment (p. 221). The latter, in her view, "has gained substantial attention in the field" with an accompanying multivariate assessment approach. These matters have also been discussed by Friedlander and Walters (2010) as well as Garber (2011), and, as Ludolph and Bow (2012) described, "most cases with issues of alienation also have either aspects of estrangement or enmeshment or both, and they term these cases 'hybrid cases'" (p. 154). The work done by these authors was important, and, for the purposes here it is underscored to be aware of these distinctions without going too far afield entertaining them.

Now, there are a number of measures for these matters as mentioned earlier in the book, the Parental Alienation Scale (Gomide, Camargo, & Fernandes, 2016), the Parental Acceptance—Rejection Questionnaire (Bernet et al., 2018), and the Rowlands' Parental Alienation Scale (Rowlands, 2019). There are also the more established Baker Alienation Questionnaire (BAQ) and Baker Strategies Questionnaire (BSQ), which were discussed as well in Chapter 4. The important thing to consider with Baker's work is that she has clearly thought about standards for scientific proof. So, considering the BAQ in a bit more detail, it was described by its author (Baker, Burkhard, & Albertson-Kelly, 2012) as a two-page paper-and-pencil instrument that was self-administered and took roughly ten minutes to fill out: "The survey is made up of 28 items designed to capture a child's extreme rejection of one parent and extreme idealization of the other" (p. 182). Also of interest were other instruments that have been developed, such as Baker and colleagues' Baker Strategies Questionnaire (BSQ) and the Relationship Distancing Questionnaire (RDQ) as described by Moné and Biringen (2012), which focused on "recollections of parental alienation during childhood" (p. 158). These measures (Baker, Burkhard, & Albertson-Kelly, 2012, p. 193) and the attributes described could contribute greatly to understanding Parental Alienation. In this author's view, however, that holds only so long as these measures describe the kind of attributes and behavior differentially, as discussed earlier in some detail. In short, what characteristics develop in PA, and then what are the behaviors that become symptomatic in PA?

In Chapter 2, a PA flow chart was provided to illustrate the kind and quality of thinking that should go into the sorting process for practitioners, professionals and researchers attempting to make the kinds of determinations described above. There were recommended considerations to work through in an objective fashion based on proofs in coming to the consideration of whether a PA IMD is present. What is now Figure 6.2 again provides an if-then process for practitioners to assemble the clinical data, findings and information before them, and to compare the characteristics and symptoms described above and those that will be further described below in order to be better able to discern PA from other conditions. These other conditions, and the phenomenon of PA itself, have been designated as Parental Estrangement (PE), Parental Denigration (PD), and adult and child forms of Alienating Behaviors (AB). Again, the latter are very detailed behaviors that have been spoken to in this chapter and acted out by adults and children in these situations.

Regardless of form, an IMD has been conceptualized as additive or cumulative, wherein individual dimensional symptoms interact with systems and subdynamics, which, across FDBP and PA, transform into a larger pathological dynamic. An IMD is admittedly a diagnosis that is difficult to perceive. Before hypotheses about such matters may be confirmed, it is suggested that practitioners, professionals, or researchers come to practice heuristics that assist in creating a more differentiated and objective framework, and gain hypotheses arrived at through a careful, studied contextual view of the interrelated-dimensional interactions. It may be a flow chart like the one above, it may be the weighed scales from Chapter 4 revisited here, or, as will be discussed in the latter pages of Chapter 7, it may be through the IMD Symbolic Language that has been created. But, whatever the convention to sketch these matters out, as a visual proof that can and should be discussed with others, it is advisable that this kind of work precedes the quantification of the

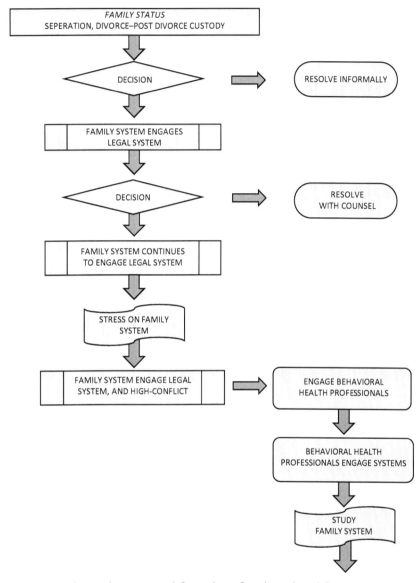

Figure 6.2 This is the proposed flow chart for clinical and forensic decision making as part of the process of determining whether there is proof of a PA IMD at each level, including ruling out such matters as Parental Estrangement (PE) and Parental Denigration (PD), and accounting for a parent's Alienating Behaviors (AB) and a child's (*ab*).

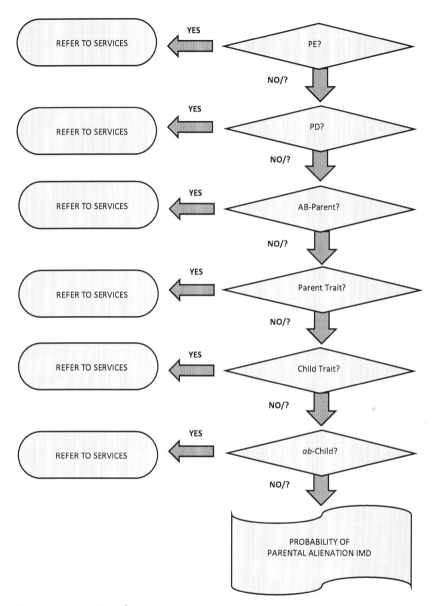

Figure 6.2 (continued)

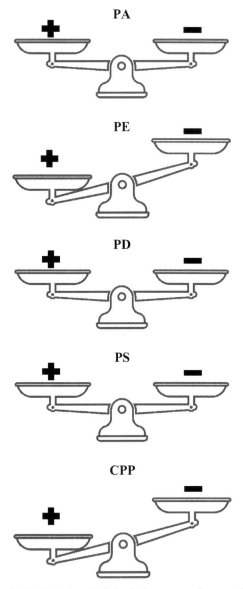

Figure 6.3 PE and CPP Weighted: If the balances on these scales are weighted toward PE and CPP, it suggests that this case is not a PA case. Instead, PE seems like the more probable hypothesis.

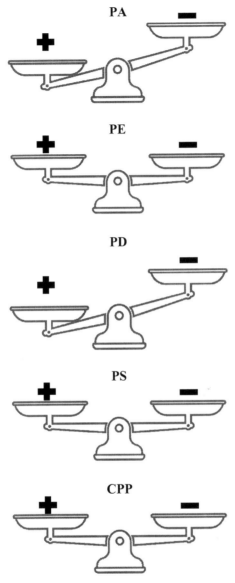

Figure 6.4 PA and PD Weighted: If the weight solely falls to PA or PD, as in this example, the findings and information collected in the case suggest perhaps a mild to moderate form of PA or PD.

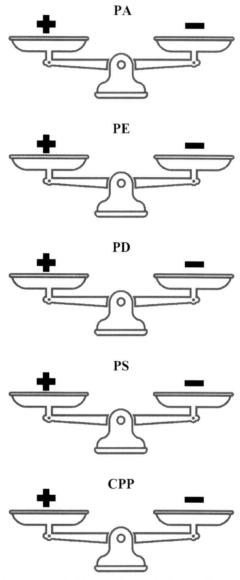

Figure 6.5 Hybrid Weighted: If there is no ability to distinguish among the weighting of these different scales, then it would appear that a hybrid case has been revealed.

variables described in the tables, various measures or the IMD Inventories©. Thus, for just these sorts of purposes, readers might consider the heuristic of weighted scales since they now have far more material to review and consider in making such designations at this point in the text.

Thus, what is revealed is a mix of both variable exclusion and inclusion criteria, rendering a delineation of whether PA is tenable or untenable. So, if there are variable criteria, these may address exclusion or inclusion by way of the weight of the evidence available, such as the accumulated data, findings and information associated with the case. It follows that system-wide PA symptoms are clarified by the accumulated weighting of individual and systems symptoms by the patterns that they create. On the one side of these scales symptomatic weighting is assigned to a variable set of exclusion criteria, while on the other side a variable weighting represents inclusion criteria.

An IMD is admittedly a difficult diagnosis to perceive in the absence of a larger contextual view of all the interrelated-dimensional interactions as noted above. To make such a determination requires proofs and careful study to confirm or disconfirm hypotheses practitioners may have. That is why these kinds of thought conventions are necessary to work out, and then inventories were created, either to provide a probability that PA exists as an IMD or to challenge and clarify the hypothesis that an IMD exists. The design and use of the IMD Inventories© have been discussed above and will be further discussed in Chapter 7 as the parallels between IMDs are explored. Finally, FDBP and PA interventions will be differentiated from one another in Chapter 8.

Parental Alienation as an IMD

Entertaining just what PA is has occupied the literature for nearly 40 years. Wallerstein and Kelly (1976, 1980a, 1980b) described it as Alignment. Gardner (1985, 2001, 2002) reported it to be a Syndrome. Kelly and Johnston (2001) described Alienated Children. Of late, the concept of PA had been proposed as both a diagnosis that resides in children and a relational problem per the group that argued for its inclusion in the *DSM-5*. Yet, as described above, there have been other conceptualizations outside of this group that have used the term PA in recent years as well.

The literature on these matters has indeed been contentious and the concept challenging to articulate. Still, at this point there have been nearly four decades of clinical focus, literature, and research on the topic that homes in on what PA is as a phenomenon. In the pages above, PA has been pieced together in order to describe an environmental context and psychological surround that involves high-conflict separation, divorce, or post-divorce custody, parenting plans, or parenting-time disputes, family and legal systems.

It was argued in Chapter 3, Chapter 4, and the current chapter that these cases should be approached in a fashion that does not diagnose the child as symptomatic and that doing so misses the point of the vast majority of the nodal family systems literature (Bateson et al., 1963; Watzlawick, Beavin, & Jackson, 1967; Hoffman, 1981; Selvini-Palazzoli et al., 1978). To diagnose the child with "the disorder" runs wholly counter to what has been discussed for decades, if not from the dawn of this theoretical orientation, within the literature on family therapy, that is, referring to an individual as symptomatic of systems' problems. Although there have been permutations, since early on in the family therapy movement such individuals have been referred to as the identified patient (Whitaker & Malone, 1953; Jackson, 1957).

In this author's view, the conceptualization that has orbited closest to the descriptions offered herein on PA has been the work done by what this author has termed "the *DSM-5* group," largely led by the works of Bernet and Baker (2013). There have been throughout references to systems considerations in many models, and a particular few even more recently (Siracusano et al., 2015; Walker & Shapiro, 2010). As noted earlier, the *DSM-5* group described two forms of PA, one diagnosable in the child and the other attributable to relationship problems. Obviously, this author disagrees with the first form, but the second form holds promise and is close to the kind and quality of conceptualization of PA that has been offered in the pages above. However, per the *DSM-5*, Relational Problems are not true diagnoses. Thus, the case has been made that PA is a complex form of diagnosis, an IMD, according to the proposal made in this book. It is a pathological dynamic unique within behavioral science and calls for a new diagnostic approach.

Parental Alienation is proposed to be an IMD formed out of the groundswell of forces that accumulate through environmental contexts and involves family and legal systems that produce a high-conflict situation related to a separation, divorce, or post-divorce custody, parenting plan, or parenting-time dispute. These forces combine in a fashion that exerts pressure and stressors on parents who are vulnerable to their collective influence. These parents respond with Alienating Behaviors. These parents, like these ABs, have been described in the literature for some time, and of late with a growing clarity that has reached the point where characteristics of parents who engage in ABs are well known, as are the behaviors in which they have engaged. The nature of the children involved has also become better understood over the years; and, what is more, the literature reviewed thus far and later on in this text has increasingly recognized the damaging effects caused by PA on these children. It is important to mention that the work of Wallerstein, Lewis, and Blakeslee (2000) should also be considered along these lines. Ultimately, the literature has described the kind and quality of interactions that culminate in the PA pathological dynamic when it has been initiated between the *ac* and the RP through the child's *alienating behaviors*.

Taking note of the pattern of diagnostic considerations described in Chapters 4 and 5, defining the pathological dynamic of the PA IMD may now be viewed as proposed diagnostic criteria informed by the tables above. As spoken to in Chapter 4, IMD diagnoses at this point in time are intended to involve a two-stage process: suspicion based on observable symptoms, and then secondarily further study of characteristics and historical variables to derive an overall probability for the IMDs presence. Consequently, IMD diagnoses are envisioned to involve at least a two-stage process, even perhaps a three-stage process; since, as discussed in Chapter 4 once a case rises to the point of suspicion (observable symptoms meet or surpass the marker of *better than chance*) best practice suggests that this determination is followed by consultation with another practitioner.

The possible observable symptom variables have been brought forward from Tables 6.1–6.6, and those will be included in Table 6.7 in order to describe the PA IMD via initial criteria for suspicion I-IV that may suggest the practitioner in the case has a good scientific reason, a marker of *better than chance*, to have concerns about the presence of a pathological dynamic. Other variable characteristics and history follow in criteria V-VII based on the known literature regarding Parental Alienation. As noted, establishing these criteria requires further study by the practitioner or another member of the multidisciplinary team, and in the case of PA the option of the additional Family—Legal Systems Subdynamic is possible to include in certain particularly unsettled and prolonged cases. Once these criteria have been studied, analysis follows based on conformance to the diagnosis in Table 6.7 and/or the broad conformance to Tables 6.1–6.5/6.6, or perhaps the outcome of the IMD Inventory—PA©. These methods are intended to arrive at a quantitative probability for the PA IMD that is considered in concert with the studies of a multidisciplinary team.

There has been a discussion of the necessity to establish what is, and what is not, PA by way of applying the concept of variable criteria to the prospects associated with this multidimensional interrelated healthcare-legal situation. Arguments have been made about how to compile preliminary data, information, and observations, and then weigh the potential for the existence of a PA IMD compared with concepts like those described under CPP, PD, PE, PS, and even hybrid cases. At the same time, it has been emphasized that this

Table 6.7 Proposed PA IMD Diagnosis

The fundamental aspect of Parental Alienation is that it is a family systems diagnosis that involves a child whose parents are engaged in a high-conflict separation, divorce or post-divorce custody proceedings; and in the course of these proceedings the child's presentation changes noticeably followed by engaging in alienating behaviors toward one parent, often referred to as the rejected parent. In addition, the other parent who is often referred to as the alienating parent, also engages in alienating behaviors toward the rejected parent for the apparent purposes of limiting information about the child or children these parents share, encouraging the rejection of this parent, and limiting the other parent's contact. Parental Alienation does not hold in cases in which the parent only denigrates the other parent to the children and does not engage in other alienating behaviors. The child has also not changed, nor does the child engage in alienating behaviors. Parental Alienation does not apply, in cases in which the child's rejection of the parent is justifiable as in conditions of estrangement such as abandonment, abuse, neglect, or witnessing intimate partner violence.

As an Interrelated Multidimensional Diagnosis (IMD), this diagnosis is meant to be made fully only after a two-stage process. The first stage, suspicion, is reached by a better than chance occurrence of observable symptoms across criteria I–IV. The second stage requires further study of characteristics and history to determine an overall probability for the diagnosis, which addresses the additional considerations involved with criteria V–VII. Also, if the case has been stalled in the legal system for an extended period of time, six months or more, additional optional criteria may be used to demonstrate the weight of these concerns and the legal system's impact on the case itself. If, then, the whole of variable criteria meet a probability of .50+ and/or more probable than not, then the PA IMD should be made.

SUSPICION

I. The parents are engaged in a high-conflict separation, divorce or post-divorce custody proceeding, which means
   A. Parents have had failed mediations,
   B. Parents had undergone psychological assessments, or
   C. Parents have had court-imposed settlements.
II. One or both parents have engaged in the following Alienating Behaviors (ABs):
   A. Failing to give information about the children,

SUSPICION

    B. Rewarding disrespectful behaviors in the child (of rejection toward the RP[16]),

    C. Insulting or belittling the RP toward the children,

    D. Sharing personal/judicial information with or confiding in the child,

    E. Making decisions without consulting the RP,

    F. Preventing visits, or

    G. Hindering telephone contact.

III. One or more children have the following observable attributes or characteristics:

    A. The child is between the ages of eight and sixteen, +/- one year,

    B. The child was observed to noticeably change during a period of time with regard to her or his behavior and statements (described in *abs* and below), and the change is so dramatic it tends to be confounding to the RP (given the prior good quality of the child–RP attachment), extended family, and others who knew the child previously (family friends, educators, coaches, or other practitioners and professionals).

    C. The child observably idealizes the AP in actions and words in a disproportionate fashion, describes the AP in positive terms and the RP in negative terms, and exhibits a general inability to entertain ideas and opinions outside of the AP's sphere of influence (a noticeable dependency).

    D. The child's opinions tend to be voiced in black-and-white terms.

    E. The child presents with a hollow or shallow, put on, "happy" affect.

IV. One or more children have engaged in the following alienating behaviors (*abs*):

    A. The child feels free to openly state hatred toward the RP and does so.

    B. The child has been permitted by the AP to engage in hostile or rude behavior toward the RP and the RP's extended family—there are no bounds to these expressions.

    C. These children tend to sound coached and/or have stilted accounts, as well as employ adult phrases or words often used by the AP.

    D. The child's reports of shortcomings of the RP allegedly possesses sound:

        i. Perceptibly absurd, frivolous, hollow, trivial, or weak, and/or

        ii. Like imitations, or slightly different variations, of those made by the AP.

    E. The child resists or refuses visits with the RP.

(Continued)

Table 6.7 (Continued)

FURTHER STUDY

V. The alleged AP may have a number of the following attributes or characteristics:
   A. Has been diagnosed with a personality disorder or its traits that are largely in Cluster B of the *DSM* series,
   B. Has demonstrated a posture toward the failed relationship in which he or she experienced the separation or divorce as embarrassing or humiliating, and responds with reprisals toward the former partner,
   C. Under the stress of the legal process (high conflict), may see a regression from a prior level of functioning and may engage in less productive parenting behaviors, and
   D. May demonstrate difficulties with reality testing per practitioners involved with the case.
VI. The alleged RP may have a number of the following attributes or characteristics:
   A. Tends to be passive and withdrawn, and this holds true in the face of conflict,
   B. May be less involved and more distant in the relationship with the child(ren),
   C. May be immature, egocentric, and somewhat rigid, and,
   D. May act like a Counter Productive Parent (noun) or engage in Counter Productive Parenting (verb).
VII. Other attributes, behaviors, or characteristics that require further study to establish:
   A. The parent may:
      i. Interrogate the child after visits to the RP,
      ii. Interfere in the child's symbolic contact with the RP,
      iii. Seek caregivers for the child as an alternative to the RP, and
      iv. Seek accomplices for alienating (e.g., new partner, extended family, etc.).
   B. The child may:
      i. Express no ambivalence or regret about her or his behavior or the changes in circumstances surrounding the family,
      ii. Insist that her or his actions, expressions, feelings, and thoughts are her or his own,
      iii. Singly express the wish to terminate the relationship with the RP,
      iv. Also report openly that the AP has been harmed by the RP,
      v. Express the desire to speak to the lawyers or the judge about her or his wishes, with the belief these wishes will be granted.

OPTIONAL REVIEW (see Table 6.6: Family–Legal System Optional Subdynamic)

---

period of investigation and hypothesis generation should be met with appropriate caution and scientific neutrality, given the powerful currents that exist in these cases, and that there may even be event horizons associated with the work on these cases. Dynamics certainly powerful enough to sway or render ineffective practitioners and professionals working on such cases were suggested in Chapter 4 when describing splitting and triangulation.

Parental Alienation is a cumulative process similar to many other scientifically studied processes, much like a naturally occurring wildfire and its results; it could even be seen as a work of art, a symphonic performance. In turn, the end result is not all there is to the situation. It is a process that builds over time with the unfortunate accumulation of weighted variables, and it sets a family system on a course that creates this pathological dynamic. The cumulative nature of such complex dynamics has been argued in the prior chapter regarding the creation of FDBP, which, like PA, has an environmental context involving multiple systems (family and healthcare), as well as parents and children with certain characteristics. In turn, bringing forward the metaphor from Chapter 3, the blind people each may have identified a different interrelated dimension of the whole process that transforms into the pathological dynamic that makes up the PA Interrelated Multidimensional Diagnosis.

The aforementioned conceptualization of FDBP was described as "a forerunner of the more sophisticated practice of wedding individual diagnoses and group, social, family, and legal dynamics together into an integrated, coded conceptualization" (Bütz, Evans, & Webber-Dereszynski, 2009, p. 37). It is, once more, ultimately expressed as a pathological dynamic and a new form of diagnosis (Bütz & Evans, 2019).

As with the FDBP IMD, in order to measure the PA IMD, rather than designating every variable's origin in the literature in the tables above, a representative set of literature was pulled together to create not only these tables but also an IMD Inventory© that describes the probability of a PA IMD. With the assistance of a colleague (Bütz & Miller, 2019b), this author will describe the IMD conceptualization by way of an outcome that is *more probable than not* as a base marker and by other features described in Chapter 5 and those that will be elaborated in Chapters 7 and 8. The conformance of this literature to these variables will be discussed as part of the supporting literature for these IMD Inventories©.

As it stands, the constituent variables that create, and symptomatically differentiate, PA from other diagnoses and family systems dynamics in this day and age are knowable. Moreover, with what is now known, PA can be described by way of environmental context, parent characteristics, alienating behaviors,

Figure 6.6 With Parental Alienation, it may be argued that each theoretical model each has had a piece of the elephant, with Alignment, Parental Alienation Syndrome, Alienated Child, and Parental Alienation via proposals for *DSM-5*. Perhaps now with a systemic interpretation, the practitioners, professionals, and researchers involved with this work may be able to mutually benefit from one another. This image has been reproduced with the permission of Sam Gross.

child characteristics, subdynamics, and the quality and kind of pathological dynamic from whence the term obtained its name. What remains is for the cumulative pathological dynamic to be recognized as an IMD by the courts, practitioners, professionals, and researchers. That is, it would be recognized not only to create understanding, but also in order to facilitate intervention in cases to serve these children's health and welfare as well as their best interests, and to stem their suffering.

Notes

1. Parent Alienating Behaviors (see p. 429).
2. Italics added to reference for emphasis.
3. Italics added to reference for emphasis.

4. The material has been adjusted to place it in an ordered sequence to promote the clarity of these findings.
5. Rejected Parent.
6. Rejected Parent.
7. Italics added for emphasis.
8. Rejected Parent.
9. Obviously rejected parent.
10. In order to clearly differentiate children from parents, and children's actions from those of parents, this convention of a lower-case italicized abbreviation will be used in the remainder of the text. The Alienated Child is not one-and-the same with the concept of Kelly and Johnston (2001); but it is simply a broadly descriptive term used from here on. The other benefit of this form of abbreviation will become apparent when in the latter part of Chapter 7 IMD Symbolic Language will be discussed.
11. See pp. 399–400 for clarification.
12. Italics added for emphasis.
13. Italics added by author for emphasis.
14. Alienating Parent.
15. Targeted Parent.
16. Rejected Parent.

Parallel Characteristics and Variables

7

Factitious Disorder by Proxy and
Parental Alienation

One purpose of this chapter is to clarify the cumulative nature of an IMD as an observable phenomenon that can be recognized by trained practitioners, professionals and researchers. Another purpose is to blur or cloud the distinctions between FDBP and Parental Alienation in a fashion that suggests that they are included under the symptomatic tenets of an IMD, as described in Chapter 4, in order to show that IMDs all have the same basic structure. Going back to the first chapter of the book, an IMD was defined as a set of diagnoses[1] that holistically describe interrelated individual and system characteristics. These characteristics, together with subdynamics, cumulatively create a multidimensional pathological dynamic that is described as an Interrelated Multidimensional Diagnosis.

Throughout the text, stress has been underscored as a crucial, really elemental, factor driving the various circumstances that, under the right conditions, ultimately lead to an Interrelated Multidimensional Diagnosis. So stress, the right quanta or accumulation of stress, is fundamental to the emergence of an Interrelated Multidimensional Diagnosis. Without the influence or impact of stress, either historically or in the interrelated multidimensional situations that unfold, IMDs would not, could not, exist. In addition, there are family systems with particular traits in certain states and there are parents as well as children with certain traits in certain states. Both the system and the individuals interact with stressors, which are engendered by intra-familial and extra-familial interactions with other systems, such as healthcare and legal systems, that may create subdynamics. In turn, the stresses associated with these interactions over time produce actions or behaviors in one or both parents that lead to certain actions, behaviors or responses toward a child or children. When these actions manifest in the child as certain behaviors or states, a pathological abusive dynamic has been created. This is the moment when an IMD may be said to emerge, i.e., *a punctuated steady state*. In this author's view, a threshold event is the act of inducing illness in a child, as in FDBP, or a child engaging in the act of denigrating communication toward an RP, as in Parental Alienation. Threshold events such as these have been described as punctuated steady states, which connotes that either the parent or the child has been transformed, and thereby the family system has been transformed as well as a result of the culmination of interrelated dynamic and static variables that occur across successive dimensions.

Interrelated Multidimensional Diagnoses are progressive phenomena, but, rather than being causal in a linear sense, they indicate a cumulative probabilistic approximation in a nonlinear sense. At this point it is not argued that there would be a notable quanta of this or that symptomatic variable criterion formed out of a series of patterns that come together. Some matters, such as what particular stress in the past interacted with a certain stress or stressors in the present to set a parent on the course of inducing or mimicking illness in her or his child, may never be knowable. Or, as but another example of many, the particular stressor that was paired with a certain AB directed at a child from an AP that propelled the child down the path of engaging in their own set of *abs* directed toward the RP in PA may also never be knowable. There are simply too many dynamic and static variables comprising the variable symptomatic criteria that have been proposed. In some cases, it may be possible to identify time frames and events that are hypothesized to interact with these proposed criteria and events. Perhaps threshold, so to speak, flashpoint events serve as the moment the pathological dynamic became apparent, yet endeavors to gauge IMDs at this point are best viewed from a hypothesis-driven probabilistic approach.

The transition from a transformative state to a punctuated steady state has been described, and even so, in this author's view, knowing when such instances occur with any measure of precision will be rare and unusual. Instead, it will be more realistic to note patterns in time and each IMD's unique variable criteria in order to arrive at a probabilistic model of whether or not the phenomenon even exists in a case. As will be discussed later in this chapter, the nature of these efforts will be more hypothesis-driven and probabilistic in this nascent stage of development, with the aim of assisting practitioners, professionals and researchers in identifying Interrelated Multidimensional Diagnoses.

As described, there is stress, in both the historical sense, given its impact on certain parents in these systems, and in the situational sense, between individuals and systems. Stresses and other more static variables, such as characteristics, represent symptoms that constitute the primary ingredients for these pathological dynamics to unfold. We have already discussed the threshold event when an IMD has been realized, and, to be clear, such a threshold event is hardly the end of the process. If left to propagate without intervention, IMDs tend to grow into more and more pathological dynamics over time and to assimilate more individuals and systems. This part of the life of an IMD will be addressed in more detail next chapter. These statements are made here to propose the conceptual arc of an IMD's life, the formative period, and the time in which it emerges as well as its potential to impact more and more individuals and systems.

 ## Stress, History, and the Nexus of an IMD in Time

The initial focus of this chapter has been to describe how stress is a primary ingredient for the characteristics and symptoms that form an IMD, and that all IMDs hold this in common. Thus far, stress has been referred to generically, although there are conceptualizations and models too numerous to mention that describe all different kinds of stress. Given the discussion so far, it has likely become evident that situational stress is a significant factor in Interrelated Multidimensional Diagnoses. It is, however, just as important to consider stress within the context of *time*; what is meant by this statement is not just the "current" notion of time but also the idea of what occurs across time. Time is a critical consideration in any reference to change processes, and its manifestations are often overlooked in the literature (Slife, 1981, 1994, 1995; Boscolo, Bertrando, & Thorne, 1993; Hartocollis, 1972; Lehmann, 1967). How is stress considered within the context of time? There are a number of different ways to conceptualize this since certain critical periods are often discussed via epigenetics or related topics (Belsky, 2019; Kumsta, 2019; Erikson, 1963, 1980, 1982). There are generically necessary stresses too, as in bone growth and character development, and then there are traumatic stresses (Friedman, 2013). There are also circumstances in time in which all three of these situations come into play.

There are the stressors involved with development and those experienced in less than optimal family dynamics that create long-standing arrests, often represented as personality disorders or traits. We have previously discussed change in the *DSM* itself, and in this case it is important to note that in prior editions of the

DSM personality disorders or traits were diagnosed on what was referred to as Axis II. It is important for the reader to be aware that as recently as *DSM-IV-TR* (2000, p. 28) Axis II was designated for addressing these maladaptive tendencies in interpersonal relationships, the use of more primitive defense mechanisms, and persistently problematic functioning that follows. Though the literature varies on this topic, the origin for these disorders and traits is generally considered to be abuse or neglect of some form that leads to a developmental arrest in the lower functioning clusters (Afifi et al., 2011; Bierer et al., 2003). These abuses occurred at an earlier time due to forces in the individual's life, forces that were stressful enough to cause the arrest and enduring enough, or epigenetically detrimental enough, to make the psychological marks of these stresses last (Belsky, 2019; Kumsta, 2019). It should be apparent by now that these arrests caused by stresses that occurred perhaps ten, twenty, or even thirty years before apply to the history of one or both of the parental figures in the IMD conceptualization. This enduring pathology, this evidence of an arrest, represents a time, or multiple times, a period of time, in a parent's early life and serves as a historical maker. If the practitioner's theoretical model is explanatory enough, these characteristics and symptoms serve as a roadmap of how the parent had been impacted in time as well. Prevention, however, has long been preferable to intervention, regardless of whether or not the aim is primary, secondary or tertiary (Caplan, 1964). Around the edges of these discussions in the literature on FDBP and PA, the specter of Intergenerational Trauma has been raised by a number of authors. Thus, arguably the most direct approach would suggest that the point of intervention is to forestall stressors and prohibit intergenerational transmission of not only the IMD but also, perhaps controversially, the historical stress itself. There are, for example, recent efforts to describe Adverse Childhood Experiences (Cerrato et al., 2017; Hughes et al., 2017; Danese & McEwen, 2012). These more recent theories seem to have their theoretical footing in perhaps the earlier work of others (Fonagy & Target, 1996; Richardson, 1948), including Anna Freud (1971):

> In our times, the analyst's therapeutic ambition goes beyond the realm of conflict and the improvement of inadequate conflict solutions. It now embraces the basic faults, failures, defects and deprivations, i.e., the whole range of adverse external and internal factors, and it aims at the correction of their consequences.
>
> (p. 203)

For practitioners, professionals and researchers, it may be informative to have this longer view of what may appear to be only points of data on characteristics and symptoms in Tables 5.4, 5.9, 6.1 and 6.2 from previous chapters that describe Background Dimensional Symptoms and Parent Individual Dimensional Symptoms. Historical references conceived of in this way also tend to provide a more accurate portrait of healthcare and legal systems, too. These systems also suffer stressors that have shaped and meaningfully described their history and functioning. For now, however, such matters are for further study, since undertaking the contemplation of the functioning and trajectories of other systems is too mind-numbingly broad to be entertained here.

The stresses experienced by these parents have a very pertinent and impactful role in IMDs, since it is proposed that these historical stresses have created a structural instability, one not only within the parent but also within the family system. An instability, that involves one or both parents, who respond poorly, regressively, to situational stressors. The *DSM Series* diagnostic criteria have long spoken to persistent, rigid patterns of behavior that are maladaptive and markedly out of harmony with an individual's culture, interpersonal community and larger society. Adaptation connotes the capacity to respond to the moment with flexibility and/or strength, to perceive the necessities involved within one's relative reality and to respond accordingly. What has been described repeatedly by the literature on FDBP and PA is that one or both parents involved are simply not able to manage an appropriate interpersonal response once in the throes of an Interrelated Multidimensional Diagnosis. There is a range here, too, as some parents may have been able to marginally maintain such a state on the one hand but could not endure the stressors they faced in the long run on the other. At the other end of this range may be parents who have never been able to tolerate stresses, and even the slightest perturbation engendered a maladaptive or pathological response.

Another form of stress has similar historical dynamics as well, but in this form it has been tied to genetic vulnerabilities in the individual and the expression of a mental illness, i.e., the Diathesis-Stress Model. For those familiar with behavioral healthcare, this theory is regularly referred to as an explanation that describes stress as a variable influence interacting with the prospect of a genetic predisposition (diathesis) toward developing a mental illness and/or its expression (Zubin & Spring, 1977). Even with more recent works on this topic that purport to go beyond its tenets (Belsky & Pluess, 2009), this author has found the work of one of this concepts' architects and proponents, Manfred Bleuler (1963), both particularly insightful and particularly humble when addressing the matter. The working definition was, of course, that, "It was supposed that various kinds of pathogenic influences on the personality would cause various kinds of psychopathological symptomatology" (p. 945).

He demonstrated a remarkable degree of scholarly consideration wherein, despite proposing this concept, he described a number of problems with it, and, among them, what follows.

> Another difficulty in research on the heredity of schizophrenics is seen in the impossibility of distinguishing between familial influences caused by heredity, and familial influences caused by an environment common to several members of a family.
>
> —
>
> This modern question—What changes the boundaries between two forms of life?—no longer suggests that all schizophrenic psychoses must be etiologically explained by a single and specific cause. Many types of trauma can destroy the dams keeping a chaotic form of life in its right place.
>
> (p. 946, 949)

Fundamentally, well back in 1963 while he was putting forth this conceptualization, he also described the complexities of doing so, noting that certain matters are inextricably woven together. Plainly, this is something that needs to be kept in mind as we entertain the concept of an IMD in the most general sense: "If we take into account what we know and if we refrain from speculating on what is unknown, we must take heredity and psychogenesis into consideration" (p. 949). His words of caution regarding scholarship, and ultimately his humility, continue to be worthy of contemplation: "Furthermore, it is quite possible that a great future discovery will disprove all that I have said" (p. 951).

Therefore, adding to the proposed conception of an IMD, here again we have another potential instability: that one or both parents may carry this hereditary and/or psychogenetic characteristic with them into the family system. These instabilities often interact poorly with situational stresses and may result in a regression in functioning by one or both parents. However, mental illness per se is not as frequent a characteristic of these parents. If there was such developmental arrest, it continues to serve as a marker of stress that remains with these parents.

 ## Three Forms of Stress and IMDs

When speaking of stress in reference to IMDs in these proposals, three types of stress are referred to: *developmental stresses, contemporary*

stresses and *situational stresses*. As the reader may readily perceive, developmental stresses are those that the parent brings with her or him from the family of origin and/or from her or his psychological history. Practitioners, professionals and researchers most readily perceive these stresses in diagnostic terms when a parent suffers from a personality disorder and/or traits, and/or there has been evidence that to some extent supports the impact of a mental illness. To be clear, the use of the term *developmental* was chosen to also describe the inherent attachment problems spoken to in the FDBP literature, which are naturally part and parcel of the diagnostic features of a personality disorder and/or traits often spoken to in the PA literature as well. There are also attachment challenges implied with mental illnesses given the developmental arrest that often accompanies the emergence of such diagnoses.

Now, there are also plenty of adults and/or parents who have had the benefit of psychoeducation, entered therapy, or in some other way attempted to resolve these matters from earlier in their lives. But within an *active IMD* the parent or parents at the center of its genesis have either regressed significantly or have never sought out the aforementioned mitigating interventions. While some of these parents may attend therapy, it is likely that the therapist would say the parent is not making progress, or the parent may well have duped the therapist via splitting, triangulation or some other means. By definition, if an IMD is in play, pathology is present, and the parent or parents at the center have not been impacted by therapeutic efforts to a meaningful degree. The therapist may be inexperienced, may not understand parental characteristics and symptoms involved with IMDs, or, worst of all, may have been split or triangulated away from a treatment team and co-opted by the parent per our discussion in Chapter 4. Hence, the earlier discussion on splitting and triangulation that is now several chapters behind us remains an important consideration. The impact of these developmental stressors is that they are internalized, and from this perspective of time it is likely that the parent continues to respond to them, to that reality, from her or his family of origin in the manner spoken to by terms such as *projection, splitting,* or *transference*. The first two imply fundamental or primitive defense mechanisms per psychodynamic language that distort reality, while transference is something we all engage in to one degree or another in viewing others and our world through the lens of our earlier relationships. This is why it may prove so difficult to get through to some of these parents who have regressed, to communicate with them at the time an IMD is active.

Contemporary stressors may be viewed in terms of the immediate environment that the parent or parents exist within at the time. These are, so to speak, run-of-the-mill stressors that all parents encounter but that in these cases often begin to mount to the point that they begin to overwhelm the parent or parents. Appreciating contemporary stresses is important to the degree that parents become overwhelmed, and their functioning begins to regress. Naturally a parent functioning at her or his best differs from one functioning at her or his worst—that is, when the latter parent has regressed in the face of mounting contemporary stressors. But some parents may only require one contemporary stressor to overwhelm them while others are more resilient and may be able to suffer half a dozen contemporary stressful setbacks and still function without perceptible regression. For example, we might have a parent who often functions in the range of dependent and avoidant traits within Cluster C of the *DSM* framework for personality disorders and/or traits. Cluster C represents a higher level of functioning than Cluster B or Cluster A. But, under contemporary stresses, these parents become overwhelmed and regress to manifest for a period of time histrionic and narcissistic traits that are within Cluster B. It follows that they become more focused on themselves than on their child or their children. The capacities of this parent under contemporary stressors are far different from a parent who, as part of her or his steady state, does not suffer from a personality disorder and/or traits. Still, under enough contemporary stress, these parents may begin to demonstrate obsessive-compulsive or even avoidant personality traits to meet the demands of the stressors, albeit such parents are likely more focused on control and order. In any event, with some exceptions this level of regression does not open up a substantial gap in their ability to see and respond to the needs of the child.

Situational stresses, then, may be seen as the proverbial straw that broke the camel's back and either precede the moment of a particular steady state or connote moments in the case where its dynamics shift to and fro like a boat in high seas. As practitioners, providers and researchers, we may never know what "the situational stressor" is or its impact on the parent when coupled with existing developmental and contemporary stressors. Nevertheless, situational stressors are important to be aware of since a change in the pattern of the child's or the parent's functioning may well follow after there is, for example, the stress associated with a change of practitioner in an FDBP case or the findings of a special master in a PA case.

Variable Responses to Stress: Exclusion and Inclusion Criteria

As one might expect, each type of designated parent responds to this combination of stressors to one extent or another with the basic conventions involved in Factitious Disorder by Proxy. The parent who abuses the child will be referred to as an Abusive Parent (AP). The other parent is often described as distant, uninvolved or remote and will be described herein as the Remote Parent (RP). So, with the basic representational scenarios described in Chapters 5 and 6 in mind, we can see that these models were built on the most frequently occurring characteristics, patterns and symptoms, with just one AP either engaging in physical or psychological abuse (PA) and one RP either remote to the situation or being psychologically abused by the AP and the child (PA). But, as both literatures have made clear, both parents can be involved in abusing the child in FDBP, and the child may even be included with symptoms à la Stockholm syndrome, whereas, in PA, both parents may be the AP and the child may respond to each variably.

How these parents participate in an IMD has to do with the developmental stressors they endured in their lives and how this history interacts with contemporary and situational stressors. In other work, this author with colleagues has also described an individual's capacities by way of their coherence, ability to manage resources, and whether or not they are in a steady or transformative state (Bütz, Schwinn, & Chamberlain, 2019; Bütz, 2017; Chamberlain & Bütz, 1998; Bütz, 1997). The relative psychological health of the parent under study has a great deal to say about how these factors play out in their day-to-day adaptation, and whether or not a parent is in a more adaptive state or a regressed state. As such, the parent's state, or parents' states, is naturally predicated on the existence and/or intensity of the Background Dimensional Symptoms in an Interrelated Multidimensional Diagnosis. In either circumstance, FDBP or PA, the questions are whether developmental, contemporary or even situational stressors are established in these dimensional symptoms, and, if so, to what degree they impact the functioning of one or both parents. Are both parents impacted by the Background Dimensional Symptoms, or is it just one?

There are several possible variations on the theme described in Chapter 5 regarding either the AP and RP, or the AP and AP. Going back to the work of Adshead and Bluglass (2005, 2001) as well as Kozlowska, Foley, and Crittenden (2006), we might ask: are these parents in a more integrated attachment state, wherein they are not so much acting in a fashion to gain attention but seeing after their child's needs in a maladaptive manner out of an earlier traumatic state that does not meet the criteria for FDBP? Kozlowska, Foley, and Crittenden (2006) described such states in this way: "parents' harmful health-seeking behaviour on behalf of their children is referred to as 'maladaptive caregiving' or 'misguided protective behaviour'" (p. 92). *Maladaptive caregiving* strikes this author as a generic enough term wherein it may also comment on mild forms of PA since there are discussions in this literature suggestive of these dynamics. It is possible in milder cases that the parent or

240 Parallel Characteristics and Variables

parents in question may have come from an intact family, or they may have been neglected or abused to a lesser degree or not at all, wherein psychological abuse may have been problematic. Regardless of the reason, the pathological dynamic has not reached beyond the threshold that the tables from the earlier chapters or the IMD Inventories© were designed to assess, i.e. a better than chance suspicion. Still, there are indications within the findings that suggest cause for concern, and supportive of a mild conceptualization. Parenthetically, and this will be spoken to in more detail later, as with any such finding from an IMD Inventory©, that finding alone will not be sufficient to make such a determination. It is this author's intent to convey that Baker's questionnaire (Baker, Burkhard, & Albertson-Kelly, 2012; Baker & Ben-Ami, 2011), the metrics from the tables in the earlier chapters, and the results of the IMD Inventory© are suggested for use in concert with a multidisciplinary team's discussion and consensus-based clinical conceptualizations. There may indeed be outliers in these teams, and that is to be expected with the complexity of these dynamics. What is being sought is majority consensus and clarity from the lead practitioners involved who will be responsible for the diagnoses of the system and individuals in the case, and ultimately the qualities associated with the intervention.

At the other end of these kinds of considerations there may be parents who are arguably more pathological and suffer from antisocial personality disorder and/or traits, and who have purposively harmed the child or children to either achieve some end or by way of abandoning, abusing, neglecting or engaging in intimate-partner violence. In FDPB this is what Rogers (2004) has spoken to regarding Malingering by Proxy, and this should be viewed as an exclusionary conceptualization that will be spoken to further in Chapter 8. It is essentially a rule-out to differentiate it from FDBP. Then, given our earlier discussions about such matters in PA, the array of abandonment, abuse, neglect and intimate violence aligns with estrangement scenarios described earlier as Parental Estrangement. These scenarios are also exclusionary wherein PE is far more common and is diagnosed with greater clarity due to the more straightforward symptomatic evidence often available in these cases. That is, of course, not always true. But, we have discussed PE as an exclusionary conceptualization when compared to PA, and PE will also be discussed further in Chapter 8.

With the considerations above, for the time being, we have two possible exclusionary criteria, which include maladaptive caregiving that does not cross the threshold but may equate to a mild form of FDBP and Malingering by Proxy. Thus, so far, we have possibilities that range from maladaptive caregiving, to mild, moderate and severe forms of FDBP, and then Malingering by Proxy. Mindful of future considerations about intervention, we plainly have exclusionary conceptualizations and inclusive conceptualizations, all of which reflect the degree of involvement by the AP and the RP when such allegations are considered, and each parent's capacities.

Similarly, although already represented in earlier chapters to one degree or another when describing PA, again we have the AP and the RP, and the basic conceptualization described in Chapter 6. Yet, again, there can be variations on this theme based on the relative health of each parent. For example, what was simply an RP can, under the right combination of stressors, regress into becoming a Counter Productive Parent. Further still, such a parent may also regress into becoming an Alienating Parent or an Abusive Parent. What is often most telling is a combination of considerations that include the degree of variables in the Background Dimensional Symptoms and the impact of developmental, contemporary and situational stressors. In this model a high-conflict case could be considered as a contemporary or situational stress, depending on its impact on the individuals and the family system. This author tends to view contemporary stressors as akin to a mood state described in a mental status interview, while situational stressors are comparable to affect. In terms of general conventions associated with describing mood and affect, mood is to affect as a prevailing climate is to the current weather. Plainly, here again, there are inclusion criteria with APs and RPs, but there are also exclusionary conceptual criteria such as the previously discussed PD, PE, PS or, conversely, Counter Productive Parenting.

 ## Family Systems in IMDs

There have often been references to family systems in FDBP and PA, but it is the rare circumstance that a family systems dynamics has been contemplated solidly (Harman, Kruk, & Hines, 2018; Griffith, 1988). In fact, as noted earlier, Griffith has made a specific conceptualization: *"a mother already possessing a somatoform or factitious disorder joins an enmeshed, authoritarian family system possessing a systemic history of exploitation of children"* (p. 423). Meanwhile, Harmon and colleagues (2018) described PA as an unacknowledged form of intimate familial violence and noted the following dynamics:

> The AP is the more likely parent to engage in controlling and coercive behaviors, display paranoid and hostile behaviors, and promote enmeshment with the child (Warshak, 2015). Indeed, the AP's behavior is the primary driver of the child's rejection of the TP (Baker & Eichler, 2016; Clawar & Rivlin, 2013).
>
> (p. 1285)

Hence, this author is of the opinion that this is an area for further study, and still there are some conceptualizations that may be useful to describe the quality of a family system's functioning in an Interrelated Multidimensional Diagnosis. Fundamentally, it has clearly been the case that in FDBP upwards of approximately 75% of these families were intact since these mothers were married (Day et al., 2017; Yates & Bass, 2017). Meanwhile, in PA the family system is no more, per se, and it is further sheering apart given the high-conflict nature of the situation that simultaneously involves divorce and separation. But then, one is left with the consideration of how did the family function prior to its division?

Attending to two well-known conceptual models we have the longitudinal work of Diana Baumrind (2013, 1991, 1971) and the family systems topology provided in David Olson's Circumplex Model (Olson, 2000; Olson, Sprenkle & Russell, 1979). Both models identify features of a family's functioning, such as how adaptive the range of characteristics the system demonstrates might be. What characteristics do these families most likely exhibit that would explain the maladaptive and pathological dynamics in the FDBP and PA IMD conditions? By asking such fundamental questions, these models are useful for conceptualizing how these families function in relation to the development of an Interrelated Multidimensional Diagnosis. Although these are two different conceptual models, this author proposes that they may identify dynamics that coincide in both conditions.

Baumrind's and Olson's Models

Baumrind (2013, 1991, 1971) identified five different conditions to describe how families functioned. She did this by characterizing the style with which they parented as Authoritarian, Authoritative, Democratic, Permissive or Disengaged. The two innermost styles, Authoritative and Democratic, were the most adaptive although Democratic families were very rare in her sample and a later finding in her research (2013, pp. 27–28). Meanwhile Authoritarian, Permissive and Disengaged parenting styles were the least adaptive. As for a literature that described family functioning in FDBP, we have Griffith's (1988) conceptualization above, which in short described an enmeshed and authoritarian familial dynamic. Considering the characteristics associated with FDBP by process of deductive reasoning, it is not conceivable that the AP in these cases can be described as Disengaged, Permissive or Democratic. This leaves the space occupied by Authoritarian and Authoritative parenting styles as a descriptor. These

Parallel Characteristics and Variables **243**

mothers are clearly overinvolved and per Griffith's description part of an Authoritarian family dynamic. But, as described above, we do have the possibilities of a mild, moderate and severe form of the FDBP IMD, wherein mild cases may well demonstrate maladaptive caregiving dynamics that would logically overlap into the outer reaches of the Authoritative style. Thus, it is suggested that FDBP functions within a range that is largely Authoritarian in moderate and severe cases, and in mild cases involving maladaptive caregiving it is possible that there is more Authoritative functioning.

The same kind of logic may well hold for the PA IMD pathological dynamic, and perhaps this is why there has been so much literature on differentiating PA from PE, and then we do also have PS, PD and Counter Productive Parenting. In the vast majority of cases PE is associated with Authoritarian, Permissive and/or Disengaged parenting styles. Next, we have the considerations of the relationship between the AP and the *ac*, which is described generally as controlling and enmeshed (Harman, Kruk, & Hines, 2018). This is not a pattern that fits with either Authoritative or Democratic parenting styles. Still, again we have the considerations of a mild, moderate and severe form of PA, and once again the milder form of this IMD would likely touch the outer reaches of the Authoritative parenting style with maladaptive caregiving. It seems most likely that under the conditions that promote PA, one part of the family system is reconfigured around the AP, who may begin to manifest Authoritarian characteristics or qualities. The descriptions above, with, of course, the exception of the citations, have limitations as they are simply based on hypothetical reasoning rooted in this author's own clinical experience, the known characteristics of these family systems, and the quality of interactions between these parents and their children. As such, it is an area of suggested further study.

So far as Olson's Circumplex Model is concerned (1980), let us consider the FDBP IMD again. In Olson's model there are characteristics of cohesion and flexibility broadly with finer distinctions that include in one corner chaotic and disengaged dynamics, in another enmeshed and chaotic dynamics, and in still another rigid and disengaged dynamics, as well as enmeshed and rigid dynamics (see Figure 7.1 below from Olson, 1980, p. 148).

Four sets of attributions are described in the most maladaptive outer ranges of this model. Three ranges are associated with functioning, with the innermost connoting health with balanced functioning, then a midrange, and unbalanced functioning (see lower right-hand corner of the figure). Plainly, the most maladaptive or pathological range of functioning includes the unbalanced regions. Considering the possibilities, again in the FDBP IMD the mother has been described as enmeshed with the child,

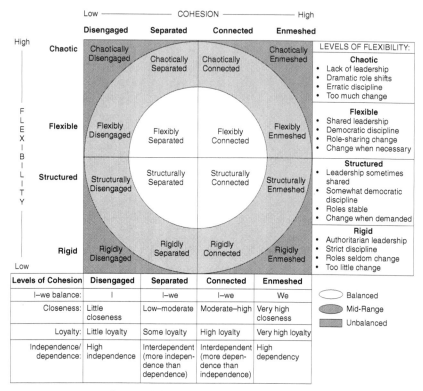

Figure 7.1 Circumplex Model by Olson (1980, p. 148).

and often the term *dependency* has been used to describe the relationship. So, this narrows the considerations down to either chaotically or rigidly enmeshed. As before, we have Griffith's description (1988), which seems to speak directly to the topological characteristics of the Circumplex Model with enmeshed and authoritarian descriptors. This narrows the field further to the region described by rigidly enmeshed functioning. We also have considerations regarding how this parent presents to healthcare providers, which, to paraphrase the literature cited earlier, suggests that these mothers are well put together and organized, not chaotic. Ultimately, this leads to but one topographical conclusion deductively: these families function in the rigidly enmeshed region. Per Olson's descriptions these families' characteristics include authoritarian leadership and high dependency.

Turning to the PA IMD, the dynamics involved here once again suggested the unbalanced region of the Circumplex figure above, but in this situation the family has bifurcated. Not only is it no longer whole, but it has been deeply divided. Its so-called premorbid functioning, however, is spoken to with the characteristics of the parents as an AP and RP, wherein the RP has been described as disengaged and separated to some degree. It is, however, unclear how the AP functioned prior to the family's separation. Thus, it is unknown how the AP's functioning shifted in order to create the new family dynamic that by most descriptions involves enmeshment with the child. Parental Alienation dynamics suggest that perhaps the family's premorbid functioning existed in the middle ground between being rigidly disengaged and enmeshed with the descriptions of rigidly separated and connected. Even so, once again this deductive hypothesis is borne from the literature on the topic and from this author's own experiences, and it obviously has limitations and suggests further study.

The discussion above suggests a range of functioning associated with these two proposed IMDs, and it is hoped these familial characteristics may well prove to be useful markers in future work on these topics. These descriptions of the range in which these families function serves as a basis for inclusion criteria, while other family dynamics may serve as an exclusion criterion once enough additional studies have been conducted to either support or refute these deductive hypotheses.

Larger Systems and IMDs

As noted in both proposed IMDs these family systems interact with larger systems such as healthcare and legal systems. These interactions are not innocuous in an IMD conceptualization, but rather contributory. In either case the IMD could not have developed without the contributory, perhaps amplifying, influence of these larger systems. In fact, the literature on FDBP shows that the child is most at risk in the healthcare system itself. The majority of mortalities associated with these cases occur in the healthcare system. The time-frame in which these dynamics are not identified the IMD has the opportunity to solidify, since on average this takes fifteen to twenty months (Bass & Glaser, 2014; Greiner et al., 2013). These interactions have certain characteristics that have been described above as a subdynamic. The subdynamic concept came from the known literature, and as before it is again the subdynamic that contains inclusion criteria that deductively lead to exclusion criteria in Table 5.7. *Time interacting with the healthcare system, the subdynamic, is the period of the most danger.*

246 Parallel Characteristics and Variables

Similarly we have the protracted nature of legal involvements with PA cases, as the citation for Gardner (2001) in an earlier chapter put a fine point on: "I have never seen a speedy decision made in a child custody dispute" (p. 67). Unfortunately, that has been this author's experience as well in PA cases. There is a fundamental lack of understanding of the phenomenon and an unfortunate impatience for these kinds of cases to be heard in courts. It has conversely been this author's experience that if there is enough time to explain PA as an IMD, and to discuss its consequences, legal officials tend to understand these dynamics. So, as in most healthcare and legal situations, thorough analysis and understanding up front tends to forestall a number of other subsequent less constructive hearings, mediations, or meetings on the matter. *But, understanding it, and taking the steps necessary to intervene are two different things.* With these delays there is also the ever higher probability that an RP who has been missing her or his child or children, and has faced one delay after another through the legal process, might feel beset. *In time,* the RP may fall prey to the ongoing contemporary and situational stressors and begin to act in the fashion suggested by Counter Productive Parenting. Also, it seems worth pointing out that these cases do not start out being high-conflict cases; rather they regress into such a state due to a multiplicity of factors. Containing these cases may prove challenging for legal officials, but there is a real need to thoroughly assess what is actually occurring in order to intervene appropriately. If intervention is unusually swift, then there is little use for the optional legal subdynamic described earlier. But, if the case moves at the customary rate with the same trepidation Gardner had spoken to nearly twenty years ago, then it is likely necessary to include the subdynamic in order to emphasize that the IMD across time will amplify and spread beyond just the two systems initially involved. In both IMDs early recognition is critical in either setting, since, if the IMD is suspected, efforts can be made to identify it and intervene appropriately, as will be discussed in the next chapter.

(rc) The Child(ren)

Now, as for the child(ren) in these cases, the argument has obviously been made earlier in this piece that the child(ren) have certain individual dimensional symptoms in accordance with Tables 5.6 and 6.4. Although literature shows most often that PA dynamics play out in a single-child family system, there are homes in which multiple children are at risk. As such, it is likely, if not probable, that each of these children may have different individual dimensional symptoms. For our purposes here,

Parallel Characteristics and Variables **247**

the majority of children in the FDBP condition will fit a certain static pattern and be between the ages of birth to eight years old per the literature. Conversely, in PA the children and adolescents are at the other end of the age continuum and have more variable characteristics. Also, the most lethal period of the FDBP IMD centers on an age in which the child is preverbal (Bass & Glaser, 2014; Greiner et al., 2013). While there are exceptions in the literature, up to and including children who have been co-opted via a Stockholm-like syndrome in FDBP, the vast majority of these children are young, and their relative mental health and decision-making are not as variable as the children and adolescents in the PA condition. Therefore, to illustrate the range of these conditions, descriptions of PA children and adolescents will follow.

As for these descriptions, they will begin with a child's strengths. There are resilient children (*rc*), much like adaptive and healthy RPs, who do not fit the typical distant and uninvolved description. These *rc*s have enough coherence and resources within them, likely coupled with external supports, that they are able to function well. The *rc* is healthy enough in such cases that even when pressed by ABs from one or both parents, they are able to resist such pressures and maintain pre-existing relations with parental figures in their lives and extended family. It is probable, too, that a child such as this has the benefit of at least one parent who has been present and stable, or perhaps an extended family member with these attributes or some other adult who is a positive and solid influence on the child (Beresford, 1994; Reid, 1993; Werner, 1993; Werner & Smith, 1992; Masten et al., 1990).

The considerations here are furthered by what will be referred to as the Naïve Child (*nc*). This is the child as described earlier in the literature who is simply too young, inexperienced or cognitively/developmentally immature to engage in *abs* to the extent that he or she does not enter into a transformative dynamic resulting in moderate to severe PA; yet pressures are potentially sufficient to allow the child to be described as suffering from inconsistently mild *abs*. In these cases, per insights offered in Chapter 6 and described fundamentally in Tables 6.4 and 6.5, the child her- or himself has not changed. On the other hand, there are older children who by their late teenage years or young adulthood have the sophistication to see through the PA dynamic and choose not to be part of it. Generally, these older teenagers and young adults would be seen as either experienced in life, an Experienced Child (*ec*) or Resilient Child (*rc*) and not subject to the PA dynamic for these reasons. Or, at least it would be discussed as something else. This leaves what will be described as the Alienated/Vulnerable Child (*a/vc*), who with the stresses in the family system, experiences the forces bearing down on her or him, and

248 Parallel Characteristics and Variables

acquiesces to the influences of the Alienating Parent or Parents (AP) for the reasons described above.

It follows that it is not simply a child who is being discussed in an Interrelated Multidimensional Diagnosis. There are characteristics and symptoms that serve as variables that, in turn, influence the quality of the child's involvement in the Interrelated Multidimensional Diagnosis. In the PA example given, we have the a/vc, a child not only subject to contemporary and situational stresses, but one who in this circumstance may well be subject to a developmental stressor that is of a similar magnitude to those that created the arrest in the development of their parent(s) in the first place. Hence, the potential beginning of an intergenerational cycle. Just as the AP's life was irrevocably changed in time by the developmental stressor he or she faced, this child is faced with a similar situation and in a state of vulnerability to the influences of the pathological dynamic foisted upon her or him by the AP's actions. The questions then become how coherently the child is put together, how well he or she is able to make use of internal and external resources, and to what degree he or she possesses resilient personal attributes that create enough of a barrier to withstand this developmental stressor and the PA pathological dynamic. Perhaps there are protective factors at work, such as naïveté with younger children (nc) and resilience in older children or even adolescents (rc). These descriptions underscore the import of the child's coherence and/or ego strength as well as her or his state at the time. These additional variables might actually hold the key to whether or not the pathological dynamic for the IMD fully develops. In the PA IMD, this author is reminded of the apocryphal story of the Dutch boy who saved his town by placing his finger in the dike (Dodge, 1865).

This is an apt metaphor to describe the experience of these children since in these cases they tend to bear the full brunt of the developmental, contemporary and situational stresses that have been described throughout this literature. Should they resist these forces, as does the Dutch boy in the fable, these children act heroically out of love for their other parent and the integrity of their family. At this stage, an IMD has not formed yet and the dynamics would be more in keeping with those articulated by Parental Denigration (PD) in Chapters 4 and 6. The AP has, by definition, been speaking of the RP in a denigrating fashion and violating the tenets of most parenting plans wherein each parent is charged with supporting and nurturing a child's relationship with the other parent. The child is still suffering psychological abuse by way of the AP's demeanor, speaking ill of the RP, and discouraging any positive feelings the child may have toward the other parent.

If and when a child's capacity to resist the onslaught of the AP's psychological abuses gives way, he or she too begins to engage in Alienating Behaviors

Figure 7.2 The little Dutch boy and the dike.

(*abs*). Not only does this child become an Alienated Child (*ac*), but they also experience a new punctuated steady state wherein the PA IMD pathological dynamic has been brought to life. The same may be said in FDBP, when the AP harms the child in order to gain attention and play the sick role in a healthcare setting. It is at this point that a new punctuated steady state begins, wherein the FDBP IMD pathological dynamic has manifested.

 ## IMD Symbolic Language and a Common Representation System

In order to help diagram these matters and find an apt shorthand by which practitioners, professionals and researchers might describe the characteristics, interrelationships and symptoms of the individuals and systems involved, this author reviewed the work done with genograms, symbolic language in mathematics and other rudimentary representations. However, none of the rudimentary symbolic languages studied appeared to be concise enough or interactively clear enough to describe these relationships. If readers have ever conducted an intake and attempted to deal with family-based information, a family therapy session, or a referral for one of these kinds of cases, they are familiar with the outpouring of information and other challenges associated with recording these matters. While genograms and mathematical symbolic language are very useful in other contexts, here even most recognized healthcare abbreviations prove to be inexpedient. In turn, this author sought to create a hybrid shorthand for those working with these families and systems that would provide meaningful symbolic chunks of information that could be unpacked and narrated subsequent to the session and/or a ready shorthand for multidisciplinary teams to communicate or debate their shared perceptions. There is certainly enough novelty within the pages of this text that this author did not feel driven to create a descriptive symbolic language, but it seemed a necessity in order to aid communication among practitioners, professionals and researchers.

As readers may well have discerned, they have already been introduced to a number of these symbols at section headings in this chapter, and a key for the basic symbols has been provided in Appendix A. It should also be noted that some conventions of healthcare abbreviations have been included, mathematical symbols substituted for other meanings, and abbreviations used throughout the text that are intended to be applied. The family and other system representations are intended to have singular cross-hatch or tick marks to indicate the number of family members or involved members of a system (see Figure 7.3), and the same markings could readily signify how many symptoms the practitioner, professional or researcher perceives at each dimension (see Figure 7.4). Other additions will likely follow if what has been proposed progresses.

Any particular resemblance to other languages, if there are such instances, are purely coincidental since this author is neither much of a linguist nor a scholar of different languages. This language is in its beginnings and has been presented in a rough form to emphasize the sketch-like nature that this shorthand will likely take. What this author refers to as IMD Symbolic Language may be written either left to right or down the page one dimension at a time, whatever direction seems most useful. Rudimentary examples follow that express a representation for the FDBP IMD described in Chapter 5 (see Figure 7.5) and for the PA IMD described in Chapter 6 (see Figure 7.6), respectively.

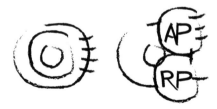

Figure 7.3 IMD Symbolic Language: Family member tick marks.

Figure 7.4 IMD Symbolic Language: Dimensional symptoms tick marks.

Figure 7.5 IMD Symbolic Language: FDBP IMD.

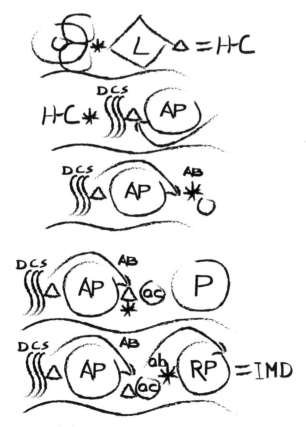

Figure 7.6 IMD Symbolic Language: PA IMD.

Note

1. In the mathematical sense.

Interventions, Motions, Policies, Procedures, and Potential IMDs

8

Much of the work in earlier chapters has focused on how to take a step back and recognize when an IMD is at work. We have looked at these phenomena as novel ideas, and the names FDBP and PA have gone by, as well as the parallel nature of an IMD's dimensional characteristics as a pathological dynamic that endangers children and affects other family members. It is, therefore, time to underscore that stemming the death and suffering that these conditions may bring is the ultimate purpose of identifying such IMDs as FDBP and Parent Alienation. If we as practitioners, professionals and researchers know that the phenomenon we are dealing with is a condition that, left unchecked, will kill potentially one in ten to one in twenty children (FDBP) or is one that will cause ongoing suffering for between twenty to forty million children as PA spreads throughout family systems into communities and other systems, is it not incumbent on larger systems to intervene? We must, of course, not only intervene but, once symptoms have been recognized to a reasonable degree of scientific certainty, do so swiftly and thoroughly.

Hopefully, by this point in the text it has become clear that this author is not suggesting a rush to judgment in any way, shape or form. Instead, just the opposite case has been made here, to establish the best facts available and pit them against the hypotheses that:

1. No IMD exists;
2. Some lesser determination of pathology exists, such as an unusual illness or maladaptive caregiving (FDBP), or maladaptive caregiving CPP or Parental Denigration (PA);

3. Some other condition is at work such as physical or sexual abuse, abandonment or neglect, or intimate-partner violence; or,
4. That the IMD of FDBP or PA exists, and that there is sufficient evidence that it is more probable than other hypotheses.

The symptoms of both proposed IMDs have been discussed, and this discussion has included an examination of not only the interrelated nature of these phenomena at the individual, system and subdynamic level, but dimensional proofs that include the particular characteristics, interrelationships and behavior that lead to pathological dynamics. In turn, the dangers associated with these pathological dynamics have been described to the extent that the impact of an IMD on individuals and systems are by now likely clear to the reader. After laying out the argument for IMDs across the last seven chapters, it is now time to describe how to resolve the pathology associated with them in reasonable fashion. However, as the reader may detect from the prior seven chapters, not all or even most parents involved in an IMD are willing and able to respond in a reasonable fashion. This point is critical for understanding the other aspects of this chapter as well, since the pathological dynamics at work in these cases are ones that require procedures, policy and the action of healthcare, legal and governmental systems to prevent them.

This author has testified in a number of legal hearings on IMDs and worked in healthcare settings dealing with IMDs, and the main issues that impede addressing IMDs are conceptualization, understanding and time. Imagine the challenge one faces in attempting to distill what lies in the pages above and getting that across within the confines of a treatment team meeting or a legal proceeding. Further, it is clear that when an IMD has become active in the fashion described there must be no compunction about coming to an intervention. To practitioners or professionals who have just tried to wrap their minds around the concept, the interventions described may sound extreme in moderate-to-severe cases. Thus, further scientific explanation is often required. To those who, after that, still find the position extreme or implausible, akin to the length of Chapters 4, 5, and 6, this author would but answer,

> "How extreme is it for parents to harm their children in order to gain attention, aware that there is a 1 in 5 chance that the child may die or be permanently disabled?"
>
> —or—
>
> "How extreme is it for parents to alienate their children from not only a good parent but a parent whom they were once bonded to, and to permanently impair the child's ability to trust themselves and others?"

These kinds of questions tend to dominate the discussion on FDBP and PA in these settings, and even so there is a range of cases that comprise each Interrelated Multidimensional Diagnosis.

Studies old and new speak to different levels of pathology. On the one hand, there is what has been referred to as maladaptive caregiving and/or milder forms of FDBP and Parent Alienation. Then, of course, on the other hand, there are severe forms of the pathological dynamic in FDBP and PA that are described in Chapters 5 and 6. It has been suggested that these determinations are best derived by the combination of a multidisciplinary team's work and one of three methods of quantitative analysis: the tables in the aforementioned chapters, a measurement such as the ones by Baker and her colleagues' questionnaires (Baker & Ben-Ami, 2011; Baker, Burkhard, & Albertson-Kelly, 2012) or others (Bernet et al., 2018; Moné & Biringen, 2012; Rowlands, 2019), or the IMD Inventories©. Such determinations would naturally include whether the pathological dynamic exists and then what level of intervention meets the needs of the case.

Procedural and policy discussions also logically follow this discussion and may guide the recognition and intervention involved with IMDs through governmental, healthcare and legal systems. In fact, though current hospital procedures are often adequate to address the FDBP IMD, how to contend with false positives and the legal process that follows appears to need further work. Child protective services agencies also need to be closely involved in these processes as well. While intervention strategies exist in PA, a comprehensive intervention strategy through legal interventions and/or a reunification process has not been thoroughly broached in a proactive fashion with motions that address each stage of the process. In turn, this author and his colleague have prepared sample motions that may be used to guide in both the identification and intervention of the PA Interrelated Multidimensional Diagnosis. Like the IMD Inventories© discussed earlier, these motions will bear the name Interrelated Multidimensional Diagnosis Motions© followed by the kind of IMD the motion is designed to address (Bütz & Rock, 2019a, 2019b).

The latter part of this chapter will address other potential IMDs, and while a number have come to this author's mind regarding particularly thorny and troublesome dynamics, there are larger issues here. For now, the focused elaboration of potential IMDs includes those that would best serve the most vulnerable, such as children, the disabled, and the infirmed, as well as long- standing wounds cultures have suffered that symbiotically harm the prospect of a larger beneficent civil society. The reader may well predict discussion of the two IMDs that have already been mentioned across the pages of this text, the first being Malingering by Proxy and the second Parental

Estrangement. In addition to recommending that both of these pathological dynamics be folded into the proposals for IMDs, this author will offer two other phenomena.

How to Intervene and the Moral Courage to Intervene

Gardner was cited earlier for describing his exceptional frustration with how courts have responded to the needs of children in PA cases. In Chapter 3, this author also described his extreme frustration with the ongoing proliferation of terms that describe FDBP Interrelated Multidimensional Diagnoses. The need to properly address these IMDs is well known, and the need to intervene has been unmistakable according to the literature on these matters, as referenced numerous times within this text. The FDBP IMD is the number one health threat that child protective service agencies address. It is the most lethal and disabling condition, but it is no less important for the quality of the impact it may have on a child's psychological health and well- being. These matters and other statistics have consistently been reported across this literature, where, depending on the study cited, between 6% and 10% of children in FDBP cases die and an equal number are permanently disabled. Further, it often takes as much as a year and a half, on average, for the pathological dynamic to be recognized and therefore for intervention to begin. Similarly, the PA literature has been building over the years and suggests strongly at this point that the number of these cases has steadily increased, touching an estimated 22 to 44 million children's lives:

> Using the percentage of parents who reported being alienated from their children in our poll (13.4%), this means approximately 22,211,287 adults are currently targets of parental alienation. Given that many parents have more than one child, our estimate also implies that there could be 22 million, 44 million, or even more children affected by this problem.
> (Harman, Leder-Elder, & Biringen, 2016, p. 65).

Others suggest that this number is much, much bigger (Siracusano et al., 2015) and that PA is a worldwide phenomenon. Think about that, and that we also have come to better know the long- term impacts on children as they become adults (Baker & Ben-Ami, 2011; Rueda, 2004), when earlier studies suggested that PA and other impacts of separation and divorce in families were just a transitional problem (Wallerstein & Kelly, 1980a). The literature building over the past twenty years paints a very different picture (Wallerstein, Lewis, & Blakeslee, 2000), not only for the children who have been impacted by being alienated but for their children as well, since there has also been a growing hypothesis regarding an intergenerational transmission of these dynamics. Parenthetically, there has been a building literature in FDBP suggesting the same. For these reasons there is little doubt of the need to intervene, and the need to intervene once an IMD pattern forms to a sufficient degree. That is, in fact, the purpose of this book and this author's earlier article with his colleague (Bütz & Evans, 2019).

If we are able to identify the pathological dynamic and build to consensus about what it looks like, how it operates, and that it is a form of abuse, then we are able to collectively intervene and not falter in the face of the kind of splitting or triangulation dynamics that in this author's view are inherent to both of these Interrelated Multidimensional Diagnoses. Establishing a consensus based on scientific study and multiple perspectives "at the table" is the purpose of defining the IMD, but it is important to do so without rushing to judgment, as has been described throughout the entirety of the arguments above. It is proposed that in coming to terms with IMDs there have been three problems. It should be plain by now that terminology and how to agree on defining the phenomenon presented as an IMD has been the first stumbling block. The next has been just how to intervene, and the third has been gathering the determination to do so once the pathology has been identified. As such, while there are interventions, protocols and reunification plans for these IMDs, the focus here will be on thoughtful follow-through rather than on specifying a certain form or type of intervention. In this author's view there are multiple roads to the same destination. Going back to our metaphors from Chapter 2, what is truly impactful in these cases is to *ensure* as practitioners and providers that the coals associated with the fires of FDBP *are out*, and that in PA the erratic sounds produced by a particularly bad Sinfonia are extinguished. Interrelated Multidimensional Diagnoses need to be contained and attended to like a campfire in the wild, and therefore observed until we are certain the coals have gone cold. Follow-through, vigilance, and a systems perspective are the means to safeguard successful lasting interventions in these cases.

258 Interventions, Motions, Policies

Let us agree for now that hypothetically an IMD has been identified as more probable than not by the IMD Inventory—FDBP© (Bütz & Miller, 2019a) or .50+, i.e., numerically a value .00 to 1.0. In that case, and despite the challenges with terminology described in Chapter 3, there are interventions that can be performed. In fact, we are able to find step-wise partial protocols in a number of the articles that have been cited throughout this text. For example, Stirling (2007) described standard considerations in these cases, and these interventions have been supplied in Table 8.1.

Once the FDBP IMD has been identified, these interventions are often accompanied by knowledge of the most common medical presentations as well (Flaherty & MacMillan, 2013, p. 591; Sheridan, 2003, p. 443). These first steps tend to be fairly clear by comparison to those seen in PA, wherein once the FDBP IMD is identified the practitioners have or will contact child protective services providers, separate the

Table 8.1 FDBP Interventions (Stirling 2007)

A list of possible interventions follows, from the least restrictive to the most restrictive. Some of these options require action by outside agencies (child protective services, private counselors, law enforcement, etc).

1. Use individual and/or family therapy while depending on a primary care physician to be 'gatekeeper' for future medical care utilization.
2. Monitor ongoing medical care usage by involving people or institutions outside the medical practice to alert the physician gatekeeper about health care issues. . . .
3. Admit the child to an inpatient hospital setting or a partial hospital program, where his or her actual signs and symptoms can be monitored (as opposed to the signs and symptoms reported by the parent) . . . .
4. Involve child protective services. . . .
5. Place the child in another family setting permanently.*
6. Prosecute the offending parent and incarcerate her or him, thus eliminating access to the child.*

---

* With comments that have been made previously and that will follow, this author disagrees with this recommendation unless there has been the finding of severe FDBP IMD.

child from the parent, begin treating the illness, and address the parent as a second level of intervention that is often deferred to child protective services.

With PA situations on the other hand, the involvement of child protective services as a member of a multidisciplinary effort is not nearly so clear given the often-muddled view of psychological abuse in these cases. There are allegations that appear to be "he said/she said" scenarios, and in many situations PE cases tend to be more straightforward if there has been a well- researched, established or known history. In PA cases, while there may be findings that cumulatively are suggestive across the tables in Chapter 6, or findings from one of the measures mentioned earlier, or a more probable than not outcome on the IMD Inventory-PA©, without a multidisciplinary focus that has the weight of the Court's ability to intervene, the pathological dynamic will continue.

Effective intervention in PA cases requires the unusual step of a proactive Court that weighs the evidence presented, recognizes the pathology of the dynamic, and takes action to stall any further degradation and/or fracture of the blended family system post-divorce/separation. Assisting the Court in these situations requires the use of assessment and knowledgeable experts and therapists who understand PA to assist attorneys in attempting to clarify these matters. The case needs to be made to the Court, and the Court needs to make a ruling in order for intervention to gain a sound footing and be successful. Often, this requires an expert in PA and at minimum a desk review addressing these matters. More often, these cases also require the involvement of a therapist and the affidavits of educators and other professionals, and then an expert to clarify the pattern. Getting an assessment conducted or a therapist involved may well prove problematic, since often APs will not support these efforts if they have joint or sole custody. As stated throughout the literature, there are a myriad of tactics used by APs to hinder and obfuscate detection of PA and prevent intervention. For these reasons, practitioners need to know what they are doing when encountering these cases, have sufficient expertise and knowledge of PA, and have a sound understanding of the paramount importance of remaining neutral so as not to be split or triangulated.

So the question that the practitioners have to answer is whether or not PA is an active IMD in the case and are there enough observable symptoms to suspect it. To assist with this are the tables in Chapter 6, the aforementioned measures, and/or the IMD Inventory-PA© that is

260 Interventions, Motions, Policies

currently under development (Bütz & Miller, 2019b). If that determination has been made and/or a solid enough case established based on what has been described above in this text, then what is it that the Court is being asked to do? Again, that centers on what degree of pathology is being addressed. Is it a mild, moderate, or severe case? What are the child's placement arrangements in the parenting plan, and is the parenting plan visitation schedule being exercised in keeping with the Court's plan? This author and his colleague have drafted sample IMD Motions-PA© to contend with just such questions (Bütz & Rock, 2019b), and still the case will have to be made by counsel with the assistance of experts and practitioners. Clawar and Rivlin (2013b) have done a particularly nice job capturing the numerous challenges involved in their text. Warshak (2015) has also explained how the prospect of outpatient therapy may be rendered useless in these cases:

> Case studies and clinical experience suggest that psychotherapy while children remain under the care of their favored parent is unlikely to repair damaged parent—child relationships and may make things worse. . . . No study has demonstrated effectiveness of any form of psychotherapy in overcoming severe alienation in children who have no regular contact with the rejected parent.
>
> (p. 243)

We have this from Warshak (2015) as well:

> The court should be informed that psychotherapy is most likely to be effective if (a) there have been no prior failed attempts, (b) the parent with whom the child is aligned is likely to cooperate and support the child's treatment and progress, and (c) the child has ample time to experience care and nurturing from the rejected parent. On the other hand, if one of more attempts with psychotherapy have already failed to remedy the problem, if the aligned parent is likely to sabotage treatment, and if the child is empowered to avoid contact with the rejected parent, the court should understand that ordering another round of psychotherapy without changing the amount of contact the child has with each parent is unlikely to remedy the problem and may postpone effective intervention until it is too late.
>
> (p. 243)

Such examples are replete in the literature and have made it very clear what the Court needs to be apprised of in these cases; but evidence is needed that describes the status of a case and what form of PA IMD is in play, that is, mild, moderate, or severe. When Warshak described no failed attempts at therapy and noted that the other parent may well support therapy, deductively it is reasonable to consider that he was speaking of a mild form of Parent Alienation. Yet, later in the very same passage, if the AP may be expected to sabotage therapy and the *ac* is empowered to avoid contact with the RP, at minimum it is likely that the degree of PA is moderate to moderately severe. These are all critical variables to be clarified before first educating and then asking for the Court's assistance with intervention. Those practitioners and professionals weighing into these cases should be clear that once PA has become the new steady state for the blended family, the Court's clear and decisive intervention will be a necessity. Practitioners and professionals should be aware of a scenario that has been known to play out in these cases, even with the above considerations. An expert has been called in to testify about a desk review, and per the discussions above there has been enough material to reach the opinion of suspected PA. Then, in this author's experience one of two things tends to happen, either in court or after the proceeding. The first is that counsel for the parent suspected of engaging in ABs would object to any further work done by the expert in the case because they are already biased, regardless of the dispassionate approach that this expert may have taken to the desk review. This often happens during the proceeding. The second is that after the proceeding the judge rules against this expert continuing to work on the case because the parent suspected of engaging in ABs would not be comfortable with that professional's continued work on the case and their counsel has objected. Plainly, either version of the scenario plays right into the kind of splitting and triangulation discussed above, since of course the parent suspected of engaging in ABs would object to a neutral review...

Other Considerations and Mild IMDs

Within recent weeks, this author has had several cases in which the determinations of counsel were that PA was active, and one included a report written by a guardian ad litem. In such cases, rather than start off with an assessment or rely on the interpretation of the therapist involved, this author suggests a desk review of the documentation with all of the applicable legal documents, educational records and records from healthcare providers. By the way, this is the same kind of recommendation that has been in place in FDBP cases for some time. After conducting somewhere between four and eight hours of document review, it was apparent to this author that one of these cases involved PD and the

262 Interventions, Motions, Policies

other involved Parental Estrangement. The children were too young, and the interrelated pattern of individuals and systems on multiple dimensions made it clear that the disturbances in each of these cases were emanating from either the abuse or the denigration of the AP. Behaviors that were historically consistent with the actions of one or the other parent in each dyad. The children in these cases were indeed being engaged or involved, but they were not engaging in *abs*; instead their contact with the other parent was being blocked and manipulated through various ploys. Consistent with the literature on these matters, despite the young age of these children, these cases had been before each Court for at least a year, if not more, and each of these APs were repeating previously established woefully maladaptive behaviors.

In PA cases, the child or children in question are most often over the age of seven or eight, and they are engaging in the *abs* that were discussed at length in Chapter 6. It is clear that in PA there are one or two APs engaging in ABs, there is a corresponding RP often, and systems are involved, certainly a legal system, but at times also healthcare or behavioral healthcare systems. Thus, to reach a more probable than not outcome for PA on an IMD Inventory©, these elements must be present. But, as the cases in the prior paragraph suggest, there are conditions in which this threshold is not met by the inventory's base marker of beyond chance. Such findings either suggest another form of abuse such as PD or PE, as in the cases above, or a mild form of Parental Alienation. This is why there have been references throughout that both IMDs exist within a range, that there are variable characteristics or symptoms, and that *IMDs themselves are also intended to be variable*. Returning to the example of PA, the IMD concept is intended to describe a range of pathology from mild to severe as Gardner suggested many years ago (2001, pp. 62–63). So, IMDs that do not meet the criteria for more probable than not require further consideration, since these cases may suggest a mild form of PA. The question that would naturally follow is what aspects of an IMD, or tables within an IMD's individual, system and subdynamic characteristics and symptoms description, are looked at to support the hypothesis of a mild diagnosis?

Such considerations fall back to the table structures spoken to in Chapters 5 and 6, bringing FDBP back into the discussion. There are tables in each case with certain characteristics or symptoms that are more closely correlated with an IMD finding of more probable than not, or even whole tables that correlate more highly with such a finding. It is a sensible conclusion that, for example, there would be a higher correlation with the final diagnostic table for each IMD with the IMD Inventory©, i.e., Tables 5.12 and 6.7. These tables fundamentally reflect each IMD's base criteria. These tables would deductively have a high correlation with the more probable than not finding that

Interventions, Motions, Policies **263**

describes the pathological dynamic, but this may not hold in some cases, or there may be other tables that have better correlations. So, if there is an outcome on the IMD Inventory© that is subthreshold, but there are findings that include these particular characteristics and symptoms and/or tables that are highly correlated with the IMD's pathological dynamic, it is more likely that a mild IMD hypothesis is supported.

Just like the potential for mild IMDs, there are findings within the IMD Inventories© that will suggest more severe pathology as well. *More probable than not, or a preponderance of the evidence, in shorthand, means an outcome that has a better than 50% probability.* But what about findings that reflect a more severe pathology or that meet a higher legal standard? It is highly unlikely that these inventories will ever reach the standard of *beyond a reasonable doubt,* but these inventories may well suggest a level of confidence that is *clear and convincing.* To be plain, just because a questionnaire or an inventory has produced a finding that suggests either more probable than not or clear and convincing, there is obviously the necessity to factor in clinical judgment and the input of a multidisciplinary group to review these outcomes and come to a clinical healthcare—legal determination as well.

The FDBP multidisciplinary team suggested should at minimum have an expert on FDBP, legal counsel from the local County attorney's office, a child protective services caseworker with a high level of sophistication about these matters, a pediatric healthcare specialist and at least one, if not two, behavioral health providers who are trained in forensics and family dynamics, and who are ideally coupled in such a fashion that they are able to assess the needs of the entire family system, i.e., each behavioral health provider has complementary areas of expertise. Naturally a subset of this multidisciplinary team makeup would ideally be involved in PA cases, or where such teams do not exist the involvement of a guardian ad litem or a parent coordinator, at least, would be useful. With the latter situations, it would be very useful to have a Court's order indicating their role in the case as a guardian ad litem or a parenting coordinator. These practitioners and professionals tend to be more effective when they have the capacity to investigate, make modest determinations in the case, and suggest further assessment if need be (Nichols, 2014; Carter, 2011; Ackerman, 2006). Use of the IMD Inventories© is conceived of in a fashion similar to the kinds of findings produced by more significant psychological assessment instruments and/or tests. Those outcomes may be used to describe certain symptoms, even to suggest diagnoses, but they are not intended to be used alone for making diagnoses (American Educational Research Association, American Psychological Association, & National Council on Measurement in Education, 2014). The same holds with the IMD

Inventories©, and by design they are intended to be used when accompanied by a multidisciplinary healthcare—legal discussion and general consensus. Obviously, not everyone will agree with the findings or the hypothesis-driven discussion, but, if the majority of a multidisciplinary group is in agreement, it is likely that an IMD is at work. Intervention naturally flows from the quality of knowledge that has been identified, and it is unwise to consider one without the other. Just as not all cases have the same IMD dynamic, not all interventions are the same for this range of pathology.

FDBP Intervention and Reunification

Before addressing intervention and reunification, it is recognized that thus far this author has not brought forward literature that soundly describes FDBP as an IMD in a fashion that designates mild, moderate or severe instances of the pathological dynamic. It has been alluded to but not firmly stated apart from the mild presentation discussed simultaneously with PA's mild form. Mild forms do not meet the .50 threshold amid the assembled tables from Chapter 5 or the IMD Inventory©, nor do they meet the legal language of more probable than not due to the preponderance of the evidence. Yet, the findings are near this threshold and are concordant with aspects of the tables described in Chapter 5 or the IMD Inventory© that are highly correlated with such a finding. Moderate cases are, of course, above this threshold but near it in Factitious Disorder by Proxy. The severity of the symptoms and the proposed diagnostic criteria in Chapter 5 are not as prevalent. Severe cases obviously exceed the more probable than not threshold for findings via the tables from Chapter 5 or the IMD Inventory© at a level that approaches, and may well speak to, the language of clear and convincing in the law. These determinations may also be supported by symptoms that are medically recognized as more lethal, and most, if not all, criteria are met for the proposed diagnostic criteria.

Taking up intervention and reunification in FDBP cases, this author has been particularly taken by the work of Adshead and Bluglass (2005, 2001) as well as Kozlowska, Foley, and Crittenden (2006). They have attempted to describe these parents in understandable terms and to describe a range of pathology by making use of the Adult Attachment Inventory (AAI) and a clinical assessment in order to gain insights into these parents. It follows that if there are mild, moderate and severe cases, then these parents require different levels of intervention predicated on the severity of the case and clinical judgment. There were indications, for example, that by gauging the origin of the parents' conflicts, intervention strategies could be developed for parents for whom years ago it was seemingly a foregone conclusion that they could never continue to be parents. These groups of practitioners have argued that these parents need to be understood, and that if that step is taken then, as Adshead and Bluglass (2005) stated,

> We would argue for the development of psychological treatment services for all maltreating parents, to include psychological therapy, psychoeducational interventions and medications where appropriate, and an active approach to risk management.
>
> (p. 332)

Kozlowska, Foley, and Crittenden (2006) had indeed taken this a step further in their work with Rosie and the Andersons; Rosie, the child, had been placed in foster care for three months, and then we have the following:

> Therapy with the couple over a period of two years occurred while Rosie was returned to the family, and the parents agreed to specific court requirements. These included regular school attendance, review by a specified doctor when Rosie was ill, and cessation of all unnecessary medical treatments and investigations. Rosie remained in the care of the government department with some features of parental responsibility, including educational and medical care, being shared with, and specifically allocated to, her father. The parents attended all sessions as a couple, and some sessions were attended by the entire family.
>
> (p. 101)

These therapeutic efforts focused on addressing feelings, working on each parent's family of origin by way of working through their childhoods, the quality of the marital relationship, shared responsibility when presenting for healthcare, family therapy sessions with the aim of addressing what happened to Rosie, and "normal" interactions, as practiced with healthcare providers.

Bass and Glaser (2014) also described interventions with parents from the perspective of early recognition and management, and proposed the following (paraphrased considerations and the numbers here were used by this author to suggest an order of operations in a mathematical sense):

1. The potential of a child's return to the parents depended on parental capacity and the parents' response to the intervention and treatment service offered.

266 Interventions, Motions, Policies

2. Therapeutic needs of the child, active rehabilitation, followed by the needs of both the child in question and the siblings to have a truthful narrative about the parents' actions, and in some cases separation from one or both parents. Support for the loss of relationship with their parents in the immediate situation, and with older children addressing guilt, potential complicity, and the reality of the FDBP dynamic.
3. Therapeutic needs the family may have, which include the generally conceived of "remote parent's" processing of a renewed awareness of the family, the abuses to the children, potential feelings of guilt for the lack of awareness and support of the abusive parent. The support needed if the remote parent shifts into the role of the child's or the children's primary parent, day-to-day activities and routines, and increased care provided to the other siblings that have typically been neglected should be addressed. Then, a new narrative was conceived of as a healthy necessity for the family to move on.
4. Needs of the abusive parent to first of all address the harm caused, the loss of relationships they experienced, and the potential for feelings of guilt, shame, or suicidal ideations. If these are absent, it is cause for concern and should be addressed. It was noted that these individuals do have histories of abuse and neglect, and the development of characterological traits and, as such, self-reflection tends to be difficult. It follows that as the outcome of an assessment process therapeutic efforts are needed to address the range of pathology suggested by the characteristics and symptoms the parent may well possess. (p. 7)

As the reader is able to see, these steps in the therapeutic process seem to mirror those provided to the Andersons by Kozlowska, Foley, and Crittenden earlier (2006). It may be evident but, essentially with what has been described, the scaffolding for a rudimentary flow chart of reasons supporting reunification and a treatment plan to do so have been provided.

These are hopeful conceptualizations that suggest, perhaps arguably, mild to moderate cases of an FDBP Interrelated Multidimensional Diagnosis. The descriptions provided herein of these authors' work move forward as if reunification is a possibility. But, first things must come first, and that is the health and welfare of the child or children and the assessment of the parents. It is, therefore, suggested that in these cases when an analysis of some combination of the tables described in Chapter 5 or the IMD Inventory© achieves results, and there is consensus among the multidisciplinary team that some form of FDBP IMD exists, then the child and/or children need to be removed from the parents for a minimum period of time until further investigation and parental assessments may be conducted. Also, it is strongly suggested that charges are filed so that the case has legal standing and the child or children are afforded the oversight of child protective services and a guardian ad litem, or the like, knowledgeable in these pathological dynamics. The nature of the aforementioned investigations has been addressed in the literature reasonably well for the past twenty years or so, with the exception of looking for the proof-based assembly of characteristics and symptoms that lead to an IMD's pathological dynamics. That much should be fairly straightforward. The assessment of the parents requires some suitable amalgam of the processes described by Bass and Glaser (2014), Kozlowska, Foley, and Crittenden (2006), and Adshead and Bluglass (2005); these include a thorough, even searching, social history and an Adult Attachment Inventory (AAI), as well as other instruments, inventories and tests. Logically, each parent will have strengths and weaknesses, the family system will likely have a plottable family dynamic on the Circumplex Model, and there may be other considerations. Once completed, these assessments should be presented to the multidisciplinary team for intervention and reunification determinations to be made. These determinations again should address the behavioral health status of the parents, their capacity to accept their role in the FDBP dynamic, the wrongdoing associated with it, their willingness to participate in treatment, and the degree to which they are open to change.

By openness to change, this author is speaking to models such as the one put forward by Prochaska and DiClemente (1983; Prochaska, DiClemente, & Norcross, 1992), which spelled out an individual's psychological preparedness for meaningful change. They outlined stages such as precontemplation, contemplation, preparation and action. Addressing a parent's capacity on this dimension will be a pivotal determination, and it should not only be included in these assessments, but weighted accordingly in the assessment process, since, as Prochaska, DiClemente, and Norcross (1992) have put it, "We have concentrated on the phenomenon of intentional change as opposed to societal, developmental or imposed change" (p. 1102).

By addressing the questions directly above, the multidisciplinary team will likely be able to determine whether or not one or both parents are able to be safely reunified with the child, or really children, what conditions need to be in place for the potential time frame for the reunification, and the interventions that may be necessary should there be a notable regression and the re-emergence of prior pathological dynamics. Still, and although it may be obvious, with an FDBP IMD finding, in all such cases the nature of any intervention is whither reunification, plain and simple. Even though this may be true it is suggested to a multidisciplinary team that its thoughts dwell on each parent's recognition of wrongdoing and openness to change. These are two critical matters that influence the kind and quality of interventions possible in these cases. It is entirely conceivable that the findings from the clinical investigation may lead to an outcome where the IMD Inventory© finding and the multidisciplinary team come to the determination of a mild form of FDBP prior to these parental capacity assessments. Yet, soon after that determination has been made one or both parents refuse to acknowledge their actions and/or the wrongfulness of their acts, and are wholly unwilling to participate in any assessment and subsequent treatment process. The opposite is possible as well, albeit unlikely, and practitioners and professionals working with these families need to be prepared for such possibilities.

It follows that determining the existence of an FDBP IMD is one thing; but then how these multidisciplinary teams suggest the Court intervene is another, and the Court's determination is still another. While procedures in the hospital are seemingly clear in ensuring a child's safety, given the different suggested levels of intervention for mild, moderate and severe cases and their somewhat imperfect treatment in the literature, what may not be so apparent is how to deal with these realities once the parent or parents and child or children are reunited during the period of intervention. The aforementioned literature spoke to, by the Court's order, the family working with one designated pediatric medical practitioner at regular intervals until such time as the case has made a final determination one way or the other. The therapists involved would hopefully have designated roles, certain frequency for contact, and topics to be addressed as part of the reunification plan. How often the multidisciplinary team would reconvene, or some derivation thereof, is another matter, too, that would be decided by the Court's order. In turn, there is a wide array of variables to be addressed in these cases, of which these are but a few examples based on the literature. It was for these reasons that this author felt the need to develop IMD Motions© with his colleague (Bütz & Rock, 2019a, 2019b), so as to capture the multifaceted nature of such cases and to do so in a readily accessible fashion. While there are generally intuitive realities that mild cases will be more likely to fully reunify and severe cases may well result in one or both parents' rights being terminated; each case is unique with more or less fragile children of different ages coupled with parents who may well have very different capacities. Interventions will need to be crafted to the particulars of each case. The suggestions from the multidisciplinary team for the particulars of a reunification plan, if there is one, are best represented in the Court's order with time frames, therapeutic modalities, and necessary oversight. Further, it is suggested that the time frame for reunification fits with conventional child protective services cases, and pertains to procedures for maintaining parental rights and for terminating parental rights.

What is being suggested here in many ways sounds like any number of child protective services reunification processes, but there are a few exceptions that should be recognized by all involved: first, the complicated nature of the FDBP IMD and what was involved to recognize it and intervene; second, the level of systemic pathology implied by simply making such a designation; and, third, how lethal the pathological dynamic may prove to be should it be revived if those within the multidisciplinary team relent in their vigilance.

PA Intervention and Reunification

When it comes to parental alienation, we have a similar set of dynamics at work. Fortunately, Gardner (2002, pp. 192–193) laid out a set of criteria that described PA's mild, moderate and severe forms. Also, to add a more quantitative set of thresholds accompanied by qualitative descriptions, many of the conventions described in FDBP broadly hold in PA as well, including conventions suggested from the tables in Chapter 6, augmented by the measures previously discussed for PA, and the IMD Inventory-PA©. It follows that, when considering mild, moderate and severe forms of the PA IMD, practitioners and professionals make use of an amalgam of those qualitative descriptions offered by Gardner such as: the suggested diagnostic criteria from Chapter 6, quantitative metrics that express values in mild cases below a threshold of .50 for more probable than not, but, have other findings that are highly correlated with positive outcomes. A moderate finding would naturally be above the threshold for more probable than not, and severe reflects a finding in excess of those that approach or speak to clear and convincing evidence. Multidisciplinary teams, or approximations thereof in these cases, will have to work out what combination of these outcomes they are most comfortable with as part of an evidentiary process.

Akin to the model suggested for FDBP IMD interventions and that reunification process, the use of a multidisciplinary team in a PA IMD case would certainly be desirable. But, often in these cases there is the reality of factions, the absence of child protective services, and the lack of a neutral knowledgeable

270 Interventions, Motions, Policies

practitioner. In these cases, therefore, some have argued that a guardian ad litem be included early on for just this reason to ensure not only the best interests of the child or children but their health and welfare as well (Nichols, 2014). Regardless of the team working on these cases, aside from the counsel for one parent or the other whose duty is to their client, even knowledgeable practitioners and professionals will at times be hard-pressed to maintain a neutral position despite the dicta of ethical practice. This is where in these discussions quantitative evidence, such as the tables from Chapter 6, measures that have been mentioned and the IMD Inventory-PA$^©$, may prove useful in clarifying matters and suggesting the severity of the case. Motions bent on establishing this severity and halting the pathological dynamic would be the next natural step; but the content of these motions would depend greatly on the parties and the PA IMD's severity. With mild cases it may be possible to work out a reasonable solution, visitation schedule and use of local behavioral healthcare practitioners with appropriate so-called carrots and sticks in the orders and a multidisciplinary therapeutic focus. In more moderate-to-severe and severe cases, a number of programs in the nation have been developed to deal with just these sorts of cases where the child simply refuses to spend any time at all with the RP (Friedlander & Walters, 2010; Judge & Deutsch, 2016; Sullivan et al., 2010; Warshak, 2018, 2010). These sorts of programs, however, may have differing levels of efficacy per the literature, and what is or is not addressed by each program may vary. These programs offer an approach analogous to an extended therapeutic weekend retreat. But there is seemingly not a consistent intervention for the AP, and there needs to be one aside from simply time away from the ac(s). These programs also do not speak to consistent aftercare for the AP, RP and ac(s), and, in this author's view, they need to. It seems a necessity to have a treatment plan that speaks to the arc of the therapeutic process, thus what happens before a program, what happens during one of these programs and what happens afterward for a period of at least six months. So, there is a need for a description of what happens prior to the time the RP and the ac(s) attend one of these programs. There also needs to be a treatment plan for reunification that describes what happens after they return from the treatment program, and which practitioners will be part of the therapeutic activities. Likewise, there also needs to be a discussion about what therapeutic progress the AP needs to make in order to start feathering in supervised visitation at some point, followed by benchmarks for unsupervised contact, and consequences for regressions and/or continued ABs. Sanctions are often spoken of during these programs, or immediately thereafter, but they are not clarified over the next three to six months. There is a whole dialogue in the literature on sanctions that APs must face if interventions are to be effective in moderate to severe cases. Such sanctions include reduced time with the *ac* and financial penalties, and these notions are tied to ABs, limiting contact, and a continued pattern of alienation. Obviously, the severity of the disincentive interventions for the AP is dependent on the severity of alienation in the particular case. As such, these treatment plans again need to be addressed through motions made, orders ruled on, and the efforts of a multidisciplinary team of sorts.

A Model for Reunification in PA

Once, roughly a year prior to taking on the project of writing this text, this author was approached in three different moderate-to-severe cases of PA to describe a plan for reunification. It was this author's initial take that surely reunification protocols had been developed from start to finish that already included sample motions and orders. It was imagined that identification, education and stalling the process would come first, followed by more intensive work, and then a period of aftercare to ensure that the "sinfonia" of PA played no more. Logically, the intervention process would begin by identification and be followed by psychoeducational efforts that would include the AP, RP and *alienated child(ren)*. This level of intervention is in many cases not possible without motions to the Court that identify the PA IMD and set initial steps of intervention and the scaffolding for a thorough reunification plan. Dependent on the severity, there are a range of options from working with local knowledgeable therapists and a cooperative type of multidisciplinary team in mild cases, on to the more significant programs discussed previously, with a period of preparation, program attendance and aftercare that leads to a graduated reunification schedule inclusive of sanctions with the Alienating Parent. Perhaps, there may even be the unfortunate need for further motions and orders that outline more intensive sanctions for continued efforts at alienation and non-cooperation up to, and including, a protracted period of no- contact and conditions that would lead to terminating parental rights as well.

No matter how much this author searched the literature and spoke to practitioners and professionals, there was no model that this author was able to uncover that addressed all these components of a reunification process. There was no set of sample motions or orders that this author was able to find that outlined a treatment plan for reunification from start to

272 Interventions, Motions, Policies

finish. There were motions tied to certain programs and other orders that addressed a part of the arc of interventions proposed here, but none that progressively dealt with education, intervention and aftercare in the way envisioned by this author. There were also resources that discussed therapeutic contemplations (Woodall & Woodall, 2017), a few particularly good overview chapters on reunification by Albertson-Kelly and Burkhard (2013) and Sauber (2013), and another on psychoeducational work with children (Baker & Andre, 2013), as well as two very good reference books that touched on a number of topics (Baker & Sauber, 2013; Lorandos, Bernet, & Sauber, 2013).

Considering what these resources did offer—and, in particular, this author is focused on the work of Albertson-Kelly and Burkhard (2013), Baker and Andre (2013) and Sauber (2013)—a few common elements ran through these treatments of the subject:

> Ensuring that the site for reunification and therapeutics is a safe place; Ensuring that the practitioners involved are neutral and knowledgeable on the topic; Maintaining a systems focus; The utility of psychoeducation; Managing the *ac*; Re-aligning parent roles for the AP and the RP; Addressing the alienation process and the narrative surrounding it; The need for ongoing work with the AP, the RP, and the *ac*; and Working toward co-parenting and stabilizing new family roles.

There were wrinkles addressed in this literature, too, but there was no per se identifiable start-to- finish model that included motions for an intervention process to gauge the degree to which the PA IMD had abated with consistent and ongoing involvement by a multidisciplinary team of sorts. If, indeed, recent discussions about FDBP and PA being intergenerational phenomena hold true, then these cases require additional vigilance. It is not just an episode of FDBP or PA. Instead, what has been argued herein is that these are IMDs and as such each manifestation began with background developmental and contemporary stresses, and, should the pathological dynamic become active, *it is after a change in state in at least one individual and the family system.* The treatment focus should be proactive rather than reactive and informative, with a planned level of follow-through that ensures that the IMD pathological dynamic is put to rest. In turn, this author developed an approach that was proposed to these parties and the courts, and designed to be proactive, informative, and with planned follow-through. Its outline has been provided below.

Introduction

The reunification process begins only after there has been sufficient evidence of a confirmed PA IMD dynamic that is more probable than not, and this finding derives from a documented triage analysis, which includes a flow chart and weighted considerations (see Figures 2.1, 4.1–4.3, 6.2, and 6.3–6.5) and is confirmed by variable exclusion and inclusion criteria across the tables in Chapter 6. This is a broad overview, and there are specific details not included in this outline. It is recommended that this process is six (6) months from start to finish. *None of the work proposed should be done without expert consultation and collaboration with one of the described intensive programs.* It is suggested that motions include the following steps and corroborating support from the literature as well as case law.

A. Define and Clarify Parental Alienation

This is largely for the Court's informational purposes, and includes the following articles, several of which include case law that counsel for either side may present (Baker, 2013b; Baker & Sauber, 2013; Clawar & Rivlin, 2013; Gardner, 2001, 2002; Lorandos, Bernet, & Sauber, 2013; Lowenstein, 2013; Warshak, 2015)

B. Parental Alienation Is Psychological Abuse

See Chapter 6, and the section on *Psychological Abuse.*

"No treatment of what is, and what is not, PA would be reasonably inclusive without considering the matter of psychological abuse, or what is often termed emotional abuse in the literature. While background or environment has been used to describe the conditions that set these dynamics in motion, the outcome of these dynamics when PA is created is the pathological psychological abuse of the child or children involved. It is hard to imagine that the purposive exploitation of a child by a parent to achieve a certain result in court is not both a pathological dynamic and psychological abuse. As Kelly and Johnston (2001) have stated: 'Whether such parents are aware of the negative impact on the child, these behaviors of the aligned parents (and his or her supporters) constitute emotional abuse of the child' (p. 257)."

(Baker & Ben-Ami, 2011; Baker, Burkhard, & Albertson-Kelly, 2012; Baker & Verrocchio, 2015; Harman, Kruk, & Hines, 2018; Kelly & Johnston, 2001). Case History is Consistent with Parental Alienation After Triage

Based on case material, see Figures 6.3, 6.4 and 6.5.

C. Pre-Intensive Program Reunification Work

This will require a schedule and early efforts toward psychoeducation with the *ac*(s), RP and AP, and work with the RP on what is referred to as Counter Productive Parenting (Albertson-Kelly & Burkhard, 2013; Baker & Andre, 2013; Clawar & Rivlin, 2013; Sauber, 2013).

D. Intensive Reunification Program

There are a number of intensive programs, and each has its own unique features, fees, policies and procedures (Friedlander & Walters, 2010; Judge & Deutsch, 2016; Sullivan et al., 2010; Warshak, 2018, 2010).

E. Post Reunification Program Aftercare

This will require a schedule and efforts to follow the interventions performed in the more intensive program and adherence to the program's advisements with continuing psychoeducation, reunification sessions and work on Counter Productive Parenting. Plainly, this will reasonably involve ongoing work with the *ac*(s), the RP and the AP.

F. Sanction Schedule for Alienating Parent Noncompliance

There are a variety of ways to go here, but most successful programs include financial and visit time sanctions, and some include reduced or even supervised parenting time in the final parenting plan (see Gardner [2001] and Warshak [2015] above).

G. Firm Time Frame for Final Parenting Plan (180 days from start to finish)

What lies above was intended as an outline for intervention and reunification, and as expected there are a number of adjustments that can be made to what has been described, other literature to rely upon, and other conventions to follow. It was also imagined that a motion, and ultimately an order, was written and issued based upon this outline and the input of the parties discussed earlier in this chapter. The IMD Motions© for PA (Bütz & Rock, 2019b) were designed to one degree or another to follow such a model, with a three-stage motion process that addresses the prospect of reunification.

Procedures, Policy, and the Best Interests—Health and Welfare of Children

If there is a new way of conceptualizing how pathological IMDs impact the lives of children and their families, then there is also a need for policies and procedures that address these children's health and welfare at a basic level with FDBP interventions, and a new way of handling PA cases with the recognition that it is no longer acceptable for these cases to be prolonged in a way that predictably deepens pathology. Gardner's (2001, p. 67) statements earlier in the text about these cases are well taken. There is a need to have a policy discussion around what is in these children's best interests and procedural discussions to ensure that these cases no longer linger in the courtroom. It is fairly clear what would happen in FDBP cases without intervention. But, as discussed in Chapter 6 the harm that comes to children in PA cases psychologically is just as tangible. Their behavior becomes emblematic of the long-known dynamic of identifying with the aggressor (Freud, 2018/1936b). These children are no longer themselves but rather hollow rigid imitations of their abusers; that mimic the AP's affect, mood and sentiments, without remorse in severe cases. Not only have these children lost themselves in favor of the superimposed identity of the AP, but damage has been done to the *ac's* ability to trust, to free her- or himself from a dependent and enmeshed relationship with the Alienating Parent. As such, changes need to be made to policies and procedures that ensure recognition of these children's struggles and their well-being. The children, of course, are the paramount consideration in such situations, but real and personal damage is done to these parents, families and communities if these dynamics are left to run. This includes the impacts large and small on healthcare and legal systems as well as the practitioners and professionals involved in these systems.

Policy change would start at the level of recognition that IMDs are inherently dangerous to our children, families and communities. Therefore, we need practices and procedures in place within our healthcare and legal systems to arrest these dynamics in their mild forms, preferably, but soundly intervene per the literature's guidance in moderate and severe cases once the dynamic of an IMD has been revealed with reasonable scientific certainty. This includes not only, crossing a threshold of more probable than not, but even more suggestive findings, coupled with the considerations of a multidisciplinary team. Procedural changes would follow current guidance on how to intervene in an FDBP case, while at same time also ensure that these cases are immediately referred to child protective services and that these parents are afforded the opportunity to respond to the situation before them given the known rate of false positives. There are legal procedural matters addressed in these cases, but at times these procedural safeguards are not followed or adhered to by local authorities. So, an IMD Motion© has been developed for cases with an initial finding of an FDBP IMD to ensure that these procedural safeguards are regularly adhered to. In turn, these matters are dealt with at the level of healthcare systems in coordination with child protective services and the practitioners and professionals involved. On each such FDBP case, there really does need to be a timely secondary review to ensure that a multidisciplinary team has not rushed to judgment despite a positive finding in their review of tables and/or the suggested IMD Inventory©. Given the rarity of these cases, it is suggested that such reviews be conducted by a collaborative multidisciplinary team from a neighboring county or healthcare facility. If there are concerns, those are built into whatever reunification plan has been constructed through a court's order so that there is a level of oversight on these cases outside of those immediately involved. These are confusing cases where, as Meadow (1977) had pointed out in his initial writings on the topic, it is easy to rush to premature healthcare conceptualizations in an attempt to aid a vulnerable infant and caring mother. In the case of false positives, reaching the conclusion of an FDBP prematurely can, and has, caused considerable harm to the attachment relationship between parent and child, and also may overlook exotic and rare disorders that are not easily recognized.

Perhaps this author's perceptions are limited to regional considerations as a preface to the discussion that follows about legal systems. Yet, one of the chief concerns this author has in PA cases is that there is still a tendency toward the tender years' doctrine. Further, new models are being talked about where there is the implicit assumption of shared custody or parenting (Meyer, Cancian, & Cook, 2017), which is not useful, or even possible, in PA cases that are of a moderate or severe nature. The legal system seems to lean or skew in one direction or another before the case is even heard. As such, the first procedural issue is to buttress the legal system's attention to cases involving high conflict, and in these cases especially attention needs to be paid to defend not only the best interest standard but such standards for scientific evidence as the Daubert Standard. All too often, it has been this author's experience that custody assessments have no scientific underpinnings to them whatsoever, and the report is simply an accumulation and/or amalgamation of different opinions leveled by people close to the case and a few therapists who may be either sucked into the family system or stand as objective practitioners. But there are no scientific instruments or tests administered, no scientific process for observations, and in the end a report is produced that is a subjective document rather than one that meets the current standards for scientific evidence. It may be necessary for courts to require certain proofs in these cases as part of the review process.

It is also a procedural recommendation that when high-conflict cases are identified they are automatically fast-tracked in order to minimize the perpetuation of acrimony and vexatiousness. It should be recognized that these cases will be challenging, and so firm limits and boundaries need to be set with these cases' counsels. National guidance should be followed to ensure consistency (American Psychological Association, 2010; American Bar Association, 2008; Martindale et al., 2007). Once the case has been fast-tracked, the focus will be the best interest of the child standard, and expert reports and testimony will be expected to meet the standards for scientific proof indicated in Daubert as well as other related standards of scientific proof. By definition, this means assessment of the parents involved in these cases to the extent where a determination can be made about whether or not they have attributes such as those seen in PA as but one example. It is also suggested that a standard of proof be developed, as discussed earlier, for a threshold; and if evidence suggests that the PA IMD exists, the court has procedures for how to deal with it expediently. Once cases are at the level of moderate PA or beyond, there are boundaries that can, in reality, only be set by the court or its delegates, including, perhaps, guardians ad litem, parent coordinators or special masters who have been given appropriate powers by the court to attend to the orders that have been issued. Boundary setting involves ensuring that regular contact occurs and that the quality of that contact is appropriate, and other such matters. Obviously, in most cases the child's best interest includes having a relationship with both parents, but in thorny moderate-to-severe cases this may not be possible; and that needs to be recognized by the Court and boundaries drawn with APs to this effect. Otherwise, there is the prospect that continued efforts to remediate the AP will fall along the lines of the state of affairs prior to the *Adoption and Safe Families Act*, when arguably children's interests languished as parents made negligible progress and had regular unproductive interactions with the Court. Family law courts are obviously preferable, where judges and those involved with the court have specialized knowledge on such specific matters.

Future IMDs

Turning to the topic of suggested additional IMDs, two have already been proposed and discussed to one extent or another across the pages of this text. It is important in this author's view to address the phenomenon of Parental Estrangement. Although there are programs in place such as child protective services as well as those that address intimate-partner violence, estrangement remains more prevalent than Parental Alienation. Also, the behaviors that create estrangement are far more damaging to children and adolescents. Further, if these cases are not handled properly, the offending parent who has engaged in these behaviors may be reintroduced to the children unchanged. What message does our society send to our children when we fail them in such a fundamental way? There were reasons the child was estranged, and yet in a number of cases with only a brief period of separation children may be put into a situation in which they are supposed to reunite with such a parent or parents who have not attended parenting classes or participated in their own personal therapy, which is at least psychoeducational, and have not received any intervention that would lead to some experience or understanding of what the children have been through. In these scenarios children are simply reintroduced in a way that appears to be endorsed by the system of care, and this abuses the children's trust all over again. It is not simply that a child has been neglected or abused, has witnessed interpersonal violence or has been abandoned; it is that these children who do not trust or want to interact with an Estranged Parent (EP) are forced to do so. They are forced to accommodate that parent rather than be protected by the system of care. This has a tremendous negative impact and requires attention as an IMD above and beyond the impacts of abuse, neglect, intimate-partner violence and abandonment. If estrangement has been earned, and legitimately documented, then these children deserve to be understood and PE recognized as an Interrelated Multidimensional Diagnosis.

Consider, also, Malingering by Proxy (MBP), which Rogers has discussed for some time. It is suggested that this particular pathological dynamic can be discriminated from FDBP, and the concept may be discerned by way of the motivation involved. The motivation is for personal gain, and the personality structure of the abusive parent would suggest antisocial or nearby characterological traits such as narcissism rather than the array seen in other aspects of Cluster B. Obviously, this literature would need to be further developed in order to place it under the heading of an IMD, with requisite background characteristics, individual symptoms, systems, interactions, subdynamics and ultimately the pathological dynamic that would result.

There are a number of possible IMDs that have not been discussed so far. Even with the spirited proposal that has been made herein by introducing FDBP and PA, it may well be considered a step too far to go beyond doubling the number of IMDs suggested here. Bearing these reservations in mind, two other IMDs will be put forward in the remaining pages of this text: Undue Influence and Intergenerational Trauma. Both phenomena have been in the literature for some time, and as PE and MBP were each dealt with at an earlier point in this text in a manner that prepared the way, so Undue Influence and Intergenerational Trauma will be addressed here briefly to simplify these phenomena and show how they fit within the IMD heuristic in a manner that would be of service.

Undue Influence

There has been a good deal of work on the matter of Undue Influence (UI), and those who are familiar with it understand that there are infirmed or disabled individuals whose health, welfare, and wishes are often impacted by their children or a caregiver. Arguably, one way of looking at UI is that there has been a reversal of roles from what has been described in FDBP or Parental Alienation. Further, systems, subdynamics and a pathological dynamic are involved in UI, which in many cases in the United States is considered a crime. How to describe a UI? Obviously, we have the individual's children and/or caretaker, the individual who is under the influence of this person or persons in a way that interacts with both healthcare and legal systems, subdynamics born out of these interactions with both systems, and then the pathological dynamic that subverts the individual's free will and wishes.

The literature on these matters has been developing over many years. In fact, an article from *Bifocal* (Quinn, 2014), "A Journal of the American Bar Association Commission on Law and Aging," noted that California's laws on these matters date back to 1872. This article also described a number of matters associated with how to define UI conceptually and legally, and it noted that the topic had been under review in California. The article in *Bifocal* described, first, research conducted on UI and, second, what was reported as "landmark legislation modernizing the definition of undue influence." Quinn, the author of this piece, noted that in this legislation the following main considerations would be addressed in these cases:

1. The vulnerability of the victim.
2. The influencer's apparent authority.
3. The actions or tactics used by the influencer.
4. The equity of the result.

The basics of UI have been addressed also in the journal of *International Psychogeriatrics*, which had offered an excellent article (Peisah et al., 2009), "The Wills of Older People: Risk Factors for Undue Influence." This article enumerated the following factors:

280 Interventions, Motions, Policies

1. Sequestration and isolation of the impaired person such that outside contact is inhibited (e.g., telephone numbers are changed or disconnected or telephone contact with the impaired person is limited by the carer; the house in which the impaired person lives is heavily barred or no one ever seems to be home);
2. Previously trusted family members or friends are no longer favored or trusted by the cognitively impaired person;
3. Family conflict is present . . .
4. Physical and/or psychological dependency on a caregiver.

(p. 10)

This work went on to catalog the kinds of vulnerabilities these elderly people face, and then described the kind of circumstances that tend to surround wills that involve Undue Influence. With the foregoing discussion on FDBP and PA, the characteristics and symptoms from IMDs are hopefully coming to the fore in the reader's mind. In these cases we have children or caregivers who have particular attributes and engage in certain behaviors. We have vulnerable adults, family systems with certain dynamics, and those systems' interactions with healthcare and legal systems. Then, we have the interactions that occur across multiple dimensions that produce abusive pathological dynamics that rob the infirmed or disabled persons of knowledgably exercising their free will and wishes toward those whom they have the most affection or trust for in their lives. It is no secret that we have a whole generation of baby boomers who are about to face the prospect of aging and infirmity, and it is proposed that as a society we may well wish to get ahead of this IMD, which could devastate generations to come due to the divisiveness and greed of a few.

Intergenerational Trauma

Turning to Intergenerational Trauma, what is perhaps debatably being addressed here are matters where a people have suffered from the impact of either colonization or genocide to a significant degree, and these people carry this experience with them as part of their current identity and reality. There has been much work on Intergenerational Trauma (IT) in the last thirty years, and in no way, shape or form is this author interested in culturally appropriating such a significant matter. Rather, the hope is to bring light to it and to perceive its contours as an IMD more readily. With IT there is a more

Interventions, Motions, Policies **281**

complicated set of multidimensional interactions that happen both within a generation and in the next generation and perhaps beyond, as the community identity of these people has been disrupted and traumatized. Here, we have individuals acting for systems on communities of people that result in either traumatic subjugation or death. These matters involve cultural, governmental and societal systems that in turn impact the individual and the family, and the family within their own cultural community. The result is a pathological dynamic that continues to live on into future generations once initiated. As Eduardo Duran has indicated (2006; Duran & Duran, 1995), this work involves a different cultural perspective and understanding of the nature of trauma:

> These concepts all present the idea that when Trauma is not dealt with in previous generations, it has to be dealt with in subsequent generations. Initial research by the above-mentioned Israeli studies indicated that not only is the trauma passed on intergenerationally, but it is cumulative. Therefore, there is a process whereby unresolved trauma becomes more severe each time it is passed on to a subsequent generation.
>
> (p. 16)

Duran has described that what is symptomatic of this IMD is internalized oppression. The literature on this concept has been building over the years regardless of the terms attached to it (Williams-Washington, 2010; Danieli, 1982; Nadler, Kav-Venaki, & Gleitman, 1985; Tong, 1971). Duran's own work has indicated that IT has proven to be explanatory for the experiences of Native Americans, an array of other cultural groups (Nagata, Kim, & Wu, 2019; Graff, 2014; Estrada, 2009; Carrillo & Tello, 2008; Danieli, 2007; Nakata, personal communication, 1989; Takata, personal communication, 1989; Tong, 1971). To articulate IT as an IMD will require a more prominent treatment of subdynamics and systems than those described for the FDBP and PA Interrelated Multidimensional Diagnoses.

Although other potential IMDs come to mind, for now these considerations will have to do, or they may hopefully be left to others to address. Still, there are considerations to be dealt with on how individuals, systems and subdynamics interact in a fashion that creates a pathological dynamic, which, if allowed to continue and spread, harms not just the individual, not just the family, but ever larger social systems. It is this author's hope that this work will be joined by other practitioners, professionals and researchers with the aim of addressing significant pathology in a way that reduces human suffering. Given the scope of an IMD's potential impact and how it potentially propagates to include intergenerational transmission, this author challenges colleagues to join in this endeavor in order to improve the level of care supplied to current and future generations.

References

Abdulhamid, I., & Siegel, P. (2006, April 24). Munchausen syndrome by proxy. *eMedicine*. Retrieved from www.emedicine.com/ped/topic2742.htm

Abidin, R. R., Austin, W. G., & Flens, J. R. (2013). The forensic uses and limitations of the parenting stress index. In *Forensic uses of clinical assessment instruments* (pp. 346–379). New York: Routledge.

Ackerman, M. J. (2006). *Clinician's guide to child custody evaluations*. New York: John Wiley & Sons.

Adshead, G. (2005). Evidence-based medicine and medicine-based evidence: The expert witness in cases of factitious disorder by proxy. *Journal of the American Academy of Psychiatry and the Law*, 33(10), 99–105.

Adshead, G., & Bluglass, K. (2005). Attachment representations in mothers with abnormal illness behaviour by proxy. *The British Journal of Psychiatry*, 187(4), 328–333.

Adshead, G., & Bluglass, K. (2001). A vicious cycle: Transgenerational attachment. Representations in a case of factitious illness by proxy. *Attachment and Human Development*, 3, 77–95.

Afifi, T. O., Mather, A., Boman, J., Fleisher, W., Enns, M. W., MacMillan, H., & Sareen, J. (2011). Childhood adversity and personality disorders: Results from a nationally representative population-based study. *Journal of Psychiatric Research*, 45(6), 814–822.

Albertson-Kelly, J., & Burkhard, B. (2013). Family reunification in a forensic setting. In Baker, A. J., & Sauber, S. R. (Eds.). *Working with alienated children and families: A clinical guidebook* (pp. 232–251. New York: Routledge.

Alexander, R., Smith, W., & Stevenson, R. (1990). Serial Munchausen syndrome by proxy. *Pediatrics*, 86(4), 581–585.

Allen, B. P., & Potkay, C. R. (1981). On the arbitrary distinction between states and traits. *Journal of Personality and Social Psychology*, 41, 916–928.

284 References

Allen, D. M. (2011, September 14). The family dynamics of patients with borderline personality: Why do some people create havoc in their relationships? *Psychology Today*. Retrieved from www.psychologytoday.com/us/blog/matter-personality/201109/the-family-dynamics-patients-borderline-personality

American Bar Association. (2008). *A judge's guide: Making child-centered decisions in custody cases*. Chicago, IL: American Bar Association.

American Educational Research Association, American Psychological Association, & National Council on Measurement in Education. (2014). *Standards for educational and psychological testing*. Washington, DC: American Educational Research Association.

American Prosecutors Research Institute & National Center for the Prosecution of Child Abuse. (2004). *Investigation and prosecution of child abuse*. Thousand Oaks, CA: Sage Publications.

American Psychiatric Association. (2013). *Diagnostic and statistical manual of mental disorders* (Fifth Edition). Arlington: American Psychiatric Association.

American Psychiatric Association. (2000). *Diagnostic and statistical manual of mental disorders* (Fourth Edition, Text Revision). Arlington: American Psychiatric Association.

American Psychiatric Association. (1996). *DSM IV sourcebook: Volume 2* (Revised Edition). Arlington: American Psychiatric Association.

American Psychiatric Association. (1994). *Diagnostic and statistical manual of mental disorders* (Fourth Edition). Arlington: American Psychiatric Association.

American Psychiatric Association. (1987). *Diagnostic and statistical manual of mental disorders* (Third Edition, Revised). Arlington: American Psychiatric Association.

American Psychological Association. (2010). Guidelines for child custody evaluations in family law proceedings. *The American Psychologist*, 65(9), 863–867.

Anderson, A. P. A., Feldman, M. D., & Bryce, J. (2018). Munchausen by proxy: A qualitative investigation into online perceptions of medical child abuse. *Journal of Forensic Sciences*, 63(3), 771–775.

Artingstall, K. A. (2016). Munchausen by proxy and other factitious abuse: Practical and forensic investigative techniques. Boca Raton, FL: CRC Press.

Artingstall, K. A. (1999). Understanding the complicated domain of MBP. In *Practical aspects of Munchausen by proxy and Munchausen syndrome investigation* (pp. 3–38). New York: CRC.

Artingstall, K. A. (1995). Munchausen syndrome by proxy. *FBI Law Enforcement Bulletin*, 64, 5–11.

Asher, R. (1951). Munchausen's syndrome. *Lancet*, 1(6), 339–341.

Australian Platypus Conservancy. (2019). *Evolution & Names*. Campbells Creek, Victoria, https://platypus.asn.au/evolution-names/ (Retrieved June 4, 2019).

Ayoub, C. C., Alexander, R., Beck, D., Bursch, B., Feldman, K. W., Libow, J., et al. (2002). Position paper: Definitional issues in Munchausen by proxy. *Child Maltreatment*, 7, 105–111.

Ayoub, C. C., Schreier, H. A., & Alexander, R. (2002). Guest editor's introduction: Munchausen by proxy. *Child Maltreatment*, 7, 103–104.

Baker, A. J. L. (2013a). Parental alienation research and the Daubert standards. In Lorandos, D., Bernet, W., & Sauber, S. R. (Eds.). *Parental alienation: Handbook for mental health and legal professionals* (pp. 322–347). Springfield, IL: Charles C. Thomas.

Baker, A. J. L. (2013b). Introduction. In Baker, A. J., & Sauber, S. R. (Eds.). *Working with alienated children and families: A clinical guidebook* (pp. 1–7). New York: Routledge.

Baker, A. J. (2010). Adult recall of parental alienation in a community sample: Prevalence and associations with psychological maltreatment. *Journal of Divorce & Remarriage*, 51(1), 16–35.

Baker, A. J. L. (2007). Knowledge and attitudes about the parental alienation syndrome: A survey of custody evaluators. *The American Journal of Family Therapy*, 35(1), 1–19.

Baker, A. J. L. (2006). Patterns of parental alienation syndrome: A qualitative study of adults who were alienated from a parent as a child. *The American Journal of Family Therapy*, 34(1), 63–78.

Baker, A. J. L., & Andre, K. (2013). Psycho-educational work with children in loyalty conflict: The "I don't want to choose" program. In Baker, A. J., & Sauber, S. R. (Eds.). *Working with alienated children and families: A clinical guidebook* (pp. 149–165). New York: Routledge.

Baker, A. J. L., & Ben-Ami, N. (2011). To turn a child against a parent is to turn a child against himself: The direct and indirect effects of exposure to parental alienation strategies on self-esteem and well-being. *Journal of Divorce & Remarriage*, 52(7), 472–489.

Baker, A. J. L., Burkhard, B., & Albertson-Kelly, J. (2012). Differentiating alienated from not alienated children: A pilot study. *Journal of Divorce & Remarriage*, 53(3), 178–193.

Baker, A. J. L., & Eichler, A. (2014). College student childhood exposure to parental loyalty conflicts. *Families in Society: The Journal of Contemporary Social Services*, 95(1), 59–66.

Baker, A. J. L., & Sauber, S. R. (Eds.). (2013). *Working with alienated children and families: A clinical guidebook*. New York: Routledge.

Baker, A. J. L., & Verrocchio, M. C. (2015). Parental bonding and parental alienation as correlates of psychological maltreatment in adults in intact and non-intact families. *Journal of Child and Family Studies*, 24(10), 3047–3057.

Baker, A. J. L., & Verrocchio, M. C. (2013). Italian college student-reported childhood exposure to parental alienation: Correlates with well-being. *Journal of Divorce & Remarriage*, 54(8), 609–628.

Bala, N., Birnbaum, R., & Martinson, D. (2010). One judge for one family: Differentiated case management for families in continuing conflict. *Canadian Journal for Family Law*, 26(2), 395–450.

286 References

Bala, N., Hunt, S., & McCarney, C. (2010). Parental alienation: Canadian court cases 1989–2008. *Family Court Review*, 48(1), 164–179.

Bass, C., & Glaser, D. (2014). Early recognition and management of fabricated or induced illness in children. *The Lancet*, 383(9926), 1412–1421.

Bass, C., & Halligan, P. W. (2007). Illness related deception: Social or psychiatric problem? *Journal of the Royal Society of Medicine*, 100(2), 81–84.

Bass, C., & Jones, D. (2011). Psychopathology of perpetrators of fabricated or induced illness in children: Case series. *The British Journal of Psychiatry*, 199, 113–118.

Bass, C., & Wade, D. T. (2019). Malingering and factitious disorder. *Practical Neurology*, 19(2), 96–105.

Bateson, G. (1972). *Steps to an ecology of mind: Collected essays in anthropology, psychiatry, evolution, and epistemology.* Chicago: University of Chicago Press.

Bateson, G., Jackson, D. D., Haley, J., & Weakland, J. H. (1963). A note on the double bind—1962. *Family Process*, 2(1), 154–161.

Bateson, G., Jackson, D. D., Haley, J., & Weakland, J. H. (1956). Toward a theory of schizophrenia. *Behavioral Science*, 1(4), 251–264.

Baumrind, D. (2013). Authoritative parenting revisited: History and current status. In Larzelere, R. E., Sheffield Morris, A., & Harrist, A. W. (Eds.). *Authoritative parenting: Synthesizing nurturance and discipline for optimal child development.* Washington, DC: American Psychological Association.

Baumrind, D. (1991). The influence of parenting style on adolescent competence and substance use. *Journal of Early Adolescence*, 11, 56–95.

Baumrind, D. (1971). Current pattern of parental authority. *Developmental Psychology*, 4, 1–103.

Belsky, J. (2019). Early-life adversity accelerates child and adolescent development. *Current Directions in Psychological Science.* doi:10.1177/0963721419837670.

Belsky, J., & Pluess, M. (2009). Beyond diathesis stress: Differential susceptibility to environmental influences. *Psychological Bulletin*, 135(6), 885–908.

Bembenek, S. (2018, March 27). Einstein and the quantum: He helped invent the concept, but struggled until his death with the idea of a probabilistic universe. *Scientific American, Observations.* Retrieved April 12, 2018, from https://blogs.sci entificamerican.com/observations/einstein-and-the-quantum/

Ben-Ami, N., & Baker, A. J. L. (2012). The long-term correlates of childhood exposure to parental alienation on adult self-sufficiency and well-being. *The American Journal of Family Therapy*, 40(2), 169–183.

Beresford, B. A. (1994). Resources and strategies: How parents cope with the care of a disabled child. *Journal of Child Psychology and Psychiatry and Allied Disciplines*, 35, 171–209.

Bernet, W. (2013). Forward. In Baker, A. J., & Sauber, S. R. (Eds.). *Working with alienated children and families: A clinical guidebook* (pp. vii–ix). New York: Routledge.

Bernet, W. (2010). *Parental alienation, DSM-5, and ICD-11.* Springfield, IL: Charles C. Thomas.

Bernet, W., & Baker, A. J. L. (2013). Parental alienation, DSM-5, and ICD-11: Response to critics. *Journal of the American Academy of Psychiatry and the Law*, 41(1), 98–104.

Bernet, W., Gregory, N., Reay, K. M., & Rohner, R. P. (2018). An objective measure of splitting in parental alienation: The parental acceptance—rejection questionnaire. *Journal of Forensic Sciences*, 63(3), 776–783.

Bernet, W., Verrocchio, R. C., & Korosi, S. (2015). Yes, children are susceptible to manipulation: Commentary on article by Clemente and Padilla-Racero. *Children and Youth Services Review*, 56, 135–138.

Bernet, W., von Boch-Galhau, W., Baker, A. J. L., & Morrison, S. L. (2010). Parental alienation, DSM-5, and ICD-11. *American Journal of Family Therapy*, 38(2), 76–187.

Bernstein, L. (1958, December). What makes opera grand? *Vogue*, 120–124.

Bierer, L. M., Yehuda, R., Schmeidler, J., Mitropoulou, V., New, A. S., Silverman, J. M., & Siever, L. J. (2003). Abuse and neglect in childhood: Relationship to personality disorder diagnoses. *CNS Spectrums*, 8(10), 737–754.

Binggeli, N. J., Hart, S. N., & Brassard, M. R. (2001). *Psychological maltreatment of children*. Thousand Oaks, CA: Sage Publications.

Biondi, M., Gaetano, P., Pasquini, M., & Picardi, A. (2018). The SVARAD scale for rapid dimensional assessment: Development and applications in research. In Biondi, M., Pasquini, M., & Picardi, A. (Eds.). *Dimensional psychopathology* (pp. 1–28). New York: Springer Publishing.

Birnbaum, R., & Bala, N. (2010). Toward the differentiation of high-conflict families: An analysis of social science research and Canadian case law. *Family Court Review*, 48(3), 403–416.

Black, T., Saini, M., Fallon, B., Deljavan, S., Theoduloz, R., & Wall, M. (2016). The intersection of child custody disputes and child protection investigations: Secondary data analysis of the Canadian incidence study of reported child abuse and neglect (CIS-2008). *International Journal of Child and Adolescent Resilience*, 4(1), 143–157.

Blashfield, R. K., Keeley, J. W., Flanagan, E. H., & Miles, S. R. (2014). The cycle of classification: DSM-I through DSM-5. *Annual Review of Clinical Psychology*, 10, 25–51.

Bleuler, M. (1963). Conception of schizophrenia within the last fifty years and today. *Proceedings of the Royal Society of Medicine*, 56, 945–952.

Bools, C. (1996). Factitious illness by proxy: Munchausen syndrome by proxy. *The British Journal of Psychiatry*, 169(3), 268–275.

Bools, C., Neale, B., & Meadow, R. (1994). Munchausen syndrome by proxy: A study of psychopathology. *Child Abuse and Neglect*, 18, 773–788.

Boscolo, L., Bertrando, P., & Thorne, S. T. (1993). *The times of time: A new perspective in systemic therapy and consultation*. New York: WW Norton & Co.

Bow, J. N., Gould, J. W., & Flens, J. R. (2009). Examining parental alienation in child custody cases: A survey of mental health and legal professionals. *The American Journal of Family Therapy*, 37(2), 127–145.

Bowen, M. (1972). Toward the differentiation of self in one's own family. In Framo, J. (Ed.). *Family interaction: A dialogue between family researchers and family therapists* (pp. 11–173). New York: Springer Publishing.

Breiding, M. J., Basile, K. C., Smith, S. G., Black, M. C., & Mahendra, R. R. (2015). *Intimate partner violence surveillance: Uniform definitions and recommended data elements,*

288 References

version 2.0. Atlanta, GA: National Center for Injury Prevention and Control, Centers for Disease Control and Prevention.

Bricklin, B., & Elliot, G. (2002). *The perception—of—relationships—test. (PORT) and Bricklin perceptual scales (BPS), current and new empirical data on 3,880 cases, 1961–2002.* Furlong, PA: Village.

Bricklin, B., & Halbert, M. H. (2004). Perception-of-relationships test and bricklin perceptual scales: Validity and reliability issues, part II of two parts. *The American Journal of Family Therapy, 32*(3), 189–203.

Briere, J. (2019). *Treating risky and compulsive behavior in trauma survivors.* New York: The Guilford Press.

Bursch, B. (2014). Munchausen by proxy and factitious disorder imposed on another. *Psychiatric Times, 31*(8), 16–18.

Bütz, M. R. (2017). Nonlinear dynamics retrospective impact on psychological theory and practice, and, a roughed out formula for crises. In *Quaderni di matematica (vol. 29), overlapping of mathematics and humanities.* Rome, Italy, Goodyear and Arizona: Aracne editrice International.

Bütz, M. R. (2014). Dealing with the reality of the DSM-5, clinically and ethically. *The National Psychologist, 23*(4), 17.

Bütz, M. R. (1997). *Chaos and complexity, the implications for psychological theory and practice.* Washington, DC: Taylor & Francis.

Bütz, M. R. (1995). Hegemonic therapy, not recognizing the symbol: A case study of a Russian family's attempt to self-organize. *Journal of Family Psychotherapy, 6*(2), 33–48.

Bütz, M. R. (1993a). The vampire as a metaphor for working with childhood abuse. *American Journal of Orthopsychiatry, 63*(3), 426–431.

Bütz, M. R. (1993b). Practical applications from chaos theory to the psychotherapeutic process, a basic consideration of dynamics. *Psychological Reports, 73*(2), 543–554.

Bütz, M. R. (1993c). Chaos theory's implications for psychological transformation: Process, perspective and Symöbia. *Studies in Psychoanalytic Theory, 2,* 3–18.

Bütz, M. R. (1992a). Chaos, an omen of transcendence in the psychotherapeutic process. *Psychological Reports, 71*(3), 827–843.

Bütz, M. R. (1992b). The fractal nature of the development of the self. *Psychological Reports, 71*(3 Suppl.), 1043–1063.

Bütz, M. R. (1991). Negotiation as a therapeutic technique in brief couples therapy. *Mediation Quarterly, 8*(3), 211–223.

Bütz, M. R., Carlson, M. J., & Carlson, J. (1998). Self-organization and symbolic representation in family systems. *The Family Journal, 6*(2), 106–115.

Bütz, M. R., Chamberlain, L., & McCown, W. G. (1997). *Strange attractors: Chaos, complexity and the art of family therapy.* New York: John Wiley & Sons.

Bütz, M. R., & Evans, B. F. (2019). Factitious disorder by proxy and parental alienation, the argument for interrelated multidimensional diagnoses. *Professional Psychology: Research and Practice, 50*(6), 364–375. https://doi.org/10.1037/pro0000250

Bütz, M. R., Evans, B. F., & Webber-Dereszynski, R. L. (2009). A practitioner's complaint and proposed direction: Munchausen syndrome by proxy, factitious disorder by proxy, and fabricated and/or induced illness in children. *Professional Psychology: Research and Practice*, 40(1), 31–38.

Bütz, M. R., & Miller, R. (2019a). *Interrelated multidimensional diagnosis inventory—factitious disorder by proxy (IMDI-FDBP)*. Currently in development see Retrieved from www.imd-i.org

Bütz, M. R., & Miller, R. (2019b). *Interrelated multidimensional diagnosis inventory—parental alienation (IMDI-PA)*. Currently in development. Retrieved from www.imd-i.org

Bütz, M. R., & Rock, K. (2019a). *Interrelated multidimensional diagnosis motions—factitious disorder by proxy (IMDM-FDBP)*. Currently in development. Retrieved from www.imd-m.org

Bütz, M. R., & Rock, K. (2019b). *Interrelated multidimensional diagnosis motions—parental alienation (IMDM-PA)*. Currently in development. Retrieved from www.imd-m.org

Bütz, M. R., Schwinn, C., & Chamberlain, L. (2019). *Transforming Crisis Theory: Moving from stasis to developmental adaptation*. Unpublished manuscript.

Bütz, M. R., & Tynan, W. D. (2019). Integrating behavioral healthcare and primary care, appropriate balance on what model is driving care, and, the whole spectrum is coming through the door . . . *Journal of Clinical Psychology in Medical Settings*. doi:10.1007/s10880-019-09679-3

Calvo, F., Karras, B. T., Phillips, R., Kimball, A. M., & Wolf, F. (2003). Diagnoses, syndromes, and diseases: A knowledge representation problem. In *AMIA annual symposium proceedings* (Vol. 2003, p. 802). Bethesda, Maryland: American Medical Informatics Association.

Caplan, G. (1964). *Principles of preventive psychiatry*. New York: Basic Books.

Carragher, N., Krueger, R. F., Eaton, N. R., & Slade, T. (2015). Disorders without borders: Current and future directions in the meta-structure of mental disorders. *Social Psychiatry and Psychiatric Epidemiology*, 50(3), 339–350.

Carrey, N. (2011). Coasting to DSM-5 — parental alienation syndrome and child psychiatric syndromes: We are what and who we define. *Journal of the Canadian Academy of Child and Adolescent Psychiatry*, 20(3), 163.

Carrillo, R., & Tello, J. (Eds.). (2008). *Family violence and men of color: Healing the wounded male spirit*. New York: Springer Publishing.

Carter, D. K. (2011). *Parenting coordination: A practical guide for family law professionals*. New York: Springer Publishing.

Cerrato, F., Aluisio, G., Casadio, P., Di Girolamo, G., Valente, S., De Ronchi, D., & Atti, A. R. (2017). Adverse childhood experiences, personality disorders and addiction: Which relationship? *European Psychiatry*, 41, S200.

Chamberlain, L., & Bütz, M. R. (1998). *Clinical chaos, a therapist's guide to nonlinear dynamics and therapeutic change*. Philadelphia, PA: Brunner, Mazel.

Chiczewski, D., & Kelly, M. (2003). Munchausen syndrome by proxy. *The FBI Law Enforcement Bulletin*, 72(8), 20–25.

Clarke, C., & Skokauskas, N. (2010). Paediatric symptom falsification ('Munchausen syndrome by proxy')-psychiatric manifestations. *British Journal of Medical Practitioners*, 3(4), 39–43.

Clawar, S. S., & Rivlin, B. V. (2013a). *Children held hostage: Identifying brainwashed children, presenting a case, and crafting solutions*. Chicago, IL: American Bar Association.

Clawar, S. S., & Rivlin, B. V. (2013b). Questions most commonly asked by targeted parents, programing/brainwashing, parents, attorneys, judges and children. In Clawar, S. S., & Rivlin, B. V. (Eds.). *Children held hostage: Identifying brainwashed children, presenting a case, and crafting solutions* (pp. 365–374). Chicago, IL: American Bar Association.

Clemente, M., & Padilla-Racero, D. (2015). Are children susceptible to manipulation? The best interest of children and their testimony. *Children and Youth Services Review*, 51, 101–107.

Cobb, M. (2015, June 23). Sexism in science: Did Watson and Crick really steal Rosalind Franklin's data? *The Guardian*.

Coyne, J. C. (1982). A brief introduction to epistobabble. *Family Therapy Networker*, 6(4), 27–28.

Crutchfield, W. (1985, January 6). Orchestras in the age of jet-set sound. *New York Times*. Retrieved from www.nytimes.com/1985/01/06/arts/orchestras-in-the-age-of-jet-set-sound.html

Cuthbert, B. N., & Insel, T. R. (2013). Toward the future of psychiatric diagnosis: The seven pillars of RDoC. *BMC Medicine*, 11(1), 126.

Dahir, V. B., Richardson, J. T., Ginsburg, G. P., Gatowski, S. I., Dobbin, S. A., & Merlino, M. L. (2005). Judicial application of daubert to psychological syndrome and profile evidence: A research note. *Psychology, Public Policy, and Law*, 11(1), 62–82.

Dallos, R., & Vetere, A. (2012). Systems theory, family attachments and processes of triangulation: Does the concept of triangulation offer a useful bridge? *Journal of Family Therapy*, 34(2), 117–137.

Danese, A., & McEwen, B. S. (2012). Adverse childhood experiences, allostasis, allostatic load, and age-related disease. *Physiology & Behavior*, 106(1), 29–39.

Danieli, Y. (2007). Assessing trauma across cultures from a multigenerational perspective. In *Cross-cultural assessment of psychological trauma and PTSD* (pp. 65–89). Boston, MA: Springer Publishing.

Danieli, Y. (1982). Families of survivors and the Nazi holocaust: Some short and long term effect. In Spielberger, C. D., Sarason, I. G., & Milgram, N. (Eds.). *Stress and anxiety* (Vol. 8, pp. 405–423). Washington, DC: Hemisphere.

Darnell, D. (1998). *Divorce casualties: Protecting your children from parental alienation*. New York: Taylor Publishing.

Daubert v. Merrell Dow Pharmaceuticals. 509 U.S. 579, 113 S. Ct. 2795 (1993).

Day, L. B., Faust, J., Black, R. A., Day, D. O., & Alexander, A. (2017). Personality profiles of factitious disorder imposed by mothers: A comparative analysis. *Journal of Child Custody*, 14(2–3), 191–208.

Dell, P. F. (1987). Maturana's constructive ontology of the observer. *Psychotherapy*, 24(3), 462–466.

de Maat, S., de Jonghe, F., Schoevers, R., & Dekker, J. (2009). The effectiveness of long-term psychoanalytic therapy: A systematic review of empirical studies. *Harvard Review of Psychiatry*, 17, 1–23.

DeMatteo, D., & Edens, J. F. (2006). The role and relevance of the psychopathy checklist—revised in court: A case law survey of U.S. courts (1991–2004). *Psychology, Public Policy and Law*, 12(2), 214–241.

Demby, S. (2009). Interparent hatred and its impact on parenting: Assessment in forensic custody evaluations. *Psychoanalytic Inquiry*, 29(6), 477–490.

Dike, C. C., Baranoski, M., & Griffith, E. E. (2005). Pathological lying revisited. *Journal of the American Academy of Psychiatry and the Law*, 33, 342–349.

Dimsdale, J., Creed, F., & DSM-V Workgroup on Somatic Symptom Disorders. (2010). The proposed diagnosis of somatic symptom disorders to DSM-V to replace somatoform disorders in DSM-IV—a preliminary report. Author's response to letters from Shröder and van der Feltz-Cornells. *Journal of Psychosomatic Research*, 68, 99–100.

Dimsdale, J., Creed, F., & DSM-V Workgroup on Somatic Symptom Disorders. (2009). The proposed diagnosis of somatic symptom disorders in DSM-V to replace somatoform disorders in DSM-IV, a preliminary report. *Journal of Psychosomatic Research*, 66(6), 473–476.

Dodge, M. M. (1865). *Hans Brinker or the silver skates*. New York: Scholastic, Inc.

Dombrowski, S. C., Gischlar, K. L., & Mrazik, M. (2011). Munchhausen syndrome by proxy. In *Assessing and treating low incidence/high severity psychological disorders of childhood* (pp. 53–79). New York: Springer Publishing.

Donald, T., & Jureidini, J. (1996). Munchausen syndrome by proxy: Child abuse in the medical system. *Achieves of Pediatric and Adolescent Medicine*, 150, 753–758.

Drozd, L. M., & Olesen, N. W. (2010). Abuse and alienation are each real: A response to a critique by Joan Meier. *Journal of Child Custody*, 7(4), 253–265.

Drozd, L. M., & Olesen, N. W. (2004). Is it abuse, alienation, and/or estrangement? A decision tree. *Journal of Child Custody*, 1(3), 65–106.

Drozek, R. P. (2019). *Psychoanalysis as an ethical process*. New York: Routledge.

Duran, E. (2006). *Healing the soul wound: Counseling with American Indians and other native people*. New York: Teachers College Press.

Duran, E. (1990). *Transforming the soul wound: A theoretical/clinical approach to American Indian psychology*. Berkeley, CA: Folklore Institute.

Duran, E., & Duran, B. (1995). *Native American postcolonial psychology*. New York: SUNY Press.

Dye, M. I., Rondeau, D., Guido, V., Mason, A., & O'Brien, R. (2013). Identification and management of factitious disorder by proxy. *The Journal for Nurse Practitioners*, 9(7), 435–442.

Eichner, M. (2016). Bad medicine: Parents, the state, and the charge of medical child abuse. *UC Davis Law Review*, 50, 205.

292 References

Ellis, M. E., & Boyan, S. (2010). Intervention strategies for parent coordinators in parental alienation cases. *The American Journal of Family Therapy*, 38(3), 218–236.

Engel, M. (1972). Forward. In Bateson, G. (Ed.). *Steps to an ecology of mind: Collected essays in anthropology, psychiatry, evolution, and epistemology*. Chicago: University of Chicago Press.

Erikson, E. H. (1982). *The life cycle completed*. New York: W. W. Norton.

Erikson, E. H. (1980). *Identity and the life cycle*. New York: W. W. Norton (Originally published in 1959).

Erikson, E. H. (1963). *Childhood and society*. New York: W. W. Norton (Originally published in 1950).

Ertelt, T., & Van Dyke, D. (2013). Understanding the complexity and controversy of parental alienation. *Psyccritiques*, 58(26), No Pagination Specified.

Estrada, A. L. (2009). Mexican Americans and historical trauma theory: A theoretical perspective. *Journal of Ethnicity in Substance Abuse*, 8(3), 330–340.

Faedda, N., Baglioni, V., Natalucci, G., Ardizzone, I., Camuffo, M., Cerutti, R., & Guidetti, V. (2018). Don't judge a book by its cover: Factitious disorder imposed on children-report on 2 cases. *Frontiers in Pediatrics*, 6, 110.

Fairbairn, W. R. D. (1944/1952). Endopsychic structure considered in terms of object-relationships. In *Psychoanalytic studies of the personality* (pp. 82–132). London: Routledge & Kegan Paul.

Fairbairn, W. R. D. (1941/1951). *A revised psychopathology of the psychoses and psychoneuroses in an object-relations theory of the personality*. New York: Basic Books.

Feldman, M. D. (2004). *Playing sick? Untangling the web of Munchausen syndrome, Munchausen by proxy, malingering, and factitious disorder*. New York: Routledge.

Feldman, M. D., Bibby, M., & Crites, S. D. (1998). 'Virtual' factitious disorders and Munchausen by proxy. *Western Journal of Medicine*, 168(6), 537–539.

Ferrara, P., Vitelli, O., Bottaro, G., Gatto, A., Liberatore, P., Binetti, P., & Stabile, A. (2012). Factitious disorders and Münchausen syndrome: The tip of the iceberg. *Journal of Child Health Care*, 17(4), 366–374.

Fidler, B. J., Bala, N., & Saini, M. A. (2013). *Children who resist postseparation parental contact: A differential approach for legal and mental health professionals. American psychology-law society series*. New York: Oxford University Press.

Fire. (2019, April 18). *In Oxford online dictionary*. Retrieved from www.lexico.com/en/definition/fire

Fire. (2019, April 21). *In Wikipedia*. Retrieved from https://en.wikipedia.org/wiki/Fire

Fisher, G. C., & Mitchell, I. (1995). Is Munchausen syndrome by proxy really a syndrome? *Archives of Disease in Childhood*, 72, 530–534.

Fisher, R., Ury, W. L., & Patton, B. (1992). *Getting to yes: Negotiating agreement without giving in*. New York: Penguin.

Fivaz-Depeursinge, E., & Favez, N. (2006). Exploring triangulation in infancy: Two contrasted cases. *Family Process*, 45(1), 3–18.

References 293

Flaherty, E. G., MacMillan, H. L., & Committee on Child Abuse and Neglect. (2013). Caregiver-fabricated illness in a child: A manifestation of child maltreatment. *Pediatrics*, 132(3), 590–597.

Fonagy, P., & Target, M. (1996). Predictors of outcome in child psychoanalysis: A retrospective study of 763 cases at the Anna Freud Centre. *Journal of the American Psychoanalytic Association*, 44(1), 27–77.

Ford, C. V. (2011). Deception syndromes. *The American Psychiatric Publishing Textbook of Psychosomatic Medicine: Psychiatric Care of the Medically Ill*, 291.

Ford, C. V. (2005). Deception syndromes: Factitious disorders and malingering. In *Textbook of psychosomatic medicine* (pp. 297–309). Washington, DC and London: American Publishing Press.

Frances, A. (2013). Newsflash from APA Meeting: DSM-5 has flunked its reliability tests. *The Huffington Post*, May 8, 2013.

Frances, A. (2009). Whither DSM-V? *The British Journal of Psychiatry*, 195, 391–392.

Freud, A. (2018/1936a). *The ego and the mechanisms of defense.* New York: Routledge.

Freud, A. (2018/1936b). Identification with the aggressor. In *The ego and the mechanisms of defense* (Vol. 51, pp. 117–131). New York: Routledge.

Freud, A. (1971). The infantile neurosis: Genetic and dynamic considerations. In *The writings of Anna Freud* (Vol. VII, pp. 189–203). New York: International University Press.

Freud, A. (1967). *The ego and the mechanisms of defense, [1936].* New York: International Universities Press.

Freud, A. (1928). *Introduction to the technic of child analysis* (L. Pierce Clark, Trans.). New York: Nervous and Mental Disease Publishing Co (Original work published 1927).

Freud, S. (1961). The ego and the id. In *The standard edition of the complete psychological works of Sigmund Freud, volume XIX (1923–1925): The ego and the id and other works* (pp. 1–66). London: Hogarth Press.

Freud, S. (1910). *The psycho-analytic view of the psychogenic disturbance of vision.* Standard Edn, Vol. XI. London: Hogarth Press.

Friedlander, S., & Walters, M. G. (2010). When a child rejects a parent: Tailoring the intervention to fit the problem. *Family Court Review*, 48(1), 98–111.

Friedman, M. J. (2013). Finalizing PTSD in DSM-5: Getting here from there and where to go next. *Journal of Traumatic Stress*, 26(5), 548–556.

Frye, E. M., & Feldman, M. D. (2012). Factitious disorder by proxy in educational settings: A review. *Educational Psychology Review*, 24(1), 47–61.

Garber, B. D. (2011). Parental alienation and the dynamics of the enmeshed parent—child dyad: Adultification, parentification, and infantilization. *Family Court Review*, 49(2), 322–335.

Gardner, R. A. (2003). Does DSM-IV have equivalents for the parental alienation syndrome (PAS) diagnosis? *American Journal of Family Therapy*, 31(1), 1–21.

Gardner, R. A. (2002). Denial of the parental alienation syndrome also harms women. *American Journal of Family Therapy*, 30, 191–202.

294 References

Gardner, R. A. (2001). Should courts order PAS children to visit/reside with the alienated parent? A follow-up study. *American Journal of Forensic Psychology*, 19, 61–106.

Gardner, R. A. (1998). *The parental alienation syndrome: A guide for mental health and legal professionals* (Second Edition). Cresskill, NJ: Creative Therapeutics.

Gardner, R. A. (1985). Recent trends in divorce and custody litigation. *Academy Forum*, 29, 3–7.

Gates, G. (2012). Family formation and raising children among same-sex couples. *National Council of Family Relations*, 51(1), F1–F4.

George, C., Kaplan, N., & Main, M. (1994). *Adult Attachment Interview Protocol* (Fourth Edition). Berkeley, CA: University of California at Berkeley, Department of Psychology.

Glancy, G. D., Ash, P., Bath, E. P., Buchanan, A., Fedoroff, P., Frierson, R. L., Harris, V. L., Hatters Friedman, S. J., Hauser, M. J., Knoll, J., Norko, M., Pinals, D., Price, M., Recupero, P., Scott, C. L., & Zonana, H. V. (2015). AAPL practice guideline for the forensic assessment. *The Journal of the American Academy of Psychiatry and the Law*, 43(2 Suppl.), S3–S53.

Gleick, J. (1987). *Chaos: Making a new science*. New York: Viking Penguin.

Godbout, E., & Parent, C. (2012). The life paths and lived experiences of adults who have experienced parental alienation: A retrospective study. *Journal of Divorce & Remarriage*, 53(1), 34–54.

Gomide, P. I. C., Camargo, E. B., & Fernandes, M. G. (2016). Analysis of the psychometric properties of a parental alienation scale. *Paidéia (Ribeirão Preto)*, 26(65), 291–298.

Gordon, M. B. (2017). *The kids aren't alright: A correlational study evaluating the relationship between high-conflict divorce and child adjustment* (Doctoral dissertation, William James College).

Gould, S. J., & Eldredge, N. (1993). Punctuated equilibrium comes of age. *Nature*, 366(6452), 223–227.

Gould, S. J., & Eldredge, N. (1972). Punctuated equilibria: An alternative to phyletic gradualism. *Essential Readings in Evolutionary Biology*, 82–115.

Graff, G. (2014). The intergenerational trauma of slavery and its aftermath. *The Journal of Psychohistory*, 41(3), 181.

Green, R. (2006). Parental alienation syndrome and the transsexual parent. *International Journal of Transgenderism*, 9(1), 9–13.

Greiner, M. V., Palusci, V. J., Keeshin, B. R., Kearns, S. C., & Sinal, S. H. (2013). A preliminary screening instrument for early detection of medical child abuse. *Hospital Pediatrics*, 3(1), 39–44.

Griffith, J. L. (1988). The family systems of Munchausen syndrome by proxy. *Family Process*, 27(4), 423–437.

Grundhauser, E. (2017, November 6). Remembering, with fondness, the 'worst orchestra in the world'. *Atlas Obscura*. Retrieved from www.atlasobscura.com/articles/portsmouth-sinfonia-classical-music-eno-orchestra

Guntrip, H. (1968). *Schizoid phenomena, object relations and the self.* London: Karnac Books.

Guntrip, H. (1961). *Personality structure and human interaction: The developing synthesis of psychodynamic theory.* New York: International Universities Press, Inc.

Hamilton, J. C., Feldman, M. D., & Janata, J. W. (2009). The ABC's of factitious disorder: A response to Turner. *The Medscape Journal of Medicine*, 11, 27.

Harman, J. J., Kruk, E., & Hines, D. A. (2018). Parental alienating behaviors: An unacknowledged form of family violence. *Psychological Bulletin*, 144(12), 1275–1299.

Harman, J. J., Leder-Elder, S., & Biringen, Z. (2016). Prevalence of parental alienation drawn from a representative poll. *Children and Youth Services Review*, 66, 62–66.

Hartocollis, P. (1972). Time as a dimension of affects. *Journal of the American Psychoanalytic Association*, 20(1), 92–108.

Herlihy, B., & Corey, G. (2014). *ACA ethical standards casebook.* Hoboken: John Wiley & Sons.

Herman, J. (1992). *Trauma and recovery.* New York: Basic Books.

Hetherington, E. M., & Kelly, H. (2002). *For better or for worse: Divorce reconsidered.* New York: W. W. Norton.

Hoffman, L. (1985). Beyond power and control: Toward a 'second order' family systems therapy. *Family Systems Medicine*, 3(4), 381–396.

Hoffman, L. (1981). *Foundations of family therapy: A conceptual framework for systems change.* New York: Basic Books.

Hoffman, P. D., Fruzzetti, A. E., Buteau, E., Neiditch, E. R., Penney, D., Bruce, M. L., & Struening, E. (2005). Family connections: A program for relatives of persons with borderline personality disorder. *Family Process*, 44(2), 217–225.

Hone, D. (2013, June 21). How a new species is named. *The Guardian*, published. Retrieved from www.theguardian.com/science/lost-worlds/2013/jun/21/dinosaurs-fossils

Hora, T. (1957). Contribution to the phenomenology of the supervisory process. *American Journal of Psychotherapy*, 11(4), 769–773.

Horgan, J. (2012). *What Thomas Kuhn really thought about scientific 'truth'.* London: Scientific American Blogs, Nature Publishing Group.

Houchin, T. M., Ranseen, J., Hash, P. A. K., & Barnicki, D. J. (2012). The parental alienation debate belongs in the courtroom, not in DSM-5. *Journal of the American Academy of Psychiatry and the Law*, 40(1), 127–131.

Howe, J. (2017). De-Junking MSBP adjudication. *Arizona Law Review*, 59, 201–234.

Howe, R. B., & Covell, K. (2014). Parental alienation and the best interests of the child. In Miller, M. K., Chamberlain, J., & Wingrove, T. (Eds.). *Psychology, law, and the wellbeing of children* (pp. 155–170). American Psychology-Law Society Series. New York: Oxford University Press.

Hughes, K., Bellis, M. A., Hardcastle, K. A., Sethi, D., Butchart, A., Mikton, C., Jones, L., & Dunne, M. P. (2017). The effect of multiple adverse childhood experiences on health: A systematic review and meta-analysis. *The Lancet Public Health*, 2(8), e356–e366.

296 References

Huynh, K. (2006). *Munchausen syndrome by proxy*. University of Iowa Healthcare Physician Assistant Program. Retrieved from www.medicine.uiowa.edu/pa/sresrch/Huynh/Huynh/sld001.htm

Jackson, D. D. (1957). The question of family homeostasis. *The Psychiatric Quarterly*, 31(1 Suppl.), 79–90.

Jaffe, P. G., Ashbourne, D., & Mamo, A. A. (2010). Early identification and prevention of parent-child alienation: A framework for balancing risks and benefits of intervention. *Family Court Review*, 48(1), 136–152.

Janet, P. (1889). *L'automatisme psychologique: essai de psychologie expérimentale sur les formes inférieures de l'activité humaine*. Paris: Alcan.

Johnston, J. R. (2003). Parental alignments and rejection: An empirical study of alienation in children of divorce. *Journal of the American Academy of Psychiatry and the Law Online*, 31(2), 158–170.

Johnston, J. R. (1994). High-conflict divorce. *The Future of Children*, 165–182.

Johnston, J. R. (1993). Children of divorce who refuse visitation. In C. Depner & J. H. Bray (Eds.), *Non-residential parenting: New vistas in family living* (pp. 109–135). Newbury Park, CA: Sage.

Johnston, J. R., & Campbell, L. (1988). *Impasses of divorce: The dynamics and resolution of family conflict*. New York: Free Press.

Johnston, J. R., & Kelly, J. B. (2004). Commentary on Walker, Brantley, and Rigsbee's, 'A critical analysis of parental alienation syndrome and its admissibility in the family court'. *Journal of Child Custody*, 1(4), 77–89.

Johnston, J. R., Lee, S., Olesen, N. W., & Walters, M. G. (2005). Allegations and substantiations of abuse in custody-disputing families. *Family Court Review*, 43(2), 283–294.

Johnston, J. R., Walters, M. G., & Friedlander, S. (2001). Therapeutic work with alienated children and their families. *Family Court Review*, 39(3), 316–333.

Jones, K. (2012). Dimensional and cross-cutting assessment in the DSM-5. *Journal of Counseling and Development*, 90, 481–487.

Judge, A. M., & Deutsch, R. M. (Eds.). (2016). *Overcoming parent-child contact problems: Family-based interventions for resistance, rejection, and alienation*. Oxford: Oxford University Press.

Kelly, J. B. (2003). Parents with enduring child disputes: Multiple pathways to enduring disputes. *Journal of Family Studies*, 9, 37–50.

Kelly, J. B., & Johnston, J. R. (2001). The alienated child: A reformulation of parental alienation syndrome. *Family Court Review*, 39, 249–266.

Kerlinger, F. N. (1979). *Behavioral research a conceptual approach* (Third Edition). Boston, MA: Harcourt School.

Kernberg, O. (1968). The treatment of patients with borderline personality organization. *International Journal of Psycho-Analysis*, 49, 600–619.

Kernberg, O. F. (1967). Borderline Personality Organization. *Journal of the American Psychoanalytic Association*, 15, 641–684.

Kernberg, O. (1966). Structural derivatives of object relationships. *International Journal of Psycho-Analysis*, 47, 236–252.

Khoury, B., Lecomte, T., Fortin, G., Masse, M., Therien, P., Bouchard, V., & Hofmann, S. G. (2013). Mindfulness-based therapy: A comprehensive meta-analysis. *Clinical Psychology Review, 33*(6), 763–771.

Klein, M. (1946/1975). *Notes on some schizoid mechanisms in envy and gratitude and other works.* London: Hogarth.

Koetting, C. (2015). Caregiver-fabricated illness in a child. *Journal of Forensic Nursing, 11*(2), 114–117.

Kohut, H. (1971). *The analysis of the self.* New York: International Universities Press.

Korpershoek, M., & Flisher, A. J. (2004). Diagnosis and management of Munchausen's syndrome by proxy. *Journal of Child and Adolescent Mental Health, 16*(1), 1–9.

Kozlowska, K., Foley, S., & Crittenden, P. (2006). Factitious illness by proxy: Understanding underlying psychological processes and motivations. *Australian and New Zealand Journal of Family Therapy, 27*(2), 92–104.

Kraemer, H. C., Noda, A., & O'Hara, R. (2004). Categorical versus dimensional approaches to diagnosis: Methodological challenges. *Journal of Psychiatric Research, 38*(1), 17–25.

Kraemer, S. (1987). Splitting and stupidity in child sexual abuse. *Psychoanalytic Psychotherapy, 3*(3), 247–257.

Krahn, L. E., Bostwick, J. M., & Stonnington, C. M. (2008). Looking toward DSM—V: Should factitious disorder become a subtype of somatoform disorder? *Psychosomatics, 49*(4), 277–282.

Kucuker, H., Demir, T., & Resmiye, O. (2010). Pediatric condition falsification (Munchausen syndrome by proxy) as a continuum of maternal factitious disorder (Munchausen syndrome). *Pediatric Diabetes, 11*(8), 572–578.

Kuhn, T. (1962). *The structure of scientific revolutions.* Chicago: Chicago of University Press.

Kumsta, R. (2019). The role of epigenetics for understanding mental health difficulties and its implications for psychotherapy research. *Psychology and Psychotherapy: Theory, Research and Practice, 92*(2), 190–207.

Kwawer, J. S. (2019). The interpersonal legacy of chestnut lodge. *Contemporary Psychoanalysis, 55*(1–2), 86–98.

La Roche, M. J., Fuentes, M. A., & Hinton, D. (2015). A cultural examination of the DSM-5: Research and clinical implications for cultural minorities. *Professional Psychology: Research and Practice, 46*(3), 183–189.

Lampel, A. K. (1996). Children's alignments with parents in highly conflicted custody cases. *Family and Conciliation Courts Review, 34,* 229–239.

Lawlor, A., & Kirakowski, J. (2014). When the lie is the truth: Grounded theory analysis of an online support group for factitious disorder. *Psychiatry Research, 218*(1–2), 209–218.

Lazenbatt, A. (2013). Fabricated or induced illness in children: A narrative review of the literature. *Child Care in Practice, 19*(1), 61–77.

Leichsenring, F., & Leibing, E. (2003). The effectiveness of psychodynamic therapy and cognitive behavior therapy in the treatment of personality disorders: A meta-analysis. *American Journal of Psychiatry, 160,* 1223–1232.

298 References

Leichsenring, F., & Rabung, S. (2008). Effectiveness of long-term psychodynamic psychotherapy: A meta-analysis. *Journal of the American Medical Association*, 300, 1551–1565.

Lehmann, H. E. (1967). Time and psychopathology. *Annals of the New York Academy of Sciences*, 138(2), 798–821.

Lopez, T. J., Iglesias, V. E. N., & Garcia, P. F. (2014). Parental alienation gradient: Strategies for a syndrome. *American Journal of Family Therapy*, 42(3), 217–231.

Lorandos, D. (2014). Parental alienation. In Morewitz, S. J., & Goldstein, M. L. (Eds.). *Handbook of forensic sociology and psychology* (pp. 323–344). New York: Springer Science + Business Media.

Lorandos, D. (2013). Parental alienation and North American law. In Lorandos, D., Bernet, W., & Sauber, S. R. (Eds.). *Parental alienation: Handbook for mental health and legal professionals* (pp. 348–424). Springfield, IL: Charles C. Thomas.

Lorandos, D., Bernet, W., & Sauber, S. R. (2013). *Parental alienation: The handbook for mental health and legal professionals* (Vol. 1116). Springfield, IL: Charles C Thomas Publisher.

Lowenstein, L. F. (2015). How can the process of parental alienation and the alienator be effectively treated? *Journal of Divorce & Remarriage*, 56(8), 657–662.

Lowenstein, L. F. (2013). Is the concept of parental alienation a meaningful one? *Journal of Divorce & Remarriage*, 54(8), 658–667.

Lucire, Y. (2000). The bearing of Daubert on sexual abuse allegations. *Australian Journal of Forensic Sciences*, 32(2), 45–57.

Ludolph, P. S., & Bow, J. N. (2012). Complex alienation dynamics and very young children. *Journal of Child Custody: Research, Issues, and Practices*, 9(3), 153–178.

Mahoney, M. J. (1991). *Human change processes, the scientific foundations of psychotherapy*. New York: Basic Books.

Martindale, D. A., Martin, L., Austin, W. G., Drozd, L., Gould-Saltman, D., Kirkpatrick, H. D., Kuehnle, K., Kulak, D., McColley, D., Siegel, J., Stahl, P. M., Hunter, L., & Sheinvold, A. (2007). Model standards of practice for child custody evaluation. *Family Court Review*, 45, 70–96.

Masten, A. S., Morison, P., Pellegrini, D., & Tellegen, A. (1990). Competence under stress: Risk and protective factors. In Weintraub, S. (Ed.). *Risk and protective factors in the development of psychopathology* (pp. 236–256). Cambridge: Cambridge University Press.

Maturana, H. R., & Varela, F. J. (1987). *The tree of knowledge: Biological roots of human understanding* (Second Edition). Boston, MA: Shambhala.

Meadow, R. (1998). Munchausen syndrome by proxy abuse perpetrated by men. *Archives of Disease in Childhood*, 78(3), 210–216.

Meadow, R. (1995). What is, and what is not, 'Munchausen syndrome by proxy'? *Archives of Disease in Childhood*, 72, 534–540.

Meadow, R. (1977). Munchausen syndrome by proxy the hinterland of child abuse. *Lancet*, 2, 343–345.

Meier, J. S. (2010). Getting real about abuse and alienation: A critique of Drozd and Olesen's decision tree. *Journal of Child Custody*, 7(4), 219–252.

References 299

Meister, R. (2003). *Therapeutic interventions for children with parental alienation syndrome* (Richard A. Gardner, Ed., p. 433). Cresskill, NJ: Creative Therapeutics, 2001.

Mermis, B. J. (2018). Developing an integrative level—dimensional taxonomy model for rehabilitation psychology research and practice. *Rehabilitation Psychology, 63*(1), 1–15.

Meyer, D. R., Cancian, M., & Cook, S. T. (2017). The growth in shared custody in the United States: Patterns and implications. *Family Court Review, 55*(4), 500–512.

Minuchin, S. (1974). *Families and family therapy.* Cambridge, MA: Harvard University Press.

Minuchin, S., Rosman, B., & Baker, L. (1978). *Psychosomatic families: Anorexia nervosa in context.* Cambridge, MA: Harvard University Press.

Moné, J. G., & Biringen, Z. (2012). Assessing parental alienation: Empirical assessment of college students' recollections of parental alienation during their childhoods. *Journal of Divorce & Remarriage, 53*(3), 157–177.

Money, J., & Werlwas, J. (1976). Folie à deux in the parents of psychosocial dwarfs: Two cases. *Bulletin, American Academy of Psychiatry Law, 4,* 351–362.

Murphy, G. E., Woodruff, M., Herjanic, M., & Fischer, J. R. (1974). Validity of clinical course of a primary affective disorder. *Archives of General Psychiatry, 30,* 757–761.

Nadler, A., Kav-Venaki, S., & Gleitman, B. (1985). Transgenerational effects of the holocaust: Externalization of aggression in second generation of holocaust survivors. *Journal of Consulting and Clinical Psychology, 53*(3), 365–369.

Nagata, D. K., Kim, J. H., & Wu, K. (2019). The Japanese American wartime incarceration: Examining the scope of racial trauma. *American Psychologist, 74*(1), 36–48.

Nazem, S., Spitzer, E. G., Brenner, L. A., & Bahraini, N. H. (2014). Beyond categorical classifications: The importance of identifying posttrauma symptom trajectories and associated negative outcomes. *The Journal of Clinical Psychiatry, 75*(9), 947–949.

Nichols, A. M. (2014). Toward a child-centered approach to evaluating claims of alienation in high-conflict custody disputes. *Michigan Law Review, 112*(4), 664–688.

Nydahl, L. O. (2012). *The way things are: A living approach to Buddhism.* New Alresford, England: John Hunt Publishing.

Olson, D. H. (2000). Circumplex model of marital and family systems. *Journal of Family Therapy, 22*(2), 144–167.

Olson, D. H., Sprenkle, D. H., & Russell C. (1979). Circumplex model of marital and family systems: I. Cohesion and adaptability dimensions, family types, and clinical applications. *Family Process, 18,* 3–28.

Pagnell, C. (2006). *Fabricated and/or induced illness in children: Theoretical basis of FII is unsound.* Retrieved August 7, 2006, from http://truthinjustice.org/fabricated.htm

Palermo, G. B., & Kocisc, R. N. (2005). *Offender profiling: An introduction to the sociopsychological analysis of violent crime.* Springfield, IL: Charles C. Thomas.

Pankratz, L. (2006). Persistent problems with the Munchausen syndrome by proxy label. *Journal of the American Academy of Law, 34*(1), 90–95.

Parnell, T. F. (1998). The use of psychological evaluation. In Parnell, T. F., & Day, D. O. (Eds.). *Munchausen by proxy syndrome: Misunderstood child abuse* (pp. 129–150). Thousand Oaks, CA: Sage Publications.

300 References

Peisah, C., Finkel, S., Shulman, K., Melding, P., Luxenberg, J., Heinik, J., Jacoby, R., Reisberg, B., Stoppe, G., Barker, A., Firmino, H., & Bennett, H. (2009). The wills of older people: Risk factors for undue influence. *International Psychogeriatrics*, 21(1), 7–15.

People of the State of Illinois v. B. T. (No. 1-05-0638; 2005, September 23).

Pepiton, M. B., Alvis, L. J., Allen, K., & Logid, G. (2012). Is parental alienation disorder a valid concept? Not according to scientific evidence. A review of parental alienation, DSM-5 and ICD-11 by William Bernet. *Journal of Child Sexual Abuse*, 21(2), 244–253.

Pienaar, C. E. (2013). *An analysis of evidence-based medicine in context of medical negligence litigation* (Doctoral dissertation, University of Pretoria).

Planck, M. (1920). The genesis and present state of development of the quantum theory. *The Nobel Prize*. Retrieved April 13, 1920, from www.nobelprize.org/prizes/physics/1918/planck/lecture/

Pleak, R. R. (2012). Transgender persons. In Ruiz, P., & Prim, A. (Eds.). *Disparities in psychiatric care: Disparities in psychiatric care* (pp. 107–115). Philadelphia, PA: Lippincott Williams & Wilkins Company.

Plewes, J. M., & Fagan, J. G. (1994). Factitious disorders and malingering. In Hales, R. E., Yudofsky, S. C., & Talbott, J. A. (Eds.). *Textbook of psychiatry* (Second Edition). Arlington: American Psychiatric Association.

Popper, K. (1985). Falsificationism versus conventionalism. In Miller, D. (Ed.). *Popper Selections*. Princeton, NJ: Princeton University Press. (Original work published in 1934.)

Prochaska, J. O., & DiClemente, C. C. (1983). Stages and processes of self-change of smoking: Toward an integrative model of change. *Journal of Consulting and Clinical Psychology*, 51, 390–395.

Prochaska, J. O., DiClemente, C. C., & Norcross, J. C. (1992). In search of how people change: Applications to addictive behaviors. *American Psychologist*, 47(9), 1102–1114.

Proskauer, S., & Bütz, M. R. (1998). Feedback, chaos, and family conflict regulation. In Chamberlain, L., & Bütz, M. R. (Eds.). *Clinical chaos, a therapist's guide to nonlinear dynamics and therapeutic change*. Philadelphia, PA: Brunner, Mazel.

Quinn, M. J. (2014). Defining undue influence: A look at the issue and at California's approach. *Bifocal*, 35(3). Retrieved August 17, 2018.

Rand, D. C. (2010). Parental alienation critics and the politics of science. *American Journal of Family Therapy*, 39(1), 48–71.

Rand, D. C., & Feldman, M. D. (1999). Misdiagnosis of Munchausen syndrome by proxy: A literature review and four new cases. *Harvard Review of Psychiatry*, 7(2), 94–101.

Reamer, F. G. (2018). *The social work ethics casebook: Cases and commentary* (Second Edition). Washington, DC: NASW Press.

Reed, G. M. (2010). Toward ICD-11: Improving the clinical utility of WHO's international classification of mental disorders. *Professional Psychology: Research and Practice*, 41(6), 457–464.

Reed, G. M., First, M. B., Elena Medina-Mora, M., Gureje, O., Pike, K. M., & Saxena, S. (2016). Draft diagnostic guidelines for ICD-11 mental and behavioural disorders available for review and comment. *World Psychiatry*, 15(2), 112–113.

References **301**

Reich, W. (1951). On counter-transference. In *Classics in psychoanalytic technique* (pp. 153–159). New York: Jason Aronson.

Reich, W. (1949). *Character analysis*. New York: Orgone Institute Press.

Reid, J. B. (1993). Prevention of conduct disorder before and after school entry: Relating interventions to developmental findings. *Development and Psychopathology*, 5, 243–262.

Richardson, H. B. (1948). *Patients have families*. New York: Commonwealth Fund.

Robins, P. M., & Sesan, R. (1991). Munchausen syndrome by proxy: Another women's disorder? *Professional Psychology: Research and Practice*, 22(4), 285–290.

Roesler, T. A., & Jenny, C. (2008). *Medical child abuse: Beyond Munchausen syndrome by proxy*. Itasca, IL: American Academy of Pediatrics.

Rogers, D., Tripp, J., Bentovim, A., Robertson, A., Berry, D., & Goulding, R. (1976). Non-accidental poisoning: An extended syndrome of child abuse. *British Medical Journal*, 1, 793–796.

Rogers, R. (2004). Diagnostic, explanatory, and detection models of Munchausen by proxy: Extrapolations from malingering and deception. *Child Abuse & Neglect*, 28, 225–239.

Rogers, R., Sewell, K. W., & Gillard, N. D. (2010). *Structured interview of reported symptoms, test manual* (Second Edition). Lutz, FL: Psychological Assessment Resources.

Roid, G. (2003). *Stanford-Binet intelligence scales: Fifth edition, examiner's manual*. Itasca, IL: Riverside Publishing.

Rosenberg, D. (1995). From lying to homicide: The spectrum of Munchausen syndrome by proxy. In A. V. Levin & M. S. Sheridan (Eds.). *Munchausen syndrome by proxy: Issues in diagnosis and treatment* (pp. 13–37). New York: Lexington.

Rosenberg, D. A. (1987). Web of deceit: A literature review of Munchausen syndrome by proxy. *Child Abuse & Neglect*, 11, 547–563.

Rowen, J., & Emery, R. (2014). Examining parental denigration behaviors of co-parents as reported by young adults and their association with parent—child closeness. *Couple and Family Psychology: Research and Practice*, 3(3), 165–177.

Rowlands, G. A. (2019). Parental alienation: A measurement tool. *Journal of Divorce & Remarriage*, 60(4), 316–331.

Royal College of Psychiatrists. (2006, July 11). *Munchausen's syndrome by proxy is no medical myth*. Presented Royal College of Psychiatrists Annual Meeting 2006 Glasgow, Scotland.

Rueda, C. A. (2004). An inter-rater reliability study of parental alienation syndrome. *The American Journal of Family Therapy*, 32, 391–403.

Saini, M., & Birnbaum, R. (2007). Unraveling the label of 'high-conflict': What factors really count in divorce and separated families. *Ontario Association of Children's Aid Societies Journal*, 51(1), 14–20.

Saini, M., Johnston, J. R., Fidler, B. J., & Bala, N. (2012). Empirical studies of alienation. In Kuehnle, K., & Drozd, L. (Eds.). *Parenting plan evaluations: Applied research for the family court* (pp. 399–441). New York: Oxford University Press.

Sanders, L., Geffner, R., Bucky, S., Ribner, N., & Patino, A. J. (2015). A qualitative study of child custody evaluators' beliefs and opinions. *Journal of Child Custody: Research, Issues, and Practices*, 12(3–4), 205–230.

302 References

Sanders, M. J., & Bursch, B. (2002). Forensic assessment of illness falsification, Munchausen by proxy, and factitious disorder, NOS. *Child Maltreatment, 7*(2), 112–124.

Sauber, S. R. (2013). Reunification planning and therapy. In Lorandos, D., Bernet, W., & Sauber, S. R. (Eds.). *Parental alienation: The handbook for mental health and legal professionals* (pp. 190–231). Springfield, IL: Charles C. Thomas.

Scaife, J. (2012). *Deciding children's futures: An expert guide to assessments for safeguarding and promoting children's welfare in the family court.* New York: Routledge.

Schreier, H. A. (2000). Factious disorder by proxy in which the presenting problem is behavioural or psychiatric. *Journal of the American Academy of Child and Adolescent Psychiatry, 395,* 668–670.

Schreier, H. A. (1997). Factious presentation of psychiatric disorder: When is it Munchausen by proxy? *Child Psychology and Psychiatry Review, 23,* 108–115.

Schreier, H. A., & Ayoub, C. C. (2002). Casebook companion to the definitional issues in Munchausen by proxy position paper. *Child Maltreatment, 7,* 160–165.

Schreier, H. A., & Libow, J. A. (1993). Munchausen syndrome by proxy: Diagnosis and prevalence. *American Journal of Orthopsychiatry, 63,* 318–321.

Schwartz, K. (2015). The kids are not all right: Using the best interest standard to prevent parental alienation and a therapeutic intervention approach to provide relief. *Boston College Law Review, 56,* 803.

Searles, H. F. (1978). Concerning transference and countertransference. *International Journal of Psychoanalytic Psychotherapy, 7,* 165–188.

Searles, H. F. (1955). The informational value of the supervisor's emotional experiences. *Psychiatry, 18*(2), 135–146.

Selvini-Palazzoli, M., Boscolo, L., Cecchin, G., & Prata, G. (1978). *Paradox and counterparadox: A new model in the therapy of the family in schizophrenic transaction* (E. V. Burt, Trans.). New York: Jason Aronson.

Shah, I. (1989). *The Dermis Probe.* London, UK: Octagon Press, Limited.

Shapiro, A. F., Gottman, J. M., & Carrere, S. (2000). The baby and the marriage: Identifying factors that buffer against decline in marital satisfaction after the first baby arrives. *Journal of Family Psychology, 14,* 59–70.

Shedler, J. (2010). The efficacy of psychodynamic psychotherapy. *American Psychologist, 65*(2), 98–109.

Sheerin, J. (2006, July 11). *Expert warns of threat of Munchausen's syndrome by proxy.* Cardiff; Scottish Press Association.

Sheridan, M. S. (2003). The deceit continues: An updated literature review of Munchausen syndrome by proxy. *Child Abuse and Neglect, 27*(4), 431–451.

Siegel, E. V. (2019). *Transformations: Countertransference during the psychoanalytic treatment of incest, real and imagined.* London: Routledge.

Siegel, P. C., & Fischer, H. (2001). Munchausen by proxy syndrome: Barriers to detection, conformation and intervention. *Children's Services: Social Policy, Research and Practice, 4*(1), 31–50.

Siracusano, A., Barone, Y., Lisi, G., & Niolu, C. (2015). Parental alienation syndrome or alienating parental relational behaviour disorder: A critical overview. *Journal of Psychopathology, 21*(3), 231–238.

Slife, B. D. (1995). Newtonian time and psychological explanation. *The Journal of Mind and Behavior*, 45–62.

Slife, B. D. (1994). Free will and time: That 'stuck' feeling. *Journal of Theoretical and Philosophical Psychology*, 14(1), 1–12.

Slife, B. D. (1981). Psychology's reliance on linear time: A reformulation. *The Journal of Mind and Behavior*, 27–46.

Sorias, S. (2015). Overcoming the limitations of the descriptive and categorical approaches in psychiatric diagnosis: A proposal based on Bayesian networks. *Turkish Journal of Psychiatry*, 26(1), 1–12.

Sousa Filho, D. D., Kanomata, E. Y., Feldman, R. J., & Maluf Neto, A. (2017). Munchausen syndrome and Munchausen syndrome by proxy: A narrative review. *Einstein (Sao Paulo)*, 15(4), 516–521.

Staff. (May 24, 2015). Mythical animals that turned out to be real. *Animal Planet*; Silver Spring, Maryland: Discovery Communications, LLC, http://www.animalplanet.com/tv-shows/monster-week/mythical-animals-that-turned-out-to-be-real/ (retrieved June 4, 2010).

State of Delaware vs. McMullen (DEF. ID. 0507014155; 2006, January 1).

Stirling, J. (2007). Beyond Munchausen syndrome by proxy: Identification and treatment of child abuse in a medical setting. *Pediatrics*, 119, 1026–1030.

Sullivan, M. J., Ward, P. A., & Deutsch, R. M. (2010). Overcoming barriers family camp. *Family Court Review*, 48(1), 116–135.

Sutherland, E. E. (2005). Undue deference to experts syndrome. *Indiana International & Comparative Law Review*, 16, 375–421.

Symphony. (2019, April 18). *In Oxford online dictionary*. Retrieved from www.lexico.com/en/definition/symphony

Tolin, D. F. (2010). Is cognitive—behavioral therapy more effective than other therapies? A meta-analytic review. *Clinical Psychology Review*, 30(6), 710–720.

Tong, B. R. (1971). The ghetto of the mind: Notes on the historical psychology of Chinese America. *Amerasia Journal*, 1(3), 1–31.

Turner, M. A. (2006). Factitious disorders: Reformulating the DSM—IV criteria. *Psychosomatics*, 47(1), 23–32.

US Department of Health and Human Services. (1997). Adoption and Safe Families Act of 1997. *Public Law*, 105–189.

Utley, T. (2005, July 15). How could an expert like Roy Meadow get it so terribly wrong? *The Telegraph*.

Van de Schoot, R., Kaplan, D., Denissen, J., Asendorpf, J. B., Neyer, F. J., & van Aken, M. A. (2014). A gentle introduction to Bayesian analysis: Applications to developmental research. *Child Development*, 85(3), 842–860.

Velsor, S., & Rogers, R. (2018). Differentiating factitious psychological presentations from malingering: Implications for forensic practice. *Behavioral Sciences & the Law*, 37(1), 1–15.

Vennemann, B., Bajanowski, T., Karger, B., Pfeiffer, H., Köhler, H., & Brinkmann, B. (2005). Suffocation and poisoning—The hard-hitting side of Munchausen syndrome by proxy. *International Journal of Legal Medicine*, 119(2), 98–102.

Viglione, D., Giromini, L., Gustafson, M. L., & Meyer, G. J. (2014). Developing continuous variable composites for Rorschach measures of thought problems, vigilance, and suicide risk. *Assessment*, 21(1), 42–49.

Vijoen, M., & van Rensburg, E. (2014). Exploring the lived experiences of psychologists working with parental alienation syndrome. *Journal of Divorce & Remarriage*, 55(4), 253–275.

Volz, A. (1995). Nursing interventions in Munchausen syndrome by proxy. *Journal of Psychosocial Nursing*, 33(9), 51–58.

von Bertalanffy, L. (1968). General systems theory: Foundations, development and application. New York: Braziller.

Walk, A. E., & Davies, S. C. (2010). Munchausen syndrome by proxy: Identification and intervention. *NASP Communique*, 39(4), 1–20.

Walker, L. E., & Shapiro, D. L. (2010). Parental alienation disorder: Why label children with a mental diagnosis? *Journal of Child Custody: Research, Issues, and Practices*, 7(4), 266–286.

Wallerstein, J. S., & Kelly, J. B. (1980a). *Surviving the breakup: How parents and children cope with divorce*. New York: Basic Books.

Wallerstein, J. S., & Kelly, J. B. (1980b). Effects of divorce on the visiting father-child relationship. *American Journal of Psychiatry*, 137(12), 1534–1539.

Wallerstein, J. S., & Kelly, J. B. (1976). The effects of parental divorce: Experiences of the child in later latency. *American Journal of Orthopsychiatry*, 46(2), 256.

Wallerstein, J. S., Lewis, J., & Blakeslee, S. (2000). *The unexpected legacy of divorce: A 25 year landmark study*. New York: Hyperion.

Warshak, R. A. (2018). Reclaiming parent—child relationships: Outcomes of family bridges with alienated children. *Journal of Divorce & Remarriage*, 1–23.

Warshak, R. A. (2015). Ten parental alienation fallacies that compromise decisions in court and in therapy. *Professional Psychology: Research and Practice*, 46(4), 235–249.

Warshak, R. A. (2010). Family bridges: Using insights from social science to reconnect parents and alienated children. *Family Court Review*, 48, 48–80.

Warshak, R. A. (2001). Current controversies regarding parent alienation syndrome. *American Journal of Forensic Psychology*, 19, 29–59.

Watson, J. D., & Crick, F. H. (1953). Molecular structure of nucleic acids. *Nature*, 171(4356), 737–738.

Watzlawick, P. B., Beavin, B. J., & Jackson, D. (1967). *Pragmatics of human communication: A study of interactional patterns, pathologies, and paradoxes*. New York: W. W. Norton.

Waugh, M. H., Hopwood, C. J., Krueger, R. F., Morey, L. C., Pincus, A. L., & Wright, A. G. (2017). Psychological assessment with the DSM—5 alternative model for personality disorders: Tradition and innovation. *Professional Psychology: Research and Practice*, 48(2), 79–89.

Weakland, J. (1976). Toward a theory of schizophrenia. In Sluzkiand, C. E., & Ransom, D. D. (Eds.). *Double bind: The foundation of the communicational approach to the family*. New York: Grune and Stratton.

Wechsler, D. (2008). *Wechsler adult intelligence scale—fourth edition: Technical and interpretive manual*. San Antonio, TX: Pearson.

Werner, E. E. (1993). Risk, resilience, and recovery: Perspectives from the Kauai longitudinal study. *Development and Psychopathology, 5*, 503–515.

Werner, E. E., & Smith, R. S. (1992). *Overcoming the odds: High risk children from birth to adulthood*. Ithaca: Cornell University Press.

Whitaker, C. A. (1989). *Midnight musings of a family therapist*. New York: W. W. Norton.

Whitaker, C. A., & Malone, T. (1953). *The roots of psychotherapy*. New York: Blakiston, McGraw Hill Book Co.

Whitcombe, S. (2014). Parental alienation: Time to notice, time to intervene. *The Psychologist, 27*(1), 32–34.

Whitcombe, S. (2013). Psychopathology and the conceptualization of mental disorder: The debate around the inclusion of parental alienation in DSM-5. *Counselling Psychology Review, 28*(3), 6–18.

Widiger, T. A., & Simonsen, E. (2005). Alternative dimensional models of personality disorder: Finding a common ground. *Journal of Personality Disorders, 19*, 110–130.

Wiener, N. (1961). Cybernetics, or control and communication in the animal and the machine (Second Edition). New York: Wiley.

Williams-Washington, K. N. (2010). Historical trauma. In Hampton, R. L., Gullotta, T. P., & Crowel, R. L. (Eds.) *Handbook of African American Health* (pp. 31–50). New York: Guilford Press.

Wollert, R. (2006). Low base rates limit expert certainty when current actuarials are used to identify sexually violent predators: An application of Bayes's theorem. *Psychology, Public Policy, and Law, 12*(1), 56–85.

Woodall, K., & Woodall, N. (2017). *Understanding parental alienation: Learning to cope, helping to heal*. Springfield, IL: Charles C. Thomas.

World Health Organization. (2018). *International classification of diseases* (Eleventh Edition). Geneva, Switzerland: World Health Organization.

Yamada, K. (2005). *The gateless gate: The classic book of Zen koans*. New York: Simon & Schuster.

Yates, G. P., & Bass, C. (2017). The perpetrators of medical child abuse (Munchausen syndrome by proxy)—a systematic review of 796 cases. *Child Abuse & Neglect, 72*, 45–53.

Yates, G. P., & Feldman, M. D. (2016). Factitious disorder: A systematic review of 455 cases in the professional literature. *General Hospital Psychiatry, 41*, 20–28.

Zubin, J., & Spring, B. (1977). Vulnerability: A new view of schizophrenia. *Journal of Abnormal Psychology, 86*(2), 103–126.

Appendix A
Key IMD Symbolic Language

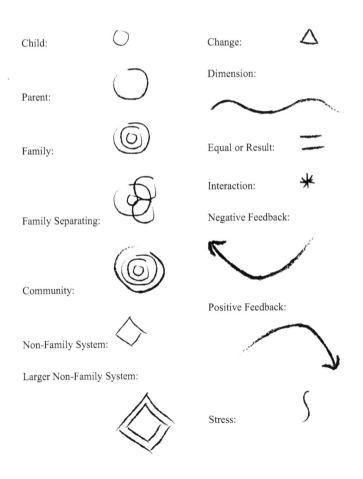

Index

Abnormal Illness Behavior by Proxy (AIBP) 2, 53, 67, 68, 72, 138, 142, 157, 199, 201
abuse 5, 9, 18, 24–25, 28, 49, 61, 65, 69, 78, 83, 86, 101, 114, 124, 125, 126, 132, 144, 149, 168, 169, 170, 183, 187, 197–198, 206–209, 211–213, 214, 234, 240, 257, 262, 278; physical 5, 33, 43–44, 46, 54–56, 61, 65, 69, 70, 71, 72, 83, 86, 119, 131, 139, 141, 142, 143, 145–148, 155, 158, 183, 207, 212, 213, 239, 266; psychological 24–25, 131, 185, 207, 211–212, 239, 248–249, 254, 259, 273; sexual 17, 79, 86, 117, 141, 142, 183, 202, 207, 212, 254
Abusive Parent (AP) 18, 124, 127, 208, 239, 241, 266, 278
Adoption and Safe Families Act 17, 204, 277
Adshead, G. 53, 67–68, 105, 107, 133, 142, 144, 149, 164, 239, 264–265, 267
Adult Attachment Inventory (AAI) 264, 267
aftercare 270–272, 274
against medical advice 168–169
Airy Experiment 39
Alienated Child ((AC), Kelly and Johnston) 2, 13, 25, 40, 48, 77, 78, 84–85, 88, 89, 91 (Fig. 3.4), 92, 110, 175, 178, 179, 192, 193, 194, 197, 209, 221, 228 (Fig. 6.6), 229
Alienated/Vulnerable Child (*a/vc*) 247–248
Alienating Behaviors (ABs/*abs*) 14, 16, 19, 25, 27 (Fig. 2.1), 36, 37, 46, 47, 48, 84, 89, 112, 116, 122, 123, 127, 179, 181, 186 (Table 6.2), ABs 187–191, ABs 191 (Table 6.3), *abs* 193–196, 197, 199, *abs*

200 (Table 6.5), 204, 205, 211, 212, 215, 217 (Fig. 6.2), 222, 223, PA Diagnosis 224–226 (Table 6.7), 227, 228, 249
Alienating Child (*ac*) 249, 271
Alienating Parent (AP) 16, 37, 83, 84, 86, 90, 104, 127, 179, 181–186, 187, 189, 195, 208, 224, 229, 241, 248, 271, 274, 275
alignment 2, 6–8 (Figs. 1.4–1.5), 10, 11, 13, 77, 78, 79, 80–81, 91 (Fig. 3), 110, 221, 228 (Fig. 6.6)
Alternative Model for Personality Disorders (AMPD) 98–99
American Academy of Pediatrics (AAP) 70
American Professional Society on the Abuse of Children (APSAC) 63, 69, 133, 158, 159, 188, 189
American Psychiatric Association 18, 19, 23, 50, 53, 54, 57, 59, 61, 63, 71, 78, 79, 84, 92, 98, 101, 106, 119, 132, 136, 137, 139, 141, 150, 158, 160
American Psychological Association iii, xiv, 211, 263, 277
Artingstall, K.A. 55, 57, 109, 135, 141, 148, 152, 159, 164
attachment 67–68, 69, 86, 115, 141, 142, 144, 148, 172, 200, 225, 237, 239, 276
Ayoub, C.C. 53, 63, 66, 67, 72, 133, 150, 151, 158, 159

Background Dimensional Symptoms17, 145, 152, 157, 164, 169, 179, 180, 235, 239, 241; FDBP 141–143, 148; PA 88–90, 180

310 Index

Baker, A.J.L. 11, 19, 36, 37, 39, 40, 77, 78, 88, 89, 90, 110, 111, 113, 116, 121, 122, 123, 124, 133, 176, 181, 185, 187, 188, 189, 193, 202, 211, 212, 213, 214, 215, 222, 240, 241, 255, 257, 272, 273, 274

Bala, N. 36, 77, 87, 182, 185

Bass, C. 58, 61, 62, 63, 68, 69, 71, 139, 140, 141, 142, 143, 144, 150, 157, 161, 163, 164, 165, 166, 168, 242, 245, 247, 265, 267

Bateson, G. 1, 22, 117, 222

Baumrind, D. 165, 242–245

Bayesian statistics 135, 173

Ben-Ami, N. 11, 18, 122, 124, 176, 185, 188, 189, 212, 240, 255, 257, 273

Bernet, W. 19, 22, 40, 77, 78, 87, 88, 89, 90, 103, 110, 123, 124, 133, 178, 195, 202, 214, 222, 255, 272, 273

Bernstein, L. xvii, 33, 37

best interests of the child 270

better than chance 45, 133, 170, FDBP Diagnosis 171–172 (Table 5.12), 223, PA Diagnosis 224–226 (Table 6.7), 240

Bleuler, M. 23, 235

blind men and elephant 74, 90, 91 (Fig. 3.4), 228 (Fig. 6.6)

Bluglass, K. 53, 67–68, 142, 144, 149, 164, 239, 264–265, 267

Bools, C. 55, 59, 67, 68, 145, 148, 150, 152

Bow, J.N. 37, 48, 77, 86, 122, 125, 175, 192, 193, 209, 211, 214

brainwashing 12, 16, 49, 82, 83, 187

butterfly effect 96

Caregiver-Fabricated Illness in a Child (CFIC) 67, 70, 72, 73 (Fig. 3.2), 138, 157

case examples: Factitious Disorder by Proxy 4–5, 40–44; Parental Alienation 6–8, 17, 45–52

causality 24–25

Chamberlain, L. 24, 93, 97, 188, 239

chaos theory 96

Child Alienating Behaviors (abs) 200 (Table 6.5)

Child Abuse in Medical Settings (CAMS) 2, 53, 67, 70, 72, 138

Child Individual Dimensional Symptoms: FDBP 149, 153, 154 (Table 5.6), 152, 166, 167 (Table 5.10), PA 196–199, 200 (Table 6.4)

child protective services 14, 159, 211, 255, 258 (Table 8.1), 259, 263, 267, 269, 275, 276

Circumplex Model 242–244

Clawar, S.S. 47, 124, 181, 187, 213, 241, 260, 273, 274

Counter Productive Parenting (CPP) 126, 186 (Table 6.2), 205–208, 214, 226 (Table 6.7), 241, 243, 246, 274

court(s) see legal proof (burden, standard)

Darnell, D. 16–17

Daubert Standard 38, 41, 105–112, 136, 210, 276, 277

Decision Tree (Drozd and Olesen) 126, 205–208

denigration 13, 17, 25, 26–27 (Fig. 2.1), 28, 48, 82, 83, 124, 126, 189, 195, 201, 203, 205, 207, 214, 215, 216–217 (Figure 6.2), 248, 253, 262

Deoxyribo Nucleic Acid (DNA) xvii, 6

diagnosis (IMD): suspicion 43, 55 (Table 3.1), 66, 132–133, 145 (Table 5.1), 148 (Table 5.2), 151, 155 (Table 5.7), 167 (Table 5.11), 169, 170, 171 (Table 5.12), 223, 224–225 (Table 6.7), 240; Further Study 54, 132–133, 169, 170, 171–172 (Table 5.12), 198, 223, 224–226 (Table 6.7), 235, 242, 243, 245

Diagnostic and Statistical Manuals (DSM): DSM-5 23, 57, 60, 61, 62, 67, 72, 75, 78, 86–90, 91 (Fig. 3.4), 98–101, 122, 132, 133, 139, 159, 160, 161, 202, 221, 221–222, 228 (Fig. 6.6); DSM-IV-TR 31, 54, 57, 63, 65, 66, 67, 77, 119, 137, 150, 158, 234; DSM-IV 11–12, 31, 103; DSM-III 57

Diathesis-Stress Model 23, 235

Drozd, L. 37, 77, 79, 124–127, 176, 188, 191, 193, 195, 205–208, 212, 214

DSM-5 Group (Parental Alienation) 89–90, 202, 222–223

DSM Series 67, 77, 132, 143, 166, 186, 226, 235

Duran, E. 198–199, 281

Dutch Boy 248–249

Einstein, A. 4

elephant and blind men 74, 90, (fig. 3.4), 228 (fig. 6.6)

epistemology 24, 29

estrangement 13, 25, 26–27 (Fig. 2.1), 37, 46, 50, 124, 125, 126, 192, 201, 202, 205–208, 214–217 (Fig. 6.2), 224, 240, 256, 262, 277–278

Index   **311**

Evans, B. F. xiii, xvi, 2, 3, 25, 31, 32, 38, 41,
54, 67, 72, 78, 89, 94, 95, 96, 100, 105,
107, 112, 118, 119, 121, 125, 134, 135,
137, 138, 139, 150, 195, 209, 227, 257
Experienced Child (*ec*) 247

Fabricated and/or Induced Illness in
children (FII) 2, 15, 31, 41, 53, 54, 56, 67,
68, 70, 105, 108, 136, 137, 138, 157
Factitious Disorder 54, 57, 60–61, 67, 69, 71,
72, 77, 143, 144, 159, 160, 165, 166, 241
Factitious Disorder by Proxy (FDBP) 2, 8,
10, 12, 14, 15, 16, 18, 19, 24, 31, 40, 41,
42, 43, 54, 55 (Table 3.1), 57, 58, 64, 65,
66, 69, 72, 104, 105, 106, 119, 120, 135,
Chapter 137–173, FDBP Diagnosis
171–172 (Table 5.12), 231, 238, 264
Factitious Disorder Imposed on Another
(FDIA) 2, 53, 59–63, 67, 92, 160
Factitious Psychological Presentation 161, 173
Fairbairn, W.R.D. 50, 113, 114
false positives 70, 107, 109, 150, 255, 276
Family–Legal System Optional Subdynamic
(Parental Alienation) 203–204, 204
(Table 6.6), 223, 226
family therapy 22–24, 113, 115, 117, 118,
222, 249, 258 (Table 8.1), 265
FDBP Pathological Dynamic 151–153, 156
(Table 5.8), 158, 168, 169
Feldman, M.D. 16, 18, 60, 61, 141, 149, 158,
161, 164
Figures 3 (1.1 Max Planck), 4 (1.2 Sir Roy
Meadow), 6 (1.3 Watson and Crick),
7 (1.4 Wallerstein; 1.5 Kelly), 26–27
(2.1 PA Flowchart), 41–44 (2.2–2.10
FDBP PowerPoint Slides), 63 (3.1
Model of Illness Deception), 73 (3.2
MSBP/FDBP Gordian Knot), 76 (3.3
Platypus Paradox), 91 (3.4 Blind men
and elephant), 126–128 (4.1–4.3 PA
Weighing), 162 (5.1 Model of Illness
Deception), 161 (5.2 FDBP table
redistribution), 162 (5.3 Elaborated
Model of Illness Deception), 207 (6.1
Drozd and Olesen's Decision Tree),
216–217 (6.2 PA Flowchart), 218–220
(6.3–6.5 PA Weighing), 228 (6.6 Blind
men and elephant), 244 (7.1 Circumplex
Model), 249 (7.2 Dutch boy at the dike),
250 (7.3 IMD Symbolic Language family
tick marks), 251 (7.4 IMD Symbolic

Language dimensional tick marks), 251
(7.5 IMD Symbolic Language FDBP),
251 (7.6 IMD Symbolic Language PA)
fire (metaphor) 29–33, 257
flowchart (Parental Alienation) 26–27 (2.1 PA
Flowchart), 216–217 (6.2 PA Flowchart)
Fisher, R. 23
Frances, A. 72, 75
Freud, A. 23, 113, 114, 199, 234, 275
Freud, S. 23, 113, 114

Garber, B.D. 77, 87, 89, 122, 125, 178, 182,
184, 209, 211, 214
Gardner, R. 12, 13, 17, 18, 19, 37, 39, 46, 48,
49, 50, 77, 81–84, 86, 88, 89, 103, 104, 110,
134, 185, 187, 201, 202, 203, 209, 211, 213,
221, 246, 256, 262, 269, 273, 274, 275
Glaser, D. 58, 68, 69, 141–142, 143, 144–145,
150, 165, 166, 168, 245, 247, 265, 267
Gordian Knot 72–73
Gould, S. J. 97
Griffith, J.L. 143, 241, 242, 243
guardian ad litem 177, 204 (Table 6.6), 261,
263, 267
Guntrip, H. 51, 113, 114

Halligan, P.W. 61, 62, 63 (Fig. 3.1), 140–141,
162 (Fig 5.1), 162 (Fig. 5.3)
Harman, J.J. 18, 124, 176, 212, 241, 243,
256, 273
Heisenberg 39
high-conflict 26–27 (Fig. 2.1), 34–35, 110,
123, 175–177, 180 (Table 6.1), 192, 203,
204 (Table 6.6), 210–211, 216–217 (Fig.
6.2), 224 (Table 6.7)
Hoffman, L. 2, 29
Horgan, J. 3, 15
Howe, J. 139, 158
Hwang, K. 22
hybrid case (Parental Alienation) 125, 130
(Fig. 4.3), 214, 220 (Fig. 6.5), 223
hypotheses 5, 28, 84, 128 (Fig. 4.1), 131, 135,
164, 171 (Table 5.12), 182, 206, 215, 218
(Fig. 6.3), 221, 227 (Table 6.7), 232, 245,
253, 254, 257, 262, 263, 264

identification with the aggressor 196–200
if-then 25, 215
IMD Symbolic Language 249–251
individual Characteristics/Symptoms 121,
133, 139, 144, 149, 153, 154 (Table 5.5),

312 Index

154 (Table 5.6), 165 (Table 5.9), 167 (Table 5.10), 186 (Table 6.2), 200 (Table 6.4), 246
individual-individual 2, 94
individual-system 94, 101
intergenerational 198, 234, 248, 257, 272
Intergenerational Trauma (IT) 198, 234, 278–279, 280–282
Internalized Oppression 198–199, 281
International Classification of Diseases (ICD) 10 137; 11 110, 122–123, 139
Interrelated Multidimensional Diagnoses (IMD): suspicion/further study (two-step process for diagnosing) 132–133, 171–172(Table 5.12), 221–226 (Table 6.7), 238–241
Interrelated Multidimensional Diagnostic Inventories© 135, 240, 263; Interrelated Multidimensional Diagnostic Inventories–Factitious Disorder by Proxy©- 157, 170, 173, 258, 264, 266, 268, 276; Interrelated Multidimensional Diagnostic Inventories–Parental Alienation©- 204, 223, 227, 259–260, 262, 269–270
Interrelated Multidimensional Diagnostic Motions© 255, 260, 268, 270–275
intervention xviii, 17, 23, 68, 70, 86, 89, 99–101, 109, 118, 123, 124, 132–133, 142, 193, 198, 203, 210, 211, 221, 228, 233, 234, 237, 240, 246, Chapter 253–277

Jenny, C. 53, 67, 69–70
Johnston, J. 8, 13, 14, 28, 34–36, 37, 48, 77, 78, 83–85, 86, 87, 88, 89, 92, 110, 121, 122, 124, 126, 175, 176, 177, 179, 180, 182, 183, 184, 185, 187, 188, 192, 193, 195, 202, 209, 210, 211, 212, 221, 229, 273
Jones, D. 69, 71, 139, 141–144, 164, 166, 168
Jung, C.G. 198

Kelly, J.B. 7, 7 (Fig. 1.5), 11, 13, 14, 28, 36, 37, 48, 77, 78, 80–81, 83–85, 86, 88, 89, 92, 110, 121, 122, 124, 126, 133, 134, 175, 176, 177, 179, 180, 181, 182, 183, 184, 187, 188, 192, 193, 195, 202, 209, 210, 211, 212, 221, 229, 257, 273
Kernberg, O. 50, 113, 114
Kozlowska, K. 68, 143, 144, 149, 164, 239, 264, 265, 266, 267
Kuhn, T. 3, 86

legal proof (burden, standard): beyond a reasonable doubt 263; clear and convincing evidence 263–264, 269; more probable than not xviii, 133, 151, 152, 171, 224, 227, 258, 259, 262, 263, 264, 269, 273, 275; preponderance of the evidence (better than chance) 45, 133, 170, FDBP Diagnosis 171–172 (Table 5.12), 223, PA Diagnosis 224–226 (Table 6.7), 240, 263, 264; standards for proof 26–27, 41–45, 74, 96, 105–112, 119, 120, 125–131, 139, 170, 214, 215, 216–217, 221, 254, 267, 277
Lewis, J. 11, 22, 223, 257
Lopez, T.J. 37, 46, 47, 98, 122, 189–191, 213
Lorandos, D. 11, 77, 110, 181, 213, 272, 273
Ludolph, P.S. 37, 48, 77, 86, 122, 125, 175, 192, 193, 209, 211, 214

Mahoney, M. 24
maladaptive caregiving 143, 239–240, 243, 253, 255
Malingering by Proxy (MBP) 59, 163, 240, 255, 278
McCown, W. 24, 93
Meadow, R. 4–5(Fig. 1.2), 9–10, 14, 15, 31, 39, 55 (Table 3.1), 58, 59, 69, 71, 75, 107, 134, 137, 145 (Table 5.1), 148 (Table 5.3), 150, 153, 154 (Table 5.5), 158, 168, 276
Medical Child Abuse (MCA) 2, 18, 19, 53, 67, 69–71, 72, 109, 138, 157
Meier, J. 11, 78, 86, 125, 176, 201, 205, 214
metaphor 16, 22, 28–37, 74, 90, 126, 138, 197, 227, 248, 257
Milan Group 22
more probable than not xviii, 133, 151, 152, 171, 224, 227, 258, 259, 262, 263, 264, 269, 273, 275
motivation (FDBP) 160–164
multidisciplinary 70, 259, 263, 270
multidisciplinary team 158, 170, 223, 240, 250, 255, 264, 266–268, 269, 271, 272, 275, 276
Munchausen's Syndrome by Proxy (MSBP) 5, 9, 14, 15, 31, 32, 38, 53, 54, 56, 57, 58, 63, 64, 65, 66, 69, 70, 71, 72, 73, 75, 77, 90, 105, 106, 109, 110, 136, Chapter 137–173

Naïve Child (nc) 247
neglect 234, 254
Nobel Prize 4
nonlinear dynamics 96

Index **313**

objectivity- 24–25, 150, 160
objects (psychoanalytic and psychodynamic), Bad, Good, Primary, Split 114–115
Olesen, D.W. - 37, 77, 79, 124–127, 176, 188, 191, 193, 195, 205–210, 212, 214
Olson, D.H. 165, 243
orchestra xvii, 28–29, 33–34, 36–37
Other Conditions That May be a Focus of Clinical Attention 62, 101

Parental Alienation (PA)2, 9, 12, 16–18, 19, 24–25, 26–27 Flowchart (Figure 2.1), 28, 40, 45–50 Case Example, 77–79, 85, 86–87, 88–90, 91 (Fig. 3.4), 92, 93, 98, 103, 110, 111, 122, 124, Chapter 175–229, 231, 232, 245, 256, 262, 269, 273, 278, 279
Parental Alienation Disorder 90, 92
Parental Alienation Relational Problem 90
Parental Alienation Syndrome (PAS) 2, 12, 19, 39, 48, 77, 78, 81–84, 91 (Fig. 3.4), 103, 202, 209, 228 (Fig. 6.6)
Parental Denigration (PD) 25, 26–27 Flowchart (Figure 2.1), 124, 126, 205, 207–208, 214, 215, 216–217 (Fig. 6.2), 248, 253
Parental Estrangement (PE) 13, 25, 26–27 Flowchart (Figure 2.1), 37, 46, 50, 124, 126, 208–210, 214, 215, 216–217 (Fig. 6.2), 240, 262, 277–278
Parental Sabotage (PS) 125, 205–208
Parent-Provider (Healthcare) System Subdynamic (FDBP) 149, 155 (Table 5.7), 167 (Table 5.11)
pathological xv, xvii, 2, 5, 9, 13, 14, 36, 94, 99, 116, 127, 164, 181, 182, 211–212, 235, 240, 243
pathological dynamic: described 2–3, 9, 11, 23–25, 28–29, 89, 94–96, 97–98, 104, 112, 121, 131–132, 156, 161, 178, 212, 215, 227, 231–233, 240, 242, 253–256, 257, 263, 275, 278–280, 281; FDBP 25, 28, 120, 134, 151, 152, 156 (Table 5.8), 157, 159, 168, FDBP Diagnosis 169–173, 264, 266–267, 269; PA 25, 28, 79, 89, 175, 187, 188, 202, 204, 211, 212, 213, 214, PA Diagnosis 221–227, 228, 243, 248–249, 259, 270, 272, 273
pathological lying 71, 139, 144, 165 (Table 5.9), 166, 172 (Table 5.12)
Pediatric Condition Falsification (PCF) 53, 56, 64–66, 67, 69, 70, 71–72, 73 (Fig. 3.2), 138, 146, 147, 155, 157, 158, 159

perception 1, 38, 185, 194, 202, 250
personality disorder/traits: antisocial 166, 181, 240, 278; borderline 116–117, 165 (Table 5.9), 172 (Table 5.12), 180, 181–182; Cluster A 238; Cluster B 36, 46, 144, 166, 186 (Table 6.2), 226 (Table 6.7), 238, 278; Cluster C 238; histrionic 165 (Table 5.9), 172 (Table 5.12), 181, 238; narcissistic 165 (Table 5.9), 172 (Table 5.12), 180, 181–182, 238
phenomena xiv, xv–xvi, xvii, xviii, 1–3, 5, 9, 10, 11, 15, 18, 21, 24, 28, 29, 31–33, 37, 38, 39, 53, 54, 56, 58, 66, 70, 77, 79, 86, 90, 91, 93, 94, 96, 98, 104, 105, 109, 112, 122, 124, 134, 135, 157, 179, 188, 198, 201, 205, 214, 232, 253, 254, 256, 272, 278–279
physics xvi, 4
Planck, M. 3–4
Platypus 74, 76–77, 90, 92
Platypus Paradox xvii, 60, 68, 74–77 (Fig. 3.3), 138, 164
policy 31, 137, 173, 254–255, 275
Portsmouth Sinfonia xvii, 34
probabilistic approach 29, 134–135, 165, 169, 173, 232
programming 12–13, 47, 49, 82–84, 85, 187
proliferation (terminology) 56, 63–73, 74, 77, 161, 256
Proposed FDBP IMD Diagnosis 169–173
Proposed PA IMD Diagnosis 221–227
psychoanalytic 113–115, 118
psychodynamic 22–23, 50, 114, 158, 237
psychological surround xvii, 175–181, 191, 197, 201–203, 204, 211, 212
punctuated equilibria 97
punctuated steady state 96–98, 232, 249

Rand, D. 25, 77, 187, 202
reality 1, 14, 24–29, 39, 78, 79, 100, 143, 150, 182, 186 (Table 6.2), 196, 201, 226 (Table 6.7), 235, 237, 266, 269, 277, 280
Reed, G.M. 139
Rejected Parent (RP)37, 46–49, 51, 88, 112, 127, 181, 182, 183, 184–185, 186 (Table 6.2), 193–195, 196, 203, 205, 224, 229, 260
relational problems 95, 100, 101–105, 118, 222
Remote Parent (RP) 239, 266
Resilient Child (rc) 247

314 Index

re-unification 257, FDBP 264–269, PA 269–275
Rivlin, B.V. 47, 124, 181, 187, 213, 241, 260, 273, 274
Roesler, T.A. 53, 67, 69–70
Rogers, R. 32, 38, 55 (Table 3.1), 58–60, 105, 112, 120, 121, 134, 138, 145–146 (Table 5.1), 148 (Table 5.3), 150, 153, 154 (Table 5.5), 156, 160–164, 165, 209, 240, 278
Rosenberg, D.A. 58, 63, 65–66, 135, 138, 141, 144, 149, 158, 160, 164
Rueda, C.A. 202, 211, 257

Saini, M. 36, 39, 77, 78, 87, 121, 178, 182, 183, 185, 209, 210
sanctions 204 (Table 6.6), 270–271, 274
scales (Weighted) 128–130 (Figs. 4.1–4.3), 218–220 (Figs. 6.3–6.5)
science 1–8, 21, 23, 25, 31, 39, 65, 74, 76, 86, 92, 100, 103, 108–109, 114, 169, 222
Searles, H. 51, 113
Selvini-Palazzoli, M. 118, 222
Sensitive Dependence on Initial Conditions 96
separation test 44, 173
sets (mathematical) xviii, 94, 250, 265
Sheridan, M.S. 32, 55 (Table 3.1), 63, 65, 66, 69, 71, 138, 141, 144, 145 (Table 5.1), 147 (Table 5.2), 148 (Table 5.3), 153, 154 (Table 5.5), 259
Sinfonia 34, 175, 257, 271
sourcebook 12, 31
splitting 50, 80, 112–118, 123, 178, 227, 237, 257, 261
steady state xvii, 96–98, 197, 232, 238, 249, 261
Stirling, J. 18, 53, 67, 70–71, 258 (Table 8.1)
Stockholm syndrome 239
stress: contemporary xvii, 236–238, 241, 272; developmental 236–238, 239, 248; situational xvii, 233, 235, 236–238, 239, 241, 246, 248
subdynamics xv, xvii, 2, 28, 38, 39, 89, 90, 94–96, 101, 104, 112, 120, 133, 139, 150, 156, 158, 164, 169–173, 178, 215, 228, 231, 278, 279, 281
supervised visitation 44, 172 (table 5.12), 270, 274

symbolic language xviii, 92, 215, 229, 249–251, 307 (Appendix A, Key)
symphony (metaphor) 29, 33–37, 39, 50
syndrome 12, 61, 78, 82, 84, 85, 101–104, 106, 108, 136
system-individual 2, 94, 101
systems xvi, xvii, xviii, 2–3, 131, 241–246

Tables 55–56 (3.1), 145–146 (5.1), 147 (5.2), 148, 152 (5.3, 5.4), 153, 154 (5.5), 154 (5.6), 155, 156 (5.7, 5.8), 165 (5.9), 167 (5.10), 167 (5.11), 171–172 (5.12), 180 (6.1), 186 (6.2), 191 (6.3), 200 (6.4, 6.5), 204 (6.6), 224–226 (6.7), 258 (8.1)
time xviii, 4, 17, 33, 204 (table 6.6), 233–236, 237, 246
transformation 97, 196–201
transformative state 98, 197, 232, 239
trauma 61, 117, 119, 139, 142, 197–198, 199, 209, 233–234, 236, 239, 278–279, 280–281
triangulation 112–118, 178, 227, 237, 257, 261
two-step process (for diagnosing) 132–133

Undue Influence (UI) 279–280
Ury, W.L. 23

variable criteria xviii, 73, 112, 123, 125, 127, 151–156, 171–172 (Table 5.12), 214, 221, 223–226 (Table 6.7), 232
V Codes 54, 100
Velsor, S. 160–164
video surveillance 171–172 (Table 5.12)
von Bertalanffy, L. 22, 97

Wallerstein, J. 7 (Fig. 1.4), 9, 11, 13, 14, 77, 80–81, 84, 110, 133, 134, 176, 221, 223, 257
Warshak, R. 37, 77, 89, 180, 187, 202, 203, 211, 241, 260, 261, 270, 273–274
Webber-Dereszynski, R. 3, 31, 32, 38, 41, 54, 67, 72, 89, 94–95, 100, 105, 107, 118, 121, 134–135, 137, 139, 150, 209, 227
Whitaker, C. 22, 222
Wiener, N. 22

Yates, G. 58, 71, 141, 145, 157, 160–161, 242